THE MAMMOTH BOOK OF BATTLES

Also available

The Mammoth Book of Classic Science Fiction
The Mammoth Book of Golden Age Science Fiction
The Mammoth Book of Vintage Science Fiction
The Mammoth Book of New Age Science Fiction
The Mammoth Book of Fantastic Science Fiction
The Mammoth Book of Modern Science Fiction
The Mammoth Book of Private Eye Stories
The Mammoth Book of Great Detective Stories
The Mammoth Book of Spy Thrillers
The Mammoth Book of True Murder
The Mammoth Book of True Crime
The Mammoth Book of True Crime 2
The Mammoth Book of Short Horror Novels
The Mammoth Book of True War Stories
The Mammoth Book of Modern War Stories
The Mammoth Book of the Western
The Mammoth Book of Ghost Stories
The Mammoth Book of Ghost Stories 2
The Mammoth Book of the Supernatural
The Mammoth Book of Astounding Puzzles
The Mammoth Book of Terror
The Mammoth Book of Vampires
The Mammoth Book of Killer Women
The Mammoth Book of Zombies
The Mammoth Book of Historical Whodunnits
The Mammoth Book of Werewolves
The Mammoth Book of Frankenstein
The Mammoth Book of Golden Age Detective Stories
The Mammoth Book of Contemporary SF Masters
The Mammoth Book of Astounding Word Games

The Mammoth Book of

BATTLES

Edited by
Jon E. Lewis

Carroll & Graf Publishers, Inc.
New York

Carroll & Graf Publishers, Inc.
260 Fifth Avenue
New York
NY 10001

First Carroll & Graf edition 1995

ISBN 0–7867–0278–8

Printed and bound in the United Kingdom

10 9 8 7 6 5 4 3 2 1

Contents

Acknowledgements

The editor has made every effort to locate all persons having any rights in the selections appearing in this anthology and to secure permission from the holders of such rights. Any queries regarding the use of material should be addressed to the editor c/o the publishers.

Parts of this work previously appeared in the partwork *War Monthly*, unless otherwise stated all material is copyright © Marshall Cavendish Partworks Ltd.

'The Relief of Ladysmith' is an extract from *Great Military Battles* by Howard Green. Copyright © 1971 Leo Cooper Ltd. Reprinted by permission of the publishers.

'Tsushima' is an extract from *Great Battles of the 20th Century*, edited by Barrie Pitt. Copyright © 1977 Phoebus Publishing and BPC Publishing Ltd.

'The Somme' is an extract from *A Sergeant-Major's War* by Ernest Shephard. Copyright © The Crowood Press. Reprinted by permission of the publishers.

'Battle of Britain 1940' by Christopher Dowling was first published in *Decisive Battles of the Twentieth Century*, edited by Noble Frankland and Christopher Dowling, Sidgwick & Jackson, 1976. Copyright © 1976 Dr Christopher Dowling. Reprinted by kind permission of the author.

'Stalingrad' and 'Ardennes' are extracts from *World War 1939–45: A Short History* by Peter Young. Copyright © 1966 Brigadier Peter Young. Reprinted by kind permission of Mrs Mary Delion and London Management and Representation Ltd.

'El Alamein' is an extract from *Decisive Battles of the Western World* by J. F. C. Fuller, Vol III. Copyright © 1974 J. F. C. Fuller. Reprinted by permission of David Higham Associates.

'Imjin River' by A. H. Farrar Hockley and E. L. Capel is an extract from *Cap of Honour* by David Scott Daniell. Copyright © 1951 David Scott Daniell and 1975 The Gloucestershire Regiment.

'Ia Drang' by Ian Westwell was first published in *The Elite: Special Forces of the World*, Marshall Cavendish 1987. Copyright © 1987 Marshall Cavendish Ltd. Reprinted by permission of Marshall Cavendish Ltd.

'Jerusalem' by Ashley Brown was first published in *The Elite: Special Forces of the World*, Marshall Cavendish 1987. Copyright © 1987 Marshall Cavendish Ltd. Reprinted by permission of Marshall Cavendish Ltd.

'Hamburger Hill' is an extract from *Vietnam: The Decisive Battles* by John Pimlott, Marshall Editions, 1990. Copyright © Marshall Editions Developments Ltd 1990. Reprinted by permission of Marshall Editions Developments Ltd.

'Wireless Ridge' is an extract from *2 Para Falklands* by Maj-Gen John Frost, Buchan & Enright Publishers Ltd. Copyright © 1983 by Maj-Gen John Frost.

'Desert Storm' is copyright © 1995 Jon E. Lewis.

Introduction copyright © 1995 Jon E. Lewis.

Introduction

If war is not an inevitable part of human nature, it is an enduring one. The profession of arms is man's oldest, and the moments in the last three millennia when peace has existed across the globe have been few. The twentieth century, the timespan covered by this book, differs from its predecessors only in that it has been even more war torn; it has also been the age in which warfare has, thanks to technological advance, reached new destructive depths.

Modern warfare is not quite synonymous with the 1900s; the 'industrialization' of slaughter began with the American Civil War of the 1860s, when entire ranks of close-pressed troops were felled by the Gatling gun. This was but a portent, however, and the mechanics and methods of mass slaughter would only truly proliferate as the new century turned. The replacement of cavalry by artillery, the invention of the aircraft, the tank, missile technology and the atomic bomb are peculiar to this age of violence and have transformed the killing power of armies into realms unimaginable by those who took the field at Agincourt, or even Gettysburg and Bull Run. Technology has not just given humankind more powerful arms, it has changed the ways – the strategy and tactics – in which war is waged. This is perhaps most clearly seen in the addition of airpower to land warfare, leading to the theory and practice of the Wehrmacht's *Blitzkrieg* (lightning war), and its several descendants, including the AirLand Battle Doctrine of the US armed forces, used so devastatingly in Operation Desert Storm (1991). And, as the war in the Persian Gulf proved – if proof were needed – with its skies traversed by Scud and Cruise missiles, war is becoming increasingly automated, due to breakthroughs in robotics, electronics and computer technology. War by remote control is no longer science fiction. A book of battles of the twenty-first century will have a very different content.

In this century, however, no war has yet been won without the small but necessary business of the mud soldier. And I would argue that the strain on that soldier over the last hundred years has become greater and greater. War is increasingly unendurable, because it is increasingly lethal and increasingly far removed from anything the soldier undergoes in ordinary civilian life. Most of the post-1950s generations have no experience of war beyond images on the television screen, leaving the soldier isolated from his (and sometimes her) peers. War, as the general said, is hell. It always has been, and it is only getting worse.

I have never been in a battle, never heard, in Churchill's phrase, 'a bullet whistle'. I find myself in awe of those who have, but also find that sometimes, through their eyes, I can get a glimpse of the intensity and uniqueness of combat, and what it means to have taken part in history. To read the testimonies of 'those who were there' seems the very least that the rest of us can do. Accordingly, a number of the 42 battles described on the following pages are eye-witness accounts. The rest are by a distinguished company of military historians, or soldiers who have taken up the pen in place of the sword. As for the battles selected, most are important twentieth-century clashes of arms which have changed the course of wars and thus our times. Some of these are directly decisive – like the naval battle of Tsushima (1905) which saw the spectacular sinking of the Russian fleet, like El Alamein, like Stalingrad – while others are indirectly so. The battle of Dien Bien Phu (1953) was a relatively small engagement, but the shock of losing it broke the morale of the French army and people, and ended France's reign as a colonial power in the Far East. But I have also selected a few remarkable, if obscure, 'non-decisive' battles which deserve to be better known (the epic Kokoda Trail, 1942, being a case in point), and others which seem typical and illustrative of the war in which they were fought (Hamburger Hill, Vietnam 1969). Taken together they make a history of war, its nature and its art, in our century. It is perhaps the last in which the human factor, the courage of soldiers and the tactics of battlefield commanders, will be of supreme importance. This book is dedicated to those who fought and fell in the battles it describes.

Jon E. Lewis
October 1994

1
The Boer War

The Relief of Ladysmith (1900)

Howard Green

Occasioned by the discovery of vast reserves of gold and diamonds in an area of South Africa outside British jurisdiction, the Anglo-Boer War (1899–1902) began as an exercise in imperial humiliation, with the volunteer Boer army scoring impressive successes over Queen Victoria's regulars. Not the least of these was at Ladysmith where Sir George White and 12,000 troops were shut in on 2 November 1899. In an effort to relieve the situation in South Africa – where imperial forces were also under siege at Mafeking and Kimberley – the British government dispatched two divisions and appointed General Sir Redvers Buller, Adjutant-General in the War Office, as Supreme Commander. A vastly experienced soldier (Buller had won a VC in the Zulu War), he decided to take personal command of the campaign to relieve Ladysmith, making his forward base at Frere, south of Colenso, where the Boers had blown the bridges and entrenched themselves on the north bank of the Tugela River.

By mid-December 1899 Buller was ready to relieve Ladysmith. His first plan was to send a brigade up to Colenso, ten miles to the north to 'demonstrate' his intention of forcing the Tugela there while he

marched the whole of the rest of his army off to the west, intending
to cross the river at Potgeiters Drift, 11 miles from Frere and so come
round the Boers' right flank in the Tugela Heights – a goodish plan,
but it overlooked the Boer mobility and the positions of observation
they could have used along the line of the hills.

However, on 13 December, he heard of the defeats at Magers-
fontein and Stormburg, the beginning of the 'Black Week', and
then realized that he was Commander-in-Chief in the whole of South
Africa, and not only in Natal. Clearly he was indirectly responsible
for these defeats and he felt that something must be done quickly to
counteract them. A quick success was imperative and its news must
arrive in London very soon.

Accordingly he abandoned the Potgeiters Drift plan entirely and
decided to attack Colenso with his whole strength. He rode up
from Frere to Chieveley on the 14th and that afternoon he told
his brigadiers that he would attack Colenso in the morning and,
having crossed the Tugela, bivouac on the far bank. It was to be
his first great attempt, and he led out next morning the finest and
largest force which any British general had handled since the Alma.
Four brigades of four battalions each, two regular cavalry regiments
with six regular and five other batteries of field artillery with 16 naval
guns under command made up a force of 21,000.

The plan was simple. A line of three brigades was to advance to
the river and across it where possible. Objectives allotted to each
brigade were very vague and almost unspecified.

The left brigade consisting of three Irish regiments and the Border
Regiment moved out to their left-front, trying to find a ford which a
local civilian thought he knew well. He was wrong, and disappeared,
and the brigade blundered on into the 'Loop', an area surrounded on
three sides by a great curve of the unfordable Tugela, a mile long and
half a mile wide. The Boers around two sides of the 'Loop' waited
until the brigade had halted well inside the trap, and had sent one of
the scouts out to find a ford. Then fire opened, heavy casualties were
caused and in spite of gallant attempts by companies and individual
men to rush forward down to the water's edge, not one man reached
it, and not one man of the enemy was seen. The brigade withdrew,
badly shaken.

The centre brigade, of four typical English country regiments,
Queen's, Devons, West Yorks and East Surreys, fared scarcely
better. Under the cover of the village of Colenso itself they advanced

well for a while, making for the two bridges, rail and road, that crossed the river 500 yards beyond the last houses. The fact that no battalion in this brigade had been given a specific bridge as an objective was of little matter, as all were held up soon after leaving the cover of the houses and gardens, by rifle fire from across the river. The two leading battalions, Queen's and Devons, infiltrated up the water's edge and the two bridges but could not cross, while the reinforcing West Yorks only added to the targets along the river bank. Not a man crossed the river.

On the right the Fusilier Brigade, of Royal, Scots, Welsh and Irish Fusiliers, advancing sometime after the other two brigades were in action, had orders to probe for the river and act as a right flank guard. Its latter task was unnecessary and like the other brigades it too was held up by accurate rifle fire from across the river and pinned to its ground. A flanking movement by one battalion out to the right petered out.

Three brigades were now halted short of, or only just up to, the river bank, not a man was over the water and the enemy was still concealed in the superb cover in the foothills over the river.

But the biggest disaster of all occurred in the centre, between the English and the Fusilier Brigades. Here Colonel Long, commanding the artillery, had been ordered to support with two batteries the advance of the centre and right brigades. He was a zealous and dashing officer with very distinct ideas of his own on the tactical employment of guns. His previous battle experience, always against natives whose rifles were usually obsolete and their marksmanship rudimentary, had taught him to fear little from defensive small-arms fire.

His principle, always successful previously, of getting his guns up into action quickly, close to the enemy, was put into practice yet again. Getting his two batteries forward at the trot he quickly got in front of the brigades he was supposed to support and advanced across the open plain in line, eventually outdistancing the Fusilier and the English Brigades by nearly a mile.

Seven hundred yards from the line of the tree-covered river bank and well short of the cover provided by the houses, gardens and railway station, in full view, with no infantry near him and the nearest cavalry far out on his right flank he halted, and his 12 guns, neatly drawn up as though on Queen's Parade at Aldershot, meticulously carried out all points of drill. The teams were led away to a donga 300 yards in the rear and Colonel Long was about to open fire at the clear, low, scrub-covered hills only a few hundred yards away, and where he thought the enemy might be.

The Boers anticipated his order to fire by a few seconds, and several hundred of the finest marksmen in the world, firing from behind cover, opened up. Heavy casualties occurred at once, among the first being Colonel Long, who was mortally wounded. He and those that could be moved were carried back to the donga where the horses were sheltering, and where he died that evening.

The gun detachments, as might be expected, fought their guns to the end despite devastating casualties. Their target was the low hills beyond the river, 800 yards away – wherein the enemy casaulties were negligible – and they fired until their ammunition was exhausted. Then, withdrawing to the shelter of the donga, they waited, the guns silent. Captain Reed, one of the battery captains, galloped up some scratch teams to pull out the guns, but was driven back losing seven men out of 13, and 13 horses out of 22. Buller then called for volunteers from his staff to bring the guns in, and miraculously two were saved. Their casualties, though, were heavy, among them Lieutenant Roberts, son of the field-marshal, who died in hospital two days later. The VC was awarded to him after his death, as it also was to three other officers and a driver. Among the Indian bearers who carried back the wounded was a young man called Gandhi, who learned here the hatred of violence that made him so successful in his campaign of non-violence in India, 26 years later. The remaining ten guns were left out on the plain, and after dark were removed by the Boers who used them against the British at Ladysmith a month later. At dusk the centre and right brigades withdrew as best they could, and next morning the force marched back to Chieveley.

Nine hundred men were killed or wounded with 250 missing. The latter were mostly wounded who could not be moved from the donga or the 'Loop' and who were taken prisoner.

The disaster at Colenso, when none of the 16 battalions reached their objective and ten of the 12 field-guns were lost was General Buller's greatest defeat. As a result of the 'Black Week' Lord Roberts was ordered out to South Africa as Commander-in-Chief. On his arrival it was thought that he did not remove Buller from his command because Lieutenant Roberts had been killed whilst on Buller's staff, and he feared that a removal might be taken personally.

Buller was much depressed by this defeat. It was the third in a week – the 'Black Week' – and he was deeply disappointed that a resounding success had not been achieved, to show alongside the two defeats elsewhere. His never-optimistic nature now became defeatist and he informed London and his goal, Ladysmith, that he could not succeed, advised the latter to destroy all documents, fire away all ammunition and to surrender. He sat back, not knowing what to do next. Severely reprimanded by Downing Street for his defeatist attitude he awaited supercession, but none came. Instead yet another division was ordered out in reinforcement.

Its Commander was Major-General Sir Charles Warren. He was a difficult man to get on with, with a distinct tinge of acerbity in his temper and tongue. Buller was brusque, with an overbearing manner and the frequent clashes between them must have been most unedifying to those of their staff who overheard them.

Roberts had telegraphed Buller to remain on the defensive and attempt no further advance until he, Roberts, and the new division had arrived. But Buller, however, being somewhat affronted by his coming supercession in the Chief Command by Roberts, whom he knew and disliked, suddenly changed drastically his recent defeatist policy for the relief of Ladysmith. He determined to have another try while still his own master. Telling his army that he had found the key to Ladysmith, he left Chieveley on 10 January for the west, marching along the line of the river barrier. Reinforced by Warren's division he had now 30,000 men, 20,000 of whom he took with him.

It was a slow and tedious march. Usually the leading unit had reached its night's destination before the last wagons had marched out of the previous camp, and it took five days to cover the 16 miles to Springfield, where Buller set up his advanced HQ.

Not only was the vast column frequently in sight from the Tugela Heights on its right, but the incessant dust cloud indicated its whereabouts. The Boers marching through the hills on the far side of the river kept up with the British, having no difficulty whatever in assessing their enemy's moves and intentions. When the British halted, they halted too, and the two marches were parallel – the only difference being that every British move was seen in full view whereas the movements of the Boers were not only invisible but their presence largely unsuspected.

Pushing on from Springfield the army reached the village and ridge of Spearman's, opposite two drifts over the river and beyond which were a high and imposing series of hills. Several days were spent here while preparations were made to cross the Tugela. The two drifts available had to have their approaches widened and metalled, water points set up on the far bank, roads improved, bakeries built, the Boers having as perfect a view from the hills of the preparations and obvious intentions of their enemy as they could possibly wish. During these five days of waiting (when the infantry and artillery were much employed in finding work parties for the sappers building or expanding the crossing and other works) the cavalry crossed to the north bank and probed for the enemy.

Buller now took an extraordinary step. He handed over the command of the whole force at Spearman's to Warren, leaving him only with his normal divisional staff to command a large force, and convoy it across a difficult river into rugged unreconnoitred country in which a dangerous enemy might or might not be lurking. He withdrew from the growing camp to his new headquarters at Springfield, some four miles away.

Meanwhile the cavalry found no sign of the enemy on one of the great mountains, Tabanyama, the most westerly of the group. The cavalry Brigade Commander, Lord Dundonald, reported this to Warren, asked for reinforcements and permission to push on and round the north side of the range of hills. It was a sensible and feasible tactical move. But this was too enterprising for Warren and he not only refused both reinforcements and permission but severely reprimanded Dundonald for presumption. However, he did send one brigade on a rather half-hearted attack on Tabanyama, which was recalled for no apparent reason when within sight of success.

During these days while the crossings were being enlarged, and the Tabanyama operations were carried out, General Buller frequently rode over from Springfield to see Warren, bombarding him with advice, suggestions, and criticisms – but no orders. Warren seemed quite unable to make up his mind as to the best tactical course to take, and Buller became more and more impatient. Finally Warren selected the next hill to Tabanyama, Spion Kop, for attack, although he admitted he did not like the look of it. Buller acquiesced, thankful to have some plan made at last.

On the late evening of 23 January, the Lancashire Brigade of Royal Lancasters, Lancashire Fusiliers, South Lancashires and Thorneycroft's Mounted Infantry left camp, and started to climb the hill, the most formidable, and the highest in the whole range,

1,500 ft above the river. The night was dark, a fine drizzle was falling and the going very difficult. Moreover, the Brigade Commander, Major-General Woodgate, an ex-Royal Lancasters CO, was 55 years of age and in poor health. The operation bore many similarities to the disaster of Majuba, 19 years earlier.

Spion Kop has three very steep sides, with one convenient and less acute shoulder up which the brigade climbed. Towards the end of the climb the hill flattens out considerably, the top being a shallow inverted saucer. At the farther (northern) end the high ground runs away into a long narrow saddle, terminating in a pronounced knoll. To the east and 200 ft below the main hill, and quite separate from it, rises another small feature, Aloe Knoll.

Advancing on a two-battalion front, the Royal Lancasters on the left and the Lancashire Fusiliers on the right followed by Thorneycroft's Mounted Infantry and led by the Brigade Commander in person, the brigade reached the first 'flattening out' without incident after climbing for most of the night. Owing to their weight and the noise inseparable from carrying them, many of the picks and shovels were dumped, but the men were still encumbered with greatcoats and ammunition, though not with rations or water. At about 6 a.m. the thick dawn mist gave the impression that the summit had been reached, the only Boer encountered had been bayoneted and the men ordered to give three cheers to indicate success to Warren below.

An hour or so later the mist suddenly lifted to disclose the summit 200 yards further on up the hill. The ensuing movement on to the hilltop in the now broad sunlight warned the main enemy force on the far side of the hill and on the plain below of the occupation, and they immediately started to climb the Aloe Knoll and the north-western end of the main feature at the end of the saddle. From the former they were soon able to accurately enfilade the shallow trench being built on the summit by the Lancashire Fusiliers on the right, while the Royal Lancasters, prolonging the line to the left, came under accurate though frontal fire from the knoll at the far end of the saddle. From Tabanyama Hill, 3,000 yards to their left front across the intervening valley, an enemy battery enfiladed both battalions.

The extreme rockiness of the hill precluded any serious trench digging although both battalions scraped together some skeleton forms of breastwork two feet high. The picks left behind would now have come in useful, although the Lancashire Fusiliers could only have protected themselves from the accurate enfilade fire from Aloe Knoll by changing direction through 90 degrees. Even then it is doubtful whether much entrenching could have been done under this fire.

Thorneycroft's Mounted Infantry passed through the two battalions and tried to reach the far end of the inverted saucer, but were prevented from doing so by the fire from the north-west knoll. A few men from the two left-hand companies of the Royal Lancasters managed to crawl forward individually, around the left (outer) flank of the MI, meeting some success but also meeting enemy scouts who had crept up along the saddle on to the far segment of the saucer. Attempting to relieve this complete hold-up, the South Lancashires were ordered forward to support. They too were quickly pinned down before reaching the three forward battalions. About an hour after the two forward battalions had commenced their trench digging, General Woodgate was mortally wounded, standing at the right of the Lancashire Fusiliers trench – the nearest man to Aloe Knoll. He was carried down the hill and died in hospital some days later.

Woodgate left chaos behind him in the command on the hill and Colonel Crofton, CO of the Royal Lancasters, as the senior officer present, assumed command. Losing his head he sent a panic signal to Warren below: 'Reinforce at once or all is lost. General dead.' Buller intercepted this message before it reached Warren and he rode over with his usual advice, suggesting that an officer more vigorous than Crofton should be appointed. Warren chose Thorneycroft, and as he was junior to Crofton heliographed to him his promotion to Brigadier-General. The news of his promotion reached Thorneycroft later but he neglected to tell Crofton.

Later in the day Warren sent up the Middlesex to the summit, and the Scottish Rifles to work round the right flank, in order to relieve the pressure on the Lancashire Fusiliers. They were unsuccessful, however, and not only added to the general confusion on the hill, but also further confused the problem of command. Colonel Hill of the Middlesex was senior to both Crofton and Thorneycroft.

When Hill arrived he assumed command at the eastern end of the summit, while Thorneycroft was commanding with vigour at the other end. They did not meet for several hours. The commander of the brigade to which the Middlesex and Scottish Rifles belonged, Major-General Talbot-Coke, felt that he too should ascend the hill to see his two battalions and was then, of course, the senior officer present. However, he did not attempt to take command and the delicate point as to who was in fact the commander on the hilltop was never settled.

During the afternoon the CO of the 60th Rifles (from yet another brigade), acting on his own initiative and without orders from any superior officer, moved his regiment far out to its right and, climbing a long low ridge, came up behind the Boers on Aloe Knoll, causing them considerable casualties from long-range fire. The Boers, seeing the British were in front of and now apparently behind them, were about to leave the Knoll, when General Buller rode up to Warren and demanded to know who had ordered the 60th on its lone though effective mission. On hearing that the CO had done so without orders Buller immediately and peremptorily ordered the battallion to withdraw, on the grounds that he would not tolerate such independence, almost amounting to impertinence.

At dusk the problem of who in fact was in command on the hilltop became acute. General Talbot-Coke advised Colonel Hill, whom both believed to be in charge, to retire to the plain during the night. Thorneycroft at the other end of the hill had now run into Crofton. Both felt that they should stay for some time yet and therefore sent a heliograph message to Warren for orders. Warren had by now heard from Hill, advising retirement, yet Thorneycroft was, as far as Warren knew, in command. However, Warren took Hill's advice and ordered withdrawal. As the left-hand units were on their way down they met Hill, who, having by now changed his mind, ordered them back. Thorneycroft came along and met Hill and, after a considerable wrangle, the latter had to admit that Thorneycroft as a Brigadier-General was the senior. The withdrawal continued.

And so the British left their objective leaving 300 dead behind them. Probably at about the same time, the Boers, quite certain that the British troops were immovable, withdrew too, and for several hours Spion Kop remained unoccupied. At dawn next day a Boer scout, finding the hill empty, signalled to his commander below and the hill was re-occupied.

It must be remembered that Woodgate's brigade did not capture Spion Kop. It took possession of it on finding it untenanted after the climb – and there remained unmolested for some hours. Had the Lancashire Fusiliers only advanced another 300 yards over the top to the far rim, they would have reached the edge of the plateau and so seen the Boers leave their laager on the plain below when commencing their climb. To assault such a slope against the fire of the defending British infantry was an impossible task for the enemy, no matter how mediocre the British shooting. But Woodgate did not see the obvious advantage he held.

Amongst the might-have-beens that are found in every account of every defeat must appear Warren's failure during the day to visit the hilltop where seven of his battalions, parts of his three brigades, were closely in action. A firm grip of the situation taken there must have shown a general with dominance how the battle could be controlled. The *junta* of five or six colonels on the site was quite incapable of doing so.

By 4 a.m. the next morning the last battalion had left Spion Kop, and rejoined the camp at Spearman's. When it was all over Buller moved Warren's command away to the east again, and out of range of Boer guns.

After Spion Kop a curious psychological change came over the Boers along the Tugela. They knew they had successfully invaded Natal, had surrounded and were now successfully besieging behind them a garrison of 8,000 British soldiers, had won resounding victories at Colenso and Spion Kop, all in less than three months. Their morale should indeed have been high. But it wasn't.

Many of them felt they had done enough and that their farms and families were now again top priority. Many applied for, and got, leave for 'private affairs' and went back to Transvaal. Others, more fearful, wondered whether they had not taken on too much. They felt that their invasion of friendly territory and then the defeats of their enemy would sooner or later bring retribution on them from the ever-growing and professional British Army. These Boers did not apply for leave. They quietly left their comrades in the hours of darkness and also rode back to Transvaal. By the time the next British advance took place there were only 4,000 Boers to face Buller's 20,000 British soldiers.

Unlike his behaviour after Colenso, Buller did not have a fit of deep depression following his defeat at Spion Kop. Instead he decided to have another go at a small hill, Vaal Krantz, six miles farther to the east.

Vaal Krantz was much lower than Spion Kop and had it been captured the cavalry could comfortably have passed round both its east and west extremities. They would then have found themselves in a plain with little or no obstacles in front of them and from where they could have taken the Boers in the rear and from both flanks.

After a week's rest and excellent rations of vegetables and fresh meat, the British soldiers were full of high spirits and very ready to go again. But the attack on Vaal Krantz was miserably slow.

It began at 6 a.m. when Wynne's Brigade (which had been Woodgate's and had led the assault on Spion Kop) advanced up to the Tugela, making a feint attack. It advanced well towards a smaller hill to the right of the Vaal Krantz but failed to draw the Boer fire.

A pontoon bridge was then built in front of the main hill and Buller led the remainder of his forces across it. It took time for the several thousands of men, in double file only, to cross the swaying bridge and the horse-drawn guns had to go very slowly. The Boers were left in no doubt as to where the attack would come.

The day passed into afternoon, the sun got hotter and hotter, the crossing of the bridge took longer and longer and Buller's natural pessimism returned. He decided to give up any idea of an attack in force that day, and told General Lyttelton, the commander of the leading brigade: 'You'll never carry the hill before dark, we had better put it off.' Lyttelton replied: 'Let me go now, and I'll guarantee I'll be on the top of Vaal Krantz by 4 o'clock.' Buller let him go.

The Durham Light Infantry led the attack and, after stiff resistance from the naturally very thinly spread Boers, reached the top of the ridge – soon followed by the Rifle Brigade – at precisely 4 o'clock.

But the position now became like Spion Kop. The top of the hill was taken but no reinforcements arrived and the Boers on the next hill were able to enfilade the Rifle Brigade. Buller, with his customary pessimism, ordered Lyttelton to withdraw – but Lyttelton ignored the order, and advised an additional attack on Green Hill whence the fire enfilading the Rifle Brigade was coming. But Buller would have nothing to do with such a common-sense suggestion, and decided to leave Lyttelton, exposed and unsupported, with no attempt to help him, on the hill all night. Buller then went to bed.

It was a very similar situation to that at Sulva Bay in the Gallipoli campaign in 1915, when 900 Turks on a low but clearly defined ridge several hundred yards inland from the beach held up two British divisions for three days before Turkish reinforcements arrived.

During the night the enemy concentrated his force, and all his guns, to defend Vaal Krantz. But for Lyttelton's tactical skill, another Spion Kop would have developed. Next day Buller vacillated all the morning between telling Lyttelton to withdraw and 'asking' him to hang on, and then reached the nadir of his professional incapacity. He telegraphed Roberts, who had just arrived in Cape Town 700 miles away, asking him what he should do and could he have tactical advice on a situation Roberts did not know, on ground he had never seen. Roberts replied that Buller must do what he could to relieve Ladysmith, his prime task, and that he was the best judge of the situation.

Buller's next step was at least positive. He relieved Lyttelton's brigade on Vaal Krantz with Hildyard's, which spent that night improving their positions on the ridge. On relief Lyttelton and Major Wilson (later to be CIGS in 1918) went to see Buller, who was dining. He asked them to share his champagne and enquired how they had got on. Lyttelton was very angry that Buller had failed to support him and so avoided victory, but the champagne worked wonders and Lyttelton and Wilson returned to their lines.

The next day Warren was sent out personally on reconnaissance, and returned with some sketches he had made of enemy-held territory. Buller saw them, and making only a sarcastic comment, called a Council of War of his brigadiers and Warren. Some advised going on, though most advised withdrawal. Buller, glad to have his mind made up for him by a democratic vote, ordered withdrawal. The troops got back across the Tugela without disturbance, the pontoon bridges were dismantled, and Buller's army marched back to Chieveley again.

Vaal Krantz, the third major defeat for Buller in trying to relieve Ladysmith, was much less costly than either Colenso or Spion Kop. Thirty men only were killed with some 300 wounded. The loss of prestige was negligible, it was already very low. Ladysmith was getting used to disappointments and Roberts had his hands full.

The new Boer position holding the Tugela around Colenso was extended two miles further to the east than they had done when Colenso was attacked in December. Buller, now in an optimistic period of thought decided to out-flank this long extension to the east.

A cavalry reconnaissance secured a hill five miles from Chieveley, and Buller arrived with his telescope. The result of his observations was that he ordered everyone back to Chieveley, intending to advance again with his whole army, eastward, along the south bank of the river, as he had done to Spearman's before Spion Kop, hoping to find a crossing.

But the next day when he intended to start was very hot, and the start was postponed for 24 hours. Then for three days the army crawled eastward parallel to the river, but well to the south. The Boers had, unwisely, left their excellent positions on the north bank and, crossing over, occupied lines not nearly so good in the open country to the south of the river.

On the 18th the British Army turned left and attacked the new Boer lines with two brigades. The Boers nervously conscious that they had their backs to the river turned and fled. For two days they were not followed and were allowed to get clear away over the river.

By the 20th Buller was not only in possession of the south bank of the river for several miles, but there was no sign of the enemy on the north bank. He could have crossed anywhere he liked by building pontoon bridges at the most suitable sites, suitable both from an engineering point of view and for tactical reasons. But he moved back almost to Colenso where he built one bridge only, leading directly into a hollow surround, enclosed by hills. Despite the expressed opinions of his staff on the unsuitability of this site, he took no notice and 15 battalions and 40 guns got across without opposition. But if anything more than a rearguard were to oppose them they would indeed be in trouble. But Buller was over the Tugela, his army now very experienced, the weather was gradually cooling, the Boers were obviously failing, and Ladysmith was only seven miles away. The end was in sight.

For three months since the Boers invaded Natal and its withdrawal from Talana Hill at Dundee the British Army had, with the single exception, at Caesar's Camp and Wagon Hill, suffered nothing but setbacks. The retreat to Ladysmith, Elandslaagte, Lombard's Kop, Nicholson's Nek, Pepworth, the armoured train, Colenso, Spion Kop and Vaal Krantz had all seen the superiority of the Boer fighting.

But now, over the Tugela at last, everything was to change. The advance through the hills and the actual relief of Ladysmith was pursued with energy, speed, concentration and success. In contrast to the previous 80 days of marching, bivouacking, marching, attacking, marching, withdrawing, covering a tragic 30 miles, littered with defeats, repulses, casualties, depression, the new phase was to be indeed different. The seven miles to Ladysmith was to take seven days only, four successful brigade attacks were to be carried out, the Boers were constantly kept on the run, less than 1,800 total casualties were suffered, of which the vast majority were wounds, frequently not serious. Press correspondents, painfully accustomed to witness assaults that failed, could hardly believe their eyes.

The brigades attacked in succession four sizeable hills, Wynne's Hill, named after the brigade commander, with Green Hill, were the first to be assaulted and it gave the most trouble. It is in fact two abutments of the same feature. Between them is a small re-entrant which peters out before it reaches the summit. The Royal Lancasters led the attack on the twin hills, the left two companies reaching the crest without great difficulty. The right companies were held up by Boer trenches and the rather steeper slope, with much more difficult going. The CO, who had only taken over the command that morning (Colonel Crofton having gone to Brigade in place of General Wynne, wounded earlier in the day), went up to the left companies to assess the situation and make a plan for a flank movement to release the right companies. While there and holding a brief 'O-Group' conference he was shot and mortally wounded. The bullet came almost from the rear, and undoubtedly one of the Boers holding up the right companies whose position was not so far forward, saw the O-Group with all its paraphernalia of officers with swords and maps and took the wonderful opportunity. Shortly after the CO's death the right companies were able to move again and the hill was captured.

Next day the Irish Brigade came through and the Royal Inniskilling Fusiliers took Inniskilling Hill a mile further on. This regiment too had considerable resistance to overcome and suffered many casualties. The hill is much more bare than Wynne Hill, with no trees, bushes or grass, and the Boers must have had great difficulty in finding positions. There is no top soil whatever on the rock, no digging was possible, and the graves are like those on Spion Kop, the bodies being covered with stones and rocks. However, Inniskilling Hill and Wynne being held and forming a strong flank protection, the next hill, Railway Hill, another mile on, was the objective for three days later.

But the plan was changed and the fourth hill, Pieters Hill, of which

Railway Hill was an off-shoot, was the next objective. Its capture must 'pinch out' Railway Hill and clearly Buller was beginning to show some tactical knowledge and to use his experience. Indeed his staff could hardly recognize the man they had served for the past two months. His previous pessimism, vacillation and indecision seemed to have disappeared and he had a firm grasp of the operations. He dictated his orders at speed and omitted nothing.

The Fusilier Brigade advanced up to, and captured, Pieters, the Irish Fusiliers losing many men. The Scots Fusiliers and the Dublin Fusiliers supported them, and the Dublin Fusiliers were able to open fire on the Boers still on Railway Hill from the rear. The West Yorks had assaulted this hill as a feint attack, and while containing the Boers thereon, had allowed Buller's 'pinch out' tactics to be successful. Buller then followed up his success with the kind of pressure that no one in his army had ever seen or suspected before. Gunfire continued through the night, and next morning, the 28th, the Boers disintegrated, fleeing across the plain past Ladysmith.

That afternoon Lord Dundonald's cavalry brigade entered Lady-smith. The 92 days of operations were over, and success had at last reached Buller. He had relieved Ladysmith.

The sudden change in Buller's attitude was quite extraordinary. His normal pessimistic, introvert, rude nature could not stand a rebuff or failure or opposition. Hence his colossal defeat at Colenso, his first engagement in the South African War, affected him deeply, greatly shaking his self-confidence and inducing indecision. He remained the same man for two months, setback following setback, his doubts always remaining.

Then the first success, when after returning to Chieveley from Vaal Krantz he got his army across the Tugela without opposition. His sudden elation, optimism, vitality, showed him to be a man whom success encouraged, a man who did not like, perhaps couldn't take, hard knocks, but who thrived on good news. Never was there a clearer case of nothing succeeding like success.

2
The Russo-Japanese War

Tsushima (1905)

C. P. Campbell

The great sea battle that was fought on 27 May 1905 in the straits dividing Tsushima island from Japan ended with the complete destruction of a first-class European battle squadron by the navy of a country with only 50 years of modern industrial and organizational experience. In those 50 years warship design had progressed from wooden sailing-ships firing cannon broadsides to steel steam-powered battleships, equipped with wireless, fire-control systems and mounting guns capable of engagement at ranges over five miles. When the battle came it was a clash of design ideas and tactical doctrines, but above all of two different social systems' will to win. As the Japanese commander, Admiral Togo, wrote after the battle, 'The *Mikasa* [Togo's flagship] and the 11 others of the main force had taken years of work to design and build, and yet they were used for only half an hour of decisive battle. We studied the art of war and trained ourselves in it, but it was put to use for only that short period. Though the decisive battle took such a short time, it required 10 years of preparation.'

On 30 January 1902 Japan announced the conclusion of an alliance with Great Britain. The Royal Navy's tactical doctrines and British shipbuilding practice had already permeated the thinking of those directing Japan's emergence as a world naval power. Japan's transformation from a medieval to a modern state had proceeded at breakneck speed. They had imported 200 years of Europe's industrial revolution wholesale, but in choosing their military mentors – Germany for the army, and Britain for the navy – they had chosen well. There had even been a modern naval action for Japan to test and show her efficiency at sea.

In 1894 the Chinese Empire seemed on the verge of breaking up. Korea and the vast Manchurian hinterland were tempting targets for Japanese military ambition. The Japanese successfully convoyed a large army to Korea in August, 1894, until the Chinese Admiral Ting sought battle off the mouth of the Yalu River.

When the time came, however, the contest was not so clear; Admiral Ting adopted outdated tactics, throwing away his advantage in gunpower, and the Japanese Admiral Ito decided the action by out-manoeuvring and encircling the Chinese line of battle. Four Chinese ships were sunk by gunfire and one by collision, but their battleships proved the value of armour against hits from smaller guns. Ito's flagship, the *Matsushima*, was hit three times by 12-in and once by 10-in shells, causing great damage and over a hundred casualties. Both fleets retired, but Japan was left in command of the Yellow Sea and free to continue her military adventure in Korea.

The prize of the Liaoutang Peninsula, with the ice-free port, Port Arthur, at its base, was snatched away when the European powers put on diplomatic pressure to 'protect' China. The wound to Japanese pride was deepened when, as soon as Port Arthur had been returned to China, Russia bullied the ailing Empire into allowing the Trans-Siberian Railway to be completed to Vladivostok across Manchuria. By March 1898 the Russians were in Port Arthur itself and developing an ice-free naval base to complement Vladivostok, 300 miles to the north. The Japanese, however, had already started a programme of naval expansion which would bring their fleet up to six new battleships, six armoured cruisers, and eight light cruisers by 1903.

Russia watched with alarm, and commenced production in Baltic yards of eight battleships. In contrast to the Anglophile Japanese, these ships were strongly influenced by French practice, with pronounced tumblehome and high freeboards (high hulls bellying out at the waterline), long waterline armour belts, and massive masts and built-up superstructures.

The Russo-Japanese War began on the evening of 8 February 1904. Japanese destroyers in two waves made a precision night attack against the Russian First Pacific Squadron lying in the roadstead of

Port Arthur. Seven battleships, six cruisers, and 25 destroyers lay anchored in the harbour, their lights blazing and their defences woefully ill-prepared. Only three torpedoes found their mark, but they crippled three battleships. The *Tsarevitch*, *Retzivan* and *Pallada* settled on the shallow bottom, stranded without dry-dock facilities, and for a vital month the Japanese controlled the Yellow Sea and began the transfer of their armies to the mainland.

When the dynamic Admiral Makarov arrived in March to take command of the dispirited Russian fleet, the squadron was roused from its somnolence and the damaged battleships were raised in coffer-dams. As the new spirit and the renewed threat to their lines of troop transports became evident to the Japanese, they redoubled their efforts to block the harbour. Admiral Togo was forced to use his ships in close blockade, with its wear and tear on his vessels (although keeping the crews combat trained), and face the increasing hazards of Russian minefields. However, on their few sorties out of harbour, the lack of skill of the Russian commanders was painfully obvious. Coming out in the battleship *Petropavlovsk* to cover the return of a disastrous destroyer sortie, Makarov led his whole squadron over a freshly laid minefield. There was a muffled explosion under the flagship, then suddenly two vast explosions threw a great chunk of the battleship's superstructure into the air. The big ship heeled over and slid to the bottom, her propellers still turning, taking Makarov with her.

His ability had been the Pacific Squadron's hope, and with his death the offensive power of the fleet, even to stop a landing on the peninsula behind the port, collapsed. 'The squadron went back to slumber in the basins of the inner harbour,' wrote an observer.

The Japanese, however, had their problems. Togo's repeated attempts to block the harbour with suicide assault blockships had failed. The battleships *Habuse* and *Yashima* were claimed by mines. The Vladivostok cruisers were harrying troop transports. It was clear that the Russians were gathering a fleet in the Baltic to come to the aid of embattled Port Arthur, and Togo was still forced to keep his fleet concentrated should the new if reluctant Russian commander, Admiral Vitgeft, attempt a breakout.

It was not Togo, however, who had to make the first move. Vitgeft received direct orders from the Tsar to take the squadron to Vladivostok and, led by minesweepers, the fleet left harbour on 10 August 1904. There was little hope aboard the Russian ships and already Japanese scouts were signalling the news of the attempted break-out to Togo's battle-squadron, now steaming north to engage. Togo had hoped the Russian fleet could be kept inside harbour where it would be destroyed or captured by the besieging army. Now his Combined Fleet, the entire battleship strength of Japan, would have to accept battle, with the threat of the Baltic Fleet still to come. He could afford to lose no more ships.

The Japanese purpose would be served by barring the way out, if not destroying the Pacific Squadron in battle. Suitably the opposing heavy squadrons opened fire at extreme range, with the Russian gunnery surprisingly accurate. As the long daylight action continued and the opposing fleets manoeuvred for the best position, the Japanese were taking serious punishment. Mutual destruction would bring Togo a tactical victory but would lose him the strategic object.

Then suddenly, with darkness beginning to fall, two 12-in shells struck the Russian flagship *Tsarevitch*, killing every man on the bridge. Of Vitgeft only a bloody piece of one leg remained, and the battleship lurched out of control, turning the battle-line into a milling throng. After minutes of utter disorder, Admiral Prince Uhtomski, flying signals from the bridge-rails of *Pereviet* (the signalling masts had been shot away), led the squadron back to Port Arthur as *Retzivan* and *Pobieda* put up a gallant rearguard. Japanese destroyers closed in for the kill, but in the darkness the Russian stragglers managed to regain the harbour they had so recently left. The crippled *Tsarevitch*, hit by over 15 12-in shells, was interned in German Kiau-Chow, and two cruisers suffered similar fates. The sortie had been a fiasco, but until the hit on *Tsarevitch* the Russians had held their station. With their leadership gone, their fighting ability collapsed. The Vladivostok squadron was brought to action on 14 August, but again this resulted in a Russian defeat. The cruiser *Rurik* was sunk and the cruiser *Gromoboi* ran aground. All that was left was the cruiser *Rossiya* and three Russian admirals, unable to reach Port Arthur, where the leaderless Russian battleships had retired to lick their wounds.

The humiliations in the East made the dispatch of reinforcements inevitable. The Russian confidence of 1904 that the 'yellow monkeys' would be crushed had been shattered by Admiral Togo Heiacho and his British-built battleships. In the Baltic a force of new first-class battleships were under construction, while older cruisers and battleships were undergoing refits. If Port Arthur held out, and a powerful new fleet could come to the rescue, Japan might still be denied her mainland ambitions.

The man appointed to command this 'Second Pacific Squadron', Rear-Admiral Zinovei Petrovitch Rozhdestvenski, faced immense problems in even getting his ships ready for sea. Food and clothing had to be procured for the fleet's 12,000 seamen, and machinery prepared for an ordeal beyond any design endurance. In the brief periods of manoeuvres nothing had gone right, with ships colliding and wildly inaccurate gunnery. The overriding problem, however, was coal. Great Britain, with her virtual monopoly of high-grade smokeless Welsh coal, had declared it contraband, but not before the Japanese had built up large stockpiles. The Royal Navy's dominance in the world's oceans was maintained by a strategic chain of coaling stations. Russia had none and only a fitful access to 'neutral' French and German colonial ports. The Baltic Fleet would have to cover 19,000 miles of sea, round the Cape and across the Indian Ocean, consuming 17,000 tons of coal per 1,000 miles. The bunkering capacity of the most modern Russian battleship was 1,063 tons. The solution was a fleet of 60 German colliers dispatched in succession to meet the slow-moving fleet at prearranged rendezvous between Libau in the Baltic and Port Arthur on the other side of the globe.

On 15 October 1904 Rozhdestvenski raised his flag on *Kniaz Suvorov* and, with flags waving and bands playing, the fleet steamed out of Libau to avenge the humiliations in the East. It comprised seven battleships – the recently completed *Suvorov, Aleksandr III, Borodino, Orel* and *Oslyaba*, and the *Sissoi Veliki* and *Navarin*, with two armoured cruisers, *Admiral Nakimoff* and *Dmitri Donskoi*, four light cruisers, *Aurora, Svietlana, Zhemtchug* and *Almaz*, plus seven destroyers and nine transports. The modern battleships mounted four 12-in and seven 6-in guns in paired turrets and had complete waterline armour belts 10 inches thick. The pronounced tumblehome and built-up superstructures, following French design practice, made them bad seakeepers. The overloading of coal and stores added to the miseries of the voyage.

Once at sea, the morale and incompetence of the fleet was revealed to the world when fantastic rumours of a Japanese torpedo attack were taken seriously. To the men on the bridges who remembered the surprise night attack on Port Arthur, however, an attack from British bases did not seem that fantastic. In the North Sea the repair ship *Kamchatka* lost contact with the main fleet, and her frantic signals of sighting torpedo-boats (in fact a Swedish steamer) reached the line of battleships just as they ran into British trawlers working off the Dogger Bank. Wild alarm seized the Russians and equally wild gunnery tore into the trawlers. The voyage had opened in fiasco, and meanwhile Britain seemed on the brink of war.

At Tangier the fleet divided. Admiral Velkerzam was ordered to take the older shallow-draught ships through the Suez Canal and rendezvous at Nossi Bé on the northern tip of Madagascar. At a halting pace the main squadron crawled around the coast of Africa. Ships got lost. Engines broke down. Sailors went made in the heat, cursing the back-breaking ritual of coaling from the faithful German colliers. Inside the ships coal was piled everywhere, 'not up to the neck but over the ears', as an officer wrote, blinding and choking, but, worst of all, making any combat training impossible.

At Nossi Bé the divided squadron rejoined and learned the news that Port Arthur had fallen. Worse still, the coaling arrangements had broken down and the fleet was stuck. All the Russian Admiralty could do was dispatch a 'Third Pacific Squadron' under the command of Rear-Admiral Nebogatov. The fleet did manage an epic crossing of the Indian Ocean, coaling at sea from lighters, until on 9 May, off the coast of French Indo-China, Nebogatov's 'tubs' caught up to further embarrass Rozhdestvenski.

On 23 May the Russians coaled off the China coast for what was going to be the last time. The force heading into the battle-zone was organized in four divisions. The first, led by Rozhdestvenski's flagship *Suvorov*, comprised the battleships *Aleksandr II*, *Borodino*, and *Orel*. The Second Division was commanded by Admiral Velkerzam aboard the *Oslyaba*. The unfortunate admiral had succumbed to a tropical disease on the day of the last coaling, but Rozhdestvenski kept this information from the fleet. The *Sissoi Veliki*, *Navarin*, and *Admiral Nakhimoff* followed the dead admiral's flagship. In *Nicolai I* Nebogatov led the Third Division, *Apraxin*, *Seniavin* and *Ushakoff*, while Admiral Enquist, in the *Oleg*, commanded the eight cruisers.

On board the *Mikasa*, flagship of the Combined Fleet lying in the anchorage of Masan on the Korean mainland, Togo directed the operations to meet Rozhdestvenski's ships, now heading for Vladivostok. The most likely route, the Tsushima Strait separating the island of that name from Japan, was divided into boxes, each patrolled by Japanese cruisers. The Tsugau Strait and the northern route around the top of Japan itself was left thinly protected, but it was a gamble that would pay off. The Russian crews prayed for fog to conceal the seven miles of the ships under their black smoke haze until they reached the safety of Vladivostok, which now seemed like the promised land. But for Rozhdestvenski merely to evade Togo and take refuge in another Port Arthur might merely repeat the fate of the First Pacific Squadron. The Russian admiral had at least to inflict some damage on the enemy, so the squadron's speed was adjusted so that it would enter the zone of maximum danger at daylight on 27 May 1905.

A Japanese armed merchant cruiser, the *Shinano Maru*, made the first contact at 0330. The wireless message reached Togo in the *Mikasa* – 'The enemy sighted in section 203, he seems to be heading for the eastern channel.' Ninety minutes later Togo led the battleships of the First Division out of Masan, the *Mikasa*, *Shikishima*, *Fuji*, and *Asahi*, the armoured cruisers *Kasuga* and *Nisshin*. Vice-Admiral Kanimura led the Second Division, the armoured cruisers *Izumo*, *Azuma*, *Tokira*, *Yagumo*, and *Iwate*. The cruisers *Naniwa*, *Takachino*, *Tsushima* and *Akashi* made up the Third Division. Every ship was fuelled and armed for maximum combat efficiency and able to make 18 knots, in contrast to the worn-out Russian ships' nine or ten. Togo's fleet could bring to action 16 12-in guns, and 112 8-in and 6-in guns. The Russians had 26 12-in, 10-in and 121 8-in and 6-in. Any disparity in gunpower mattered little, however; it was how the rivals used their gunpower that would decide the battle.

Togo's operations officer, Commander Akiyama, had set a seven-stage trap for the Russians to sail into. The battle would open with torpedo and destroyer attacks and the third phase would be the direct fleet engagement. The remaining stages envisaged the piecemeal destruction of any survivors who might break through towards Vladivostok. The Russian fleet was detected too late for torpedo attacks, but shadowing cruisers forced Rozhdestvenski into weakening his formation. Fearing an attack, he ordered a manoeuvre designed to give him the advantage of crossing the 'T' of the main Japanese force that must be waiting somewhere ahead. When the shadowing cruisers disappeared, the Russian admiral ordered the First and Second Battleship Divisions to make an eight-point turn to starboard to bring the ships in line abreast. As *Suvorov* began the turn, the Japanese cruisers reappeared and the order to the Second Division was contradicted. The Russian captains could not execute the change with any kind of precision and, as Nebogatov wrote, 'The enemy continued to turn to port and lay parallel to our mob, since this is the only word to describe our formation.' Thus the Russians were suddenly steaming towards Togo's battlefleet at a closing speed of 24 knots in a ragged battle formation exposed on the port side.

It was not Togo's intention to make a north–south broadside pass which, although it might damage the weaker Russian ships, would leave them travelling in the direction of Vladivostok. At 1355 the Japanese line swung to port, following the *Mikasa* in line ahead. Rozhdestvenski meanwhile had ordered the First Division to increase speed and come out from behind the weaker line to his left and take up battle formation in one line ahead. Then, as Togo reached the chosen position, the battle ensigns were unfurled, and in a breathtaking manœuvre the whole Japanese line swung round 180 degrees, turning in succession, with the *Mikasa* leading. At the moment of the turn they were helpless targets, but only the lighter Russian shells were making hits. Coming out of their turn, one after the other, the Japanese ships opened a slow deliberate fire at a range from 5,000 to 6,000 yards. Then they put on speed, sprinting north-east at 15 knots across the head of the labouring Russian column. The classic manœuvre that the pirates of the Inland Sea had known for centuries, crossing the 'T', had been achieved.

As the Japanese gunners found the range, the leading Russian ships were subjected to a fearful battering. *Suvorov* and *Oslyaba* were soon set ablaze, while, on board, stunned Russian seamen struggled with primitive damage-control procedures. At 1455 *Suvorov* fell out of line on fire. At 1505 *Oslyaba* sank, throwing the following ships into chaos. *Aleksandr III* turned to port to escape under the smoke haze and slip behind the stern of the Japanese line, all steaming in perfect formation at 15 knots, all guns in action. As they looped back to intercept them, only the *Suvorov* was left in sight, still fighting back with one remaining 12-in gun and a few remaining 12-pounders. From the shattered bridge the severely wounded Rozhdestvenski was carried to a gun turret.

An hour later the missing Russian main body was resighted and forced to turn away south-east as Togo's ships poured fire into them at a range of 1,000 yards. *Aleksandr III* was forced out of formation until, at 1800, it capsized and sank. The *Orel* was raked with fire and the *Borodino* burned until her exploding magazines ripped the ship apart. At the same time the gallant *Suvorov* was being finished off with torpedoes. The agony of the battleships could not relieve the cruisers *Oleg* and *Zhemtchug*, set ablaze, and the sinking of several auxiliary ships.

At darkness, with Vladivostok still 300 miles away, Admiral Nebogatov, in the old *Nicolai I*, attempted to achieve some sort of order from the decimated survivors of the First and Second Divisions and his still largely intact Third Division. The gathering darkness, however, brought the torpedo-boats. Pressing home vicious attacks at ranges under 300 yards, the Japanese sank *Navarin* and *Sissoi Veliki*. Admiral Enquist, in the *Oleg*, led *Zhemtchug* and *Aurora* away from the slaughter out by the southern exit of the Tsushima Strait, but the cruisers *Admiral Nakhimoff* and *Monomakh* were scuttled on the island of Tsushima itself.

At dawn the next day Nebogatov's shattered fleet was found again by the Japanese battlefleet. The tragic Rozhdestvenski lay critically wounded in the destroyer *Bedovi*. By 1115 the Japanese had formed a great circle around the Russian ships. There was no other choice. A white tablecloth was run up on *Nicolai I*, but Togo did not cease fire until the Russians had stopped their engines. Victory was complete when the unconscious Admiral Rozhdestvenski was carried into captivity. Of the 12 Russian ships that had made up the battle-line, eight had been sunk and four captured. Four cruisers had been sunk, three scuttled and Enquist's three escaped to the Philippines and were interned in Manilla. One cruiser, the *Almaz*, and two destroyers reached Vladivostok. The Russians lost 4,830 men killed, 7,000 prisoners and more interned. The Japanese lost three torpedo-boats, 117 killed and 585 wounded.

What had happened? How had two battlefleets – on paper, at least, evenly matched – met and fought with such an uneven outcome? The reports of the British naval attachés who had gone into action with the Japanese fleet were eagerly studied, and they indicated several things: that Russian gunnery had been surprisingly accurate at long range but had rapidly deteriorated as soon as the Russian ships themselves took damage; high-explosive shells had caused the most damage, and a high proportion of Russian shells found their target but failed to explode; that shells, not torpedoes, were the deciders; that both sides had fought bravely, but that the Japanese were vastly more competent than their opponents. All this was true, and the reports strongly influenced naval thinking up to the start of the First World War and beyond, however, the Second Pacific Squadron had been disadvantaged from the very start.

The ships were worn out by the voyage from across the world. Of the men themselves, many were sick. Ironically, after the repeated stops and the backbreaking task of coaling, the Russians had gone into action with too much, some of it stacked on the decks in bags. The Japanese, taking the advice of a Royal Navy report by Admiral Fisher, had actually dumped coal, losing weight to fighting trim and giving them the crucial speed advantage which allowed Togo's in succession turn and the foiling of Russian evasive manoeuvres. The Japanese had concentrated fire on the Russian flagships, and as soon as they had been battered out of line, their squadrons' formation and fighting qualities fell to pieces.

Finally, the initiative and competence of the Japanese commanders and seamen was something that could not be quantified in the reports drafted by naval attachés. As they had closed for action, Admiral Togo had been urged to take cover as he stood on the exposed bridge. He shook his head. 'I am getting on for sixty, and this old body of mine is no longer worth caring for. But you are all young men with futures before you, so take care of yourselves and continue living in order to serve your country.' The Imperial Japanese Navy was a curious mixture of Royal Navy traditions of understatement and Oriental determination to triumph. Togo had signalled to the fleet: 'The rise and fall of the Empire depends upon the result of this engagement. Do your utmost, every one of you.'

3
The First World War

Nun's Wood (1914)

Peter Banyard

It is not often in the history of warfare that elite corps clash head on. The occasions when they do such as at Waterloo when the British Guards faced Napoleon's Imperial Guard are usually well-recorded and dramatic struggles. Yet 11 November 1914, when Prussian Guards broke the line held by 1st British (Guards) Brigade, during the First Battle of Ypres, is not the date of a well-remembered contest. This may be because neither side had much to celebrate at the end of the day or because the British brigade contained so few actual guardsmen that they could plead that it was hardly a fair contest. But, although the battle lacked the drama of an equal stand-up fight between the Guards of two Royal Houses, it was nevertheless a moment in the First World War during which the Germans were within an ace of seizing a decisive advantage.

It had long been a basic tenet of German military thinking that France and her Allies in the West must be crushed swiftly in any general conflict, so that the German Army would be free to turn on Russia. When this strategy was frustrated in September 1914 by the Anglo-French victory on the Marne, General Helmuth von Moltke, the younger, was replaced as Chief of the German General Staff by General Erich von Falkenhayn. Although von Falkenhayn realized that he had little chance of driving the Western Allies from the field during 1914, he knew that the capture of the Channel ports would prevent any easy reinforcement of the French from Britain and might provide Germany with an advantage which could, eventually, be decisive.

The Allies, whose command was co-ordinated in Belgium and Northern France by the irrepressible French General Ferdinand Foch, were concerned not only to parry the threat to the ports but also to liberate and hold as much of Belgium and France as they could – however high the cost. The result of these decisions in high places was a series of bloody engagements in Flanders beginning on 19 October and collectively known as the First Battle of Ypres. Throughout the battle the Germans enjoyed a numerical and material advantage over the Allies and, despite Foch's repeated attempts to counter-attack, began to exert a near intolerable pressure on the Allied line. Through October and into early November fresh German troops pressed attack after attack on the severely strained Anglo-French forces holding the infamous Ypres Salient. By 11 November the Allies and particularly the British had no reserves left worth the name. They were logically a beaten army.

During the night of 9/10 November the Germans inserted a fresh, elite Army Corps into the line opposite Gheluvelt. The move was carried out in secret and the troops were Pomeranians and West Prussians of 4th Division and the men of Lieutenant General von Winckler's Guard Division. They were commanded by General Baron von Plettenberg of the Guard Corps and their role was to be spearhead of a great, final assault to break the Allied line. Other German units to the north launched an attack on 10 November to keep the French busy and prevent them from reinforcing the weak British formations in the path of the Prussian steamroller. Early on the morning of 11 November the long lines of guardsmen formed up well to the rear of their front line as a powerful preliminary barrage plastered the British trenches. Although German forces to the south were meant to join in the attack, they made only a half-hearted attack and the real blow was delivered by the Guard and 4th Divisions. Together they made up 25 battalions – at least 17,500 infantry – as they advanced astride the Menin road, east of Ypres.

The entire available British forces in the path of the attack (from 1st and 3rd Divisions) including reserves, cavalry and cooks totalled no more than 7,850 men and only a proportion of these were in the fire trenches. Besides this all British units were now very reduced after three weeks constant fighting. Although new armies were being formed in England there were no reinforcements left for the old

Regular Army which was withering away under continuous attrition. Most British battalions could muster only 200–300 men from their original wartime establishment of more than 900 and they had already used up all their trained reinforcements. Besides this all British units were exhausted by long exposure to battle without relief and their clothing and health had suffered in the rain and sleet. It had proved impossible to feed front-line units promptly and adequately during First Ypres and there was a very marked German superiority in the available quantity of shells and guns. All in all it was remarkable that any British troops kept on fighting.

But the professionals of the British Regular Army were very accomplished soldiers. They were not all heroes but constant indoctrination with regimental and unit loyalty made them, in general, as loyal and enduring as soldiers can be. They were also experts with their weapons as seen in the famous 'rapid fire'. In the 'mad minute' of rapid fire on the rifle range the best of them could hit a target with 30 shots; it must have been a spectacular feat, using a bolt-actioned rifle and three magazine changes. They had also been given practice with the bayonet and were prepared to use it. But fond hopes for a war of maneuver had led British military theorists to rely too heavily on shrapnel rather than high explosives (HE) – which was more effective on earthworks. In fact, the Royal Artillery was hampered by a dire shortage of shells of any sort, but the more readily available shrapnel was effective enough against massed formations, even if not much good for softening up prepared defenses.

The German Army should have been able to match the British in military virtue. The Prussians were picked troops of unusual size and courage. They were to display an enthusiasm for the bayonet at least equal to the British, and they were backed by far greater resources in artillery. But their counter-battery work was defective and the British guns were seldom shelled during the day. There was also, at least among the Prussian Guard, a certain narrowness of military outlook which is best illustrated by the fact that, in spite of new regulations, it prided itself on sticking to the methods of the 1870–1 Franco-Prussian War. It was ironic that in 1906 a German military theorist had described 'clockwork guards from Potsdam' as being soldiers of the past. Throughout 11 November the Prussian Guard, relying chiefly on courage and discipline, seems to have been confused and dismayed when called upon to show initiative and flexibility.

The British had also made primitive beginnings at defense in depth. Their front line was pitifully inadequate by later standards and consisted of a single, shallow and roughly continuous trench. This was not revetted by timber or sandbags and so was a death-trap under bombardment as near misses collapsed it, burying defenders. There were no proper communications trenches and no buried telephone cables for safe contact with supporting batteries. Then the GOC 1st Corps, Lieutenant-General Sir Douglas Haig, had one of his rare flashes of imagination. He ordered engineers to construct vestigial strongpoints in a chain immediately behind the lines. These five strongpoints were revetted and surrounded by a single fence of barbed wire; this was not much by later standards but it made them almost impervious to infantry assault in 1914, unless they had been softened up by artillery.

So there were a few shocks in store for both sides when the German bombardment began at dawn (a little after 0630) on the 11th. As the barrage built up, the British, who had been taken by surprise, soon felt the lack of buried cables as their telephone links to the rear were swiftly destroyed. Many of their infantry were forced out of the dangerous front-line trenches to shelter in nearby woods. It was the heaviest bombardment which the Germans had mounted at Ypres. Lieutenant William Congreve of the Rifle Brigade wrote: 'I never have seen the like before . . . the shrapnel played up and down our lines exactly as one waters a line of flowers, backwards and forwards. Also there were heaps and heaps of crumpets, crumps and super-crumps – all over the place they were.'

At 0900 the barrage began to lift towards the rear areas and the British infantry ran forwards from sheltered positions to firing positions in the trenches. In most places they were in time to see the Germans advancing out of the morning mist. For most of the attackers this spelled disaster. The braver and more determined they were the greater their losses would be. The magnificent 4th Division of Pomeranians and West Prussians was to suffer most. Their 12 battalions (about 8,500 men) received the staggering blow of a full minute's 'rapid fire' from eight and a half British battalions (about 4,600 men). After that, they tried to advance in 'a sort of dazed way as if they were drugged' until a last attempt at 1600, but they never came near the British trenches, although some of their companies took 75 per cent casualties.

Winckler's Guard Division had considerably better fortune; 4th

Prussian Guard Grenadier Regiment was the only part of the division to attack south of the Menin road, and it soon received its first unnerving experience of rapid fire. The regiment's official account records that it 'at once suffered such heavy losses that the first two attacks made no headway.' But, the success of the rest of the Prussian Guard north of the Menin road forced the British to retire. At the end of the day, and after much bitter fighting with 4th Royal Fusiliers, 1st Royal Scots Fusiliers and 1st Northumberland Fusiliers, 4th Prussian Guard Grenadier Regiment managed to take and hold a small section of the British front line south of the Menin road.

North of the Menin road the full weight of 2nd Prussian Guard Grenadier Regiment's three battalions fell on 2nd Battalion, The Duke of Wellington's Regiment. Some 2,100 Prussians reached the British trenches before the 846 defenders could come forward from their shelter in the woods to man them. The leading (Fusilier) battalion of 2nd Guard Grenadiers pressed on over the British front line into Weldhoek Wood. As it went on into the wood this battalion became more and more heavily engaged by its British opponents and its losses became heavier by the minute amid the dense undergrowth. All might still have gone well for the Prussians if their following 1st Battalion had come up in support. Amazingly these picked troops declined to come forward because of shrapnel fire from the British 1st Division's artillery. It is hard to believe that unsighted guns suffering from shell shortage could have put up a deadly and continuous barrage, but it was evidently quite enough for 1st Battalion which did no more than occupy the already captured British front line. A few of the Fusilier battalion's survivors escaped back to join it before evening.

It was the rest of Winckler's Guard Division that was to punch a big hole in the British line. Opposed to them was the British 1st (Guards) Brigade with 1st Battalion, The King's (Liverpool) Regiment, at right angles to their northern flank. This was where the epic clash of Guard against Guard should have taken place but, in the event, it was hardly a real test. For there were only about 200 guardsmen on the British side and they were the survivors of 1st Battalion, The Scots Guards. The rest of the so-called Guards Brigade was made up of the men from two badly mauled Scots line regiments – 1st Cameron Highlanders and 1st Black Watch – the whole brigade amounted to no more than 800 men. The Prussians moved against them with two full-strength regiments, each of three battalions. Some of the Prussian force was used for an attack on the 456-strong 1/King's which quickly shot down its assailants and maintained its position throughout the day.

The mass of the Prussian 1st and 3rd Foot Guard Regiments had very little opposition to face before reaching the British lines. The three 18-pounder gun batteries of 41st Brigade, Royal Field Artillery (2nd Division) were out of touch with the infantry but, realizing that something was up, were firing shrapnel on their 'night lines' (preset traverse and elevation to be used in emergency, these 'night lines' brought down fire in likely places in No Man's Land). This did not stop the lines of Prussians, as Major H. C. Rochfort-Boyd of 41st Brigade, RFA, noticed: 'The German Infantry moved forward at a shuffling run through the mist – then, without firing but using the bayonet with a sort of grunting cheer, they closed with and passed over our front line.' Rochfort-Boyd was able to escape on this occasion and doubled back to his battery with the news that the line was broken.

The fight between Scot and Prussian for the front line was short but very bitter. *Domprediger* Baumann, chaplain of the 4th Prussian Guard Division, was impressed by it: 'Our Brothers [the British] are cold-blooded and tough and defend themselves even when their trenches are taken, quite different to the French.' Only five Scots Guardsmen came back from the fire-trench alive. The survivors of the Scottish regiments quickly fell back upon the garrisons of the newly built strongpoints and fortified battalion HQs. This new British concept of defense in depth was to save the day for them. The German breakthrough was bottlenecked between the Black Watch strongpoint held by a lieutenant and 40 men of that regiment in the north, and a combined battalion HQ at Verbeck Farm in the south which was stoutly defended by battalion COs Lieutenant-Colonels C. E. Steward and D. L. McEwan and their staffs of the Black Watch and Cameron Highlanders.

To all intents and purposes, the Prussian Guard were through the British line and it seemed that they might go on to Calais. At this point the difference in training and experience began to tell. Most British units and individuals seemed to know exactly what they should do but the Prussians, who had been effective in storming the carefully defined objective of the British line, seemed to become confused when they stumbled upon the unexpected. They had not known about the existence of the Black Watch strongpoint and they suffered heavy casualties passing it – they were unable to take it. As they pressed on they were enfiladed by the survivors of the Scottish regiments from the edges of Glencorse Wood and the majority of them stumbled thankfully into the sanctuary of the undefended Nonne Bosschen (Nuns' Wood). From the edges of the Nonne Bosschen the Prussians could actually see the last obstacle between themselves and complete breakthrough – the three 18-pounder batteries defended only by their gunners. But at this critical moment the British kept their nerve while the Germans failed to realize their opportunity.

The British gunners made no attempt to limber up and run for it. In the front line, 1/King's made no move to fall back and cover their exposed flank; indeed the battalion diary merely noted that it was 'supported on the right by the Prussian Guard.' For the gunners, Lieutenant P. H. Murray (orderly officer to the 39th Brigade, RFA) did a lightning horseback reconnaissance of the German position. Once they knew that the enemy was in the Nonne Bosschen the British batteries concentrated their fire on it and sent out dismounted parties of gunners, cooks, stragglers and veterinaries to use their rifles against any attack.

Between 0930 and 1000, between 700 and 900 Prussians of 1st Foot Guard Regiment were assembling in the Nonne Bosschen. There were other parties of Prussians both to east and west. Ahead were the British batteries protected by small groups of riflemen amounting to about 30 bayonets all told. But the Foot Guards knew nothing of this and milled about the wood in confusion lashed by shrapnel and convinced that they were faced by numerous enemies. After 1000 the British commanders calmly built up the forces around the wood until a threatening German spearhead became a beleaguered and beaten mob.

The strongpoints still holding out behind the Germans made their communications difficult and added to the uncertainty of their position. On their right flank they might have gone into Polygon Wood and taken 1/King's in the rear but this option was soon closed to them by Lieutenant-Colonel C. B. Westmacott, commanding 5th Brigade (2nd Division). He immediately sent 5th Field Company, Royal Engineers, and 2nd Connaught Rangers to line Polygon Wood and protect the flank of 1/King's. Westmacott's divisional commander, Major-General Charles C. Monro, ordered three companies of Highland Light Infantry, the divisional cyclists and 1st Coldstream

Guards to be placed at his disposal for counter-attack. General Monro also moved 2nd Oxfordshire and Buckinghamshire Light Infantry right across the battlefield to the western edge of the Nonne Bosschen.

Meanwhile Brigadier-General Charles FitzClarence, commander of the ill-fated 1st (Guards) Brigade, found the Prussians almost in his HQ and appealed to his divisional commander, Major-General H. J. S. Landon (1st Division), for help. General Landon sent the 1st Northamptonshire Regiment. These units sound more impressive than they were, for all had been heavily engaged very recently (the Coldstream battalion was only about 100 strong), but the balance of strength was tilting against the Germans.

Meanwhile, casualties were mounting in the Nonne Bosschen. Small parties of Prussian infantry which tried to work their way forward out of the wood had been met by accurate shrapnel from 41st Brigade and rifle fire from its dismounted groups. This was enough to convince the Prussians that they faced serious opposition and they began, methodically, to dig fire positions on the edge of the wood to prepare for a full-dress assault. Time was running out for this as British reinforcements hurried to the spot and the Allied artillery began singling out the Nonne Bosschen for heavy bombardment. As many guns of 41st Brigade as could register sent shrapnel into the wood (one of the batteries had been given 24 rounds of 'experimental' 18-pounder HE and much of this was used in and around the Nonne Bosschen). Farther away, 35th Heavy Battery (four 60-pounders) NW of Westhoek joined in the shelling. Elsewhere, 51st Battery (39th Brigade) and 22nd Battery (34th Brigade) found time to send contributions crashing into the German positions and French 75 mm field guns added their quick-firing help. The German shelling was heavy at times but their counter-battery work and target indication left much to be desired, so that Allied casualties were light, but many German shells rained in on the luckless Prussians in the Nonne Bosschen.

While the Prussian strength was being sapped, their counter-attackers were forming up. The 2/Oxfordshire Light Infantry (Lieutenant-Colonel H. R. Davies), 306 strong, arrived behind the guns of 41st Brigade at about 1300. When Col. Davies learned of the situation he eagerly formed his men up for an assault to clear the Nonne Bosschen. By one of the strange coincidences of war, 2/Oxfordshire were the direct descendants of the 52nd Light

Infantry which had dealt the mortal blow to Napoleon's Imperial Guard at Waterloo by leading a charge into their flank. Traditions are long remembered in British regiments and 2/Oxfordshire were eager to add the scalp of the Prussian Guard to that of Napoleon's veterans. Just before 1500 the battalion moved off and charged the western edge of the Nonne Bosschen.

The Foot Guards may have been adversely affected by the shelling and have lost most of their officers but they put up very little resistance to the disciplined assault. The Light Infantrymen moved steadily through the wood, killing or capturing all who stayed to meet them and sustaining very few casualties (they had only five killed and 22 wounded from all causes, including shellfire, on the 11th). Once through the wood 2/Oxfordshire found 1/Northamptonshire on their right and the doughty 5th Field Company, RE, on their left. These troops pressed on together and cleared Prussian resistance up to the old British support lines and relieved the Black Watch strongpoint, which was still holding out. Just as they prepared to retake the old front line they were caught by shrapnel from the guns of the French 9th Corps near Frezenberg. It took time to send word to the French guns that they were shelling their friends and the final attack was stillborn. Early next morning Brig.-Gen. FitzClarence was killed while trying to organize a new attack and the project was abandoned.

So the great German attack of 11 November gained them less than a mile of front to a depth of less than 300 yards. Their casualties had been fairly heavy and some of them provided the British with grisly proof of the splendid physique of the Prussians. Second Lieutenant Titherington of 2/Oxfordshire complained that three of the Prussians he had had to bury were over 7 ft tall while many of their wounded proved too long for the British stretchers and ambulances.

The battle of Nonne Bosschen was one of strange and sometimes meaningless coincidences. Its very date, 11 November, seems oddly prophetic of Armistice Day 1918 and it resulted in a clash between two so-called Guard formations on very unequal terms. But these strange coincidences mean nothing when one recalls how close 11 November 1914 came to being the date when the Prussian Guard broke the British line and won a decisive victory. It was only because the Prussians did not realize how close they were to success that they did not grasp it. For one of them realization was blinding and bitter.

Feldwebel-Leutnant Schwarz was wounded and captured. As he was led past the guns of 16th Battery, 41st Brigade, he saluted and spoke to Major W. E. Clark. He asked where the British reserves were. Major Clark pointed silently to the guns. Unbelieving, Schwarz asked what troops stood behind. The curt answer was 'Divisional HQ!' Amazement and disappointment made the German exclaim, 'Heilige Gott!'

Gallipoli (1915)

Nigel Bagnall

The order to 'fall in' came ringing down to the men of the 10th Australian Battalion resting on the lower decks of HM battleship *Prince of Wales*. They were approaching the Gallipoli peninsula. There was only a dim glow from the stars as the men calmly assembled and formed into dark, shapeless groups. Between these were the smaller Naval beach parties, whose duty it was to put the men ashore. After the final breathless orders, the Australian and New Zealand Army Corps (ANZACs) clambered down the improvised ladders and ship's gangways into the waiting barges.

The expedition was made for a number of reasons. The Russians were asking Britain for aid against the invading Turks. At this time the British War Cabinet were alarmed at the seemingly endless war of bloody attrition in France. Alternative strategies were needed. And an attack on the Turks would help the Russians, make new British Allies in the Balkans and raise home morale. The War Cabinet were unsure about the attack but it was First Lord of the Admiralty Winston S. Churchill's enthusiasm that convinced them. But although the concept was bold, it was marred by indecision, delay and bad planning. Time was lost and with it the chance of surprise and success.

By March 1915 the Turks were alerted to possible British intentions after a failure by the Fleet to force past the Turkish forts and minefields defending the Dardanelles. This unmistakable warning had been realized by the Turks, who, under their energetic German commander, Marshal Liman von Sanders, began improving their defenses.

The Turkish Fifth Army were to defend the Dardanelles, a 50-mile peninsula with mountainous cliffs falling down into the sea. The ground was rugged and scrub-covered, with little cultivation. All landing sites were dominated by Turkish defenses. Three of their six divisions were on the peninsula, two on the Asiatic mainland and one astride the narrow isthmus of Bulair.

Reports of the preparations for the expedition reached the Turks from their agents. They secretly watched the gathering concentrations of shipping, troops and stores at Alexandria and the island of Lemnos. Exactly where the enemy planned to land remained a mystery. Fearing the effects of the supporting naval bombardment, von Sanders had ordered each division to remain concentrated – maintaining only the minimum forces necessary near the coastline. His defences were to be mobile. With this in mind, he exercised his 60,000 troops with forced marches, developed the paths and bridle tracks on the peninsula into roads, and assembled barges at specially chosen harbors. At the same time, the field fortifications were strengthened by all means possible – mainly by night. Stores were not plentiful, so considerable improvisation was necessary. Torpedo heads were used as mines. Wire and posts were taken from fences enclosing the cultivated areas, and pressed into service as assorted obstacles – both above and below the water line.

General Sir Ian Hamilton, Commander of the 78,000-strong BEF, planned to make two converging attacks at the southern end of the peninsula. The first would be by the British 29th Division. They were to make five separate but simultaneous landings on small beaches near Cape Helles. The ANZACs were to mount the second attack near Gaba Tebe. It was hoped that these separate actions would link up to roll the Turks back along the whole length of the peninsula. Two diversionary operations were also planned. The French contingent would land near the ruins of Troy on the Asiatic mainland, while the Royal Naval Division in transports accompanied by warships, feinted at Bulair.

Late on the afternoon of 24 April the armada, assembled in Mudros Bay, set sail. At 1000 on the 25th the three battleships and seven destroyers carrying the 3rd Australian Brigade, which formed the assault wave, stopped short of the peninsula. The final preparations for disembarkation were completed. Each of the battleships had towed astern three steam pinnaces – in addition to her own. These now took in tow the ships' boats which had already been lowered. Once alongside, they waited to receive the assembled troops.

Thanks to the rigorous rehearsals there was no confusion. As the midshipman in the stern reported each boat full, the officer in charge ordered 'Cast off and drift astern.' The boats fell behind until arrested by the hawsers connecting them. Once in position the battleships moved slowly towards the shore, each ship trailing four tows. At about 0430, the ships came into line. They were about 3,000 yards from the coast. The signal was given for the tows to cast off and make for the beach. Like so many snakes, they slowly forged their way ahead packed with men – gunwales almost flush with the water. Behind them, until the water became too shallow, the warships followed to cover the final approach. Thirty minutes after the tows had left the battleships, the seven destroyers moved forward right behind them ready to disembark their troops 20 minutes later in a second wave.

General Sir William Birdwood, commander of the ANZACs, planned to land 4,000 men of the 1st Australian Division in three successive waves, on a front of about 2,000 yards. The essence of his plan was speed and surprise. There would be no preliminary naval bombardment. Once ashore, the troops were to strike rapidly inland for some 2,000 yards and secure three prominent hill features. Having captured these, the main body would be passed through and the advance extended over comparatively easy ground for a further 3,000 to 4,000 yards. This was to be the limit of the first day's objectives.

Exactly what happened next remains in dispute. Some blame a northerly current, others a last-minute and largely unknown change of plan, while a Turkish source attributes it to deception on their part. They claim that they found and moved a previously positioned British marker buoy – causing the battleships to anchor too far north. Whatever the cause, instead of approaching the shore over a 2,000-yard front just south of the Ari Burnu promontory, the boats crowded together in the direction of the promontory itself.

This error became apparent to some of the troops and naval officers in the landing boats. But it was too late for the majority to do more than hope to reach the beach before the Turks saw them. Fifty yards from the water line the pinnaces cast off and the boats were rowed in by the sailors until grounding on the shelving beach. During this final approach they were seen. The Turks opened fire from the high ground. Scrambling out of the boats – often into several feet of water – the Australians struggled to the shore and rushed across the beach to take cover where they could. After quickly reorganizing and discarding their heavy packs, they charged the Turkish trenches on the foreshore and bayoneted the enemy. Then, heaving themselves up the steep, broken slope by the roots and branches of trees or shrubs, they doggedly pressed inland as ordered.

Not all the men were so lucky. Some of the packed boats were hit by Turkish machine-gun fire and their occupants suffered severely. Other boats ran aground at the foot of sheer cliffs. The troops were forced to move along the beach until they could find an exit. One effect of this was that the sheer cliffs protected them from Turkish guns. It caused confusion and delay, however, sub-units became hopelessly mixed, and objectives impossible to identify.

But by 0600 the Australians had secured the first ridge and began to infiltrate the second. On the left flank the greatly outnumbered Turkish survivors were falling back in disorder. Waves of Australians were landing unhindered. Some 4,000 men were already ashore and the advance inland gathered strength. By 0700 small groups of Australians had reached the third ridge. Looking down, they could see the Dardanelles only three miles away. Success appeared within reach. But the situation was to change.

The Australians' progress was delayed and then halted by the growing confusion on the beach. As a result of landing on a beach only a few hundred yards long instead of one of 2,000, the confusion and delay in bringing ashore the two follow-up brigades was immense. The control organization ashore had all but collapsed. Wounded were beginning to flow back in an ever-increasing stream and choked the beach from where many of them could not be moved. Others were loaded into boats which were meant to land further reinforcements. The one hospital ship was soon full. Successive waves of troops were landing in an increasingly chaotic manner and – on coming ashore – could be given no precise orders in the absence of any clear knowledge as to what the situation was inland.

The beach itself soon became a scene of confusion. Heaps of hastily dumped ammunition and stores lay around. Among these lay the dead. Overhead the sky was rent with the flash of shrapnel, and the air hummed with bullets. Fortunately, most of the Turkish fire was wild and casualties were not heavy. The same sanctuary was not available farther out to sea where fountains of water were thrown up around the tows operating to and from the ships.

The New Zealand Brigade was part of the reinforcements. They were given the job of lengthening the line to the left of the Australian 1st Division. The transports with their field guns on board were delayed in the face of the Turkish guns, and the New Zealanders were to feel the full bitterness of being subjected to enemy shellfire with no means of retaliation. Eventually some support was given by an Indian Mountain Battery which skilfully maneuvered themselves into seemingly inaccessible vantage points. Unloading, they would fire a dozen or so shots and be down the gully and up to a new position before the Turks could find them.

Of greater impact than even the chaos on the beach was perhaps the arrival of 34-year-old Mustafa Kemal Pasha, Commander of the Turkish 19th Division. Like all able commanders, he contrived to arrive at the critical part of the front when most needed. Alerted by the sound of gunfire from Gaba Tepe where the Australians had first landed, he at once alerted the 19th Division and at 0630 received orders to send one battalion to the heights of Ari Burnu, where the leading Australians were reported to have arrived. Kemal instinctively sensed that a major threat had developed. Far more than one battalion would be needed.

Disregarding orders, he gave instructions for the whole division to move to the coast and he himself led the first regiment which was ready towards the threatened key ridge. On arrival, he ordered the men to rest after their forced march over broken ground while he continued on his way, accompanied only by his ADC, a second officer and an orderly. Then he saw some Turkish troops fleeing towards him. Confronting them he demanded to know why they were running away. The reason was clear enough. Their ammunition was exhausted and the Australians were close behind. This explanation did not satisfy Kemal. He ordered them to fix bayonets and lie down and take up firing positions as the leading Australians came into view. The Australians did the same and unwittingly lost the initiative to the Turks.

Then Kemal ordered an officer to bring up his resting regiment at the double. They soon arrived at the position. The small band of Australians – isolated and unable to resist the ever-increasing weight of Turkish fire – withdrew to the next ridge. It was held by their countrymen. But they were widely dispersed and largely uncoordinated.

From about 1000 the Turks started to push against the Australians' left flank and filter round the seaward slopes of Baby 700 – the main hill feature held by their leading troops. A little later the second Turkish regiment started to arrive. The Turks mounted a series of savage counter-attacks. Baby 700 was lost but retaken again by two companies newly arrived from the beaches.

By now the Turks were arriving in increasing numbers and Baby 700 changed hands no fewer than five times before the Australians were finally driven off. The Australians and the New Zealanders, who had joined them during the afternoon, were suffering heavy casualties. No more than scattered and mixed up elements of seven battalions were trying to stem the advance of most of the Turkish 19th Division which were attacking in massed waves. Silhouetted against the sinking sun, they screamed 'Allah' as they advanced. They were cut down *en masse* but successive waves continued the frenzied attacks over the corpses of their fellows.

Neither side were taking prisoners. Groups of ANZACs were cut off and could not repel the Turkish charges any longer. They died where they fought. The firing line was indeterminable. Isolated groups of Australians and New Zealanders clung grimly to a number of key features as night fell and a steady drizzle set in. In the tangled gullies, when not actually fighting, men dug for their lives until, trumpets blowing and still calling on 'Allah!' the Turks again surged forward. One New Zealander remembers how they would counter these attacks by running forward themselves 'cursing in loud round English and very bad Arabic.' Many strange duels were fought that night. One Turkish rush was stemmed by a small band commanded by a corporal armed with nothing more effective than a pick-handle.

Not only the fighting men showed such tenaciousness. From the firing line it took two and a half hours to get a wounded man back onto the beach. Ignoring both bullets and shells, carefully threading their way down the twisting tracks made ever more treacherous by the endless rain, the stretcher bearers and doctors worked unstintingly. Only the most severe cases could be dealt with on the crowded beaches. Many a man, when asked whether he was badly hurt, replied quietly that 'he was all right,' then died uncomplaining.

Shortly after 2200 General Birdwood came ashore at the request of his two Australian and New Zealand divisional commanders. He found a demoralized force, tired and shaken by the day's events and disorganized by the confusion on the beach. But he was taken aback when it was proposed that there should be an immediate evacuation. Tired themselves, neither the divisional commanders nor their brigadiers believed their men could resist the renewed Turkish counter-attack. They all believed this would be mounted in overwhelming strength by fresh troops at daybreak. With no reinforcements to replace their own exhausted and fragmented units, there seemed no alternative but to evacuate and save what they could. Reluctantly Birdwood agreed. He dictated a message to Hamilton recommending that re-embarkation should start immediately.

In response to this totally unexpected proposal, Hamilton held a conference with his principal advisors. Among them was Rear-Admiral C. F. Thursby, his naval commander. The Admiral was emphatically opposed to evacuation. He did not regard it as being administratively feasible. The men were tired and disorganized and it was a dark and stormy night. Control on the crowded beaches would be virtually impossible. Under such conditions the losses could be dreadful. Hamilton needed no further persuasion. His instructions were explicit and ended with the exhortation: 'You have got through the difficult business, now you have only to dig, dig, dig, until you are safe.'

Admiral Thursby was given the job of delivering the message. He landed on the right of the ANZAC position. Here he saw for himself the chaos and suffering which had provoked such despair among the commanders. They felt too much was being demanded of their men. However, he found Birdwood cheerful, though not exactly hopeful, and the two divisional commanders more inclined to stay and fight it out.

What had not been allowed for was the courage and resolution of the troops. Had the order to evacuate been given it is probable that it would have been received with incredulity – possibly even contempt. In the succeeding days' fighting the few orders to withdraw which were given were usually queried and as frequently countermanded.

Although it was known that their own landing and that of the British at Helles should converge, it was as well that neither Birdwood nor his men counted on getting any early help as a result of this plan. The initial British landing had resulted in appalling casualties. The survivors were fighting as grimly as the ANZACs themselves to maintain their positions ashore.

Preceded by a naval bombardment, the British 29th Division had begun to land at five beaches in the vicinity of Cape Helles shortly after the Australians had got ashore at Ari Burnu. The landings at 'V' beach by the 88th Brigade were intended to be the most important. An old ruined fort dominated the beach but it was hoped that the Turkish defenders – dug in along the cliff edges as well as concealed in the fort itself – would be largely accounted for by the Navy's guns. The plan was to run the *River Clyde* – an old collier turned 'Trojan Horse' specially adapted for landing troops – as close to the beach as possible and bridge the intervening water gap with two lighters. At the same time, other troops would be landed by boat.

Because of a strong current which had delayed their arrival, there was a long interval between the lifting of the naval bombardment and the landings. This allowed the Turkish defenders to recover and take up their positions. When the *River Clyde* gently grounded, the 2,000 men of the Dublin and Munster Fusiliers and the Hampshire Regiment began to cross the improvised causeway. But as they did so, whole platoons were shot down as they raced into the withering Turkish fire. Those in the boats fared no better. The Turks had laid wire below the water and along the beach. Holding their fire until the packed boats became entangled and crowded together on the obstacles, they devastated the leading wave. There were few survivors. A handful of men managed to cross the beach and shelter under the cliffs. Others, who had been ordered to stay below and cease the senseless slaughter, remained aboard the *River Clyde*. With the brigade commander dead, any further attempt to land at 'V' beach was suspended until nightfall.

Farther north on 'W' beach the Lancashire Fusiliers suffered similar carnage. The naval bombardment had little impact on either the defenders or their defenses. Holding their fire until the last possible moment the Turks reduced the Fusiliers to a handful as they struggled through the water and wire entanglements and tried to cross the open beaches. One officer, who died later, described the scene he saw as he looked behind.

There was one soldier between me and the wire, and a whole line in a row on the edge of the sands. The sea behind was absolutely crimson, and you could hear the groans through

the rattle of musketry. A few were firing. I signalled to them
to advance. I shouted to the soldier behind me to signal, but
he shouted back that he was shot through the chest. I then
perceived they were all hit.

In spite of their appalling losses and suffering, the Fusiliers
re-formed into a thin line and began to assault the cliffs. Six VCs
were won on that desperate morning, but it is unlikely that the
survivors would have had the strength to dislodge the Turks had not
one of the companies been landed unopposed under a promontory
slightly farther to the north. From here the Fusiliers scrambled up
onto the high ground and, after being reinforced, extended this
foothold to relieve the survivors on the beach. On the other three
subsidiary beaches – 'X', 'Y' and 'S' – only light opposition had
been encountered and the few troops assigned established themselves
ashore without great difficulty.

The Turks had fought resolutely. Of the 9,000 men who had been
disembarked onto the five beaches, 3,000 had been killed or wounded
and the survivors had secured little more than precarious toeholds.
Only 'W' and 'V' beaches were linked together after dark. The troops
who had been kept on board the *River Clyde* were landed and helped
extend the bridgehead to make contact with those advancing south
from 'W' beach.

The landing of the French regiment on the Asiatic mainland near
the site of Troy occurred after a preliminary bombardment from
French warships at about 1000. There appears to have been some
delay and confusion. But by the afternoon the whole force was ashore
after encountering only light opposition. The Turkish units in this
area initially showed little of the tenacious determination which
had been displayed on the peninsula. Progress was easier for the
French. Later, however, they were unable to advance farther. After
withstanding a series of Turkish counter-attacks during the night,
they were withdrawn the following day to reinforce the right flank
of the British line on the European side of the straits. 'V' beach was
handed over to them as their base.

None of these details was known to the ANZACs. Most of them
only had time to concern themselves with their own immediate
difficulties. After the close-quarters fighting during the earlier
part of the night, exhaustion and confusion forced a lull. There
was still continuous firing. Here and there the front would flare

into angry violence. Generally, however, both sides had reached the limit of exertion. They concentrated on holding on to what they had. Some reinforcements came ashore during the night. The Wellington Regiment were disembarked and sent straight up Plugge's Plateau – a prominent feature behind the firing line. Here the sappers were already hard at work preparing a second and last line of defense. Behind this position no organized resistance would be possible.

Most of the 4th Australian Brigade was also landed but arrived in a very irregular order. Some elements came from one ship and some from another. As each platoon or company came ashore it was immediately sent under the senior officer present to the right flank where the 1st Australian Division was particularly hard pressed. In this manner units became further mixed up.

Elsewhere, the gunners labored through the night to prepare positions and improve access routes for the guns which it was hoped would be disembarked urgently. Stores and supplies poured ashore onto the congested beach. Movement was further hampered by the darkness and the running sea. It was therefore not until daylight on the 26th that the first howitzer was landed. It went into action shortly afterwards. The gun's arrival did not significantly affect the situation, but its steady, reverberating fire acted as a tonic to the hard-pressed infantrymen.

After a night of feverish activity, bitter fighting and at one time near despair, the expected Turkish dawn attack never materialized. Instead, a series of piecemeal assaults took place. These were fiercely mounted but containable because they were neither overwhelming nor sustained. The Turks had themselves suffered heavily. Further reinforcements were slow in arriving, co-ordination was difficult and the situation no clearer to them than to their enemy. The front started to stabilize. Shell scrapes became trenches, outposts became firm strongpoints, the firing was incessant. But it became possible for the troops to snatch a few moments of sleep, eat and adjust to their condition.

However immediately welcome this stabilization of the front may have been to Birdwood and his senior commanders after their earlier anxieties, it represented the first small step towards reproducing the stalemate of Western Front trench warfare which the Dardanelles expedition had been intended to break. As the days turned into weeks and then months, the deadlock became firm. The ANZACs could not materially extend their positions beyond where they had been established during the first night's fighting. The Turks had suffered the most dreadful losses as a result of repeatedly attempting to dislodge them.

In the five weeks since the expedition had begun the British and Dominion troops had suffered almost 40,000 casualties, and the French a further 20,000. Hospitals throughout the Middle East were crammed with the wounded and sick. Large numbers had been shipped back to England. The toll of sickness had arisen alarmingly. All that had been gained was a 6,000-yard-deep front across the peninsula. In the wearing heat of a Mediterranean summer swarms of flies and vultures feasted on the unburied dead that littered the battlefield and invaded every sanctuary of the living. Disease became rife, especially in the crowded conditions at ANZAC, from where an ever-increasing number of sick were having to be evacuated daily. Many of those who remained were gaunt and weak – they were barely recognizable as the same robust, exhuberant men who had so recently terrorized Cairo.

After heavy deliberations, it was decided by the War Cabinet that a great endeavor would be made to break the deadlock with large reinforcements. Three separate attacks would be mounted at the same time. First, a new landing would be made due north of the ANZAC position by two British divisions at Suvla Bay. Secondly, the ANZACs would break out and link up with the Sulva Bay landings. Finally, at Helles a holding attack would be mounted to stop the Turks switching reinforcements to the north. Including reserves available either at sea or on the adjacent Aegean islands, the Allies had some 120,000 men. Against this the Turks had an approximately equal number. About 100,000 of these were on the peninsula.

Despite great courage and impressive fighting skill by British, Dominion and Indian troops, by the end of August it was clear that the operation had failed. With certain notable exceptions the inertia of the senior commanders and the rawness of many of the troops at Suvla resulted in an over-cautious advance inland. This allowed the Turks to move their reserves to the threatened area and stem all further progress. About 1,000 men had been lost on the day of the landings. Nearly 8,000 were killed or wounded during the two days following. Another bridgehead had been established but it only served to strain the expedition's administrative resources even more and increase the need for reinforcements to maintain units at fighting strength. A break-out seemed as unrealizable at Suvla as it had proved to be at ANZAC and Helles. The weeks and months dragged on. With the approach of winter, storms added to the supply difficulties. Piers and barges were pounded and smashed on the beaches. Inland, the trenches were flooded and tracks washed away or blocked – preventing ration parties from getting forward. No sooner had the storms abated than a November blizzard swept the peninsula. The battlefields were blanketed in snow and ice. Blankets were frozen solid, weapons jammed and a lull in the fighting was enforced while men struggled to survive in the savage cold. Frostbite increased the sick-rate and deaths occurred amongst the already physically exhausted troops on both sides. One morning at stand-to, 30 men of a British battalion were found frozen to death on the fire-steps of their trenches.

Inevitably – but after much conflicting advice and painful debate – the decision to evacuate the entire peninsula was taken. Planning for such a possibility had already been put in hand. Clear, carefully considered instuctions were issued to selected officers. Unless anything unforeseen happened, the evacuation would be conducted in three stages. All surplus men, equipment and animals would begin to be withdrawn immediately. Then the force would be progressively reduced by formed units between 13 and 18 December. Finally, on the nights of 19 and 20 December the last rearguard would be withdrawn.

If the evacuation was to be undertaken successfully the highest degree of security and deception was essential. Losses of up to 40 per cent were already being expected in some quarters. Every night the outgoing barges were jammed full. But as it grew light a show of landing troops would be made. By day stores and ammunition which could not be evacuated were prepared for destruction, barricades were erected in all the principal communication trenches and a final covering position to be manned by machine-gunners was prepared.

Smoothly and methodically the evacuation continued. Only 3,000 volunteer 'Diehards' were left in each of the three divisions to hold the bridgeheads for the last 24 hours on 19 December. About 1,500 of them manned the forward trenches moving from position to position to keep up the usual pattern of fire. Others marched uphill where they could be heard and even seen to impersonate reinforcements, kept the cooking fires burning and maintained the atmosphere of general activity. To accustom the Turks to complete inactivity, periods of total silence had been imposed at irregular intervals during the preceding weeks.

Soon after dusk on the last night the rearguard started to thin out. The guns opened fire for the last time before they too were withdrawn or destroyed when this was not possible. Midnight came and the firing died down on both sides – as was usual. At 0145 the silence was broken on the New Zealand sector when the duty machine-gunner fired three rapid bursts. This was the signal for the brigade's machine-guns to withdraw. At 0200 the already sparsely populated trenches were further depleted as the infantry started to thin out. Individuals slipped away from their positions to form a shadowy stream as they flowed into the main communication trenches from the web of forward posts and trenches.

Those left behind stared into the darkness. They watched fearfully for any signs of Turkish suspicions being aroused, before it was time for they themselves to withdraw. Not all the positions could be abandoned at the same time. Those farthest from the beaches were vacated at 0130. Others, covering the more direct and short approaches, were held until 0315.

As the last of the men were being checked through the control posts manned by staff officers, a huge mine which had been tunnelled under the forward Turkish trenches was detonated. Its deafening roar abruptly shattered the silence and tension of the last few hours. The Turks took this as a signal for an all-out attack and opened fire along the entire front. They kept this up with unrelenting vigor until long after the last of 83,000 soldiers had been safely embarked from both Suvla and ANZAC. As dawn broke the Turks realized at last that their enemy had vanished. With a mixture of disbelief and awesome relief, they left their trenches to work their way down to the abandoned piles of stores and equipment lying burning and broken along the beaches.

Against all expectation of being able to surprise the Turks again, the evacuation of 35,000 men from Helles was equally successfully carried out on the night of 8 January. This was in spite of a Turkish attack taking place when the front line had already been withdrawn.

Few military expeditions create such controversy – even today – as does Gallipoli. But whether or not it was ill-conceived, hesitant in its implementation, a sad saga of 'might-have-beens', it remains an epic of heroism. Its tragedy was that it was all for nothing, but, as one New Zealander wrote, 'It was not our wasted energy and sweat that really grieved us. In our hearts it was to know that we were leaving our dead comrades behind. That is what every man had in his mind.'

Suez (1915)

Anthony Burton

In the 1973 Yom Kippur War both the Egyptians and the Israelis crossed the Suez Canal. They were not the first to do so – some 50 years before them a Turkish army had marched across the forbidding wastes of Sinai and put men on the western bank of the Canal.

In the middle of January 1915 a Turkish Expeditionary Force of 25,000 men left its base at Beersheba and prepared to cross the Sinai peninsula. Its goal was the Suez Canal – a vital link in Britain's Imperial chain. Djemal Pasha, Commander-in-Chief of the Turkish force, despite his arrogant proclamation as he left Constantinople for the front – 'I shall not return until I have conquered Egypt' – should have been under no illusions as to the magnitude of his task.

On the far bank of the Canal there was a British force much stronger than the Turks. Its base was only a few miles to the rear. The Turkish troops would find it difficult to carry sufficient stores across Sinai to maintain an offensive for more than a few days. Yet Djemal considered that the political situation was promising. Agents of the German Baron Oppenheim were busy stirring up a rebellion in Cairo which was timed to break out at the approach of the army of another Islamic Power. In the west of Egypt the Senussi tribes were revolting against the British. Djemal Pasha hoped that the infidels would soon find themselves faced with a holy war, a *jihad*, in their very midst. He had, he believed, already scored a propaganda triumph by the insulting messages he had sent to the British generals, inviting them to come out and fight in the open. Understandably, the British had ignored these suggestions and remained behind their Canal defenses.

They did not commit the error of underestimating their enemy. The contemporary issue of *War Illustrated* (13 March 1915) said: 'Whatever may be thought of his intelligence and skill, the ordinary Turkish soldier is at least no coward. He can usually die as bravely and stubbornly as men of any race.'

If German agents and the promise of a Turkish invasion could succeed in inciting rebellion in Cairo then Djemal could hope to repeat the exploits of Sultan Selim, the first Turkish conqueror of Egypt in 1517. Even if the hoped-for risings did not materialize, the Turks still reckoned on being able to seize a portion of the Canal and hold it long enough to destroy or block it. At the very least they would be able to sink some of the ships which would be trapped *en route* by the advance. Their hulks would take weeks, perhaps months, to shift. So Djemal took with him nine batteries of field artillery and one 150 mm (5.9 in) howitzer battery – supplemented by a quantity of mines – to attack the British shipping.

The Turks possessed one other advantage. They had with them as adviser the true architect of the advance to the Canal, the Bavarian Colonel Kress von Kressenstein – 'a most excellent and efficient Officer', wrote the German General Liman von Sanders. Von Kressenstein's forte was desert warfare.

The German Major Fischer saw to it that the problem of watering man and beast on the trek were overcome. Nature also helped the passage. The winter of 1914 had been exceptionally wet and the force was to find a number of springs and pools of water as it marched towards the Canal and the waiting British. Fischer had charge of 5,000 water-carrying camels. A similar number were loaded with stores and ammunition.

British Intelligence knew of the impending assault but the short range of their available aircraft made early discovery of the direction of the attack difficult. The defenders only had three Maurice Farmans, two Henri Farmans, one BE2a and seven French seaplanes at their disposal. Therefore, Djemal and Kress believed that an element of surprise might be achieved by avoiding the traditional coastal route, which would be under the guns of the British and French navies. Instead they decided to strike across the center of Sinai at the section of the Canal between Lake Timsah and the Great

Bitter Lake. This approach would provide the possibility of access to Ismailia. He who controlled that town controlled the Canal. Here were the sluices which would enable the water supply to be cut off from its whole length.

Of the three possible routes – the central, the coastal strip and the Akaba–Nekhl–Suez line – that chosen was the worst watered. Also, none of the routes was at that time more than a camel track. However, the central approach via Jifjaffa had the advantages of reasonably firm going and immunity from British naval attack.

To confuse his enemy, Djemal sent out two diversionary columns, one in the north against Kantara, the other to his south towards Kubri. Guided by local Bedouin tribesmen, the main Turkish force crossed central Sinai in two contingents, patiently laying brushwood tracks when the surface deteriorated into areas of sand dunes – sometimes several square miles in extent. It is a tribute to German organization and Turkish doggedness that the force crossed Sinai in ten days without losing a single man or animal. By the end of January the Turks were poised before their objective. Djemal then issued a flowery exhortation:

'Warriors! Behind you lie the vast deserts; before you is the craven enemy; behind him the rich land of Egypt, which is waiting impatiently for you. If you falter, death will overtake. Before you Paradise lies.'

After this rhetorical flourish Djemal gave his orders and the Turks moved forward.

On the right flank, in the north, a weak force of irregulars and Bedouin was sent with some Turkish infantry detachments to mount a feint attack on Kantara. In the south, a pack battery accompanied the 69th Regiment, 23rd Division, as it moved towards Kubri while in the center 20,000 of the best Turkish troops prepared for the attack. Kress von Kressenstein was with the first group of the central force while his fellow German, Colonel von Frankenberg und Proschlitz, accompanied Djemal Pasha and the crack 10th Division in the second contingent.

By now the British were ready for them. Small raids against Kubri (27 January) and Kantara (29th) did not disguise the Turkish intention to thrust at the center. Spies as well as aerial reconnaissance confirmed that the attack would concentrate on that sector. Accordingly, Major General A. Wilson, GOC Canal Defenses, reinforced Serapeum with the 2nd Rajputs.

Thirty thousand troops, mainly Indian, now awaited the attack along the line of the Canal. The 10th and 11th Indian Divisions were supported by the Imperial Service Cavalry Brigade and the Bikanir Camel Corps. Behind them the 42nd (East Lancashire) Division, Australian and New Zealand contingents and some Yeomanry units lay in reserve. The total overall strength was 70,000 men, but not all were fully trained. The defenders were short of artillery. There were only three batteries of Indian mountain artillery and a battery of Egyptian artillery available in the threatened sector. This deficiency was made up for by stationing British and French warships in the Canal. Eight were eventually used in this role. The most powerful of these were HMS *Ocean*, a *Canopus*-class pre-Dreadnought battleship of 12,950 tons (four 12-in, 12 6-in and 12 12-pounder guns) and HMS *Swiftsure* (formerly the Chilean Navy battleship *Constitution*, bought by the Royal Navy in 1909), 11,800 tons, armed with four 10-in, 14 7.5-in and 14 14-pounders. Other vessels involved included the *Eclipse*-class second-class cruiser HMS *Minerva* (5,600 tons), the sloop HMS *Clio*, the armed merchantman *Himalaya* and the Royal Indian Marine armed troopship *Hardinge*. *D'Entrecasteaux*, the French cruiser, and the coastguard ship *Requin* were also to be involved. The latter, together with the *Hardinge*, was destined to play an important part in the action on the central sector.

The attack began on the night of 3 February. It was cloudy and the waiting British strained their eyes into a darkness made more impenetrable by the blown sand which stung their faces and against which they had to wrap their rifles for protection. Three posts on the east bank, Tussum, Serapeum and Deversoir – two companies in each – watched for a sign of the Turkish advance. Behind them on the west bank 11 smaller posts, each manned by two platoons, covered the opposite shore – and waited. Among the 62nd Punjabis was a 30-year-old subaltern who was to achieve fame in the Second World War. The defense of the Canal was his first experience of action ('I remember the first bullet that went over my head, which made me duck damn quickly'). His name was Claude John Eyre Auchinleck.

At 0325 Arab irregulars – calling themselves the 'Champions of Islam' – disobeyed orders and gave away their positions south of Tussum by calling loudly upon Allah and cursing the infidel. After sporadic firing on both sides there was once again silence. A little after 0400, the clouds cleared and the moonlight illuminated hundreds of the attackers struggling down to the water's edge, carrying rafts and pontoons. At 0420 this party was engaged by an Egyptian artillery battery and by rifle fire and driven back. Immediately after this, larger groups appeared to the north, near Tussum. These troops tried manfully to launch their cumbersome craft – galvanized iron pontoons and rafts of kerosene tins in a simple wooden frame. Over their heads fierce fire raged between defenders and their own supporting infantry. Three boatloads succeeded in crossing the Canal but were attacked by a bayonet charge from the 62nd Punjabis and the 128th Pioneers. As Auchinleck laconically remarked, 'We were on the west bank and they came over and our men charged down the bank and put a bayonet into them – that was all.' In these engagements every Turkish soldier on the west bank was either killed or captured. At the same time as the Tussum incident the Turks launched a half-hearted attack on the Ismailia ferry post.

In the weary dawn the cost of the attack became clear. Turkish dead lay among their abandoned rafts and pontoons on the east bank. The defenders of the east bank outposts sallied forth from their perimeters. More troops crossed the Canal to support them and put paid to any surviving Turk from the eastern margins of the waterway. A torpedo boat was sent north from Deversoir to destroy any pontoons still intact.

But these British counter-attacks were halted by the appearance of a superior Turkish force. Artillery duels between the ships anchored in the Canal and the Turkish batteries continued throughout the rest of the day.

Here the Turkish artillery was efficient. Two batteries of field artillery and the 150 mm howitzer battery succeeded in hitting the outgunned 6,520-ton *Hardinge*, armed only with six 4.7-in guns. She was forced to break off action at 0845. A duel now began between the *Requin* and the Turkish battery. At first the Turks had the better of it, but at 0900 their position was betrayed by a puff of smoke. Their range was estimated and their howitzers silenced. *Requin* and the cruiser *D'Entrecasteaux* – ordered up to replace the *Hardinge* – now concentrated their fire on the assumed position of the main Turkish force. Artillery engagements were fought elsewhere on the front, particularly between HMS *Clio*'s six 4-in and two Turkish field guns which had scored some direct hits on El Ferdan railway station. At 1030 these too were silenced.

Next day, to the surprise of the watching British and Indian troops, the Turks began to retreat. Djemal had in fact ordered it on the evening of the 3rd. The speed of the withdrawal, which both Kress and Djemal believed to be necessary, left some of the Turkish troops behind. These were duly attacked and captured before they could escape from their trenches facing the Canal. The remainder of the Turkish army escaped without incident since the British were neither physically nor psychologically prepared for pursuit. Djemal fell back to Beersheba, leaving Kress in the desert with three infantry battalions and a squadron of cavalry with two mountain batteries to support. Kress's orders were to exploit his mobility to keep the enemy occupied, to hamper shipping movements and slow down preparations for any British advance across Sinai.

British casualties numbered only 32 killed and 130 wounded. Enemy losses were heavier. Kress gives figures of 192 killed, 371 wounded and 727 missing, a total of 1,290 – but the true numbers were higher, since the Turks did not record the casualties of their irregulars. British archives show that they buried 238 of the enemy dead and captured 716 prisoners. One of the dead was the German Staff Officer who had been in charge of the crossing, Captain von dem Hagen.

While Turkish expectations of a rising in their favor were certainly over-optimistic, their less ambitious plan of seizing a section of the Canal for a few days was more realizable. Therefore, their failure to come anywhere near to achieving this objective is puzzling.

Kress claimed that the sandstorm delayed his preparations, that the force lacked the training necessary for a night crossing of the Canal under enemy guns and, finally, that the use of an Arab, rather than a Turkish division was an error – the former's loyalty being suspect. While the first two of these reasons may have some plausibility the third does not bear examination. It would indeed have been more sensible to have used the 10th Division in the first place, instead of holding it in reserve to pass through the Arab 23rd (Homs) and the 25th (Damascus) Divisions after they had made an initial breach in the British defenses. The assertion, made by General Liman von Sanders among others, that Arab units went over to the British is certainly untrue. On the contrary, the crossing was bravely attempted against an entrenched enemy who had prepared the ground – even to the extent of putting range markers out in the desert – and had excellent fields of fire.

The warships were the eventual victors of their clash with the Turkish artillery. The reluctance of the Turkish troops to press their attacks later on the morning of the 3rd must be attributed to the warships' shelling accuracy, not least with their 12-pounders and smaller quick-firing guns.

Djemal Pasha and Kress von Kressenstein argued later that the raid had in any case been worth the effort. It had demonstrated the vulnerability of the Canal and had floored British assumptions as to the numbers of men who could cross the Sinai peninsula. In 1906 the British War Office had estimated that, in view of the water situation, the largest force that could cross would be 5,000 men and 2,000 camels. Technically, the expedition had been impressive and this demonstration of German/Turkish expertise made necessary the continuation of a huge British presence – first to defend and then to move out from the area of the Canal. One British commentator, Major-General Sir M. G. E. Bowman-Manifold, is generous in his praise for the Turkish achievement.

> The Turkish effort deserves admiration. To bring thousands of men, artillery and pontoon train across 140 miles of desert was creditable; to assault a front defended potentially by 70,000 men and the heavy metal of ships' armament, was audacious: to depart again with artillery and baggage intact, and a loss of not 10 per cent of infantry was clear gain and left the defenders with little to boast of.

Troops occupied in Egypt – and the next time the Canal was threatened, early in 1916, 400,000 troops were massed to oppose any expedition – were at least kept out of the European theater. This, to von Kressenstein, was reason enough for the original attack. Djemal had escaped without serious loss, while the British were to pay dearly for letting Kress von Kressenstein escape them. It is difficult to avoid the impression that the British were much too cautious in their counter-attack, even allowing for the fact that their reconnaissance capabilities were reduced by damage to the French seaplanes.

Djemal and Kress had twisted the lion's tail – and got away with it. There was little glory in the affair. But what there was must, on the Turkish side, go to those who crossed the Canal.

Nearly 60 years before the SAMs and the Phantoms, the T62s and the Centurions, a few infantrymen struggled over the one hundred yards of the Canal, paddling rafts made of kerosene tins.

Verdun (1916)

Brenda Ralph Lewis

In choosing Verdun as the main German objective for 1916, General Erich von Faikenhayn, Chief of the German General Staff and Minister for War, pre-dated the jibe that the British would fight to the last man in the armies of their allies. Falkenhayn reasoned that, for the British, the European fronts in the First World War represented nothing more than a sideshow, with the Russian, Italian and French armies as their whipping boys. The Italians and Russians, Falkenhayn believed, were already foundering on their own ineptitude. Only France remained.

'France has almost arrived at the end of her military effort.' Falkenhayn wrote to the German Kaiser Wilhelm II in December 1915.

> If we succeeded in opening the eyes of her people to the fact that in a military sense they have nothing more to hope for . . . breaking point would be reached, and England's best sword knocked out of her hand . . . Behind the French sector on the Western Front, there are objectives for the retention of which the French General Staff would be compelled to throw in every man they have. If they do so, the forces of France will bleed to death, as there can be no question of a voluntary withdrawal.

The objective Falkenhayn chose to put France in this moral and military dilemma was the massively fortified town of Verdun, on the canalized river Meuse. Verdun fitted Falkenhayn's bill admirably. It had immense historic and emotional significance for the French and formed the northern linchpin of the double defense line of fortifications built to protect France's eastern frontier after the Franco-Prussian War of 1870–1. Mount an assault here, with enough threatening potential, Falkenhayn reckoned, and the French Army would be inextricably lured to Verdun and mangled to extinction by the Germans. The mangle would be provided by a series of limited, but attritionist advances, intensively supported by artillery and spiced with surprise.

Falkenhayn's proposals appealed to the Kaiser and to his son, Crown Prince Wilhelm, whose Fifth Army had been pounding away at Verdun with little success since 1914. But the prince and his Chief of Staff, General Schmidt von Knobelsdorf, seemed to see the Verdun campaign more in terms of shattering the French with a bombardment than of bleeding them dry by attrition. Wilhelm, who wanted to attack on both sides of the Meuse, not on the right bank only, as Falkenhayn proposed, stated the campaign's purpose as 'capturing the fortress of Verdun by precipitate methods'. Compared with this fierce phraseology, Falkenhayn's notion of 'an offensive in the Meuse area in the direction of Verdun' seemed enigmatic. Despite the suitably malevolent code-name of Operation *Gericht* (Judgement) given to his offensive, Falkenhayn's essentially half-hearted approach to it planted the seeds of ultimate German failure at Verdun. Basically, that failure was rooted in Falkenhayn's timid choice of too narrow a front for the initial attack and also in his extreme parsimony in doling out reserves.

Although Crown Prince Wilhelm and others seemed to suspect this outcome, preparations for the campaign went ahead as Falkenhayn had originally planned. It did so at a pace remarkable for those leisurely times. Weeks, rather than the usual months, divided Falkenhayn's preliminary consultations with the Kaiser at Potsdam on or about 20 December 1915 from the issue of final orders on 27 January 1916 and the projected attack date of 12 February.

During this period, the Germans amassed in the forests that surrounded Verdun a massive force of 140,000 men and over 1,200 guns – 850 of them in the front line – together with 2.5 million shells brought by 1,300 munitions trains, and an air arm of 168 aircraft as well as observation balloons. A superlative standard of secrecy was achieved by deft camouflage of the guns, by the building of underground galleries to house the troops instead of the more usual, give-away 'jump-off' trenches, and by dawn-to-dusk air patrols to prevent French pilots from casting spying eyes over the area.

These gargantuan preparations were, however, being directed against a military mammoth whose teeth had been drawn. By early 1916, Verdun's much-vaunted impregnability had been seriously weakened. It had been 'declassed' as a fortress the previous summer and all but a few of its guns and garrison had been removed. This was primarily the work of General Joseph J. C. Joffre, C-in-C of the French Army, who, with others, had presumed from the relatively easy fall in 1914 of the Belgian fortresses at Liège and Namur that this form of defense was redundant so far as modern warfare was concerned. Between August and October 1915, therefore, Verdun was denuded of over 50 complete batteries of guns and 128,000 rounds of ammunition. These were parcelled out to other Allied sectors where artillery was short. The stripping process was still going on at the end of January 1916, by which time the 60-odd Verdun forts possessed fewer than 300 guns with insufficient ammunition.

The result was that on the eve of the German offensive, the French defenses at Verdun were perilously weak, from the trench-works, dugouts and machine-gun posts to the communications network and barbed-wire fences. Far-sighted men who protested at the headlong disarmament of Verdun did so in vain. One of them, General Coutanceau, was sacked as Governor of Verdun and replaced in the autumn of 1915 by the ageing and apparently more tractable General Herr. Another, Colonel Emile Driant, commander of 56th and 59th *Chasseur* Battalions of 72nd Division, 30th Corps, warned as early as 22 August 1915: 'The sledge-hammer blow will be delivered on the line Verdun–Nancy.' After his opinion reached the ears of Joffre, Driant was sharply reprimanded in December for arousing baseless fears. Gen. Herr quickly realized that Coutanceau's alarm had been perfectly justified, and that he was in dire need of reinforcements to prepare the defense line Joffre had ordered at Verdun. But Herr's pleadings did little to penetrate the cloud of smugness that swirled about the question of defending Verdun. This mood remained impervious for some weeks, despite information from German deserters about troop movements and cancelled leave and other glimpses at the dire truth.

The very last moment had almost arrived before a glimmer of sense started to seep through. On 24 January General Nöel de Castelnau, Joffre's Chief of Staff, ordered a rush completion of the first and second trench lines on the right bank of the Meuse, and a new line in between.

On 12 February, two new divisions arrived at Verdun – much to Herr's heartfelt relief – to bring French strength up to 34 battalions against 72 German. Had the German attack begun on 12 February as planned, it would doubtless have smashed through the weak French defenses to score a stunning steamroller victory.

As it was, 12 February was not a day of savage battle, but of snow-blizzards and dense mist which afforded less than 1,100 yards visibility. The Verdun area was said to 'enjoy' some of France's filthiest weather. For a week it lived up to its reputation with snow, more snow, rain-squalls and gales.

Not until 21 February – just before 0715 – did a massive shell, almost as high as a man, burst from one of the two German 15-in (380 mm) naval guns and roar over the 20 miles that separated its camouflaged position from Verdun. There, it exploded in the courtyard of the Bishop's Palace. At this signal, a murderous artillery bombardment erupted from the German lines and a tornado of fire – including poison gas shells – began to flay the French positions along a six-mile front. The earth convulsed and the air filled with flames, fumes and a holocaust of shrapnel and steel which, the Germans clearly hoped, would destroy every living thing within range. The bombardment hammered on and on until about 1200, when it paused so that German observers could see where – if anywhere – pockets of French defenders survived. Then the artillery began afresh, smashing trenches, shelters, barbed wire, trees and men until the whole area from Malancourt to Eparges had become a corpse-littered desert.

Between 1500 and 1600, the barrage intensified as a prelude to the first German infantry advance along a 4.5-mile front from Bois d'Haumont to Herbebois. The advance began at 1645 when small patrol groups came out over the 656 to 1,203 yards of No Man's Land in waves 87.5 yards apart. Their purpose was to discover where French resistance might still exist and to pinpoint it to the artillery – which would then finish off the surviving defenders. This tentative approach, the result of Falkenhayn's excessive caution, was not to the taste of the belligerent General von Zwehl, commander of 7 Reserve Corps of Westphalians. Von Zwehl, whose position lay opposite Bois d'Haumont, paid brief lip-service to Falkenhayn's orders by sending out probing patrols first, but only a short while elapsed before he ordered his fighting stormtroopers to follow them. The Westphalians surged into the Bois d'Haumont, overran the first line of French trenches and within five hours had seized the whole wood.

To the right of the Bois d'Haumont lay the equally devastated Bois des Caures. Here, 80,000 shells had fallen within one 500,000-square-yard area. In this shattered wasteland, the advance patrols of the German 18 Corps expected to find nothing but mounds of shattered bodies in the mud. Instead, they were faced with a fierce challenge from Colonel Driant's *Chasseurs*. Of the original 1,200 men under Driant's command, fewer than half had survived the artillery bombardment. Now, these survivors poured machine-gun and rifle fire at the infiltrating Germans from the concrete redoubts and small strongholds which Driant had cunningly scattered through the trees.

Similarly ferocious isolated resistance was occurring all along the front, causing the Germans more delay and more casualties – 600 by midnight – than they had reckoned possible. By nightfall on 21 February, the only hole decisively punched in the French line was in the Bois d'Haumont, where Gen. Zwehl's Westphalians were now solidly entrenched. Elsewhere, the Germans had captured most of the French forward trenches, but were held up when darkness put an end to the first day's fighting which had yielded only 3,000 prisoners.

On the next two days, the Germans attacked with far greater force and much more initiative. On 22 February they blasted the village of Haumont, on the edge of the wood, with shellfire and flushed out the remaining French defenders with bombs and flamethrowers. That same day, the Bois de Ville was overwhelmed and in the Bois des Caures, which the Germans enveloped on both sides, Col. Driant ordered his *Chasseurs* to withdraw to Beaumont, about half a mile behind the wood. Only 118 *Chasseurs* managed to escape. Driant was not among them. On 23 February, the Germans saturated Samogneux with a hail of gunfire, captured Wavrille and Herbebois, and outflanked the village of Brabant, which the French evacuated. Next day – 24 February – despite their inch-by-inch resistance, the pace of disaster accelerated for the French with 10,000 taken prisoner, the final fall of their first defense line and the collapse of their second position in a matter of hours.

The Germans were now in possession of Beaumont, the Bois de

Fosses, the Bois des Caurieres and part of the way along La Vauche ravine which led to Douaumont.

Incredibly enough, at first the magnitude of the disaster did not sink in at Joffre's HQ at Chantilly, where the Staff had persuaded themselves that the German attack was a mere diversion. 'Papa' Joffre, who had long believed a serious German offensive was more likely in the Oise valley, Rheims or Champagne, maintained his customary imperturbability to such an extent that at 2300 on 24 February, he was fast asleep when General de Castelnau came hammering on his bedroom door bearing bad news from the front. Armed with 'full powers' from Joffre, who then went calmly back to bed, de Castelnau raced overnight to Verdun.

At about the time he arrived there, early on 25 February, a 10-man patrol of 24th Brandenburg Regiment of 3 Corps walked into Fort Douaumont and took possession of it and its three guns while the French garrison of 56 reserve artillerymen slept. This farcical episode, which German propaganda exaggerated into a hard-fought victory, shocked the French into melancholic despair and realization of the true state of affairs. At Chantilly, many officers openly advocated abandoning Verdun.

There, de Castelnau drew the conclusion that the French right flank should be drawn back and that the line of forts must be held at all costs. Above all, the French must retain the right bank of the Meuse, where de Castelnau felt that a decisive defense could, and must, be anchored on the ridges. The hapless Gen. Herr was replaced forthwith by 60-year-old General Henri Philippe Pétain. De Castelnau cannibalized Pétain's Second Army with the Third Army to form for him a new Second Army.

Pétain took over responsibility for the defense of Verdun at 2400 on 25 February, after arriving that afternoon to find Herr's HQ at Dugny, south of Verdun, in a chaos of panic and recrimination. Pétain, however, judged the situation to be far less hopeless than it seemed, even though the loss of Fort Douaumont and its unparalleled observation point was a serious blow. He decided that the surviving Verdun forts should be strongly re-garrisoned to form the principal bulwarks of a new defense. Pétain mapped out new lines of resistance on both banks of the Meuse and gave orders for a barrage position to be established through Avocourt, Fort de Marre, Verdun's NE outskirts and Fort du Rozellier. The line Bras–Douaumont was divided into four sectors – the Woevre, Woevre–Douaumont, astride the Meuse, and the left bank of the Meuse. Each sector was entrusted to fresh troops of the 20th ('Iron') Corps. Their main job was to delay the German advance with constant counter-attacks.

Pétain saw to it that the four commands were supplied with fresh artillery as it arrived along the Bar-le-Duc road – which was soon rechristened 'Sacred Way'. Three thousand Territorials labored unceasingly to keep its unmetalled surface in constant repair so that it could stand up to punishingly heavy use by convoys of lorries – 6,000 of them in a single day. Along *La Voie Sacrée* came badly needed reinforcements to replace the 25,000 men the French had lost by 26 February – five fresh Corps of them by 29 February. Already, Pétain was topping up his stock of artillery from the 388 field guns and 244 heavy guns that were at Verdun on 21 February towards the peak it reached a few weeks later of 1,100 field guns, 225 80–105 mm guns and 590 heavy guns. He also set the 59th Division to work building new defensive positions.

His injection of new strategy, new blood, new supplies and new hope into the Verdun defense soon began to disconcert the Germans. In any case, their impetus was gradually grinding down. On 29 February, their advance came to an exhausted halt after the last of their initial energy had been expended in three days of violent attacks against Douaumont, Hardaumont and Bois de la Caillette.

At that juncture, apart from their own mood of 'grievous pessimism', the most damaging factor for the Germans was the French artillery sited on the left bank of the Meuse. Here, more and more Germans came under fire the farther along the right bank they advanced. The solution was obvious, as Pétain had long feared and Crown Prince Wilhelm and Gen. von Knobelsdorf had long urged. On 6 March, after a blistering two-day artillery barrage, the German 6 Reserve and 10 Reserve Corps, partly pushed across the flooded Meuse and in a swirling snowstorm, attacked along the left bank. A parallel prong of this new onslaught was planned to strike along the right bank towards Fort Vaux, whose gunners had been savaging the German left flank.

Despite a plastering from French artillery in the Bois Bourrus, the Germans sped along the left bank and swept through the villages of Forges and Regneville – ending by nightfall in possession of Height 265 on the Côte de l'Oie. This ridge was of crucial importance, since it led through the adjacent Bois des Corbeaux towards the long mound known as Mort Homme. Mort Homme possessed double peaks and offered two advantages to the Germans. First it sheltered a particularly active battery of French field guns, and secondly, from its heights there stretched a magnificent all-round vista of the surrounding countryside. This gave whoever possessed it a prize observation point.

But Mort Homme soon lived up to its grisly name. After storming the Bois des Corbeaux on 7 March and losing it to a determined French counter-attack next day, the Germans prepared another attempt on Mort Homme on 9 March – this time from the direction of Béthincourt in the NW. They seized the Bois des Corbeaux a second time, but at such a crippling cost that they could not continue.

Results were depressingly similar on the right bank of the Meuse, where the German effort faded out beneath the walls of Fort Vaux. Difficulties of ammunition supply had made the attack there limp two days behind the left bank assault. With that, the parallel effect of the German offensive was ruined.

Inexorably, perhaps inevitably, the fighting around Verdun was acquiring that quality of slog and slaughter, and of lives thrown away for petty, short-lived gains that was so familiar a characteristic of fighting in the First World War.

Both Pétain and, in his own way, von Falkenhayn, were devotees of attrition by gunpower rather than manpower, but between March and May, the struggle at Verdun, like some Frankenstein's monster renouncing its master, assumed a will of its own and reversed this preference. German casualties mounted from 81,607 at the end of March to 120,000 by the end of April, and the French from 89,000 to 133,000, as the two sides battered each other for possession of Mort Homme. By the end of May, when the Germans had at last taken this vital position, their losses had overtaken their enemy's. On the right bank of the Meuse, in the same three months, the fighting swung to and fro over the 'Deadly Quadrilateral' – an area south of Fort Douaumont – to the tune of maniacal, endless artillery barrages, never resolving itself decisively in favor of one side or the other.

The process greatly weakened both contestants. Mutinous behavior and defeatist gossip became more common in the French ranks and French officers tacitly condoned this mood. More and more Germans, many of them terrified, clumsy 18-year-old boys were becoming sickly from exhaustion, the din of the guns and the filth in which they were forced to live.

Ennervation and dismay affected the heads as well as the bodies of the two opposing war efforts. By 21 April, Crown Prince Wilhelm had made up his mind that the whole Verdun campaign was a bloody failure and ought to be terminated. 'A decisive success at Verdun could only be assured at the price of heavy sacrifices, out of all proportion to the desired gains,' he wrote. These sentiments were echoed by Gen. Pétain, who was being nagged by Joffre to mount an aggressive counter-offensive. Pétain baulked at the increase in human sacrifice which that implied and clung to the principle of patient, stolid defense. Pétain was in a difficult position. Verdun had already become a national symbol of implacable resistance to the Germans, and Pétain himself a national idol. On the other hand, Verdun was threatening to gobble up the whole French Army and it certainly presented a serious drain on the manpower being reserved by Joffre for the coming Anglo-French offensive on the Somme.

For both sides at Verdun, these falterings at the top opened the way for men more ruthlessly determined to escalate the fighting onto even more brutal levels. On 19 April, Pétain was made Commander of Army Group Center, a position which placed him in remote rather than direct control of operations. His place as commander of Second Army was taken by General Robert Georges Nivelle, whose freebooter style of warfare had caught Joffre's attention during his series of audacious, if expensive, attacks along the right bank of the Meuse. Nivelle took over on 1 May, and arrived at headquarters at Souilly with the brash announcement: 'We have the formula!' He was also responsible for a quotation attributed sometimes to Pétain: 'Ils ne passeront pas!'

Nivelle's formula displayed itself in all its gory wastefulness on 22/23 May, when General Charles Mangin staged a flamboyant attack on Fort Douaumont. After a five-day bombardment, which barely chipped the fort's defenses, Mangin's troops streamed out of their jump-off trenches straight into a hurricane of deadly German gunfire. Within minutes, the French 129th Regiment had only 45 men left. One battalion had vanished. The remnants of the 129th charged the fort and set up a machine-gun post in one casemate against which the defending Germans flung themselves in a matching mood of suicidal madness. Out of 160 *Jägers*, *Leibgrenadiers* and men of the German 20th Regiment who attempted to overcome the French nest, only 50 returned to the fort alive. By the evening of 22 May, Fort Douaumont was in French hands, but the Germans staged violent counter-attacks, capping their onslaught with eight massive doses of explosive lobbed from a mine-thrower 80 yards distant. One thousand French were taken prisoner, and only a pathetic scattering of their comrades managed to stagger away from the fort.

This bloody fiasco ripped a 500-yard gap in the French lines and greatly weakened their strength on the right bank of the Meuse. Together with the fact that German possession of Mort Homme largely nullified French firepower on the Bois Borrus ridge, the self-destructive strife at Fort Douaumont gave great encouragement to the so-called 'May Cup' offensive which the Germans planned for early June.

The inspiration behind 'May Cup' was Gen. von Knobelsdorf, who had temporarily eclipsed Crown Prince Wilhelm. As Nivelle's new opposite number, von Knobelsdorf soon displayed an equally implacable resolve to overcome the enemy by brute force. 'May Cup' comprised a powerful thrust on the right bank of the Meuse by five divisions on under half the 21 February attack frontage. Its purpose was to lift Verdun's last veil – Fort Vaux, Thiaumont, the Fleury ridge and Fort Souville.

On 1 June, the Germans crossed the Vaux ravine and after a frenzied contest forced Major Sylvain Raynal – commander of Fort Vaux – to surrender on 7 June. By 8 June, Gen. Nivelle had mounted six unsuccessful relief attempts, at appalling cost. He was stopped from making a seventh attempt only when Pétain expressly forbade it. Elsewhere – notably round the Ouvrage de Thiaumont – the fighting brought both sides terrible losses. The French alone were losing 4,000 men per division in a single action. By 12 June, Nivelle's fresh reserves amounted to only one brigade – not more than 2,000 men.

With the Germans now poised to take Fort Souville – the very last major fortress protecting Verdun – ultimate disaster seemed imminent for the French. Eleventh-hour salvation came in the form of two Allied offensives in other theaters of war. On 4 June, on the Eastern Front, the Russian General Alexei A. Brusilov threw 40 divisions at the Austrian line in Galicia, in a surprise attack that flattened its defenders. The Russians took 400,000 prisoners. To shore up his war effort, now threatened with total collapse, Field Marshal Conrad von Hötzendorf, the Austrian C-in-C, begged Falkenhayn to send in German reinforcements. Grudgingly, Falkenhayn detached three divisions from the Western Front. Meanwhile, the French had been doing some pleading on their own account. In May and June, Joffre, de Castelnau, Pétain and French Prime Minister Aristide Briant had all begged General Sir Douglas Haig, the British C-in-C, to advance the Somme offensive from its projected starting date of mid-August. Haig at last complied on 24 June, and that day the week-long preliminary bombardment began.

At this juncture, a German 30,000-man assault on Fort Souville, which had begun with phosgene – 'Green Cross' – gas attacks on 22 June had already crumpled. Despite its horrifying effects on everything that lived and breathed, the novel phosgene barrage was neither intense nor prolonged enough to sufficiently paralyze the power of the French artillery. This shortfall, together with German failure to attack on a wide enough front, their recent loss of air superiority to the French, their shrinking store of manpower and the ravages thirst was wreaking in their lines, combined to scuttle the German push against Fort Souville on 22 June. July and August saw increasingly puny attempts by the Germans to snatch the prize that had come so tantilizingly close, but all ended in failure and exhaustion. German morale was at its lowest. On 3 September, the German offensive finally faded in a weak paroxysm of effort. Verdun proper came to an end.

For the Germans, this miserable curtain-fall on the drama of Verdun was assisted by the fact that after 24 June, the exigencies of the fighting elsewhere denied them new supplies of ammunition and, after 1 July, men.

All that remained was for the French to rearm, reinforce their troops and counter-attack to regain what they had lost. By 24 August 1917, after a brilliant series of campaigns masterminded by Pétain, Nivelle and Mangin, the only mark on the map to show the Germans had ever occupied anything in the area of Verdun denoted the village of Beaumont.

During this counter-offensive, the formerly maligned forts reinstated themselves as powerful weapons of defense. As the French recaptured them, they found how relatively little they had suffered from the massive artillery pounding they had received. This discovery made forts fashionable among French military strategists once more. It did so most notably, and later mortally for France, in the mind of André Maginot, Minister for War from November 1929 to January 1931 and in that time sponsor of the Maginot Line of fortifications.

Of course, fortress-like durability was given neither to the 66

French and 43.5 German divisions which fought at Verdun between February and June 1916, nor to the terrain they so bitterly disputed for so long. Both suffered permanent scars. The land around Verdun, raked over again and again by saturation shelling – over 12 million rounds from the French artillery alone – became a ravaged, infertile lunar-like wasteland. By 1917, the soil of Verdun was thickly sown with dead flesh and irrigated by spilled blood, having claimed more than 1.25 million casualties. Between February and December 1916, the French had lost 377,231 men and the Germans about 337,000 in a scything down of their ranks. In these circumstances, the Western Front ceased to be a sideshow for the British – if it had ever been so. They were forced to assume the star role in the Allied war effort which the French had formerly played. A repetition of Verdun was simply inconceivable.

The Somme (1916)

Sergeant-Major Ernest Shephard

In the memorable phrase of Basil Liddell Hart, the Somme was the 'glory and the graveyard' of Kitchener's army. After a week's heavy shelling British troops 'went over the top' on 1 July 1916 along a 15-mile sector of the Western Front, expecting little opposition. They met instead a hurricane of German fire, and 60,000 officers and men were lost on this day alone. Their deaths secured 1,000 yards of ground. It soon became clear to the Allies that a breakthrough on the Somme, despite some French successes, was impossible and they settled down for a campaign of attrition. The battle ended on 18 November, with an Allied advance of only seven miles, won at a cost of 418,000 British and 195,000 French casualties. The Germans lost 650,000 killed or wounded. Sergeant-Major Ernest Shephard, whose diary covering the first days of the Somme offensive is extracted here, served with the Dorset Regiment. He was killed in action in January 1917 in the Beaumont Hamel sector.

Saturday 1st July 1916

Place already nearly crammed, only four dug-outs for Company, two-thirds of us slept outside, enemy sending heavy shell and shrapnel all round us. A heavy shell caught a store containing flares, etc., a big fire caught some petrol and Bangalore Torpedoes. Some troops of the KOYLI were there, ten were killed by shell, two

burnt to death. Fire continued until dawn. I got no sleep, it was
bitterly cold. Had a limited walk round at 4 a.m., roused troops as
all breakfast to be finished by 6.30. Wind change from favourable to
dead against us at 5 a.m. At 6.30 a.m. our artillery were bombarding
intensely, a most awful din. At 7.30 a.m. we moved to 'the attack'
by companies at 200 yards intervals in the order C, D, A, B. We
took the track in rear of the batteries by Brookers Pass, turned left
on and over the road, into the Authuille Wood (which we call Blighty
Wood) and followed the Dumbarton Track. A battery of artillery was
in action half way in wood, enemy sending heavy shrapnel all over
the place searching for us. (Naturally we got the thickest time, as
the 97th Bde had already debouched from the front of wood, and the
enemy guessed more to follow.) We had a number of casualties there,
and passed by a number of killed and wounded from our leading
companies. We had a terrible dose of machine-gun fire sweeping
us through wood, could not understand why. If front and second
line had been carried, enemy machine-guns would be out of action.
We found reason quick enough. Had to wait nearly two hours on
the track waiting for the brigade ahead of us to get forward, most
infernal noise all the time, had a rough time from enemy artillery.
Finally we got to Wood Post. This lies on the forward edge of the
wood, a lot of killed and wounded there. Here we had to wait again,
I went forward to see what was happening. Across the opening I saw
the last platoon of A Coy going over the open ground in front of wood
to our original front-line trench, a distance of about 120 yards. Half
of this platoon were killed and almost all of remainder wounded
in the crossing and I at once realized that some part of the attack
had gone radically wrong, as we were being enfiladed by batteries
of enemy machine-guns from the ridge on our right front held by
the enemy.

I saw the Adjutant at this moment, and sent signal to our leading
platoon to advance. We were told to cross as quick as possible. I went
on ahead, Gray the Company Orderly behind, and No. 5 platoon
behind him. How I got over I cannot imagine, the bullets were
cracking and whizzing all round me. I got bullet holes through
my clothing and equipment in several places and was hit in left
side. The ground was covered with our dead and wounded men.
When nearly over I dropped into a shell hole for breath and to see
how the platoon was getting on. Gray was shot dead alongside me,
and very few of No. 5 platoon left. I pulled two wounded men of

A Coy into the shell hole for cover, and then went on again, and got to a communicating trench. This I could not get into as it was simply crammed with troops of all units in utter confusion, some badly wounded and a number of dead. I pushed on again half left and got into our fire trench which was almost level from shell fire in places. From here I directed my Company behind to cross further to the left where the fire was not so hot, nevertheless they grew very thin in the crossing. I joined my Company Officer (2/Lt Webb) and we tried to find out from men of other units what was the situation. These were chiefly men of the Bns of 96th Bde, who should have passed through the 97th Bde (in enemy front and second line) to enemy 3rd line and Ferme du Mouquet. Of these most could only say they were the sole survivors of their Bn, but we got news that at any rate some of our own Bn had gone on to the enemy trenches, but no one knew exactly what portion of enemy trench or trenches were in our possession. There were a number of NCOs and men of C, D, and A Coy in with us. We gave orders for these to get ready to push on to enemy line, meanwhile 2/Lt Mainhood came up, and I got No. 6 and 7 platoons together, and he led them on to enemy trench. Meanwhile Captain Lancaster took command of the remnants of C, D and A Coys and they went over. By this time my No. 8 platoon had come up and I got them together with No.5 platoon and was just going to push over with them when orders arrived from Major Shute that we were to wait until he could get information from our troops in enemy line and report same to our Brigadier. A portion of the 19th Lancs now arrived (2 Companies). Some of these pushed straight through, others were stopped in time. Of the 11th Borders only one officer was left. The Colonel, 2nd in Command, and several other officers were killed. The Adjutant (we got him in) and remainder of officers were wounded. RSM also killed. We had lost most of our officers also. At this moment our Commanding Officer (Major Shute) was wounded (he had arrived in trench five minutes before with our Adjutant). Our Adjutant now took command of us, also he took command of the 11th Borders. Message from Brigade in reply to our report on situation, that we were to hold on and consolidate where we were, as owing to the Division on our right having failed in their attack our advance was impossible, as every inch of the ground in front of us was commanded by enemy.

The remainder of our Brigade, i.e. 19th Lancs, 2nd Manchesters and 15th HLI, had of course remained behind on getting orders not to push on. The 19th Lancs who had come up were now withdrawn to Blighty Wood to reorganize. Manchesters and HLI also in wood. This left remnants of us and 11th Borders to hold the line. I took charge of trench from Chequerbent St to the left of 'The Nab'. CSM Stehr took from my left to Chowbent St CSM Pedder of C Coy had been killed and CSM Mills slightly wounded in leg. My wound was not very deep. I stuck a bandage on and managed to keep going. Our troops in front are carrying on a bombing attack, bombs are being sent to them via a big underground sap called the Russian Sap.

A lovely day, intensely hot. Lot of casualties in my trench. The enemy are enfilading us with heavy shell, dropping straight on us. A complete trench mortar battery of men killed by one shell, scores of dead and badly wounded in trench, now 1 p.m. Every move we make brings intense fire, as trenches so badly battered the enemy can see all our movements. Lot of wounded in front we got in, several were hit again and killed in trench. We put as many wounded as possible in best spots in trench and I sent a lot down, but I had so many of my own men killed and wounded that after a time I could not do this. Sent urgent messages to Brigade asking for RAMC bearers to be sent to evacuate wounded, but none came, although Brigade said they had been despatched. Meanwhile the enemy deliberately shelled the wounded between the trenches with shrapnel, thus killing, or wounding again most of them. Our own Regtl stretcher bearers worked hard to take cases away. Counted all Dorsets at 1 p.m. Total 53 all ranks. At 3 p.m. the Manchesters went through the Russian Sap and made an attack, captured a portion of the Leipzig Redoubt. Brigade sent message to say we would be relieved by 15th HLI as soon as possible. Meanwhile we were to hold tight.

We needed to; literally we were blown from place to place. Men very badly shaken. As far as possible we cleared trenches of debris and dead. These we piled in heaps, enemy shells pitching on them made matters worse.

Wounded suffering agonies. I got them water from bottles of dead, a few managed to crawl away to the Aid Post in wood. At dusk we got more wounded in from the front. 8 p.m. we got shelled intensely, and continued at intervals. I had miraculous escapes. The HLI arrived at midnight. I handed care of wounded to them, and took remnants of B and C Coys, only ten NCOs and men, back via Mounteagle and Rock St, through Wood Post and over same track (Dumbarton) through Blighty

Wood, down the valley to Crucifix Corner. Arrived there at 1 a.m. on

Sunday 2nd July

Had a halt there, then on as ordered to the Authuille defences in Kintyre St. Got to top of hills, met messenger, orders to go to Blackhorse dug-outs for night, arrived there absolutely dead beat at 2 a.m. No dug-outs available, place crammed with troops of another division, camped out in the open. Very cold, had some sleep for an hour. Terrible bombardment going on all the time. The 17th HLI and 11th Borders say their Bns nearly wiped out, also the Ulster Div. who attacked Thiepval on left.

A number of our men came in at 4 a.m., some had been mixed up with other units, others had to lie in shell holes unable to budge owing to machine-gun fire, some from various jobs detailed for before the attack, and a number from the enemy trenches on relief by 15th HLI. This party had been commanded by Capt. Lancaster. He got wounded but held on and our men did very good work there. They bombed and captured a large portion of the enemy second line, and completed the capture of enemy 1st and 2nd line up to the Hindenburg Fort on right and Leipzig Redoubt on left. Very strong position held them up. We lost a lot of men there, but we have satisfaction over them as they killed a large number of the enemy. The enemy troops against us were the Prussian Guards, whom we have fought against at Ypres and previously at La Bassée. A prisoner said they only came there two days ago, and had lost heavily. Our men say they fought very bravely, and were of splendid physique, all over 6 feet in height. Also, they say enemy trenches very substantial and wanting nothing. Good dug-outs fitted luxuriously with electric lights, boarded and even wallpapered, plenty of good food, cigars, wines, in fact everything required. Plenty of German helmets as souvenirs. Enemy trenches choked with their own dead. Three Companies of 15th HLI are holding enemy trenches now, with two companies of Manchesters. At 6.30 a.m. came orders we were to be at Kintyre Trench by 7.30 a.m. On arrival there we had a roll call of the Bn. After all were in I mustered 90 all ranks, out of 201 who went into action. I lost 111 all ranks. Total casualties in Battalion reckoned as 490 NCOs and men, and 20 officers. I lost all my Platoon Sgts and three Platoon Officers.

A fine day. I reorganized my remnants, made new Platoon Sgts, etc., sent in my list of casualties and had a little sleep. Major Thwaytes now arrived and took over command of Bn. Needless to say, we are all bitterly cut up at practically losing our fine Battalion in getting to our own fire trenches. Had we lost so many in actual grip with the enemy we should have felt more satisfaction. This is a repetition of Hill 60, where we lost nearly the Battalion with hardly a fighting chance. That happened on 1st of month as well.

Of course the 8th Division caused it through not being able to capture the ridge with machine-guns on our right. Really our Division ought never to have attacked until that ridge had been gained, but either the 97th and 96th Brigade Commanders did not inform our Divisional Commander of the situation (possibly the orderly was killed or wires destroyed) or else, if our General did know and yet decided that we should carry on, he is not fit for his job.

At 2.30 p.m. an intense bombardment of our artillery started on Beaumont Hamel. At 4.30 p.m. smoke bombs were used, so I presume our troops attacked. We could see quite plainly, but no troops. The enemy retaliated on us, and we had a hot time from 'Jack Johnsons'. Great aerial activity going on. Rumour at 6 p.m. that the cavalry are in action on left. Got rations up later and just going to settle down for a decent sleep at 8.30 p.m. when we were sent for and told to be ready to move in one hour for trenches to relieve 17th HLI. All day we have been expecting to go right back out of it for the Division to reorganize. I sent a Sgt to take over our portion of trench. Our Bn is to hold our own original front line from Chequerbent St to Tyndrum St as support to 2nd Manchesters in enemy trench in front between the Leipzig and Hindenburg Forts. The 15th HLI are relieving Manchesters at 3 a.m. and are to make an attack to capture the forts. We act as supports to them with 19th Lancs and Manchesters in reserve. Stood by for orders which came at 1.30 a.m. on

Monday 3rd

We moved up via Campbell Av. and got blocked there by a company of Cheshires with 'wind up'. Hell's own bombardment going on by our artillery preparatory to the attack, and enemy retaliating heavily all round us. Got clear of Cheshires and cut across the New MG Trench. Here we found half of our men had got cut off by Cheshires and lost touch. Waited half an hour trying to connect up, nothing doing so I sent on what we had and went back to find the others. I found nine of them and they said the remainder were sure of the way on, so I decided to get the nine up. Got to Oban Av. and up to the front trench expecting to find the others there. Most terrible fire from enemy on the trench from howitzer shells dropping dead in trench, also the enemy were using gas shells, which almost stifled us. Evidently by the intense shelling from enemy, they have news of our attack and shelling this trench to prevent troops getting up. Shells dropping all round us, hairbreadth escapes. L/Cpl Lillington and Jenkins killed by one shell. The trench almost level with ground. Finally got to Chowbent St, still no sign of our men so came to conclusion they had all been killed and buried by debris in trench. I turned into Chowbent, worked way to junction of Bury Av. – Hough St, and through Hough St to Oban Av., met no one, so I put the men in a shelter for a rest, while the HLI passed up to relieve Manchesters. Now almost break of dawn. At 4 a.m. the remainder of lost party came up, so I decided to hold Hough St (instead of the fire trench), and I put two groups on duty there. Later I found my OC Coy at the Aid Post and found that he had, on arrival with first party, decided not to hold fire trench owing to intense fire, and he had put his party on duty in Chequerbent St on the right of Hough St. Time now 6 a.m., devilish row going on ahead.

The attack started at 6.30 a.m. I went along the fire trench and put out another post in the new communicating trench across the salient from Chowbent to Iona St. From there I had fine view of the attack. Apparently the HLI are getting on alright, as they have not asked for our help yet. We are getting a lot of heavy shell and machine-gun fire. I returned to Coy HQ at 11 a.m. to find the OC in a great stew over my absence. They thought I had been killed and reported me as 'Missing' to Bn HQ. Had breakfast. Enemy brought one of our aeroplanes down at noon. I have only one officer in the Company, i.e. the OC, Lt Webb. In afternoon had little sleep. Heavy shelling continues all day. At 7 p.m. message to say we are being relieved by 1st Wilts tonight, so sent guides down and made all preparations. They arrived at 9.30 p.m. and we got out fairly easily as enemy eased down a little at that time. The Wilts have a lot of raw reinforcements of officers and men. We led out via Oban Av. through Authuille, over Blackhorse Bridge and Road to Pioneer Road, Northumberland Av., skirted Martinsart and arrived Bouzincourt at midnight. Here we collected the Company, a few enemy shells dropped close by. We pushed on and got in by singing, quite exhausted, at 1 a.m. on [billets in Senlis].

Tuesday 4th

Issued rum and tea, saw men settled and slept until 10 a.m. Nasty day, very hard storms of rain and wind continued all day. Road outside my billet flooded 2 feet deep. Adjutant told me General Joffre came round here yesterday, and says it will cost us 20,000 men to take Thiepval and trenches close to it, by frontal attack. The 15th Lancs Fus. reported to have attacked there and completely swallowed up. Joffre says it is the best situated and most strongly fortified enemy position on the Western front. I see in today's paper same thing mentioned, also a paragraph mentioning the 'Dorsets' hard fight'. By what I read and hear our offensive has been quite successful generally, certain strong points are holding against us. I hear we are not going to attack Thiepval now. We are going to wedge them out from round Pozières. I felt very queer all day, have a bad attack of bleeding piles, also the relaxation is telling.

Wednesday 5th

During morning held kit inspection. Company bathed in afternoon from 2 to 4 p.m. At 5 p.m. the Bn paraded and marched via Hédauville to Forceville where we occupied huts, arrived 7 p.m. All the Brigade are here close by. Quiet night.

Thursday 6th

Fine day. During morning sorted out kits of casualties. Company parade for arms drill 10–11 a.m.

Rained hard in afternoon. Just settling for night when urgent orders arrived to be ready to move for Senlis or Bouzincourt at an hour's notice. We were ready at 9 p.m. Raining hard, fierce bombardment going on.

Friday 7th

Operation orders arrived at 3 a.m. The 19th Lancs Fus. and we go to Bouzincourt, Manchesters and 15th HLI to Senlis. Our Brigade is in Corps Reserve. Packed up, paraded and moved off at 4.45 a.m. in order B, A, D, C; marched via Hédauville direct to Bouzincourt. There we handed in packs, drew bombs and extra SAA, all ready to go. We are reserve to 49th Division, who are attacking at 8 a.m. to capture completely the Leipzig and Hindenburg redoubts. Intense bombardment going on now. I went to a high point to watch the attack. At 8 a.m. the smoke screen was flying in front of enemy trenches and the troops moved to attack. Could see nothing more. While waiting news I went to the cemetery to see what men of ours had been buried there. Only L/Cpl Woolfries from my Company. After I went over to see Lizzie, the heavy gun fire – shells so large can be seen quite plainly on leaving muzzle. After I went to billet and had little sleep. Heavy rain from 1 p.m. and all the afternoon. Lot of Colonial (Australian) artillery just come round here. We expected to move in evening, as our Brigade is now lent to the 12th Division, who are continuing the attack on Ovillers. No orders yet.

Saturday 8th

We were heavily shelled all night, some just cleared roof of billet and exploded on yard. Fritz is after Lizzie, but is a long way out. No moving orders yet. Sent for by Adjt at 10 a.m. All Bns in the Brigade are now forming two Coys out of the remnants of the four Coys to simplify work. Also all officers, warrant officers and NCOs over the complement of the two Coys are to be left behind when we go into action again, thus forming a reserve of ranks to keep the Bn going. The Adjt had already listed CSM Miller and myself as the two CSMs to stay behind, as we both have been on active service longest, Miller since start of war, and I since January 1915. I selected Sgts Stroud, Charles and Gilchrist to stay as well from my Coy. A and B Coys will be joined together and called the 'Right Company', C and D same and called the 'Left Coy'. CSM Cobb to be CSM of Right Coy, CSM Stehr to be CSM of Left Coy. We have to go back to Hédauville and be under orders of 97 Bde while the Bn is in action. I do not like the idea at all, but orders must be carried out. I turned my No. 5 and 6 Platoon into No. 3 Platoon, and 7 and 8 into No. 4 Platoon of Right Coy. Handed over all documents to Cobb. I decided to stay with Coy until they moved to go into action. Fine day. Went up to high ground to watch the fighting. Lot of observation balloons up. At 5 p.m. orders came for Bn to move tonight. I collected the party staying behind, 13 officers, 20 WOs, Cpls and Sgts, and moved off for Hédauville. Half way orderly came, orders to go to transport lines; went there, and later in night orders to move to Senlis where 97 Bde are now. Decided to go there in morning. Very heavy bombardment all night. Rather interesting to be back from trenches with transport and peep behind the scenes. Continued passage of troops and supplies all night. Had a good bivouac, slept well.

Vimy Ridge (1917)

Brenda Ralph Lewis

Four divisions of the Canadian Corps, with the 5th British Division in support, began their assault on Vimy Ridge on 9 April 1917. This six-mile hogsbacked pleat in the plains near Arras in NE France possessed an almost legendary reputation for impregnability. French forces had battered incessantly against it in 1914 and 1915, only to gain the Lorette Spur next to the Ridge and part of the slopes. They gained it in the typically wasteful and bloody style of the First World War with the loss of 150,000 men. In 1916, when the British took over from them, they, too, employed the same dismally ineffective tactics of repeated shelling, mining, raiding and skirmishing by night. The British, like the French, lost men by the thousand – 2,500 in the three days 23–26 May alone.

The slaughter of all these men, like that of millions of others on the Western Front, achieved absolutely nothing from a strategic point of view. For while the Germans remained firmly entrenched in their warren of tunnels and deep dugouts, and while they stayed strongly in possession of the crest of Vimy Ridge, which dominated the Lens–Douai Plain, they were able to keep their opponents' position in Arras, six miles away, in a constantly precarious condition.

The apparent unshakeable hold of the Germans on Vimy Ridge also maintained the Allied High Command in a mood of fuming frustration. These were men to whom territory gained equalled success, no matter what the cost, and territory lost (or like Vimy

Ridge, not captured), spelled failure. It was this rigid mentality – divorced from the realities of modern, mechanized warfare and untempered by humanitarian considerations – that helped account for the quality of attrition that so quickly characterized hostilities on the Western Front. Among the firmest exponents of attrition and the mass assault by thousands of human lemmings, was Marshal Joseph Joffre, C-in-C of the French Armies on the Front between 1914 and 1916. Joffre's methods were so successful in killing off his own troops that in 1916 he stated they could stand just one more great battle, after which France's pool of men of military age would virtually dry up.

But by the end of 1916 the French were no longer able to countenance the wholesale slaughter of their men for the sake of a few patches of gain, or, more commonly, for none at all. In 1916 alone, a year of almost unmitigated failure on the Western Front, the inconclusive battles of the Somme (1 July to 15 November) and Verdun (21 February to 24 August) had taken more than 500,000 French lives and left thousands of survivors gassed, crippled, blinded and otherwise ruined.

French patience and trust in Joffre finally ran out and he was relieved of his command. He was replaced on 12 December 1916, by General Robert Georges Nivelle. He had won instant popularity in the public imagination by master-minding two successful French counter-attacks at Verdun. Nivelle appeared to have a more mobile and more promising concept of warfare. The enemy was to be violently and repeatedly hammered by masses of artillery and assaulted by vast numbers of infantry. Nivelle's ideas seemed to herald the decisive victory for which the French now thirsted. As 1917 began, the impression mushroomed that the hour had found the man and the man could produce with one stunning strike the longed-for miracle of a complete and permanent rupture of the German lines.

In this atmosphere, the plan Nivelle conceived – that the French should mount an offensive along a 50-mile front between Soissons and Champagne – was as much of a public relations venture as a battle campaign. To draw the German reserves away from the French sector, the British were to attack along the Hindenburg Line, which was held by the German Sixth Army under General Freiherr von Falkenhausen. The Hindenburg Line skirted Queant and Bullecourt in the south, crossed Telegraph Hill, part of Vimy Ridge, and ended at the Railway Triangle about two miles east of Arras. It was intended that the British Third Army, under General Sir Edmund H. Allenby, would break through the line and advance south-eastwards towards Cambrai. At the same time, the British First Army, of which the Canadian Corps formed part, would advance towards Douai to the north-east. During these offensives – the battles of Arras which began on 9 April and cost 150,000 casualties – the Third Army succeeded in puncturing the Hindenburg Line with a dent 11 miles long and 3.7 miles deep. But, although Monchy-le-Preux and Hill 102 were also gained, the British effort round Arras fell short of most of its other objectives.

The onslaught on Vimy Ridge, on the other hand, was a brilliant success. The Ridge, which ran NW to SE from south of Givenchy to the edge of Farbus Wood, was the northernmost part of the British front. It was a depressing wasteland. The continuous struggle staged there since 1914 had pulverized it into a quagmire of mud and waterlogged pot-holes and trenches, scattered with the rotting flesh and stripped bones of thousands of unburied dead, numerous rats, lice, bugs and nits, the jagged debris of countless shells, bombs and bullets, torn-up fragments of barbed wire and corrugated iron and the empty cans and litter that were the junk of everyday living.

Early in 1917, the Canadian Corps began to replace the British on this derelict compost heap. It was assumed on both sides that they would repeat the melancholy mixture as before, and do no more than wage fruitless running warfare resulting in heavy losses. The five regiments of the German Sixth Army, who were occupying the Ridge, together with their commanders, were confident that this was the case. The German reading of the situation was well founded. The mediocre performance Allied troops had so far made in the war convinced them that incompetence was inherent in the Allied war effort. Any attack – on Vimy Ridge or anywhere else – was bound to fail.

Therefore, it was in complacent mood and without undue alarm that the Germans fended off occasional Canadian raiding of their lines and observed the quickening pace of the British build-up around the Ridge in late 1916 and early 1917. During that winter, the British dug thousands of feet of new tunnels in the chalk of Vimy Ridge, together with caves capable of housing men by the hundreds. In March, 1917, piles of ammunition and supplies were stockpiled in the area, the roads leading to it and from it bustled with activity, fresh wire barricades were erected and strongpoints reinforced. Early in April, the Allied artillery bombardment, which had been more or less continuous in the months before, suddenly intensified. The Germans' former superior firepower began to be overwhelmed. The number of rounds fired rose sharply – doubling the Allied expenditure in March and rising to a peak of 90,000 rounds on 5 April: this was three times the number pumped out by the Germans in reply. The bombardment flattened several German trenches and smashed huge gaps in the wire. Each hammering was followed up with British and Canadian forays, made in greater strength than before, to discover the damage caused.

Despite all this, the Germans concluded only that some time soon, some strenuous effort – bigger than a raid, but not so powerful and much more limited than a 'Big Push' – was about to be made. But they believed that they could deal with anything their enemies would throw at them. In this complacent mood, General von Falkenhausen not only failed to move up the best part of his reserves, but kept them so far back that they had little chance to intervene should the coming battle put the front line under impossible pressure. The men of von Falkenhausen's First Guards Reserve Division and 18th Infantry Division were in fact, still 12.5 miles behind the lines on 9 April. What was more, von Falkenhausen did not order his artillery to the rear, where they might have mounted a defence in depth, until the Canadian attack was imminent. To make the Germans' plight worse their sluggish supply system failed to deliver rations and reinforcements. They also suffered from an ammunition shortage.

The magnitude of the threat to the Germans on Vimy Ridge was considerably greater than they imagined. For one thing, their Canadian opponents possessed qualities unusual in ordinary soldiers of the First World War. The nature of Canadian society encouraged tenacity and toughness to a far higher degree than did the rigid class societies of Europe. Similarly, the plan of battle for Vimy Ridge was not the sort the Germans' experience so far had led them to expect. Though it was a set-piece offensive, it contained the uncommon element of surprise. The preliminary artillery barrage was to be much briefer than the usual days or even weeks. It would last only three minutes before the Canadians went 'over the top' and would creep forward at the rate of about 33 yards per minute. The infantry would march behind at a careful synchronized pace.

At the same time, 150 Vickers machine-guns would thicken up the barrage and spray the ground 40 yards ahead of the advance, while HE and gas shells saturated the German positions and mortars spread a smokescreen in selected sectors. The overall effect would be to provide the infantry with a devastating artillery umbrella to get them to the German front line long before they were expected.

On the night of 8/9 April, the first attack wave of Canadian troops – 15.000 men – stood packed shoulder to shoulder in the jump-off trenches in freezing and unseasonable weather. They were weighted down with full battle kit, extra ammunition and rations and – as was all too familiar – were standing knee-deep in freezing, muddy water. At 0530, a large gun coughed out a throaty signal from nearby Mont St Eloi. Immediately, 1,000 Allied guns, the heaviest of them 15-in howitzers, responded with a huge concerted roar. The air was rent with shells that whooshed over the heads of the men hunched in the jump-off trenches. The barrage speared out over No Man's Land ripping apart the semi-darkness blanketing the German front line with a flickering, flashing curtain of light. At the same time, counter-battery fire thundered down upon the German gun emplacements, and to add to the cacophony, two large mines were detonated in the German lines, tearing massive holes in the wire.

After three minutes, the guns of the 'creeping barrage' lengthened their range and the bombardment leapt 100 yards ahead. The deluge of shells pounded its way foward as the Canadians scrambled out of the trenches and moved over the mud-wastes that led up the slopes of Vimy Ridge. Their rate of advance – drummed into them by intensive training – was the same as that of the barrage. Some of the most heavily laden troops had trouble keeping up even with this crawling pace. It was snowing fairly heavily and the sticky mud beneath their feet made the Canadians slither and slide. The eight MK 1 'Female' tanks, armed with machine-guns, which were moving forward with 2nd Division, soon lumbered to a complete halt – their tracks quite unable to grip the near-liquid sludge beneath them. Three of the tanks were wrecked by German gunfire.

Overhead and in front of them, the advancing Canadians could see amber-coloured flares leaping up into the gradually lightening sky as the Germans fired desperate signals for immediate artillery support. They signalled largely in vain. The best part of the German heavy artillery – accurately plotted earlier by Allied sound ranging or aerial photography – had been neutralized or destroyed. Those

guns further back which were still intact were not in communication
with their beleaguered front line, and could not lay down fire where
it was needed. All that the German guns were able to do was to fire
at the known position of the Canadian front line, which the initial
attack wave had already left.

Only the German machine-guns, which were strongly emplaced
almost flush with the ground, were able to retaliate to any advantage.
Their answering fire streamed out among the Canadians. Many fell
dead in the mud. Even if they were not mown down in neat rows – as
had happened during infantry advances on the Somme and elsewhere
– the Canadians suffered considerable losses. For example, the 7th
Battalion of the 1st Division, which lost half its men during the
battle of Vimy Ridge, lost most of them to machine-gun fire in the
first half-mile of their advance.

The deadly machine-gun nests could only be silenced by close
personal onslaught. This tactic was extremely dangerous and likely
to be fatal to the attacker. Two Victoria Crosses won at Vimy Ridge
– both awarded posthumously – went to a 1st Division private who
crawled up to the gun-slit of a machine-gun and slammed a hand
grenade inside, and to a 2nd Division lance-sergeant who charged
another nest single-handed and bayoneted the crew.

If the machine-gunners on the Ridge were able to defend themselves adequately, the German infantry were the exact opposite.
The preliminary barrage, which had been directed with punishing
accuracy from Forward Observation Posts, observer balloons and
aircraft of the Royal Flying Corps, had smashed the German trenches
to near-oblivion along with many of their deep dugouts – most of
them unwisely placed in the first 700 yards of the front line. This
bombardment had buried hundreds of Germans alive in the dugouts
and those who managed to survive were taken completely by surprise.
They had not expected an attack to arrive for hours, perhaps days.
Several were taken prisoner while sitting down to breakfast. Others
were captured in their beds or skulking sockless, shirtless and
otherwise half-dressed in tunnels, shafts and dugouts. The shock
of surprise was quickly followed by terror, as the Germans realized
that the roarings and shudderings they could hear and feel close by
were caused by Canadians tossing Mills bombs into neighbouring
dugouts.

Germans who had been surprised underground, but who managed
to avoid capture, rushed down their tunnels to the rear in a frantic

effort to escape, carrying the dire news of disaster to gun-crews in the German artillery area of Farbus Wood. There was immediate panic and those crews able to began to pull out across the Douai Plain. The demoralization the Canadians achieved by swiftness and surprise proved a valuable, even economic, weapon in their armoury. One German machine-gun crew which opened fire a few hundred yards ahead of troops of the 31st Battalion of 3rd Division gave themselves up as soon as a Canadian fired a Mills bomb at them from his .303 rifle. Another lone Canadian, a member of the 29th (British Columbia) Battalion of the same division, achieved even easier success while reconnoitring in Farbus Wood. A short burst of bullets from his rifle, fired in the general direction of a German howitzer crew, resulted in the instant evacuation of their position.

By 1100 – after five and a half hours of battle – the German defences were in almost total disarray. Some scattered spots on the front, in the areas covered by the 2nd and 3rd Canadian Divisions, were still held by the Bavarian 79th Reserve Infantry Division, but the Germans' centre had been pushed well over the crest of Vimy Ridge. The German left wing had fallen back as far as Intermediate Position No. 11, which coincided roughly with the Canadians' 'Brown Line'. The overall picture now was that the most important parts of Vimy Ridge, including Telegraph Hill and its south-eastern contour, were in Canadian hands. Also, men of the 1st Division were swarming through Farbus Wood. There, they were performing an unprecedented function for Allied troops in the First World War – capturing German guns, several of them the much-dreaded 5.9-in howitzers.

The dictum that 'artillary conquers, infantry occupies' had for once come true – and much faster than anyone had forseen.

However, the rapid and spectacular success of the 1st, 2nd and 3rd Divisions and most of the 4th Division was not being matched on Hill 145, a vital part of the 4th Division's area. Hill 145 (475 ft), the highest point of Vimy Ridge, lay in the centre of the 4th Division's operation and was the objective of its 11th Brigade, under Brigadier V. W. Odlum. Opposing the 11th Brigade was the Reserve Infantry Regiment No. 261, a unit of the Bavarian 79th Division. The Germans were dug into strong defences – the normal three forward trenches, with a strong tunnel, the *Munchener-Lager*, between trenches two and three. On the crest and reverse slope of Hill 145 lay a twin-trench system which included the deep defences of the *Obere*

Hangstellung, the *Untere Hangstellung*, a reserves' double tunnel, and a large encampment, the *Hanseaten-Lager*. This defence system was basically no different from those faced by the other three Canadian divisions, and the method of attack used by them was the same as on Hill 145. There was, nevertheless, one crucial difference, and a difference ironically created by a Canadian commanding officer.

Before the battle began, the CO of the 87th (Montreal) Battalion of the 4th Division had requested that the artillery barrage should leave intact and undamaged a German trench of the second line, which he wished to capture and exploit. The CO seemed confident of seizing the trench – only 150 yards from the Canadian jump-off trenches – before its defenders had time to emerge from their deep tunnels and fight back. In these circumstances, the CO's request was granted. Unfortunately, in keeping this trench sacrosanct, the CO had also preserved unharmed several machine-gun nests and infantry sections of the German 5th Company of 261st Regiment. This factor, combined with German reserve machine-guns farther back on Hill 145, and the peculiarly stubborn fighting qualities of the 5th Company, brought the Canadians near to disaster.

Machine-gun fire, rifle fire and hand grenades were unleashed from the undamaged trench, slaughtering half the advancing Canadians in minutes, and producing piles of khaki corpses in front of the German position. All around them, shell-holes full of water were stained a deep red.

Despite their appalling losses, the Canadians managed to overwhelm the left wing of Regiment No. 261 and the opposition they faced narrowed down to the centre. Here, the Germans scrambled from their tunnels and viciously counter-attacked. Soon, the fighting degenerated into confusion and discernible lines of Canadians and Germans disappeared. The battle dissolved into small close-quarter skirmishes, fought by groups of isolated men. Battered battalions of the ill-fated 11th Brigade, together with neighbouring units of the 12th Brigade, on their left, broke up into scattered remnants. Of the 11th Brigade battalions, the 54th on the left flank was rapidly reduced to about 90 men, the 102nd to not many more and the manpower of the 87th was scythed in half. As for the 12th Brigade, 'A' Company of its 78th Battalion lost all its officers, either killed or badly wounded, and out of the 700 men the battalion sent into the battle, only 199 reported at the first roll call afterwards.

The 11th Brigade Commander, Brigadier V. W. Odlum, was

distraught. Reports reaching him were non-existent or scanty. As far as he could tell, the 54th, 102nd and 87th Battalions had gone up Hill 145 and disappeared. Of the 30 scouts Odlum had sent out to reconnoitre and report, only one had returned. And he brought dismal news that the Germans were still holding their Second Line on the left of the 11th Brigade's front. The major part of Hill 145 was still in German hands long after the battle plan had specified that it should have been wrested from them.

At 1450 Brigadier Odlum summoned officers of the 85th Battalion, Lieutenant-Colonel J. Warden commanding, to urgent consultations at Tottenham Tunnel, the communications trench that served as 11th Brigade HQ. The result of this anxious get-together was orders for the 85th, which consisted mainly of untried men, to prepare to take Hill 145. A covering artillery bombardment was promised but, in the event, failed to materialize.

At 1745 the 85th Battalion began to advance without the comfort and reassurance of covering fire. They ran straight into a barrage of German machine-guns. Bullets whipped through the Canadian ranks. Many men fell to the ground but the advance was not halted. Several men of the 85th had been trained in the tricky job of firing Mills bombs from rifles. This daunting marriage of two weapons had a terrifying effect on the Germans. Corporal H. M. Curll, of the 85th's 'C' Company, fired a Mills bomb to within five yards of one machine-gun crew, producing instant surrender. Curll's initiative was followed by other rifle-bombers and by the time 'C' Company got within 50 yards of the Germans' Second Line five crews had leapt from their gun positions and fled.

At nightfall on 9 April, troops of the 85th Battalion were passing over the crest of Hill 145. Isolated Germans in scattered positions on the Hill were still resisting, but their main defence effort had been effectively quelled. At 1600 on 10 April, under cover of an artillery barrage, the 44th and 50th Battalions of the 10th Brigade (4th Division) crossed over the north of Hill 145 and down the reverse slope to the *Untere Hangstellung*. A few hours later, as night closed in, Hill 145 was in Canadian hands and the 'Southern Operation', the main part of the Vimy Ridge offensive, was over. The cost had been 3,000 Canadians killed, over 4,000 wounded, and the reward, 4,000 German prisoners taken and unknown numbers killed.

The hiatus on Hill 145 had, however, put the timetable out by about 48 hours. The 44th and 50th Battalions had originally been detailed to spend 10 April carrying out the 'Northern Operation' to take the wooded knoll – known as the 'Pimple' – commanding the Souchez Valley. Because of the rescue operation on Hill 145, the attack on the 'Pimple' which was made with very heavy artillery support, did not start until 0530 on 12 April.

The weather, which had alternated between squalls of snow, hail, sleet and rain, leaden skies and brief glimpses of bright sunshine since 9 April, was now decisively in favour of the Canadians. It was snowing as the 44th and 50th Battalions, together with the 46th Battalion, struggled towards the German positions on the 'Pimple', sunk up to their knees in gluey sludge. Fortunately for them, the freezing wind was blowing the snow straight at the Germans, and their machine-gunners were so blinded and bemused by it that the Canadians were upon them before they had a chance to mount an effective defence. The ensuing fight was vicious and the result never in serious doubt. By 0900, after three and a half hours, the Canadians had taken the 'Pimple' and had completed the capture of Vimy Ridge. Their toll of casualties was now climbing towards the final figure of 10,000 which was officially acknowledged on 14 April. The Canadians had lost one tenth of the men they put into the battle. In human terms, this is a chilling toll, but in cold statistics, in terms of the ratio between sacrifice and success, nowhere near as costly as other battles in the First World War.

Already, during the night of 12/13 April, the Germans had withdrawn to their well-fortified defence line between Avion, Mericourt and Arleux, near the Scarpe River. Here, their strength was reinforced by 14 April with reserve divisions, and with one man to every 6 ft of ground, their resistance markedly stiffened. The reaction of the British High Command was to attack quickly and prise the Germans out. Three attacks were made to this end, one at Arleux (28–9 April) and two on the Scarpe (23–4 April and 3 May). They failed to dislodge the enemy. Twelve days later, on 15 May, the battles of Arras, of which these were almost the final flickers, petered to an inconclusive close, leaving the Canadian capture of Vimy Ridge very poorly exploited.

However, Arras and Vimy did have uncomfortable consequences for General von Falkenhausen. He was fired for his gross unpreparedness. The French General Nivelle of whom so much, perhaps too much, had been expected was also removed from his post after his Champagne offensive – launched on 16 April in the vilest possible weather – failed to break through the German defence-in-depth. The French lost 100,000 men and on 3 May, the French armies mutinied. On 15 May, Nivelle was replaced as French C-in-C by General Henri Philippe Pétain.

In these circumstances, with the British effort round Arras something of a damp squib and the French campaign an embarrassment and disaster, it was not surprising that so much lustre had attached itself to the Canadians' exploit on Vimy Ridge. This was, in the first place, the first Allied effort in the First World War that could even vaguely be called a success, and the gains made there proved in time to be permanent.

Vimy gave a striking demonstration of just how much could be achieved and just how quickly when warfare was conducted along intelligent, well-coordinated and efficient lines. Marshal Joffre and the other apostles of attrition had shown that sending thousands of men to certain death in the hope of swamping the enemy by force of numbers was neither necessary nor efficacious if battles were to be won.

But in practice the lessons of Vimy Ridge were forgotten as soon as they had been learned. For in the history of the First World War, the Vimy battle makes a fresh filling in a stale and melancholy military sandwich. Six months before it was fought, the battles of the Somme ended. Here, British and French troops were thrown at the enemy in droves – 350,000 of them were mown down like corn. Six months after Vimy Ridge came the battle which cost the British 250,000 men and which serves, even today, as a synonym for nauseating waste and mindless butchery – Passchendaele.

Passchendaele (1917)

Hubert Essame

Much has been written about Passchendaele, or the Third Battle of Ypres, 1917 – a lot of it by writers who were not there. In the process, they have created many myths ranging from the belief that the troops were 'lions led by donkeys', and that the generals lived in luxury chateaux whilst the soldiers died in the mud, to the claim that Field Marshal Sir Douglas Haig was a 'great master of the field' and justified in his decision not only to stage an offensive on the grand scale east of Ypres on 31 July 1917 but also to continue attacking there for a further 14 weeks. I belong to neither of these schools of thought but prefer to tell what happened to me and what I saw just north of the Menin Road in late July and August.

There was something sinister about the ruins of Ypres in 1917. The painters Hieronimus Bosch, Gustave Doré and Sidney Nolan, had they been living at the time, could, perhaps, have conveyed the eerie horror of the place. A stink of decay from the moat mixed with that of HE defiled the air. In June and July 1917 it was under day and night bombardment. Everybody going to the front had to pass either through the Menin Gate and take the road to Hellfire Corner or the Lille Gate whence a plank road called the Warrington Track ran just north of Zillebeke Lake. Men anxiously waited for the next shell as they marched over the cobble stones of the *Grande Place*. In the ramparts there was some cover from the shellfire. By night the Very lights of the front line cast a loop round the city.

Never can the point of attack have been more blatantly advertised. On 7 June we, 2nd Battalion, The Northamptonshire Regiment were in reserve for the Messines battle but not used. A few days later, we, with the rest of our division, the 8th Infantry, were moved into the line to hold the sector about Hooge and to familiarize outselves with the ground over which we were destined to attack. Our guns were so closely packed together for the coming offensive that the northern half had to fire for one part of the night and the southern half for the other. It would have been impossible otherwise for the traffic to get through. Daylight movement east of Ypres was impossible – except for individuals. On our divisional front over 2,000 men worked like moles every night burying cables, digging dugouts at Halfway House and carrying stores to forward dumps under almost continuous shellfire.

Every yard of the Menin Road and the Warrington Track was 'taped'. Abandoned wagons, corpses, dead horses and mules lined the roads. Limbs and bodies in the twisted distortion of death festooned the shell-holes. Commanding a working party on these roads was a nightmare. It was usual for over 20 per cent of the men to fail to return.

General Sir Hubert Gough, GOC Fifth Army, planned to attack on a front of seven and a half miles from the Zillebeke – Zandvoorde road to Boesinghe with ten infantry divisions. By early July he had concentrated 752 heavy and medium guns, 324 4.5-in howitzers and 1,098 18-pounders to blast his troops forward two miles by a methodical advance in three stages – to the Blue Line about 1,250 yards distant, the Black Line 900 yards farther on and finally a further 1,400 yards to the Green Line. With communications between infantry and artillery as primitive as they were, this may well seem a clumsy plan. But it should be noted that in March and May 1918 the Germans executed successful attacks along these lines on the Somme and the Chemin des Dames.

About 15 miles west of Ypres a full-scale replica of the German positions we were to attack had been marked out with broad tapes in the standing corn. Every day in hot sunshine, under the eyes of the divisional and brigade commanders, we deployed as if for the real attack, advancing behind an imaginary barrage represented by men with red flags moving forward at the rate of 100 yards in four minutes in 25-yard lifts. We had two companies forward and two companies behind them in depth – each company attacking in two waves. They were all intended to go straight through to their objectives leaving one of their four platoons to follow and deal with enemy over-run. Much emphasis was laid on the need to keep as close as possible to the bursting shells of the barrage. All officers also attended an exposition of the divisional plan on a large-scale relief model. This envisaged an advance on a two-brigade front each with four tanks. Two battalions of each brigade would take the Blue Line. Then the other two would pass through to take the Black Line. A pause would then be necessary while the artillery was moved forward. When this was done the third brigade, supported by 12 tanks, would pass through and capture the Green Line.

It had been intended to launch the attack on 25 July. Accordingly we moved back into the line about Hooge on the 23rd. The preliminary day and night bombardment had reached a crescendo. We now found that the French, who were due to attack in the north, were not ready, so the attack had to be put back to the 31st.

As a result of 1916 experience on the Somme each unit going into action left behind within easy reach a so-called 'battle surplus' or cadre consisting of understudies at every level of command from lance-corporal upwards. There were about a hundred all told. I was left behind with this party as understudy to the adjutant.

On the afternoon of 26 July a signal from brigade HQ ordered me forward at once. It was a scorching afternoon. The road as far as the outskirts of Ypres was choked with transport, raising huge clouds of dust. Just short of the railway station on the western outskirts all traffic stopped. On reaching the Lille Gate I took the Warrington Track. Not a soul seemed to be moving in the wilderness ahead. It was not a pleasant walk. The observer of a German 77 mm battery apparently thought I presented a worthwhile target and sniped at me all the way to battalion HQ by Zillebeke Lake. Here I found utter confusion. The surface shelter which housed the HQ had sustained a direct hit and the adjutant, the Intelligence officer, the signals officer and the chief clerk had all been blown up and killed or evacuated. Even the leather-faced old RSM looked off colour. But he was still able to call my attention to three jars of rum which had been smashed by the explosion – a contingency Higher Authority was likely to treat with suspicion unless vouched for by unimpeachable evidence.

My CO, 26-year-old Lieutenant-Colonel C. G. Buckle, MC, moved the HQ to a vast dugout by the ruins of Halfway House. This shelter was a triumph of engineering under the marsh, designed to hold about 3,000 men before the attack. The greater part of the battalion were already in residence. There was just room for one man to pass another and the floor was a foot deep in grey mud. Pumping went on continuously. The smell was appalling – a delicate blend of marshes, sewage and human sweat. This vast sewer was spasmodically lit by electric light.

The Germans knew all the exits and kept up a continuous bombardment on them. Every visit to the latrines outside was a dash for life; day and night a never-ending stream of men stepped over us *en route* for the hell outside. We remained in these insanitary quarters for four days – jammed shoulder to shoulder. When the light failed and the supply of candles ran out we sat in darkness.

My main worry concerned not the loss of all the paper about the attack but casualties inflicted on the battalion signallers and runners, amounting to 50 per cent a day. When, on my first night, the signal came through postponing the attack for four days I foresaw that we would probably have to start the battle short-handed. In the event the misty weather on the 27th and 28th and rain on the 30th, ominous though they were in other respects, cut down the casualty rate.

A message on the afternoon of the 30th confirmed that zero hour would be at 0350 the next day. On the previous two nights the German artillery had unleashed exceptionally heavy shelling on our form-up area. There was therefore a feeling of acute tension when we all filed out of the great dugout at about 2100 to assembly trenches just north of the Menin Road at Hooge. Just in front of the assembly trenches a party had already laid out the tapes marking the start line. It was a dark and cloudy night.

The CO, the Intelligence Officer and I moved to Birr Cross Roads in the middle of the two rear companies with our little party of signallers trailing D3 cable and carrying some unlucky pigeons in baskets. At 0300 all was quiet; half an hour later all companies had reported that they were formed up on the tapes. Suddenly at 0350 the sky behind and on our flanks erupted. The blast was so deafening that we jammed our fingers in our ears; the ground shook. We could see the flashes of the barrage in the murk ahead. There were just a few silvery streaks in the sky to the east. The swish of the 18-pounder shells tempted us to crouch down. In fact, although we could not see them, the two leading companies advancing on compass bearings were clinging to the barrage and moving forward each time it jumped a further 25 yards. The reserve companies and our own headquarters soon started to move forward in the gloom as well.

We reached what had been the German front line. Here, the wire had been blown to bits by our bombardments of the preceding fortnight. Slowly the light strengthened. We could now see about 100 yards and all around us men moved steadily forward. The going was fairly good at first. Five hundred yards farther on we found the two leading companies on their objective rounding up a number of dazed Germans. The two reserve companies now pressed through towards their objective on the Bellwaarde Ridge and soon struck a ravine of sorts full of water and surrounded by the dead stumps of Château Wood. Here were smouldering dugouts which had been treated to a barrage of Thermite (incendiary bombs) fired from mortars. There were also some pillboxes which had been knocked over by heavy artillery fire.

Ploughing through the mud, the two reserve companies could be seen approaching the crest of the ridge which was our final objective. When the CO and I reached a point on the crest they were mopping up some dugouts running along the northern edge of the wood. It was now quite light. We established HQ in a large shell-hole. I could hear a lot of machine-gun fire 100 yards or so away to our left. Evidently the battle here was not yet over. About 100 ft above our heads an RE8 scout plane was sounding its klaxon horn. Looking up I could see the pilot distinctly. The time had come to put out the ground strips indicating our HQ's position and the capture of our objective. The pilot seemed satisfied, for he put the nose of his aircraft up and made off. One of his friends failed to get back to safety. His aircraft had been caught, probably by our own shells, and was burning a few hundred yards away on our left.

I wrote 'Objective gained' and our map reference on the flimsy message form which the signals sergeant promptly attached to the leg of a pigeon which was released. I could not have said much else at the time. At that very moment Captain T. R. Colyer-Fergusson was winning his Victoria Cross just 200 yards away. As his 'B' Company approached the ridge he found himself in danger of losing the barrage which was already 100 yards ahead. Right in front of him was an enemy trench well wired and occupied by a machine-gun crew which the barrage had missed. Hastily collecting about ten men, amongst whom was Sergeant W. G. Boulding and his own orderly Pte. B. Bell, he rushed forward and gained a footing in the trench which was on the crest of the ridge. Almost at once a German company counter-attacked. Colyer-Fergusson and his little party shot down 20 or 30 of them with rifle fire and the survivors surrendered. The rest of the British company now came up. At the same time a German machine-gun opened fire on them. Leaving his men to hold the trench Colyer-Fergusson and his orderly captured the gun. He then turned the gun on to another group of Germans, killing a large number of them. A few minutes later he was hit in the head by a stray machine-gun bullet and died instantly.

Meanwhile 'C' Company on the right had also had a tough struggle for its objective. Here, Second Lieutenant Frost rushed a post which held a machine-gun which was shooting down men of 1st Battalion, The Worcester Regiment, on our right flank. Frost killed a German officer and 14 men. By now Col. Buckle had gone forward and ordered the two companies to consolidate about 150 yards ahead. The liaison officer from the Worcesters reported that they too were on their objective. It was now daylight. I could now see the 1st Battalion, The Sherwood Foresters, and 2nd Battalion, The East Lancashire Regiment, passing through us and going strong *en route* to the Black Line 1,200 yards ahead on the Westhoek Ridge.

Hours of uncertainty, misunderstanding and confusion descended on the battlefield. It took me a long time to grasp what was actually happening in front and on our flanks. Walking wounded of the Foresters and E. Lancashires said their attack was going well but that they were losing a lot of men from machine-gun fire from their east flank and, surprisingly, from their right rear as well. About 0630 these two battalions were apparently on their objective on the Westhoek Ridge but fighting was still going on. About the same time our own company in Château Wood reported that they were being subjected to very heavy machine-gun fire from their east flank. Looking back I saw our own GOC, Brigadier-General H. W. Cobham, DSO, coming towards us with his brigade major. Suddenly quite close to us the brigade major (Captain A. Holmes Scott, Royal Engineers) was killed by a machine-gun bullet.

On the edge of the tree stumps of Château Wood two tanks were bogged down. They were the only tanks I saw that day. Coming forward from the direction of Hellfire Corner there was a mass of troops from 25th Brigade (Brigadier-General C. Coffin, DSO), destined to carry forward the advance beyond the Westhoek Ridge to the Green Line. About this time my CO, while trying to find out what the situation was on our right flank, was wounded and evacuated. Fortunately Lieutenant-Colonel S. G. Latham, MC, the second-in-command, had found it impossible to restrain himself from coming forward to see if he could be of any help. He never bothered to take cover. We had breakfast – biscuits and cold boiled bacon from our haversacks washed down with cold tea. Latham then went towards the right flank to find out what was really going on there. A lot of machine-gun fire was coming from Nonnebosschen, Glencorse and Polygon Woods. Nobody seemed able to say definitely which group of trees was which. The Worcesters apparently were out of touch with 30th Division which was rumoured to have failed to take Clapham Junction.

The sound of machine-gun fire from this direction continued. About this time our signallers reported that they had line communication with brigade HQ. When I raised the instrument the brigade Intelligence officer's voice seemed far away. I gathered, however, that 30th Division had been checked but were staging another attack on Sanctuary Wood and Stirling Castle. About 1000, the guns on our own front opened up in all-out support for 25th Brigade, now said to be near the final objective for the day – the Green Line on the far side of the Hanebeek stream. Despite the obscure situation on their right flank they seemed to be doing well.

Their progress was a matter of great interest to us as we were due to relieve one of their battalions when it reached its objective. About this time we were heavily shelled. Brigade HQ ordered us to send 60 men at once to Westhoek to act as additional stretcher bearers. A steady stream of walking wounded flowed from the front. They reported that 25th Brigade's three assault battalions were on their objective but had lost a lot of men. Some said they had got their objectives but had been counter-attacked and driven back. Large numbers of Germans had been seen arriving in lorries. By now it was at least clear that they still held Glencorse Wood and Nonnebosschen. The hours dragged by in an atmosphere of continued uncertainty. A wounded officer from 25th Brigade said they were being slowly pushed back to the Westhoek Ridge. Another reported later that Brig.-Gen. Coffin had been forward with his troops all the morning and was now rallying what was left of his brigade on the Westhoek Ridge.

All day the skies had been overcast. At about 1600 it started to rain in torrents. The shell-holes rapidly filled with water. Men were soon sinking knee-deep in the mud. The prolonged preliminary bombardment had shattered the drainage system and the churned-up earth held water like a sponge. The soldiers' ground-sheet capes were poor protection. Very soon we were all soaked to the skin. Only after dark did I fully understand what had happened. The 30th Division on our right, in a maze of shattered tree stumps and wire, had lost the barrage soon after the start. All the tanks supporting them had almost immediately become immobilized in the stinking bog. In the whole day, they had advanced less than 1,000 yards to Stirling Castle after using up all their battalions. For them it had been a nightmare – almost as bad as the first day of the Somme. It was clear that the Germans still held the high ground of the Gheluvelt Plateau at Clapham Junction and Glencorse Wood. The rest of Fifth Army on our left had had better luck and advanced about 2,000 yards.

It rained all night. Soon after dawn 10th Battalion, The Cheshire Regiment (25th Division) arrived to relieve us and we moved back in small parties towards Ypres. For the moment the guns were silent. Stretcher bearers were still bringing back their heavy loads through the all-pervading swamp of glutinous mud. Compared with 25th Brigade's battalions our casualties of 13 killed and 189 wounded had been light. Altogether the division had lost 160 officers and 3,005 men, mainly due to deadly machine-gun fire from the east flank. This was a fifth of the total British loss on 31 July but we had 600 prisoners to show for it. The divisional artillery exposed in the open for six weeks before the attack had lost more men from mustard gas and HE than they had incurred in the whole preceding period from 1914.

We spent the next ten days in comparative comfort in billets in the little town of Steenvoorde near Poperinghe. The Corps commander, after congratulating us on our efforts, informed us that we would have the privilege of continuing the battle in the same area when the weather improved. I do not recall any unbounded enthusiasm at his announcement, but if anyone disapproved he kept his mouth shut. Meanwhile, the rain continued unabated. On 13 August we returned to the line of shell-holes we had captured two weeks previously with two companies forward just short of Westhoek. Conditions had been bad when we left; they were even worse now. All the holes were full to the brim with water. Everywhere it was hard going through the mud. In some places duckboard tracks sank out of sight almost as soon as they were laid. Aerial photographs showed that the Hanebeek, which had been a mere trickle on 31 July, was now a broad stream.

This time the advance to the Green Line which we had captured but failed to hold on the 31st was to be carried out immediately south of the Ypres–Roulers railway on a two-brigade front with Coffin's 25th Brigade on the right. The Northamptonshires were now attached to this brigade as a reserve. On our right Polygon Wood, Glencorse Wood and Nonnebosschen were still in enemy hands. It was abundantly clear that if the 56th Division attacking on our right failed to capture them we would once again be out on a limb and caught under fire as we had been a fortnight earlier.

The battle on 16 August remained imprinted on my mind because it was the only time I ever saw anyone in the act of winning a VC. This time we took into action only 13 officers and 400 men. Zero hour was 0445. The three attacking units of 25th Brigade, 2nd Battalion, The Royal Berkshire Regiment, 1st Battalion, The Royal Irish Rifles and 2nd Battalion, The Lincolnshire Regiment, got off on time despite being shelled when forming up. As the light strengthened, reports passed to us from brigade HQ gave the impression that all was going well and that the Hanebeek had been reached and crossed. Later, however, news came once more that they were being caught in enfilade by machine-guns on right and left flanks. Wounded and stretcher bearers passing by said that Gen. Coffin had gone forward to the hard-pressed front.

In lulls during the bombardment we could once more hear prolonged machine-gun fire from Nonnebosschen and Polygon Wood. Col. Latham therefore ordered Captain C. E. Blake to find out what the situation was there. Working his way to the right, Blake discovered that 56th (1st London) Division had found the tangled mass of dead woods around Inverness Copse and Glencorse Wood concealing considerable numbers of unlocated machine-guns which had been too much for it. There could be no doubt that Coffin's brigade was isolated 1,200 yards ahead with open flanks. The expected counter-attack came at about 0930 under a savage bombardment of shells and machine-gun fire. As the morning dragged on there could be no escaping the fact that 25th Brigade were being shot to pieces and slowly pressed back. A little after noon Gen. Coffin ordered Capt. Blake's two forward companies to come forward at once and our other two companies to join him on the Westhoek Ridge with all speed. When we arrived a terrifying situation prevailed. The German shellfire was hellish. Ours must have been just as bad for them. Our forward observation officers had now brought down a dense curtain

of fire across our front. Just behind the Westhoek Ridge the massed
Vickers guns of the Divisional machine-gun companies had opened
up with good observation and deadly effect. In the din you had to
shout to make yourself heard.

On the ridge we found Coffin standing upright in the open. He
welcomed us with a smile: 'Those two companies of yours are a fine
lot. They got here just in time.' We then discovered that he had led
the counter-attack with them and halted the Germans about 150 yards
ahead. He and Latham then took the rest of the battalion forward and
patched up some sort of line with Royal Berkshire survivors and filled
the gap between the right flank and what was left of 167th Brigade
(56th Division). Neither Coffin, nor Latham for that matter, showed
the slightest inclination to take cover or indeed of being in any way
perturbed.

About 1700 quiet descended on the front. It seemed that both sides
had had enough for the time being. The sun made a fitful appearance.
Three of Coffin's battalions had lost half their strength – the Royal
Irish Rifles had only one officer and 60 men left. They were still,
however, a disciplined body prepared to fight on. So long as Coffin
remained with them they would have gone on to the last man.

Within two weeks my battalion had lost about 330 officers and
men. Compared with other 8th Division battalions we escaped
lightly. On 16 August our divisional loss came to 81 officers and
2,074 men. When Haig inspected the infantry on 21 August only
3,950 of the 12,000 or so available three weeks previously could
be paraded. I do not recollect anything he said. According to the
Divisional History, however, he 'gave the division many words of
encouragement and thanks, inspiring all ranks by his generous
appreciation of what they had done.'

Junior officers in most battles see only the local picture. Historians
therefore tend to treat their accounts with caution. Because I had
the luck to act as adjutant in both these battles I probably got a
broader impression of what went on than most of my fellow second
lieutenants. By some fluke, a copy of the three-page report I wrote
on the battle a day or so afterwards has survived. I recollect being
very proud of this literary effort at the time and feeling somewhat
peeved when my CO signed it after only a cursory glance before
dispatch to brigade HQ. I realize that my comments are open to
the charge of bias. The loss of so many of my friends may well have
embittered me. But, I can at least say that in my limited experience

the accusation that divisional and brigade commanders ordered their men to face dangers they were not prepared to share themselves is unfair. Even in minor operations they had little scope for initiative and no option other than to obey orders. The casualty rate in battalion commanders (eight out of our 12 on 31 July), company commanders and lieutenants was proportionately far in excess of that of men in the ranks.

What I failed to understand after these two battles was why Haig chose to attack in an area of reclaimed marshland which two years' experience had already shown would revert to bog when it rained. It should have been obvious that this was no place to employ the 136 primitive tanks committed to battle here. Why did he so blatantly advertise his intention of attacking east of Ypres for six weeks before the actual assault by a vast increase in traffic, a gigantic forward build-up of dumps and a fortnight's preliminary bombardment? This mystified me at the time and still does. Having finally shown his hand and staged a fiasco on the 31 July why did he decide to go on with the battle hoping for fine weather? I was even more astonished when we came back to the muddy horror of Passchendaele in November 1917.

Cambrai (1917)

Bryan Cooper

Accusing as I do without exception all the great Allied offensives of 1915, 1916 and 1917, as needless and wrongly conceived
operations of infinite cost, I am bound to reply to the question,
what else could be done? And I answer it, pointing to the Battle
of Cambrai. *This* could have been done. This in many variants,
this in larger and better forms ought to have been done.

Such was Winston Churchill's belief in 1927 and the perspective
has only been enlarged since.

At first sight the Battle of Cambrai in November 1917 was no more
decisive than most battles fought on the Western Front. Indeed, the
initial British advance through the Hindenberg Line that gave such
promise of success, and caused church bells in England to ring
victory peals for the first time since the Boer War, was repulsed by
a German counter-attack that actually took back more ground than
had been won. But it was the means of making that original advance,
by the first-ever massed attack by tanks with close air-support and
an unregistered artillery barrage which established Cambrai as a
milestone in the history of warfare. It was a prelude to the tank's
decisive role at the Battle of Amiens in August 1918 which signalled
the final defeat of Germany.

Although the first, premature and piecemeal use of tanks by the
British on the Somme in September 1916 wasted a great chance, it

must be remembered that not only tanks were new but also the whole concept of their use. Many Allied commanders continued to disregard their potential but Field-Marshal Sir Douglas Haig, the British C-in-C, made a personal request for 1,000 improved tanks to be built during 1917. It was probably inevitable that the first tanks should be misused in wartime conditions, while those most concerned, crews, designers and commanders, learned from their mistakes. Unfortunately, this was not true of the latter during most of 1917.

The year opened promisingly for the embryo tank force. While a shortage of materials at home reduced Haigh's order, there were some 200 tanks available by March, not only improved Mark Is but also a few Mark IVs. These were similar in outline and armament, but had 50 per cent thicker armor in the vital parts, against German armor-piercing ammunition. The Tank Corps, as it was named in June, became better established with at least a rudimentary training procedure. It had also produced its first master of tank tactics and strategy in the person of Lieutenant-Colonel John Frederick Charles Fuller. As Chief General Staff Officer (GSOI) to Brigadier-General Hugh J. Elles, the Tank Corps' first and 36-year-old commander, he devised many of the principles that were to govern the employment of tanks in battle up to and during the Second World War. Fuller saw the tank primarily as a mobile fortress which could escort the infantry into the enemy's defenses and emphasized the necessity for surprise. He also saw the need to mass not disperse tanks, and preferably on ground that had not been reduced to a quagmire by constant shelling.

Such concepts were too unorthodox for most of the general staff at Haig's GHQ, especially the artillery commanders who believed that only a long and massive bombardment could soften up the enemy and cut his barbed wire as a prelude to any attack, regardless of the warning this gave. The first 1917 use of tanks was in April during the Battle of Arras, in which some 40 took part. Again strung out along a wide front, diminishing their impact, and despite individual successes, most became bogged down in the mud and unable to avoid German shellfire. At Vimy Ridge, eight tanks were to assist the Canadian Corps, but these foundered before they could even fight.

An even greater tragedy occurred at Bullecourt (NW of Cambrai) where 11 tanks were to help the 4th Australian Division. Due to a heavy snowstorm the attack was postponed for a day; the tanks stood out as easy targets against the white background on a bright clear morning. Nine were knocked out before they reached the

Hindenberg Line, and the remaining two were captured, giving the Germans their first chance to examine the new weapon. Australian infantry, following behind the tanks from which they expected protection, suffered appalling losses. They lost their faith in tanks for more than a year.

The worst tank ordeal of all came in Flanders, where the Corps took part in Haig's grand plan to break through the Ypres salient. The start of the offensive, at mine-sprung Messines Ridge on 7 June, was a great success, but 40 new Mark IV tanks were hardly needed, although they gave valuable support to the infantry. It was during the main campaign, begun on 31 July, which resolved itself into the terrible struggle for the village of Passchendaele that tanks, in common with the British Army as a whole, experienced their greatest catastrophe.

The preliminary artillery bombardment reached its highest peak of the war, when in 13 days over four million shells were fired from 3,000 guns, one gun to every six yards of the 11-mile front. This churned the ground into a dreadful condition made even worse by several weeks of non-stop rain and flooding in Flanders. Some 200 tanks were mustered for the Ypres offensive, and when it petered out at the beginning of November, hardly any remained in one piece. Most had sunk deep into the mud and were destroyed by enemy fire, to the point where the Menin Road was known as the 'tank grave-yard'. After three months of bloody fighting, total British casualties were nearly 400,000 men – for the gain of four miles of territory.

GHQ was still unable to see the true value of tanks and held on to an attitude typified by one army commander, who stated after the Ypres campaign: 'One, tanks are unable to negotiate bad ground; two, the ground on a battlefield will always be bad; three, therefore, tanks are no good on a battlefield.' The War Office in London had further doubts about whether to build more tanks. But although few realized it at the time, Passchendaele was the last of the senseless battles of attrition, fought in despair of conducting the war in any other way. For on another part of the front the Tank Corps had quietly been planning an attack in conditions of their own choosing, on dry hard ground, and according to their own tactics, that would show that indeed there was another way.

The town of Cambrai lay seven miles behind the Hindenberg Line, opposite General Sir Julian H. G. Byng's Third Army. It was a region of open, rolling countryside and firm ground covered by uncultivated grass that had seen little fighting during the war. The Germans considered their fortifications to be impregnable and were content to hold them while the Allies wore themselves out in reckless assaults elsewhere. As far back as mid-June, in a paper written on the future employment of tanks, Col. Fuller had suggested the idea of a major tank raid, not to win ground but to destroy or capture enemy troops and guns. One area he thought suitable was the country between St Quentin and Cambrai. The idea was originally turned down at GHQ, but early in August, support for it came from Gen. Byng, already thinking of an attack in the Cambrai area.

Further support came from Haig himself. As it became obvious even to him that Passchendaele was a disaster, he wanted to launch a quick operation with a good chance of immediate success in order to raise morale at home and among his own troops. He believed the Tank Corps plan might work. If it failed, he could always blame the tanks for not fulfilling their earlier promise. In such an event, it was not likely that the Tank Corps could have survived. On 13 October, he gave his approval for the attack to take place on 20 November. Conditions were now not nearly so favorable. Flanders had drained the Army's resources, most divisions were battle-weary and under strength, and on top of that the collapse of the Italian Front at Caporetto on 24 October meant rushing five British divisions to Italy to hold the line, leaving Third Army short of reserves.

Byng's intention was to break through the Hindenberg Line along a six-mile front between two canals, the Canal de L'Escaut (St Quentin) on the right and the unfinished and waterless Canal du Nord on the left. This was to be accomplished by three brigades of Mark IV tanks, followed by six infantry divisions with support from another two and three more held in reserve. While the tanks and infantry captured the two main features of the area, the Flesquières and Bourlon ridges, five cavalry divisions (40,000 horsemen) were to pour through the gap and isolate the town of Cambrai. The German forces would be cut off and rounded up, then the way would be clear to drive NE towards Valenciennes. From then onwards the plan was rather vague, but conformed to Haig's doctrine of attacking the German flanks after a breakthrough and 'rolling up the front'. Supporting the attack would be 1,003 guns, almost a third of 6-in calibre or more, and 14 squadrons (289 aircraft) of the Royal Flying Corps. This novel co-operation between tanks and aircraft was the origin of the German *Blitzkrieg* in the Second World War.

Cambrai itself was an important target, being a major communications center where four railways and a number of main roads and waterways converged, and German defenses were therefore particularly strong. They lay in a wide path, up to five miles deep, between the British front and Cambrai, with three main lines of trenches dug much wider than usual, up to 16 ft and to a depth of 18 ft. Even if tanks were used, the three defending divisions were confident that such vehicles would be unable to cross, and indeed the Mark IV only had a 10 ft trench-crossing capability. Each trench system included concrete dugouts in which were massed batteries of machine-guns and lay behind acres of dense barbed wire, nowhere less than 50 yards thick. British observers had estimated that it would take five weeks of artillery bombardment to cut down this wire in the normal way.

Col. Fuller reckoned that tanks could crush the barbed wire, although there was always a danger of it becoming entangled in their tracks. The sheer size of the trenches was the biggest obstacle. An answer was finally provided by the Tank Corps Central Workshops. Bundles of brushwood of the kind used for road repairs were bound together by thick chains to make huge 10-ft-long fascines, each weighing 1.75 tons. One would be carried on the roof of each fighting tank, to be dropped into the trenches to form a bridge across.

The fighting tanks were to operate an ingenious leap-frogging system, in sections of three. An advance tank would go forward, flatten the German wire for the oncoming infantry, then reaching the first trench would turn left and drive along the edge, firing down at the enemy to protect the two main-body tanks following 100 yards behind. The first of these would drop its fascine in the trench, cross over, and give covering fire in front of the second trench for the next tank. This in turn would cross the second trench and move forward to attack the third and last line of trenches. Meanwhile, the advance tank would have come up to drop its fascine in the third trench, leading its two companions into the open country beyond. Four platoons of infantry were to follow closely (25–50 yards) behind each tank section to capture and garrison the trenches as they were overcome. Finally, 32 special wire-pulling tanks would roll up the flattened wire with grapnels to make broad pathways for the cavalry advance. In addition to these and 378 fighting tanks, there were 54 supply carriers with nine wireless tanks, a telephone cable laying tank and two bridge layers – making a grand total of 476, the largest tank force ever concentrated.

The week before the attack was due to begin, and after ten days training in the technique described above, the tanks were brought up to the front by rail in great secrecy, arriving by night so that even the British infantry did not know of their presence. Late on the afternoon of 19 November, the tanks began to leave their lying-up positions in woods and fields and made their way to the start-line. Dawn came up very slowly, grey and overcast with a fine ground mist. The shapes of the woods and ridges ahead began to emerge out of the darkness. Coveys of partridges sprang up and larks and crows took to the sky as the British infantry began to cut through their own wire, ready for the assault. There was no sign of the Germans, hidden deep in their trenches and dugouts, confident of the protection given by long, dense belts of barbed wire.

At zero hour, 0620, there was a devastating roar as 1,000 British guns opened up, most firing for the first time, having had their targets mapped and not registered by ranging shots, while from out of the sky swept four RFC squadrons, flying low and spraying the German trenches with machine-gun fire. The Battle of Cambrai had begun. And from the beginning it was different from previous battles. The artillery barrage, instead of continuing for days and even weeks, giving the Germans time to bring up reinforcements, almost immediately began to lift towards targets farther on. At the same time, the tanks moved slowly forwards down tape-marked lanes, the sound of their engines hidden by the noise of the guns and their course set by compass. At last they were to be used in a surprise attack as the pioneers of tank development had always intended.

Right in the center and aboard 'Hilda', one of the leading tanks, was Brig.-Gen. Elles, carrying the new Corps flag and insisting on the right to lead his men into the first large-scale tank attack in history. It was one of the very few occasions in the First World War that a general did so. The sight of so many tanks lumbering out of the half-light of dawn, their huge fascines on top making them appear even more like monstrous, prehistoric animals, was too much for many of the German troops, who fled in panic. Those who remained were dismayed to find that their armor-piercing bullets could not penetrate these new Mark IV tanks. And when the tanks opened fire with their 6-pounders and Lewis machine-guns, the demoralization of the enemy was complete. A tank commander called it 'almost a cake-walk'. And it was recorded that 'the infantry had walked behind the tanks smoking and with practically nothing to do except mop up a few dugouts.'

By midday, the tanks had broken through the three trench systems as planned and advanced nearly five miles on a six-mile front, a deeper penetration than that achieved after the three months of fighting just over at Passchendaele. The day had yielded captures totalling 8,000 men, 123 guns and 281 machine-guns: two divisions had been annihilated. At HQ German Supreme Command, there was consternation. An immediate counter-attack was ordered, but the necessary reinforcements could not be brought up for at least 48 hours. Now the value of a swift surprise attack became evident.

So serious was the situation that General Erich Ludendorff, commanding the German armies, considered an extensive withdrawal of the whole Cambrai front, one which might have led to a general retreat. But the attack's success had also surprised British GHQ. In fact, many commanders refused to believe it and valuable time was lost while they awaited confirmation of reports from the front. The morning objectives, with one important exception, had been taken with such relative ease that some advanced infantry units were content to remain in the captured German trenches, so much more comfortable than their own. In some instances the infantry failed to keep up with the tanks, which later had to withdraw for lack of support. But there still remained the five divisions of cavalry massed behind the British lines waiting to advance. They had waited for such a chance in nearly every other battle previously fought. Now it had come. The great breakthrough had been made.

Unfortunately, Cavalry Corps HQ was five miles behind the front line, and local commanders were not empowered to make decisions on the spot. By the time orders came through to advance, the momentum of the attack had faltered. And in one vital sector of the center, at Flesquières, the German 54th Reserve Division was still holding out. The way should have been clear for 1st Cavalry Division to pass through the village and move on to the all-important objective of Bourlon Wood on the ridge covering the approach to Cambrai. But it was here that the one hold-up of the morning had occurred, largely due to a lack of co-operation between tanks and the infantry of 51st Highland Division, for which their commander, Major-General G. M. Harper, was largely responsible. He did not approve of tanks, just as earlier he had opposed machine-gun development, and ignored the instructions laid down by the Tank Corps. Instead of keeping his men in files close behind the tanks, to deal with German artillery, he made them follow in extended order 100 yards or more behind. They had to waste valuable time looking for the paths that the tanks had cut through the barbed wire. Meanwhile, as the tanks pressed on alone towards the crest of Flesquières Ridge, they came under fire from several German 77 mm field-gun batteries. Sixteen were destroyed (a quarter of the figure lost to gunfire), with no survivors among the crews. By the time the Highlanders advanced to this point, the Germans had regrouped and the fighting here lasted until evening. Only then, outflanked on both sides, did the defenders withdraw. But this delay prevented the cavalry advance until next day, and the chance of taking Bourlon without a fight was lost.

By nightfall on the 20th, 179 of the 378 tanks that had moved forward at dawn were out of action. Many of those remaining had fought almost continuously for 16 hours and required maintenance. In spite of the great success achieved, the infantry and cavalry had not taken full advantage of it – perhaps because no one really expected such a breakthrough after the deadlock of earlier battles. Meanwhile, on the German side, five reserve divisions were beginning to arrive around Cambrai. Haig did in fact see the danger. But having provided the British public at home with a victory, the first one for so long, he did not wish to call a halt. The offensive continued.

On the 22nd, the British attack was resumed and very nearly succeeded. With the help of tanks, the infantry managed to fight their way into Bourlon village, while several other tanks almost reached Cambrai itself. But with little by way of reserves to call on, the British offensive lost its impetus. The Germans fought back with grim determination, and for another five days the battle swung first one way, then another. The fighting reached its peak on the 27th in the village of Fontaine, almost within sight of Cambrai. The situation at Bourlon was much the same, with part of the wood and village still in enemy hands. By the end of that day it was apparent to all, even Haig, that the offensive had to be called off. There were just not enough reserves to keep it going.

One week of fighting had achieved little more than the initial success gained in the first few hours, although on the credit side, apart from ground gained, over 11,000 prisoners had been taken, together with 142 guns, 456 machine-guns, 74 trench mortars and large quantities of stores and ammunition. After a hurried conference at GHQ, it was decided to withdraw to a defensive line on Flesquières Ridge, making use of the former German trenches. As far as the British were concerned, the Battle of Cambrai was over. The remaining tanks were pulled back to prepare for entrainment to their winter quarters.

But no one had reckoned with German intentions. On the morning of 30 November, while the British were carrying out an orderly withdrawal, eight German divisions delivered a massive counter-stroke that took 6,000 prisoners and 158 guns on that day, in many ways just as sudden and surprising as the original British attack. The German plan was nothing less than to cut off and destroy all British troops in the salient formed by their advance on Cambrai. Only 63 tanks remained in the area. These were quickly rounded up and sent into action to help the infantry. They made a vital contribution to preventing what could have been a major disaster. Even so, by the time the German offensive ended in a blinding snowstorm on 7 December they had won back as much ground as they had lost and achieved a more or less even balance in casualties and prisoners, which totalled about 45,000 for both sides.

It was by no means the worst British defeat of the year, but after the promising victory of 20 November, the final result seemed just that much more of a bitter failure. There was a public outcry at home and even a Court of Enquiry which whitewashed the generals and put most of the blame on the junior officers, NCOs, and men. But this time, at least, the tanks could not be blamed. No one could deny their brilliant initial success. They suffered for it as well, particularly during the German counter-attack. Of the 4,000 officers and men of the Tank Corps who had taken part in the whole battle, a total of 1,153 were killed or wounded. Less than a third of the 476 tanks returned to base and all of them required extensive repairs. In fact, few saw action again, for the Mark IV was replaced in 1918 by the more efficient and more heavily armored Mark V. Haig had finished his Cambrai dispatch: 'The great value of the tanks in the offensive has been conclusively proved.'

4
Asian Incidents

Shanghai (1937)

Michael Calvert

The weather in Shanghai, the great international seaport by the Yangtze, was threatening. The warnings of the approach of a typhoon had been hoisted, there was low cloud at 1,500 ft with gusts of wind up to 60 m.p.h. It was Saturday morning 14 August 1937 and one of the world's largest cities was about to begin a three-month ordeal.

The start of the Sino-Japanese 'Incident' which was to cost millions of lives, and which might be said to be the start of the Second World War, is traditionally dated to the 'Double Seventh' (when Japanese troops clashed with Chinese at the Marco Polo bridge, just south of Peking, on 7 July 1937). Hostilities near Shanghai began on 13 August. The Japanese had landed about 1,300 sailors and marines to protect their interests in the International Settlement, which included the huge Toyada Cotton Mills. Just over five years before, Shanghai had been the scene of a ferocious month-long battle when a Japanese army had landed to smash a Chinese trade boycott.

General Chiang Kai-shek, eager to involve the Western Powers in the new struggle, and also to gain the attention of the world press, rapidly moved in two of the best of his German-trained divisions, the 87th (involved in the 1932 battle) and 88th. These divisions, part of General Chang Chih-Chung's 9th Army Group, assaulted the Japanese naval forces which were holding bridgeheads along the NW bank of the River Huang-P'u (Whangpoo) on 13 August.

The Huang-P'u, flowing 16 miles north, connected the great port of Shanghai (at that time the fourth largest port in the world with 3.5 million inhabitants) to the Yangtze at Wu-sung near its mouth. Opposite the Japanese warehouses, which were being besieged, and in the middle of the river, was anchored Vice-Admiral Hasegawa's flagship, the old three-funneled cruiser, *Idzumo*. This 9,580-ton warship had been built for Japan in Scottish yards at the turn of the century and had fought in the Russo-Japanese War of 1904–5. Just upstream and in line ahead were also anchored the modern American heavy cruiser USS *Augusta*, and the British *Kent*-class cruiser HMS *Cumberland* flying the flag of the Shanghai-born C-in-C, China Station, Admiral Sir Charles J. C. Little, KCB.

Other naval vessels of the Western Powers in the port included the Royal Navy light cruiser *Danae*, the destroyers *Duncan*, *Delight* and *Duchess* and the sloop *Falmouth*. These were busy ferrying their national troops to reinforce the normal peacetime detachments defending the International Settlement.

On 13 August Vice-Adm. Hasegawa had unilaterally issued an edict that no merchant shipping was to be allowed to enter the Huang-P'u River in case they smuggled Chinese troops ashore in the Japanese rear. Meanwhile several Japanese destroyers were firing broadsides from their 4.7-in guns at point-blank range into the wharves and along the jetties opposite them to hold back the Chinese attackers who had, in places, reached the go-downs (warehouses) on the water front. Chinese snipers in sampans under the wharves succeeded in killing a number of Japanese officers clad in their white uniforms while they controlled the gunfire from the bridges of these destroyers.

In the International Settlement proper, and in the separate French Concession containing most of the more luxurious night clubs, life went on as near normal as possible. At lunchtime, for instance, the European *T'aipans* (heads of thriving business houses) played liar dice in the Shanghai Club's Long Bar on the Bund (a promenade by the Huang-P'u) to decide the final arrangements of contracts and other problems requiring decisions.

With plenty of pink gin and dice, decisions could be reached quickly, saving much time in negotiations. After a Saturday's curry lunch, the Chinese compradores (buyers) and Number Ones of the firms would be telephoned and the decisions would be quickly implemented. Shanghai, in its hundred years of international history, was used to emergencies. For example, permanent steel slots had been installed in the streets so that barbed wire 'knife-rests' could be quickly fixed in to divide the settlement into defensible districts, supported by permanent concrete pillboxes to cover the wire. The only real signs of the times were the very many thousands of Chinese refugees who had fled into the city before the perimeter defenses were manned and who were filling the streets, but were being moved along into the remoter parts of the settlement by the efficient Shanghai Police. Their senior police officers were European, mostly British, while the rank and file were mainly robust Chinese and Sikhs.

On the Huang-P'u Bund European families clustered with their possessions ready to be evacuated to Hong Kong by the warships which were bringing in reinforcements. By the afternoon of the 14th the surge of Chinese refugees had reached Avenue Edward VII, which cut through the French Concession upstream opposite Pu-Tung and south of the International Settlement where the fighting was taking place.

The troops of the main Western Powers manning the perimeter were British soldiers and sailors, US Marines, Dutch Marines and *Savoia* Grenadiers from Italy. The British contingent, besides the sailors and Royal Marines who were later withdrawn, consisted of 2nd Battalion, the Loyal Regiment (North Lancashire) and 2nd Battalion, the Royal Welch Fusiliers (from Hong Kong). They were late reinforced by the 1st Battalion, Ulster Rifles and the Middlesex Regiment, some detachments of Royal Signals and HQ staff. Thirteen stalwart men of the Royal Engineers were to supervise the emplacement of more than one million filled sandbags to form the temporary blockhouses. The watertable was only a foot or two below the pavement gutters, so it was not possible to dig down to find cover from the Japanese and Chinese bombs and shells which missed their targets and landed in the Settlement.

It was agreed that this international garrison, with the exception of the French in their Concession and who liked to be different, was to be under the command of the Scottish Major-General A. P. D. Telfer-Smollett CBE, DSO, MC (later GOC Scottish Command) aided by about ten staff officers who also formed the brigade HQ for the four British battalions. In a very similar situation in Trieste during 1948, the staff was ten times as great for the same size garrison.

Suddenly, at 1600 on Saturday 14 August, a formation of four US-exported Northrop 2E attack aircraft (from 2nd Group of the

Chinese Air Force) emerged out of the 1,500 ft cloud-ceiling and made straight for the *Idzumo*. The pilots had been trained by Colonel Claire Lee Chennault (an American serving as the Inspector of the Chinese Air Force) in level bombing from a height of 7,500 ft on a fixed air speed. As the four aircraft lost height in a shallow dive, the bomb aimers, lying flat on the deck, saw through their sights the three-funneled *Idzumo* and dropped 1,080 lb bombs (which had been sold to them by the British). But they had apparently forgotten to reset their bombsights for the correct speed and lower altitude and, with the gusty air conditions in the prevailing typhoon situation, all the bombs went astray. One fell near *Augusta* damaging her with bomb splinters which killed one sailor. Another two splashed *Cumberland*. But the fourth landed on a road junction off Avenue Edward VII in the French Concession which was teeming with refugees and killed 1,123 persons besides wounding another thousand. Much of the damage was done by falling glass from the tall buildings surrounding the junction.

A second attack on *Idzumo* next day by two aircraft was just as inaccurate and disastrous. One bomb landed in the Great World Amusement Centre and a second on a luxury hotel in the Nanking Road where it killed over 250 people. A total of 1,956 Chinese and Europeans were killed, and 2,426 wounded by these six misplaced bombs. The Avenue Edward VII killing was a record for one bomb for many years to come. It was rumored at the time that Claire Chennault took part in the second raid. But whatever the truth it did not prevent him organizing, and commanding with distinction, the American Volunteer Group (AVG, more popularly known as the Flying Tigers, who fought in an unneutral manner for China in association with the British 204 Mission) from the beginning of 1941, long before Pearl Harbor. In 1943 Claire Chennault was promoted to Major-General commanding the volunteer US 14th Army Air Force in China, and, in spite of shortages of pilots and planes, drove the Japanese air forces from the Chinese skies.

Meanwhile, the Chinese offensive against the Japanese holding out among the wharves and go-downs of Hangkow continued. By 20 August Chiang Kai-shek had committed the equivalent of nine divisions to the Shanghai area, on both sides of the Huang-P'u. In support were 72 guns and 24 light tanks (British Vickers). These ramshackle but numerous Chinese forces threatened to squeeze the thin Japanese bridgehead to death. On the 23rd, Japan's hastily assembled Shanghai Expeditionary Army began disembarking two large divisions with a tank battalion and lavish heavy artillery to save the embattled landing force. It took round-the-clock attacks from 1st Combined Air Flotilla in Formosa (Taiwan) and strikes from four aircraft carriers, backed up by ceaseless naval gunfire, to prevent the multiplying Chinese armies from achieving a dramatic victory.

On 20 September no fewer than 62 'divisions' were in or heading for the theater of war. Meanwhile, three more Japanese divisions and support units had joined the struggle against the 19 Chinese formations in the Shanghai area. General Chang Chih-Chung, commander of four reinforced divisions a month before, now controlled 15 in his Central Group of Armies. Above the ground troops, Chiang Kai-shek's pilots flew up to 142 assorted American and Italian aircraft against twice their number of more modern Japanese machines. Only the introduction of even newer aircraft types began to gain Japan air supremacy in mid-September.

Western warships steaming up the Huang-P'u were surprised to find that Japanese destroyers ceased their bombardment of the Chinese as they passed and gave the usual naval compliments. When that was done they continued their firing. At sea, the concentration of seven cruisers, 17 destroyers and nine gunboats gave General Iwace Matsui (C-in-C Shanghai Expeditionary Army) complete freedom of maneuver.

The British manned two separate sectors of the international perimeter, the most important being in Chapei, north of the Suchow Creek and alongside the Japanese sector where heavy fighting was taking place. On the other side of the sector was the North Station building which had been converted into a Chinese strongpoint. The second British sector, initially manned by the Loyal Regiment, was on the extreme west of the settlement along Bubbling Well Road near Hungjao Airport where a railway bridge crossed the Suchow Creek. A zoo, which was later to be inadvertently bombed, was situated behind the Loyals' position.

The American sector lay between the two British enclaves and was manned by a US Marine Regiment which had last served with the Royal Welch Fusiliers at Peking during the 1900 Boxer Rebellion. The Dutch and Italian contingents closed other gaps in the perimeter while a strong, purposeful French force guarded the French Concession which covered the southern sector near Nantao.

But it was Chapei, where the Fusiliers soon took over from the British Marines and sailors, which was, for some months to come, in the forefront as it constituted a salient between the Chinese and the reinforced Japanese, and acted as a touch-line along which the conflict between these two Oriental countries waxed and waned. Members of the British garrison, with permission, could pay visits to either side and observe the course of the war and the methods used. But Chapei was no pleasure resort. Shells and bombs landing in this sector had caused the inhabitants to evacuate the area north of the Suchow Creek and the mass of derelict brick and black-tiled slums soon became a haunt of rats, flies and maggots as the sewers were destroyed and corpses floated to and fro between the booms in the tidal creek. Some of these unfortunates were suspected saboteurs executed by the Japanese; others were Japanese prisoners executed by the Chinese in retaliation. Between 13 August and November, when the Japanese were enlarging their bridgeheads and obtaining more elbow room, about 20 British troops manning the perimeter of Chapei were killed, mainly by Japanese bombs and shells that were misdirected, or by unexploded bombs that went off later.

Britain's China Command HQ in Hong Kong could not visualize a major war being fought between about half a million Chinese and eventually about 250,000 Japanese in the area between Shanghai and the Yangtze, complete with modern weapons, aircraft and naval support from a fleet anchored in the mouth of the Yangtze. In keeping with the niggardly defense spending of the 1930s, China Command gave orders that it was unnecessary to provide British troops with overhead cover. But Hong Kong had been forestalled in this decision, as Captain (later Major-General) Thomas G. Rennie of the Black Watch, acting Brigade Major, and Captain Howard-Vyse, the Commander Royal Engineers (CRE) had already spent thousands of Chinese dollars buying up 6 in timber struts so that overhead cover, heavily reinforced with sandbags, could be placed over the small redoubts constructed along the dangerous Chapei perimeter. This action undoubtedly saved many British soldiers' lives but, on instructions from the Chief Financial Advisor to China Command, the Hong Kong paymaster refused to pay the bill.

So when the Chief of Staff, British troops in China, Colonel (later Lieutenant-General) Noel M. S. Irwin, DSO and two bars, MC and the Chief Engineer, China Command, Brigadier Geoffrey Cathcart Gowlland, OBE, announced that they would pay Shanghai a visit,

Rennie and Howard-Vyse cooked up a scheme with the Chinese and Japanese commands, neither of which wanted to kill British soldiers, but who fully understood and had suffered from the tortuous minds of accountants in a peacetime army. The Sino-Japanese contestants organized a seemingly furious battle on the perimeter at the wide open space in front of the North Station building. All unwittingly, Gowlland and Irwin, with their solar topees and red tabs in full array, were brought to the scene of action.

At once dozens of shells were plummeted into the area by either side while first Japanese, and then Chinese aircraft bombed and strafed the edge of the perimeter. Armored cars from both sides also roared up and rained tracer bullets vaguely at each other while the infantry and gunners on either side let off their weapons in all directions. The Chinese engineers, not to be outdone, exploded a mine for full measure. Rennie and Howard-Vyse had, over the months, become inured to the sounds of battle. But Irwin and Gowlland had not. These were probably the first shots these two courageous and well-decorated senior officers had heard fired since 1919, 18 years before. Gowlland, now lying in the rubble, gripped the arm of a junior engineer officer and cried: 'This is war! This is war!' After further treatment the two shaken officers got up and were led away to a covered blockhouse where Rennie and Howard-Vyse had the necessary papers ready, complete with the requisite rubber stamps, authorizing the required expenditure. In a daze, Irwin and Gowlland duly signed and then departed back to Hong Kong.

One of the mainstays of the defense of the International Settlement was the Shanghai Volunteer Corps which included a rigorously trained, smart and durable White Russian regiment whose members had escaped from the Soviet regime. The Volunteers mainly consisted of young and energetic businessmen from the great merchant banks and business houses such as Butterfield and Swire, Hong Kong and Shanghai Bank, Jardine Matheson and other British and European firms which had done so much to develop China, taking great financial risks but also gaining great profits. The corps was formed into infantry, cavalry and armored car companies which reinforced the national contingents, especially at night and weekends when businesses were closed. They also supported the very efficient and highly motivated British-trained Shanghai Police. So, in spite of the bombing and after the evacuation of many families, business, trade and life in this city of 3.5 million carried on. But the Chinese had failed as yet to involve the Western Powers in the war. The Europeans were too engrossed nearer home with the Spanish Civil War, Mussolini's invasion of Ethiopia and the threat from Hitler. Soon after the 'Incident' started in Shanghai, Chiang Kai-shek concluded a Non-Aggression Pact with the Soviet Union which brought in a $250,000,000 loan to buy armaments. An unfortunate happening further depressed relations between Japan and Britain. On 26 August, the 6 ft 7 in British Ambassador to China, Sir Hughe Knatchbull-Hugessen (later Ambassador to Turkey and victim of the 'Cicero' espionage case) was returning to Shanghai from the new Chinese capital, Nanking, farther up the Yangtze. In spite of a large Union Jack painted on the roof of his car, a myopic Japanese pilot strafed it, and Sir Hughe was badly injured. As his driver rushed him into Shanghai by way of Chinese-held territory, the car was attacked again. The Ambassador, *hors de combat* for many months, was replaced. The Americans also suffered seven casualties when a US troop transport, the *Hoover*, was bombed and strafed by Chinese aircraft off the mouth of the Yangtze.

These military peccadilloes were bound to occur as long as the Western Powers refused to acknowledge the fact that China and Japan were gripped together in a full-scale war. The Chinese boom at Chiang-yin on the Yangtze, and the subsequent Japanese blockade of the coast, had stopped all trade and traffic up the river. In Nanking the British had stationed the 4,290-ton light cruiser *Capetown*. There were also a number of British and US gunboats which normally protected trade on the river from pirates and bandits. On 19 September a Japanese admiral, who had been trained at Dartmouth Royal Naval College, was piped aboard *Capetown*. His news was that from 0800 on 21 September all foreign nationals were liable to be bombed, as Japan extended her range of attack. The Western admirals decided to ignore the threat and stay put, but arrangements were made to move all Europeans up-river for evacuation to Canton and Hong Kong, via the newly completed Han-k'ou (Hankow)–Canton railway. *Capetown* actually left Nanking on 21 September with a large contingent of refugees for Han-k'ou and only just missed the heavy bombing of the capital the following day.

Meanwhile, the land battle around Shanghai was hotting up. The Chinese defenses between Shanghai and the Yangtze were based on a river and canal line through this low-lying marshy area of the Yangtze Delta, as far as Chiang-yin where the mouth of the Yangtze narrowed. There the Chinese had sunk a number of coasters to form a boom covered by shore batteries to prevent the Japanese Navy advancing up to Chen-chiang, Nanking and beyond (which they were eventually to do). The numerous Chinese divisions, of which there were eventually 33 in six 'army groups' deployed between Hang-chou, Shanghai and Nanking, were now holding the coast south of Shanghai in Hang-chou (Hangchow) Bay.

As the Chinese still wanted to draw the Japanese into the built-up area of Shanghai's outskirts, where street fighting was to their advantage, fierce fighting took place during the hot, steamy malarial months of the remainder of August, September and October. The Chinese lost nearly 80,000 casualties and the Japanese 30,000. While the Japanese developed their base at Wu-sung at the mouth of the Huang-P'u and extended their foothold, fighting spread all along the 70-mile front from Shanghai to Chiang-yin with the Chinese armies fully committed. Ch'ung-ming, an island astride the mouth of the Yangtze, had been captured against quite stiff opposition from the Chinese River Defense Force and was being developed into an advance naval and air base. But the Japanese, in spite of having now landed armor, could make little headway across the flooded paddy area which was intersected with small and large irrigation canals.

The Japanese now took a leaf out of the experience of Major ('Chinese') Charles G. Gordon (of Khartoum). He had successfully fought with his 'Ever Victorious Army' through the same area in 33 actions on behalf of the Chinese Emperor against the T'ai P'ing rebels from 1863–4. Gordon had found that the best method of transport both for his troops and supplies were boats which could easily penetrate land defenses based on water obstacles. The Japanese had developed light, flat-bottomed, shallow-draught landing craft, with armored sides (similar to those developed later by the Western Powers in the Second World War).

These 46 ft vessels could carry 70 men or 10 tons of cargo at 8 knots. As landing craft carriers they used ships modelled on whaling mother ships (in which the whales were normally winched out of the water and cleaned and cut up). The technique was to reverse these ships close to shore from which six to 12 landing craft could be launched to make a simultaneous landing. In this type of operation the Japanese, who had devised these craft specifically for operations on the China coast and in the great Chinese river network, were at least three years ahead of European and American development.

On 5 November 1937 four Japanese divisions (6th, 16th, 18th and 114th), supported by a naval bombardment and carrier aircraft, simultaneously made landings near Fushon, just downstream from the boom at Chiang-yin on the Yangtze and at Cha-pu in Hang-chou Bay, south of Shanghai. They thus formed a pincer movement from either side of the peninsula where the fighting for Shanghai was taking place. Both landings were opposed but the Chinese were overwhelmed. General Matsui's powerful 10th Army heavily outnumbered the defenders in the Hang-chou area.

The Japanese, with their hundreds of landing craft, quickly exploited their success and penetrated inland, relying on rivers and canals for their lines of communication. They were well supported by naval aircraft operating from Ch'ung-ming Island. The Chinese armies around Shanghai were forced to withdraw helter-skelter to avoid encirclement. They split up into two, one half making for Chen-chiang (Chinkiang) and Nanking in the Yangtze valley, and the remainder for Hang-chou, the great seaport to the south. The Chinese set fire to their sectors of Shanghai as they withdrew and destroyed bridges in their rear, but this did not delay the now waterborne Japanese.

By 11 November the Chinese had withdrawn from the environs of Shanghai apart from one unit dubbed the 'Doomed Battalion' by the press, which had been cut off in a five-storey go-down on the Suchow Creek alongside the Royal Welch Fusiliers' sector. It held out for a few days giving the press photographers a field day until arrangements were made for the survivors to be interned in Shanghai. By 12 November the Loyals' sector on Bubbling Well Road was clear of Chinese, who had been replaced by more sinister Japanese units.

During the retreat some shells and bombs had landed in the Zoological Gardens which caused the keepers to open the cages to give their captives a chance to escape. So the Loyals, and the Ulster Rifles manning the perimeter farther to the south, had the eerie experience of finding lions, tigers, bears, elephants, rhinos and wolves prowling around their blockhouses and emplacements. They certainly kept away visitors and most of the press. But the British troops rapidly rounded them up without casualties on either side, and as the fight receded, put them back into their cages or adopted a few as pets.

The Japanese followed up their success by a river assault on the Chiang-yin boom whose land defenses they had captured. At first, landing craft penetrated beyond the boom, and then, after demolitions on the boom had been carried out, Japanese gunboats started to sail upstream, supporting their army which hurried on towards the Chinese capital, Nanking, 145 miles NW of Shanghai. Advancing on a broad front the Japanese captured Su-chou on 20 November. At this stage Germany, through General Alexander Ernst von Falkenhausen (Chiang Kai-shek's military adviser 1934-8), offered to mediate between the contestants, but the Army party in the Japanese government had now begun to sense a great victory.

Japan's terms for peace were so outlandish that Chiang Kai-shek scorned them. He was still intent on carrying on protracted warfare and wearing the Japanese down until Britain and America would come to China's aid. As the Japanese forces approached Nanking and the bombing of the city intensified, clashes occurred with the warships of the Western Powers which were protecting their embassies and consulates in the capital. These culminated in the shelling of the RN gunboat *Ladybird* which rescued survivors from the sinking of the Shanghai-built river gunboat USS *Panay* by Aichi DIAI dive-bombers on 12 December. For a brief period, it seemed that both the US and Britain were on the brink of war with Japan, which was China's one hope. But, after the Japanese had apologized and paid an indemnity for the damage they had caused, both the American and British people suppressed their chauvinistic feelings and the eventual, inevitable war was postponed for another four years.

Khalkhin-Gol (1939)

Alan Lothian

Lieutenant General M. Komatsubara's 23rd Infantry Division had been destroyed utterly – scarcely one man in a hundred escaping – on the empty borderlands of the Khalkhin-Gol river between Outer Mongolia and Manchuria. It was late in 1939, while half a world away Poland bled from the new German *Drang nach Osten* (Drive to the East) and the Western democracies indulged themselves in the 'Phoney War' along the new Siegfried Line, a lonely and disgraced officer of Imperial Japan brought his life to a private end. Komatsubara might now find redemption in the agonizing rite of *seppuku*: only by ripping out his own entrails with his own short sword might he 'prove his sincerity' to the Emperor and his ancestors. But the Khalkhin-Gol disaster was too great to be atoned for by a general's suicide. It was better that it had not happened at all, and the less attention drawn to it the better. Komatsubara, announced Tokyo inscrutably, had died of 'an abdominal ailment'.

The empty steppe country around the Khalkhin-Gol river had represented the farthest fringe of Japanese expansion. China, invaded in 1937, was still unsubdued but the Imperial grip on Manchuria, annexed in 1931, was firm. Here, in the wilderness of the Mongolian Republic, might Soviet strength be tested. Thirty-five years before, Japan's crushing defeat of the old Tsarist armies had astounded the world; now, perhaps, a border pinprick might develop into a deep thrust at the Trans-Siberian Railway, severing Russia's spinal column and allowing the rich Soviet Far East with its port of Vladivostok to fall into the lap of the Emperor.

For years, Japan's highest military councils had been divided into factions advocating either a 'Strike North', at Russia, or 'Strike South', at the western colonies. Emperor Hirohito had already decided upon 'Strike South', which would in the next few years lead to Pearl Harbor, the fall of Singapore, and ultimately Hiroshima. But in the Army many officers still hankered after an attack on Russia, and the High Command of the Kwantung Army in Manchuria was no exception.

'Border incidents' spanning July–August 1938 at Lake Khasan, near Vladivostok, had shown real Soviet weakness after Stalin's terrifying purges of the Red Army. A Russian general, Lyushkov, had defected to the Kwantung Army with details of dispositions and stories of discontent. Acting first without Hirohito's knowledge, and eventually in direct disobedience, the Kwantung command launched an attack on the Russian forces which met with some success until it ran up against superior Soviet armor and airpower. Enraged, Hirohito refused to allow his air force to fly in support of his own disobedient army, and the situation was eventually settled by a diplomatic return to the status quo. But to save his officers from a catastrophic loss of face, the constant problem of the Japanese Imperial regime, he had to let them try again. After a formal cease-fire had been agreed at Lake Khasan, Hirohito approved a General Staff plan for an organized trial of strength farther west, in Mongolia, during the following summer.

The border area chosen by the Japanese staff was beside the Khalkhin-Gol river, for much of its length a frontier between Japanese-occupied Manchuria or Manchukuo to the east and the Outer Mongolian People's Republic, closely bound to Russia by a mutual-assistance pact in March 1936, to the west. At one point, however, the border bulges east of the river around the village and hill of Nomonhan. On this shallow salient, 46 miles wide, the Japanese planned to test the Soviet pledge to defend Mongolia. The country was steppe, blue-green in the summer with sturdy grass, and populated only by a few tribal herdsmen. East of the river it was more broken, with gullies, dunes, and even a few quicksands.

On 11 May 1939, a few hundred Inner Mongolian horsemen under Japanese control and accompanied by 'advisers' from Komatsubara's 23rd Division, crossed the frontier and rode as far as Nomonhan itself before the villagers alerted their border guards, based in a log fort five miles away on the west bank of the river. The following day, the invaders were driven back across the border in an action that resembled an ancient tribal feud rather than a clash between two twentieth-century super powers: whooping Tskirik horsemen riding rings around their Japanese-led Bargut enemies.

But on 14 May the Inner Mongolians reappeared in strength, and this time they had 300 Japanese cavalry as stiffening. Within a few hours the Tsiriks had been driven back to their garrison positions, and that night the local Russian adviser, Major Bykov, was called in. When he reached the picturesque border fort next morning, he found that the twentieth century had arrived at last in the shape of a Japanese air raid which terrified his Mongolian charges and left the place a ruin. Taking no chances, Bykov at once called in 6th Mongolian Cavalry Division and the few Red Army detachments available. But as these troops massed on the Mongolian side of the Khalkhin-Gol, the Japanese on the east bank melted away. On the night of 22 May, Bykov made a cautious reconnaissance in force across the river. In the quiet rough pasture of Nomonhan the Japanese were waiting. Only after fierce hand-to-hand fighting was Bykov able to fall back to the Khalkhin-Gol.

The game of cat-and-mouse continued. On 25 May Bykov cautiously moved his full strength forward and over the next two days cleared the east bank and reoccupied the deserted village of Nomonhan. By now, about 10,000 men had been involved on the Mongolian side, mainly 'constabulary' troops with a few specialist Russian companies. The border incident was rapidly escalating, and at dawn on 28 May it went a stage further. Five thousand Japanese regulars, with an accompanying tribal horde, fell on Bykov's troops before daybreak. Only the veteran Russian's canny dispositions enabled him to fall back once more to the river without complete destruction. But the panic button had already been pressed in Moscow and that same evening troops of the Soviet 149th Motorized Infantry Regiment began to arrive, to be sent straight into the fight from their trucks. All that night the battle continued, and the following morning a Soviet–Mongolian counter-attack pushed the Japanese back, once more, to the border with a loss of 400 men.

By now, Moscow was feeling real alarm. Despite accurate intelligence from his master spy Richard Sorge in Tokyo on long-term Japanese planning, Stalin understandably feared the possibility of a disastrous two-front war with Japan and Germany. Accordingly, no effort was to be spared in crushing this Japanese adventure before it threatened all of the Soviet Trans-Baikal. The first step was to release troops from the interior for the mission, and the second was to appoint a commander, someone new, outstanding, trusted, and with a fighting reputation to make. The man Stalin picked was Corps Commander Georgi Konstantinovich Zhukov.

Zhukov in 1939 was a tough, 43-year-old cavalryman turned 'tankist' and Deputy Commander of the key Belorussian Military District. Squat, barrel-chested, heavy-browed (his name came from the Russian word *zhuk*, meaning 'beetle') he had fought his way up from the ranks of the Red Army in the Civil War to distinction in every peacetime command he had held. He had been in China, perhaps in Spain; he had survived the bloodletting of the 1937 purges unscathed and was already well-known in the Red Army for his short-tempered, no-nonsense thoroughness. As 'the general who never lost a battle' Zhukov was to direct forces and fighting of unsurpassed dimensions in the Russo-German war: 1941 would see him halt Hitler's offensive outside Moscow, in 1942 he would master-mind the Stalingrad campaign, and in 1945 he would meet the Western Allies in the wreckage of Berlin as the epitome of the ruthless, crushing might of the Soviet war machine. But in June 1939, as he flew out with a small staff to Mongolia, his future career and quite possibly his life depended on victory at Khalkhin-Gol. And victory alone would not be enough. Only the utter destruction of the Japanese would satisfy Stalin.

On 5 June Zhukov arrived at HQ, Soviet 57th Special Corps, the only major Red Army formation in the area. There he found little cheer. The command was hopelessly out of touch with the front, there was not so much as a kilometer of telegraph wire in the area, co-ordination of troops was poor and reconnaissance, though inadequate, clearly showed a Japanese build-up far greater than any mere border conflict would require. Furthermore the Japanese were making full use of air superiority, both for bombing and reconnaissance. Zhukov, with papers in his pocket appointing him local C-in-C if need be, at once took charge. The Corps commander was relieved and sent home and Zhukov threw all his characteristic energies into organizing a defense.

By early July, the Japanese had about 38,000 men, 135 tanks and 225 aircraft concentrated on the frontier east of the Khalkhin-Gol.

Soviet and Mongolian forces together amounted to only 12,500 men, though Zhukov had 186 better tanks and 226 armored cars. He would need them. The Japanese plan involved sending a strong force wide around the Soviet left flank, across the river to seize the dominating high ground of Mount Bain-Tsagan. Then, as the main tank-led force attacked along the general front, this outflanking force would surround and destroy the east bank salient from its rear.

According to the Japanese schedule, offensive operations would be over by mid-July and the campaign wound up before the autumn rains. On 2 July, the first attacks pressed into the weak east bank positions and by the end of the day Japanese tanks and infantry were on the river in the Russian third line at some points. But Zhukov was too shrewd a commander to commit his reserves prematurely. Shortly before dawn on 3 July, the Soviet Colonel I. M. Afonin, Chief Adviser to the Mongolian Army, was inspecting Mongolian 6th Cavalry Division defenses on Bain-Tsagin when he stumbled upon Japanese troops who had made a surprise river-crossing by pontoon bridge. The Mongolians, without the training or equipment of their Red Army mentors, were driven off.

As the sun rose the following morning, Zhukov could not fail to appreciate the danger of the situation. The Japanese only had to roll on to the south for the hard-pressed Soviet forces on the east bank to be completely cut off. At once he ordered his armor – practically his only reserve – into action; 11th Tank Brigade was to attack from the north, 7th Mechanized Brigade from the south, and 24th Motorized Infantry Regiment from the NW through the retreating Mongolians. These forces together deployed over 300 fighting vehicles: the Japanese, on both sides of the river, had less than half that. Zhukov wrote in his 1969 memoirs: 'It was impossible to delay a counterblow since the enemy, who saw the advance of our tanks, rapidly began to take defensive measures and started bombing our tank columns. The latter had no shelter whatsoever: for hundreds of kilometres around there was not even a bush in sight.'

The speed of the triple-pronged Soviet thrust first startled, then demoralized the Japanese. From 0700 Zhukov's entire bomber force had been pounding them, and for the first time they felt the weight of the brilliantly organized Russian heavy artillery. By 0900 the advance detachments of Russian armor were arriving in the combat area and at 1045 the full attack went in. The Japanese had had little time to dig in thoroughly; their anti-tank training had always been a weak spot and now they paid the penalty. As the battle raged all that day, it was no longer the Russians who were in danger of encirclement.

An attempt at counter-attack on 4 July was broken up by Red Army aviation and artillery; worse, the single pontoon bridge they had laid across the Khalkhin-Gol was destroyed by Russian bombs. Hundreds of soldiers drowned trying to escape, and Komatsubara was lucky to get across with his HQ. Most of the 10,000-strong Bain-Tsagan assault force lay dead and wounded on the slopes of the little mountain, and when the heaviest fighting ended, on the night of 4–5 July, the Japanese had little cause to celebrate, having lost half the tanks available in Manchuria. And though Soviet 3 July tank losses had been over a hundred, the Red Army had successfully exploited glaring Japanese deficiencies in field and anti-tank (AT) artillery.

But the Kwantung Army was by no means willing to abandon its Mongolian campaign. During the remainder of July, it doubled the force committed, stripping divisions elsewhere of AT units to strengthen the Khalkhin-Gol positions. On 10 August, two full Japanese infantry divisions (7th and 23rd), a Manchukuoan brigade, three cavalry regiments, 182 tanks, 300 armored cars and three artillery regiments with over 450 aircraft were combined into the 75,000-strong Sixth Japanese Army under General Ogisu Rippo. A final general offensive along a 43-mile front was planned for 24 August, after an attack on 23 July got nowhere under Soviet bombardment.

On the Russian side of the hill final victory was far from certain. Powerful reinforcements had to be brought over poor communications from the Soviet heartland. But Stalin knew that Soviet international prestige was at stake and his new negotiations with Hitler, no respecter of weakness, had reached a critical juncture. Neither blood nor treasure would be spared. 'For Stalin,' wrote one former Red officer, 'the losses were of no importance whatsoever.'

Throughout July and August three infantry and two cavalry divisions with seven independent brigades, including five armored, as well as artillery and air force units, were assembled. This was in itself no mean feat. The Japanese, in the year before their attack, had built a railway to within a few miles of the Mongolian border. The nearest Russian railhead from which the new First Army Group could be supplied was 403 miles away. For Zhukov's coming offensive, 55,000 tons of supplies, including 18,000 tons of artillery ammunition, had to be carried along rudimentary Mongolian roads, the overworked trucks and drivers further tormented by late summer heat and the piercing dust storms of Central Asia. Such was the shortage of trucks that gun-towing tractors from the front had to be pressed into service as supply carriers.

So Zhukov laid his plans. The Japanese had attempted a great envelopment; very well, Zhukov would show them how it was done. He organized his new forces into three groups, North, South and Central, with his armored units, ready to move fast and deep, on the wings. He would be ready by 20 August, four days before the enemy. Until then he kept his plans, his troop movements, and thus his future surprise well masked by painstaking and ingenious deceptions. Fake radio signals ordering large quantities of engineering equipment misled the Japanese into thinking the Russians were digging in for the autumn. Sound effects gave the impression of heavy pile-driving work. The night movements of armored and motorized units were covered by air and artillery bombardments. All day a few tanks stripped of their silencers drove up and down until the Japanese got used to the noise. Zhukov even solemnly issued to his troops the official handbook *What the Soviet Soldier Must Know In the Defence*. By Sunday 20 August, unknown to the Japanese, quietly waiting in the jump-off positions were 35 infantry battalions, 20 cavalry squadrons, 498 tanks, 346 armored cars and 502 guns of all types.

The first the Japanese knew of the coming storm was at 0545 when 150 bombers, escorted by 100 fighters, launched a saturation raid on their forward defenses and artillery positions. Before the stunned Japanese had recovered, Zhukov's 250 heavy guns and mortars were playing on their close reserves and at 0845 his yelling infantry were surging forward behind the tanks. All along the front, the Russian waves broke through the Japanese front. The defenders were 'morally and physically suppressed' by the three-hour Red Army artillery bombardment, delivered by twice the number of defending guns which anyhow lacked the wealth of Russian ammunition.

Not that the Japanese crumbled easily. At one point a divisional attack on Japanese fortifications was bloodily repulsed and the division, probably the raw 82nd Infantry sent from the Urals, pinned down under heavy fire. Its commander begged Zhukov for new orders; Zhukov told him to continue his attack. When the divisional commander doubted the possibility, Zhukov said coldly: 'I hereby relieve you of command. Give me your Chief of Staff.' The Chief of Staff agreed to continue the attack, but the attack failed to materialize. Zhukov picked up the telephone once more: 'I hereby relieve you of your command. Wait for the arrival of a new commander.' An officer from Zhukov's own staff was sent over, and with reorganized artillery and air support, the attack succeeded despite appalling losses.

Most successful was Zhukov's Southern group. Its powerful armored forces, which included a battalion of SP guns and a company of flamethrower tanks, swept clear around the left and by 21 August were solidly established behind the Japanese operating south of the Khalkhin-Gol's east–west tributary, the Khailastyn-Gol. Two days later the Northern group, assisted by Zhukov's reserve 212th Airborne Brigade (fighting on the ground) cut its way across the Palets Heights round to join them, and the enemy were surrounded. The fighting was bitter and by no means over. Japanese in dugouts had to be burned out by the flame-throwing tanks, and surrenders were rare. But the Red Army too had a determination which took a heavy toll of 600 dead in the savage hand-to-hand fighting in the dugouts and gullies of the Palets Heights as the pincers of encirclement closed.

After a Japanese relief attempt had been beaten off by 6th Tank Brigade on 26 August all hope for the trapped troops was gone. The growing Russian air superiority alone was enough to prevent the movement of fresh Japanese troops into the battle zone. In the first week the Soviet Air Force flew 474 sorties and dropped 190 tons of bombs, modest by later standards but some of the most intense air fighting since 1918. In the dogfights of the first day five Polikarpov I16 fighters shot down two Mitsubishi A5M fighters with 82 mm RS82 rockets – the first likely instance of air-to-air rockets being lethal against aircraft.

But neither Zhukov nor his government were content with a passive containment. With bloody impatience, he set about planning the liquidation of Japanese units trapped on various patches of high ground within the perimeter. For a week the savage business of mopping up went on. In this phase too, Zhukov demonstrated his tactical skill and the technical superiority of his army. Japanese troops on the Remizov Heights had relied on the muddy bottom of the shallow Khailastyn-Gol to protect their southern flank from attack. But by night Zhukov's engineers reinforced the river bed and the tanks with their terrifying flamethrowers drove straight across, as one of the three converging assaults on the last pocket of resistance.

By the morning of 31 August, any Japanese remaining on Mongolian territory were either dead or prisoners. Of 60,000 troops trapped in the cauldron, 50,000 were later listed as killed, wounded and missing. Casualties in the veteran 23rd Division ran as high as 99 per cent. The Russians admitted casualties of 10,000 in killed and wounded throughout the campaign, but it seems likely that this was a considerable underestimate. The outnumbered Japanese Army Air Force claimed to have downed 1,200 Soviet planes (the Russian figure for their 'kills' was 660) in the four months of hostilities, but in the days before instant close-support on the battlefield this could not sway the ground-fighting.

Now, on the last day in August, Zhukov's dog-tired, grimy tank crews stared east from the border they had regained, waiting for the order to go on, while the frantic Kwantung Army HQ scraped the depots of Manchuria to find troops to stem what many feared would be a Red flood.

That order never came. In that autumn of 1939, Moscow and the world had other, more urgent problems. On the day Zhukov's pincers met behind the Japanese, Stalin and Hitler had published their Non-Aggression Pact: the Soviet dictator now believed, with unusual trustfulness, that he had bought the time he needed to prepare Russia against war. On 1 September the German *Panzers* rolled into Poland and within a few days the victorious Soviet armor was rattling back across the Trans-Siberian Railway to the new Soviet frontier in Eastern Poland – just in case.

Hirohito had to face up to more than the shock of military disaster. The Non-Aggression Pact surprised no one more than the Japanese, to whom it was a baffling breach of faith. The Prime Minister resigned in shame. Hirohito would have been more than just puzzled and disappointed had he heard Hitler ranting to his generals a few days before. 'The Japanese Emperor . . . is weak, cowardly, and irresolute. . . . Let us think of ourselves as masters and consider these people at best as lacquered half-monkeys, who need to feel the knout.' To Hitler, the Japanese defeat was no surprise. But thanks to Khalkhin-Gol, the confidence he had in his invasion of Russia was not shared by the Japanese.

Hirohito was on his own. Yet that was not entirely unsatisfactory.

The 'Strike North' army faction was discredited at last. The Kwantung Army begged to be allowed one more offensive to save its face, but this time the Emperor was firm. In Moscow once more the diplomats took over, and once more the status quo was resumed. A ceasefire was signed on 15 September. In April 1941, a Russo-Japanese Non-Aggression Pact was signed. The Soviet Far East remained safe from Japanese Imperial ambition, and throughout the coming war with Germany, American ships under Soviet flag would sail unhindered from United States arsenals to Vladivostok. Japan would strike south.

5
The Second World War

River Plate (1939)

David Thomas

Commodore Henry H. Harwood, OBE, RN, stabbed a finger on the chart aboard his flagship, the light cruiser HMS *Ajax*: 'That's where she'll turn up next,' he predicted confidently. But he was quite wrong in thinking his quarry was the German pocket-battleship *Admiral Scheer*, nevertheless the chart position was as accurate as a star sight. He further predicted – though with less skill and some luck – that the enemy ship would arrive astride the rich South American trade routes of the River Plate area on 12 December 1939. He was one day out.

The warship was, in fact, the *Admiral Graf Spee* and at the time she was 2,000 miles away celebrating the sinking of the ninth and last victim of her 12-week cruise as a commerce raider. *Admiral Graf Spee* was one of three brilliantly designed German warships: *Deutschland* (re-named *Lützow* in February 1940) was the first, launched in 1931, followed two years later by *Admiral Scheer*, then on 30 June 1934 the garlanded *Admiral Graf Spee* took to the waters of Wilhelmshaven Naval Dock. They were fine ships, and, curiously, they were the direct product of the 1919 Treaty of Versailles which forbade Germany to construct warships of more than 10,000 tons displacement.

German naval architects had evolved an entirely new type of vessel, nominally of 10,000 tons but in the event *Graf Spee* displaced 12,100 tons. A design requirement was to mount guns superior to those of a British heavy cruiser and with protective armor thick enough to withstand such a cruiser's (8-in) shells. By employing welded construction and adopting diesel propulsion in place of conventional steam-turbines, by minimizing thick belt and armor protection, sufficient weight was saved to allow a radius of action of 12,500 miles at cruising speed before the need for refuelling. *Graf Spee*'s 54,000 hp engines gave her a trial speed of 27.7 knots.

The three new warships were armed with a main battery of six 11-in (280 mm) guns in two triple turrets and a secondary armament of eight 5.9-in (150 mm) guns. They could outgun every British cruiser. They could outrun every British battleship. Only three ships in the entire Royal Navy had the speed to catch them and the guns to sink them – the First World War vintage battle-cruisers *Renown*, *Repulse* and *Hood*.

Kapitän zur See (Senior Captain) Hans Langsdorff took command of *Admiral Graf Spee* at the age of 44 in 1938, climaxing a naval career of 26 years; the captain and the ship were well matched but when put to the test of battle it was the man who failed, not the ship. *Graf Spee* sailed from Wilhelmshaven on 21 August 1939, ten days before the outbreak of war, destination mid-Atlantic, and then three days later her sister ship, *Deutschland*, sailed for a similar waiting assignment in the North Atlantic. Each was accompanied by a supply ship, the notorious *Altmark*, later captured as a prison ship, being assigned to *Graf Spee*. The pocket-battleships' tasks had been clearly defined as 'the disruption and destruction of enemy merchant shipping by all possible means.' Action with enemy naval forces was to be avoided at all costs, except to further the primary objective.

Graf Spee entered the sunshine and heat of the South Atlantic and intercepted her first victim, the SS *Clement*, off Brazil on 30 September. But the 5,084-ton ocean-going tramp steamer reported the pocket-battleship as *Admiral Scheer*, a report which confused the eight Raider Hunting Forces formed jointly by the British Admiralty and the French Ministry of Marine. The second victim was the SS *Newton Beech*, one of three ships captured and sunk on the trade routes from the Cape of Good Hope during 5–10 October. *Graf Spee* then rendezvoused with *Altmark* in mid-South Atlantic from whom she fuelled and to whom she transferred the crews of her victims.

A week later SS *Trevanion* was sunk on 22 October, then *Kapitan* Langsdorff rounded the Cape of Good Hope where the 706-ton tanker *Africa Shell* was sunk on 15 November. *Graf Spee* doubled back, refuelled from *Altmark* on 27 November NE of volcanic Tristan da Cunha island, then a few days later sank the 10,000-ton cargo liner *Doric Star*. Before the end, the liner got away the prescribed distress signal, 'R–R–R', signifying Raider.

The day after the *Doric Star* sinking, SS *Tairoa* was sunk. On 7 December *Graf Spee* sank her last victim, the 3,895-ton cargo vessel *Streonshalh*. This sinking brought her total to nine British ships and 50,089 tons. Not a single life had been lost during these sinkings, a source of great pride to Langsdorff. Many of his prisoners subsequently testified to his courteous firmness, his fairness, distinguished bearing, chivalry and professionalism.

The responsibility for the long and anxious search for the elusive *Graf Spee* in the South Atlantic fell upon Forces G, H and K. Their success depended largely upon attacked merchantmen getting off their R–R–R signal and position. In fact, Langsdorff was better informed about British warship movements. He was aware, for example, that the cruisers *Ajax*, *Achilles*, *Exeter* and *Cumberland* were operating off the South American coast, that the two heavy cruisers *Sussex* and *Shropshire* were off Cape Town and that the battle cruiser *Renown* and aircraft carrier *Ark Royal* were off West Africa.

As Commodore Harwood had predicted, Langsdorff determined to quit the mid-ocean patrol and, as if destiny was directing him to destruction, he set course for the River Plate estuary, attracted by the prospect of rich prizes. Also heading for the estuary was Harwood's squadron, one of the British Raider-Hunting Forces engaged in the ever-changing dispositions, wider-ranging even than the later *Bismarck* pursuit from the wastes of the North Atlantic to the southernmost tip of Latin America.

Early in December 1939, 51-year-old Commodore Harwood, as Officer Commanding the South American Division of the American and West Indies Squadron, flew his broad pennant in the 6,985-ton 6-in gun cruiser *Ajax*, commanded by Captain Charles H. L. Woodhouse. His two heavy 8-in gun cruisers, the 8,390-ton *Exeter* (Captain Frederick S. Bell) and the 9,850-ton *Cumberland* were at Port Stanley in case of an enemy attack to revenge the Battle of the Falkland Islands where Count von Spee's squadron was destroyed on 8 December 1914. The 6-in gun cruiser *Achilles* (Captain Edward Parry), to 7,030 tons and partly manned by 327 New Zealanders, was patrolling off Rio de Janeiro. *Ajax* had recently sailed from Port Stanley for the River Plate.

Harwood calculated after the *Doric Star* sinking that the raider could reach Rio by 12 December and be off the River Plate by the following day. Accordingly, he ordered his cruisers to concentrate. *Exeter* was instructed to leave Port Stanley on the 9th and *Achilles* was instructed to head south from Rio to join the flagship on the 10th. *Cumberland* had to remain in the Falklands to complete an imperative self-refit.

By 0600 on 12 December the three cruisers were in company 150 miles off the River Plate. The Commodore had long considered the tactics his squadron should employ on encountering a pocket-battleship. Undaunted by the greatly superior gunpower of such an adversary, he made his intentions clear in a signal to his three captains, timed 1200, 12 December: 'My policy with three cruisers in company versus one pocket-battleship: attack at once day or night.'

At dawn on 13 December the sea was tropically calm with a light swell. As the light strengthened to promise another beautiful day the three grey British cruisers formed up in line ahead, *Ajax* leading *Achilles* and *Exeter*, 2,000 yards apart, zig-zagging about a mean course of 060° at 14 knots. At 0540 crews stood down from Dawn Action Stations. Visibility rapidly increased with tropical suddenness from a few hundred yards to 20 miles. Twenty minutes before, at 0520, the squadron was in position 34°34′ S, 47°17′ W, 250 nautical miles due east of Punta del Este.

Soon after 0600 Leading Signalman Swanston on *Ajax*'s bridge sighted smoke over the horizon bearing 320°. Harwood ordered *Exeter* to investigate. She swung out of line and at 0616 she signalled by lamp: 'I think it is a pocket-battleship,' and Capt. Bell ordered Flag N hoisted to the yard-arm – 'Enemy in sight'.

Graf Spee, heading 155° at 15 knots, logged an almost identical chart position. Langsdorff held the whip hand. He had sighted the British ships 20 minutes before *Ajax* saw the smudge of smoke. At 0552, fine on the starboard bow, there were first two, then four more thin masts. The stereoptic main range-finder measured a distance of 31,000 metres (33,902 yards = 19.26 miles). By 0600 *Graf Spee* was cleared for action and some of the masts had resolved themselves into the unmistakable superstructure of HMS *Exeter* accompanied by what appeared to be two destroyers.

Now, if ever, was the time for Langsdorff to turn about and refuse action. By maintaining course he committed a cardinal error.

He went even further and decided to attack contrary to Naval Operations Command instructions. Langsdorff's senior navigator, *Korvettenkapitän* (Lieutenant Commander) J. Wattenberg, reminded him of the order to avoid even inferior enemy forces. 'I suspect a convoy.' Langsdorff explained. He ordered full speed to close the range. Phase 1 of the Battle of the River Plate had begun even before the British cruisers had sighted the enemy. At 0615 the pocket-battleship eased to port on to a course of 115° for a running action to starboard with a closing range. By now she had identified the 'destroyers' as *Ajax* and *Achilles*. Her only safeguard now lay in crushing the opposition by destroying it or putting it to flight. At 0618 the two triple 11-in turrets opened fire with a thunderous crash.

When *Exeter* identified the pocket-battleship, Capt. Bell hauled off to the west while Harwood led *Ajax* round to close the range. *Achilles* conformed to the flagship's movements throughout the action enabling the two light cruisers to concentrate their gunfire with great effect. All three ships increased speed, hoisted battle ensigns and fire was opened: *Exeter*'s 8-in guns opened at 0620, *Achilles*' 6-in at 0621 and *Ajax*'s two minutes later. The range was then about 19,000 yards (10.8 miles). Langsdorff had made no effort to maintain his range advantage and he now found himself, as Harwood intended, confronted with two divisions and the problem of whether to divide his main armament to engage them both – or to leave one unengaged. Initially, *Graf Spee* engaged both but very soon shifted fire of all six 11-in guns to *Exeter*. Her accuracy was formidable and remained so throughout the day.

Exeter's 'A' and 'B' (bow) turrets opened fire at 0620 with 'Y' (stern) turret following 2.5 minutes later. She had been steaming on boilers in Boiler Room B only and when the alarm sounded those in Boiler Room A were flashed up and connected. Full speed was ordered at 0620. With his third salvo, the gunnery officer, Lieutenant Commander Richard B. Jennings, straddled *Graf Spee* and prospects looked promising. But *Exeter* herself was under fire and *Graf Spee*'s third main salvo straddled the British ship. A minute or so later – at 0624 – *Exeter* was hit but the 670 lb shell smashed through the deck abaft 'B' turret and passed through the ship's side to the sea without exploding.

A minute later *Graf Spee*'s eighth salvo struck an almost decisive blow: within seconds *Exeter* was transformed from an efficient fighting unit into an uncontrollable machine. 'B' turret took a direct hit between the two gun barrels, putting it and eight of the crew out of action. Splinters swept the bridge killing or wounding nearly everyone there; the wheelhouse was smashed, vital communications cut. Captain Bell, wounded himself, was compelled to retire to the after-conning position where a human chain of command had to be set up.

While the 11-in salvoes were being directed at *Exeter*, Langsdorff employed his eight 5.9-in guns against the 16 6-in guns of the two light cruisers whose accuracy was such that the pocket-battleship shifted fire from *Exeter* to bring her 11-in guns to bear on *Ajax* and *Achilles*.

During this period – at about 0637 – while still under fire from *Graf Spee*'s secondary armament, *Ajax* managed to catapult into the air one of her two 124 m.p.h. Seafox floatplanes, piloted by Lieutenant Edgar D. G. Lewin; a fine evolution considering that 'X' and 'Y' turrets only a few feet away were firing at the time. Lewin and his observer, Lieutenant Richard E. N. Kearney, began their spotting reports at 0654. *Exeter*'s two Walrus seaplanes were damaged beyond repair early in the battle and had to be jettisoned. *Graf Spee*'s Arado 196 floatplane was unserviceable because of a cracked engine block and took no part in the battle.

Exeter's shooting astonished the *Graf Spee*'s officers, both for its accuracy and in particular for the rapidity of each following salvo. Her fifth salvo scored a direct hit but the shell passed through the upper part of the bridge without exploding and caused little damage. Another 8-in shell passed a metre above the armored deck, passing through the 5.5-in (140 mm) armored belt and finally exploding amidships. The ease with which this shell penetrated the armor plate contrary to expectation caused great anxiety aboard *Graf Spee*. Pocket-battleships were not, it seemed, inviolable to 8-in cruisers.

At 0632 the damaged *Exeter*, under severe pressure from the accurate German gunnery, fired her three starboard 21-in torpedo tubes. A few minutes later *Graf Spee* made a heavy alteration of course to port and steered NW under cover of smoke. This change of course prevented a 'crossing the T' situation by *Ajax* and *Achilles*. From this moment on the battle became a pursuit with the light cruisers maintaining contact with *Graf Spee* while the heavily damaged *Exeter* limped along in company. As a parting shot – at 0638 – she fired her port torpedoes, but they too missed.

During this period *Exeter* took two more 11-in shell hits. 'A' turret was damaged and put out of action and a second shell burst in the Chief Petty Officers' flat amidships starting a fierce fire. It was this shell which created the most damage: the 4-in magazine was flooded by burst water mains, all compass repeaters were out of action and Captain Bell handled the cruiser using a whaler's compass. The ship's upperworks were pierced with splinters, dead and dying littered the decks. Lieutenant Commander Jennings, now stationed on the after searchlight platform kept the single remaining 'Y' turret in action under local control. Captain Bell kept adjusting course to keep the turret bearing on the target. *Exeter* took another shell hit under the fo'c'sle, suffered flooding of several compartments and took a 7° list to starboard. Ablaze, she had taken heavy punishment, and was close to being destroyed.

At 0640, when one of *Graf Spee*'s 11-in turrets was being directed against the light cruisers, a shell near-missed *Achilles*, bursting on impact with the sea. Hundreds of splinters penetrated her thin bridge plating and the armor of the Director Control Tower, killing four ratings. Captain Parry and the Chief Yeoman on the bridge were slightly wounded and a splinter severed the halyard for the White Ensign: the battle continued to be fought under the New Zealand flag at the mainmast.

At 0656 Harwood hauled round to the north then west to maintain close range and to keep all guns bearing. He also pursued the tactic of 'chasing salvoes' – sailing towards close splashes and away from distant ones to confuse the enemy spotting. *Graf Spee* also made frequent alterations of course to throw out the British gunfire and from 0700 she made much use of smoke. Despite these tactics she continued to be struck by 6-in shells but these 100 lb projectiles inflicted relatively little damage.

By 0724 Harwood had closed the range to 9,000 yards to deliver a torpedo attack. *Ajax* turned to starboard and fired a spread of four 2-in torpedoes. *Kapitanleutnant* (Lieutenant) Rasenack on *Graf Spee*'s bridge later reported, 'They came right at us. To avoid them our captain again put them under the direct fire of our heavy guns. One of the torpedoes passed only a few metres from our side.' Langsdorff told Captain Patrick G. G. Dove, one of the 62 British Merchant Navy prisoners aboard the pocket-battleship during the battle, 'The *Ajax* and *Achilles* came at me like destroyers.'

But this daring maneuver took an ugly turn for Harwood when *Ajax* received an 11-in shell hit on the after superstructure at 0725; the shell passed through several cabins, wrecking the machinery below 'X' turret and burst in the Commodore's sleeping cabin. Damage was sustained by the 'Y' turret barbette, jamming the turret. Thus one shell effectively put both 'X' and 'Y' turrets out of action, killing and wounding many of the guns' crews. By now *Exeter* was out of the fight, her speed reduced, falling astern of the action, fires raging with 61 officers and ratings killed. *Ajax*, the flagship, had been reduced to only half her main armament. Only *Achilles* remained practically undamaged.

Langsdorff's tactics – British and German naval experts are agreed on this point – are difficult to understand because he should have turned to the southward to finish off *Exeter* before then turning his attention upon the two light cruisers. Yet he deliberately allowed *Exeter* to escape, then pointlessly sought sanctuary in a neutral harbor. Harwood continued to harry *Graf Spee* and by 0728 the range was down to only 8,000 yards (4.54 miles). *Graf Spee* was now being subjected to a deluge of accurate 6-in gunfire and the pocket-battleship even brought into action some of her six 4.1-in (105 mm) AA guns against the cruisers. It was at this stage that the Seafox spotter plane reported torpedo tracks and Harwood altered course to comb them.

Graf Spee, now on a westerly course and clearly heading for the River Plate estuary, was still maintaining accurate fire, one of her last salvoes, at 0738, bringing down *Ajax*'s mainmast with all its radio aerials. Harwood decided to break off the day action, carry out the traditional cruiser duty of shadowing, and close in again after dark. Accordingly, at 0740, 82 minutes since *Graf Spee* had opened fire, the light cruisers turned away to the east under cover of smoke but continued to maintain contact. *Exeter* set course for the Falklands and *Cumberland*, pre-empting a signal from Harwood, sailed at 1000 from the Falklands for the River Plate to take her place.

Langsdorff, who had now recovered from two slight splinter wounds and a bout of unconsciousness from shell blast, made no attempt to pursue Harwood as the cruisers broke off action. He headed for Montevideo in Uruguay at 22 knots and took stock. Senior Surgeon Dr Kartzendorff reported one officer and 35 ratings killed and 61 others wounded. In no way did these casualties reduce the fighting capacity of a ship with a complement of 1,134, but the supply of 11-in shells was only 186–31 per gun.

Damage-control reports revealed a considerable mass of minor damage by 17 6-in shell hits from *Ajax* and *Achilles* and more serious damage by the three 8-in shell hits from *Exeter*. The wireless direction-finding apparatus was damaged and nearly all galleys out of operation. The equipment for purifying lubricating oil was damaged as were the forward ammunition hoists. The armor belt and armored deck had been penetrated: there were 15 holes on the starboard side plating and 12 to port including two in the bows, the largest measuring 6.5 ft wide. Minor items of damage to guns, torpedoes, searchlight and communications was superficial. More important from the point of view of fighting efficiency was slight damage to the main range-finder, foretop, torpedo-ranging device and fire-fighting equipment.

One hit was from a practice shell from *Achilles*, probably loaded in error; it hit aft, killed two ratings, passed through half a dozen cabins and came to rest in the berth of a Petty Officer still identifiable as a drill projectile! It was the large hole in the bows which was serious because *Graf Spee* would ship water in anything for a seaway if she made a dash for Germany. Langsdorff was also worried over the ammunition shortage. He decided, entirely alone and without consultation with his senior officers, to seek shore repair facilities. *Korvettenkapitän* Wattenberg later quoted his captain: 'Our damage cannot be repaired with the means available on board. We must run into port somewhere for repairs.'

Ajax and *Achilles* continued their shadowing for the rest of the day. *Achilles* followed close to the coast. *Ajax* remained to the south to cover a possible doubling back at dusk. At 1915 *Graf Spee* fired two accurate salvoes and at 2048 another three. Sporadic firing finished at 2142 and the pursuit and shadowing phase of the battle ended when *Graf Spee* anchored off Montevideo at 2350.

While the battle and pursuit were in progress the Royal Navy was making dispositions to engage *Graf Spee* whenever she should quit Montevideo. *Cumberland* joined her consorts at 2200 on 14 December after steaming 1,000 miles in 34 hours. The 8-in cruisers *Dorsetshire* and *Shropshire*, carrier *Ark Royal*, battle-cruiser *Renown* and modern cruiser *Neptune* were all directed to the River Plate but this overwhelming strength could not concentrate there before 19 December.

Meanwhile Langsdorff was the center of an unprecedented diplomatic storm in what he later called 'the trap of Montevideo'. He had secured a 72-hour extension over the 24-hour permissible stay of a warship in a neutral port. British objections were more academic than real for they had no wish to force *Graf Spee* to sea before the 19th and the ploy of sailing a British merchant ship each day was adopted. International Law provided that merchantmen leaving port had to be given a head start of 24 hours over an enemy warship.

On 16 December Langsdorff reported to Berlin – erroneously – his belief that the British concentration of warships already lay in wait outside the harbor. *Gross-Admiral* Eric Raeder, C-in-C of the German Navy, discussed this naval dilemma with Hitler that same day and they agreed that an attempted fighting breakout to Buenos Aires was the proper course of action, failing which scuttling would be preferable to internment.

At 1815 on 17 December Langsdorff conned *Graf Spee* out of harbor with a reduced crew aboard: 800 of her company had been transferred to the German tanker SS *Tacoma* which followed close astern. Soon after the ship was outside the three-mile limit she stopped and anchored. Tugs approached. The ensign was lowered. Six fuses were lit. Boats – the last one containing Langsdorff – headed away from *Graf Spee* across the River Plate towards Buenos Aires in Argentina. Six violent explosions shattered the quiet of evening. The pocket-battleship *Graf Spee* exploded like a volcano and settled in the shallows of the estuary, deserving of a more dignified end than a scuttling. She burned like a pyre in position 34°58' 25" S, 56° 18' 01" W, four miles 117 yards from land.

Langsdorff turned to his senior navigator: 'Pilot, enter in the log book *Graf Spee* put out of service 17 December 1939 at 2000 hours.' *Ajax*, *Achilles* and *Cumberland* steamed by *en route* to Montevideo with Harwood newly knighted and promoted to Rear-Admiral on the bridge of his damaged flagship. Two days later in a suicide letter Langsdorff wrote: 'Now I can only prove by my death that the fighting services of the Third *Reich* are ready to die for the honour of the flag. I alone bear the responsibility for scuttling the pocket-battleship *Graf Spee*. I am happy to pay with my life to prevent any possible reflection on the honour of the flag.'

Lieutenant H. Dietrich found Langsdorff the following morning. He had shot himself in the right temple. He lay in full uniform stretched out on the flag of the German Imperial Navy.

Battle of Britain (1940)

Christopher Dowling

On 30 June 1940 Major-General Alfred Jodl, Hitler's closest military adviser, expressed the view that the final German victory over England was 'only a matter of time'. He had good reason to be confident. Thanks to a run of victories unparalleled since the days of Napoleon, Germany was master of Western Europe from the Arctic to the Bay of Biscay. The much-vaunted French army had been destroyed in a campaign lasting barely six weeks. The British, who had sent a token force to France and Belgium, had been bundled off the Continent. Although the greater part of the British Expeditionary Force had managed to escape, it had been compelled to abandon almost all its heavy equipment and, for the time being, was incapable of offensive action. With the fall of France Britain lost her only ally in Europe. Despite Churchill's defiant speeches, many, including President Roosevelt and his advisers, doubted whether Britain would be able to resist the expected German onslaught.

Paradoxically, the very magnitude of their triumph over France had created intractable strategic problems for the German High Command. No plans had been made for a direct attack on England because the possibility that the Wehrmacht would inflict a decisive defeat on the French army had scarcely been contemplated. At most, Hitler had hoped to occupy bases in the Low Countries and northern France from which a naval and air blockade could be mounted against the British Isles. On 21 May, after the German armour had reached the Channel coast, Hitler briefly discussed the idea of invading England with the commander-in-chief of the navy, Admiral Raeder, but he was too preoccupied with the Battle of France (which was far from over) and then with the armistice negotiations to give much thought to the matter. In any case he was convinced that the British, for whom he had a grudging respect, would recognize the hopelessness of their position and sue for peace. He was anxious to bring the war to a Speedy conclusion so that he could fulfil the mission which had always been the ultimate aim of his policy: the carving out of a great land empire in the East.

Hitler's hopes of a settlement with Britain were not finally dispelled until the third week of July, when Churchill contemptuously rejected his ill-conceived 'peace offer'. In the meantime he and his advisers had begun, in a somewhat leisurely manner, to consider possible courses of action should the British refuse to see reason. Britain, with her insular position, her powerful navy and her rapidly expanding air force, was an awkward opponent for the Wehrmacht, which, as the relative size and strength of the three armed services demonstrated, had been designed for Continental warfare. Germany's naval weakness and her lack of long-range aircraft ruled out a strategy of blockade – even if the necessary forces had been available this was bound to be a lengthy process. An invasion seemed the quickest and surest method of bringing Britain to her knees. However, in view of the Royal Navy's overwhelming superiority in surface ships, it was clear that troops could only be landed after air supremacy had been achieved and that even then the operation would be fraught with risk. Unlike some of his generals, Hitler did not regard the voyage across the Channel as merely 'an extended river crossing'. As Raeder was at pains to point out, the navy, which had been decimated in the Norwegian campaign, could provide little or no protection for the invasion fleet. Hitler lent a sympathetic ear to Raeder's arguments and it was agreed that invasion should be a 'last resort', to be launched only when the British had been softened up by air bombardment. If, as its commander-in-chief Hermann Goering boasted, the Luftwaffe was capable of knocking Britain out single-handed, the government might capitulate before the first assault troops crossed the Channel.

On 16 July Hitler announced in a directive that he had decided 'to begin to prepare for, and if necessary to carry out, an invasion of England'. The operation was to be given the codename Sea Lion and preparations were to be completed by the middle of August. The planning for Sea Lion was not marked by the inter-service co-operation and consultation which characterized Operation Overlord, the Allied invasion of north-west Europe in 1944. Goering set little store by Sea Lion and did not attend a single planning session, yet the other two services were relying on the Luftwaffe to establish the conditions for the landing. Disputes between the army and navy over the number of divisions which could be put ashore and the width of the landing front led on 1 August to the postponement of Sea Lion until the middle of September. On the same day Hitler, who was becoming impatient at Goering's dilatoriness, ordered the Luftwaffe to begin intensified warfare against England on or after 5 August. The Royal Air Force was to be overcome as quickly as possible, after which attacks were to be directed against ports; those on the south coast which might be needed for Sea Lion were, however, to be spared. Goering issued his tactical instructions for the air offensive, which he christened Eagle, on 2 August. He had so poor an opinion of the RAF that he allowed only four days for its elimination south of a line from Gloucester to London and four weeks for its total annihilation.

For the coming assault the Luftwaffe could muster some 2,500 serviceable aircraft, of which nearly 1,000 were He 111, Do 17 and Ju 88 medium bombers. In addition there were some 260 Ju 87 dive-bombers – the dreaded Stuka, which, with its menacing silhouette and blood-curdling scream, had come to symbolize the *Blitzkrieg*. The fighters comprised about 800 single-engined Me 109s and 220 twin-engined Me 110s. These aircraft were deployed in three *Luftflotten* (air fleets). *Luftflotte* 2, which was based in Holland, Belgium and northern France, was under the command of Field-Marshal Albert Kesselring, a former artillery officer who had transferred to the Luftwaffe in 1933. His genial manner had earned him the nickname 'Smiling Albert'. Further west lay *Luftflotte* 3 under Field-Marshal Hugo Sperrle, who had commanded the Condor Legion during the Spanish Civil War. It was intended that the 150 or so bombers of *Luftflotte* 5, under General Hans-Juergen Stumpff, should create a diversion by attacking targets in north-east England from their bases in Norway and Denmark. Of the three *Luftflotten* commanders, Sperrle was the only one who had flown in the First World War.

Although the Luftwaffe had officially been in existence for little more than five years it had already acquired a legendary reputation. It had played a spectacular and decisive part in the Polish, Norwegian and French campaigns; in the euphoria of victory the check it had suffered at the hands of the RAF over Dunkirk in May 1940 was soon forgotten and its significance was overlooked. Yet, formidable though it was, the Luftwaffe was in many respects ill equipped for the task which it had been given and which its leaders had embraced so readily. It had been designed not for independent strategic bombing but rather for the tactical support of the army in the field, a role which it had performed with brilliant success. Its organization, the training of its crews and the weapons with which they were provided reflected this purpose. The Luftwaffe lacked the essential instrument for an effective air offensive, a long-range heavy bomber. The medium and dive-bombers which formed its striking force did not have the necessary range, armament or bomb-carrying capacity for strategic operations and were vulnerable to the latest fighters, the dive-bombers particularly so. Had the ambitions of the first chief of the Luftwaffe General Staff, the gifted and far-sighted General Walther Wever, been realized, Germany might by the summer of 1940 have possessed a fleet of heavy bombers capable of reaching every target in the United Kingdom. As early as 1936 – the year in which the British Air Staff first issued the specification for a four-engined bomber – prototypes of the Do 19 and Ju 89 were ready for testing. However, after Wever's death in an air crash both models were scrapped and the heavy bomber programme was given a low priority.

The Luftwaffe was also severely handicapped by the limited endurance (about 80 minutes) of its standard fighter, the Me 109, which in other respects was an outstanding aircraft. The return journey across the Channel took approximately an hour; this left only 20 minutes for combat over England. The longer-ranged Me 110, on which extravagant hopes had been placed, proved incapable of holding its own against the RAF's Hurricanes and Spitfires and had itself to be protected by the faster and more nimble Me 109. As the German bombers were too vulnerable to fly without escort in daylight, their operational zone was necessarily restricted to the Me 109's radius of action – that is, to London and the south-east corner of England, where the British defences were concentrated. Moreover, owing to the comparative neglect of the fighter arm before the war, there were not enough Me 109s to provide adequate cover for the bombers, each of which needed an escort of at least two fighters. This, in effect, reduced the number of bombers that could be launched against Britain at any one time to a mere three or four hundred.

The Luftwaffe High Command was only vaguely aware of these deficiencies. Goering, who was more of a politician than an airman, greatly overestimated the strength of what he fondly regarded as 'his' Luftwaffe. He had been a dashing fighter pilot during the First World War, but he had resigned his commission in 1922 and since then had lost touch with the development of military aviation. Hitler took little interest in air warfare and was content to leave the management of the Luftwaffe entirely to his faithful party henchman. Though he was not without ability, Goering had neither the technical knowledge nor the professional experience to command a modern air force. He lacked the capacity for sustained work and concerned himself only spasmodically with Luftwaffe affairs, preferring to lead a life of self-indulgent ease on his country estate at Karinhall. His chief of staff, the youthful Hans Jeschonnek, was an ardent Nazi and was not disposed to challenge his overbearing superior. In any case, he, like the two field commanders Kesselring and Sperrle, shared many of Goering's illusions about the Luftwaffe's potential.

While the Battle of Britain was, from the Luftwaffe's point of view, an improvised operation hastily mounted with the resources to hand, the RAF had been preparing for it over a period of more than four years. By the summer of 1940 a sophisticated system of air defence had been evolved under the direction of the commander-in-chief of Fighter Command, Air Chief Marshal Sir Hugh Dowding. The cornerstone of this system was the chain of 52 radar (originally called RDF or radio direction-finding) stations which lined the coast from Pembrokeshire to the Shetlands. In the early 1930s the problem of intercepting enemy bombers before they reached their targets had seemed insoluble, since the defending fighters had to be alerted when the raiders were still well out to sea. In 1935, however, Robert Watson Watt demonstrated that radio waves might be used to detect and locate approaching aircraft. His ideas were taken up by another distinguished scientist, Sir Henry Tizard, who harnessed the new device of radar to operational requirements. Although the radar screen was not quite complete when the Battle of Britain began, it was able to provide accurate information on the distance and bearing of hostile aircraft at ranges of 70 miles or more and to give a rough indication of their height and numbers. Once the aircraft had crossed the coast their movements were tracked by the keen-eyed volunteers of the Observer Corps, whose methods Churchill rather tactlessly described as 'early Stone Age'. The Germans were aware of the existence of the radar stations – their towering masts made them an obvious landmark – but they underestimated their efficiency and did not realize how closely they had been integrated into the British defence system. Radar enabled the British fighters to be in the right place at the right time and obviated the need for standing patrols. Without its magic eye Fighter Command would have been at a hopeless disadvantage.

Information from the radar stations and Observer Corps posts was passed by means of an elaborate network of communications to the four groups into which Fighter Command was divided. The most important of these was No. 11 Group, which was responsible for the key area of London and the south-east of England. Its commander was Air Vice-Marshal Keith Park, a New Zealander, who, though very different in personality from Dowding, saw eye to eye with him on the handling of the fighter force. No. 12 Group, under Air Vice-Marshal Trafford Leigh-Mallory (brother of the famous mountaineer George Mallory), covered the Midlands; No. 13 Group, under Air Vice-Marshal R. E. Saul, Scotland and the north of England; and No. 10 Group, under Air Vice-Marshal Sir Quinton Brand, the south-west. Each group comprised a number of sectors. There were seven sector stations in No. 11 Group: Tangmere, Northolt, North Weald, Debden, Hornchurch, Biggin Hill and Kenley. The sector commander ordered aircraft into the air in accordance with the orders he received from group headquarters and directed their movements from the ground by the then advanced method of radio telephone. Although Fighter Command Headquarters at Bentley Priory near Stanmore had a general view of the situation as it developed from minute to minute, the actual conduct of the battle was left to the various groups and sectors. In addition to the radar stations, Observer Corps centres and fighter squadrons, Dowding had at his disposal the 1,500 barrage balloons of Balloon Command, and the 1,300 heavy and 700 light guns of Anti-Aircraft Command.

At the beginning of August the RAF had a front-line strength of 1,200 aircraft, nearly 700 of which were fighters. (The 500 or so bombers were not directly involved in the battle.) All but a handful of the 55 fighter squadrons were equipped with Hurricanes or Spitfires, whose eight wing-mounted Browning machine-guns were capable of destroying a bomber in a two-second burst of fire. The Hurricane has been overshadowed in the popular imagination by the more glamorous Spitfire, and it is not always recognized that it formed the backbone of the fighter defences. It was a steady, robust and highly manoeuvrable aircraft but it was inferior in performance to the Me 109. There was little to choose between the Me 109 and the Spitfire, though the system of direct fuel injection which enabled the German machine to go into a steep dive without any loss of power perhaps tipped the scales in its favour. In terms of the number and quality of their single-engined fighters and the skill and courage of the men who flew them the two sides were evenly matched. The British, however, had the greater reserves and, thanks to the forceful methods of Lord Beaverbrook, the Minister of Aircraft Production, were producing more than twice as many aircraft as the Germans. Between June and September 1940 deliveries of Me 109s averaged only 190 a month, compared with 470 Hurricanes and Spitfires.

The position as far as pilots were concerned was less encouraging. Nearly 300 fighter pilots had been lost during the Battle of France (a third of the total complement), and at the beginning of August Fighter Command was still 154 pilots below establishment, despite the welcome addition to its ranks of trained recruits from France, Belgium, Czechoslovakia, Poland, the United States and the Dominions. On the other hand the British enjoyed the advantage of fighting over their own territory: RAF pilots who baled out or crash-landed could be in action again within a few hours, whereas their opponents were marched off to prisoner-of-war camps. Similarly, many of the British aircraft that were shot down could be salvaged.

Fighter Command was fortunate in being led by men of unrivalled professional ability and experience. Dowding, who but for the outbreak of the war would have been retired in 1939, was a career officer with a keen interest in the application of science to modern warfare. Just as the Grand Fleet of the First World War was moulded by Lord Fisher, so Fighter Command was largely Dowding's creation. Austere, reserved and dedicated, he presented a complete contrast to the flamboyant and vainglorious Goering. By his tenacious opposition to the War Cabinet's proposal to send additional fighter squadrons to France after the German breakthrough in May 1940, Dowding ensured that he had sufficient forces with which to fight the Battle of Britain. Unlike their German counterparts, many of whom had army backgrounds, Dowding and his senior officers had behind them a quarter of a century of continuous service in military aviation.

The Battle of Britain, like the Battle of the Atlantic and the Battle of France, was, strictly speaking, a campaign rather than a battle. In fact it was a campaign within a campaign, for it formed part of a major German air offensive against Britain which lasted from June 1940, when the first bombs fell on British soil, to May 1941, when the bulk of the Luftwaffe was transferred to the Eastern Front in preparation for the attack on Russia. Although there is no agreement about its exact time span, the Battle of Britain consisted in essence of a series of daylight engagements fought in the skies above south-east England between 12 August and 30 September 1940. During these critical weeks the Luftwaffe sought to destroy Fighter Command in order to pave the way for a landing or for the unopposed occupation of a country paralysed by bombing. As Fighter Command could only be engaged in daylight the night raids by unescorted bombers, which began to assume a regular pattern after 24 August, cannot properly be regarded as part of the Battle of Britain, except perhaps for those that supplemented the daylight attacks on London during the last three weeks of September. After September the daylight fighting gradually died down and the Battle of Britain merged imperceptibly into the Blitz.

The prelude to the battle was an attempt by Goering early in July to wear down Fighter Command by attacking ports and shipping in the Channel. Neither side was at full strength, for the Luftwaffe had not yet completed its redeployment after the French campaign, and Dowding prudently refused to commit more than a small number of squadrons in conditions which usually favoured the enemy. The *Kanalkampf*, as the Germans called it, continued with mounting intensity until well into August. The results of these preliminary skirmishes were inconclusive. The Germans sank 30,000 tons of shipping and succeeded in establishing air superiority over the Straits of Dover in daylight, but their losses in aircraft were twice those of the British.

The Battle of Britain proper can be said to have begun on 12 August, when the Luftwaffe struck its first real blows at the RAF's fighter airfields and radar stations. Of the six radar stations attacked, one, Ventnor on the Isle of Wight, was so badly damaged that it was out of action for ten days, though this was skilfully concealed from the Germans. The Luftwaffe, however, failed to follow up the limited success it had achieved. Owing to faulty planning and slipshod staff work the long awaited Eagle Day on 13 August, which was to herald the opening of the main air assault, proved to be a flop. No attempt was made to repeat the attacks on the radar stations, and the aerodromes at Eastchurch, Detling and Andover were heavily bombed in the mistaken belief that they were fighter stations.

On 15 August the Luftwaffe made its greatest effort of the battle, flying no fewer than 1,786 sorties. Every available fighter was thrown in and for the first and last time all three *Luftflotten* were committed. The outcome was a notable victory for Fighter Command, which shot down 75 German aircraft at a cost of 34 of its own. The weakly escorted bombers of *Luftflotte* 5 came in over the North Sea expecting to encounter little or no opposition. They were set upon by fighters from Nos 12 and 13 Groups when they were still some distance from land and suffered such crippling losses that they took no further part in the battle. There was heavy fighting on 16 and 18 August before a spell of cloudy weather brought the first phase of the struggle to an end.

Although Fighter Command was putting up stiff resistance, Goering, whose wishful thinking was reinforced by wildly inaccurate intelligence estimates, believed that Dowding had only about 300 fighters left – this was less than half the true figure. By concentrating his attacks on Fighter Command's vital airfields in south-east England he hoped to draw the British into an all-out fighter action in which Dowding's remaining squadrons would be wiped out. Hitherto, on Park's instructions, the British fighter pilots had engaged the bombers and avoided combat with the Me 109s. This had driven the Germans to employ their fighters in a close escort role rather than in the offensive sweeps for which they were best suited. In order to provide the strong escorts which Goering demanded for the bombers, almost all the Me 109s in Sperrle's area were transferred to Kesselring. The Ju 87s, which had been severely mauled, were withdrawn. Further attacks on the radar stations were discouraged by Goering, who considered them a poor investment, and after 18 August they were left unmolested.

The second and most crucial phase of the battle opened on 24 August with a devastating raid by *Luftflotte* 2 on No. 11 Group's forward aerodrome at Manston, which was so badly knocked about that it had to be evacuated. During the next fortnight the Luftwaffe began for the first time to gain the upper hand. The new German tactics of maintaining continuous patrols over the Straits of Dover and of delivering feint attacks across the Channel confused the British defences. Park's fighters found it difficult to get to grips with the German bombers, which were now protected by swarms of Me 109s. The disparity in losses narrowed sharply. From 31 August to 6 September the Luftwaffe lost 225 bombers and fighters, the British 185 fighters. As bombers accounted for about half of the German figure the British losses in fighters were considerably higher. Of even greater concern than the dwindling reserves of aircraft was the wastage of trained pilots: weekly casualties were running at more than 10 per cent of Fighter Command's total combat strength and the strain of almost daily action was beginning to tell. The Luftwaffe was also causing serious damage on the ground. At Biggin Hill, which was raided six times in three days, the operations room was wrecked, hangars, workshops and barracks destroyed and nearly 70 station staff killed or wounded. Early in September the Luftwaffe was close to winning some measure of air superiority over Kent and Sussex. This would have forced Park to withdraw his squadrons to airfields north of the Thames, from which an effective defence of south-east England would have been impossible.

But on 7 September Goering relaxed the pressure on Fighter Command's ground organization by switching the main weight of the offensive to London. Shortly after 5 p.m. over 300 bombers escorted by some 600 fighters converged on the capital and dropped a hail of bombs and incendiaries on the East End and the London docks, kindling numerous fires. Fighter Command was taken by surprise and the German bomber losses were comparatively light. The blazing warehouses and oil refineries acted as a beacon for a further 250 bombers, which continued the work of destruction during the night. When dawn rose over the smoke-laden city 306 civilians were dead and 1,337 seriously injured.

There were two reasons for what, in the event, proved a disastrous change of strategy: one military, the other political. The time of decision for Sea Lion was fast approaching. Already, in the first week of September, hundreds of barges and tugs had begun to creep round the North Sea coast to the ports of embarkation in the Channel, yet the Luftwaffe had still not achieved the necessary degree of air superiority to justify launching the invasion. Goering and Kesselring, though not the more realistic Sperrle, were convinced that Fighter

Command was on its last legs and that mass daylight raids on a target as important as London would hasten their victory by forcing Dowding to expend his few remaining fighters. The possibility that ruthless bombing of the civilian population might break the British will to resist was an added inducement. The political reason for the assault on London was Hitler's demand that reprisals should be carried out for British raids on Berlin, which had themselves been ordered as reprisals for the accidental bombing of London by the Luftwaffe on the night of 24 August.

Because of unsettled weather and the growing fatigue of its aircrews the Luftwaffe was unable to sustain its daylight offensive against London. In the week that followed the big attack of 7 September there were only three days – 9, 11 and 14 September – when sizeable forces were sent over London, though it was heavily bombed every night. The raid on 9 September was a failure, but two days later the Luftwaffe inflicted greater losses than it incurred, while in the fighting on 14 September honours were even. The opposition was patchy and it seemed to the Germans that the British fighter defences were at last on the point of collapse. Encouraged by Goering's jubilant account of the Luftwaffe's recent achievements, Hitler determined to wait until 17 September before making a final decision about Sea Lion. In the meantime the raids on London were to continue.

The weather on the morning of 15 September was clear and sunny. Sensing that the day would not be devoid of incident, Winston Churchill paid one of his periodic visits to No. 11 Group's headquarters at Uxbridge. As Park accompanied the Prime Minister and his wife down to the operations room, 50 feet below the ground, he remarked: 'I don't know whether anything will happen today. At present all is quite.' Shortly after 10.30 a.m. radar plots revealed that enemy aircraft were massing over the Pas de Calais, and it soon became apparent that a major attack was imminent. The Germans neglected to carry out their usual feints and Park was able to deploy his forces to the best advantage. When the German bombers crossed the English coast at about 11.30 a.m. they were engaged by successive squadrons of British fighters and harried all the way to London. Although a considerable amount of damage was done few of the bombers succeeded in reaching their targets. After a two-hour interval, which gave the British fighters an opportunity to rearm and refuel, a second and heavier attack was launched. It too was repulsed.

One of the features of the day's fighting was the timely intervention of a wing of five squadrons from No. 12 Group, aggressively led by Squadron Leader Douglas Bader. Park, who believed in using his squadrons singly or in pairs rather than in the large formations advocated by Leigh-Mallory and Bader, had, on previous occasions, complained bitterly about the lack of support from No. 12 Group.

As the German bombers straggled back to their bases, many with their wings and fuselages riddled with bullets and with dead or wounded men on board, it became clear that the Luftwaffe had taken a severe beating. The British thought that they had shot down 185 German aircraft, and on the strength of this grossly inflated estimate 15 September has come to be celebrated as Battle of Britain Day. The actual German losses were about 50 – fewer than on 15 and 18 August. Even so, the two actions on 15 September, if not particularly significant from a tactical point of view, were strategically decisive. The German fighters had once again held their own but they had been unable to protect the bombers. There was no disguising the fact that Fighter Command, which had lost only 26 aircraft, was still very much in being and that air supremacy was as far away as ever. Furthermore, since 4 September Bomber Command had been mounting nightly attacks on the Channel ports and had sunk or damaged more than a hundred barges and transports. On 17 September Hitler postponed Sea Lion indefinitely. Two days later, after Bomber Command had struck further damaging blows, he ordered the invasion fleet to be dispersed.

The abandonment of Sea Lion (formally cancelled on 12 October) did not, as might have been expected, bring the Battle of Britain to an end, for Hitler was anxious to keep up the threat of a landing and Goering, who was not one to admit defeat, still nourished the hope that his stubborn adversary might yet be vanquished. After 15 September the Luftwaffe turned increasingly to night bombing – a tacit acknowledgement that it had failed to win the daylight battle – but daylight attacks on London and other targets by mass formations of bombers continued for another fortnight. The fighting did not go in the Luftwaffe's favour and at the beginning of October, in order to avoid further bomber losses, Goering resorted to the use of fighter-bombers, which relied on speed and altitude to evade the British defences. These raids were mere pinpricks compared with what had gone before and they served no real strategic purpose. Nevertheless the battle dragged on, its finale being the belated intervention of the Italian air force, which made two gallant but ineffectual raids on 29 October and 11 November. The crew of one of the antiquated Fiat BR20 bombers which was shot down over East Anglia presented an incongruous spectacle: they wore steel helmets and were armed with bayonets.

There were many reasons for the Luftwaffe's defeat in the Battle of Britain: Goering's muddled strategy and his boundless capacity for self-delusion; the failure of the Germans to destroy or neutralize the British radar screen; the shortage of Me 109s and their unsuitability as bomber escorts; the high courage and superb morale of Fighter Command's pilots and ground crews, whose belief in ultimate victory never wavered; and, not least, the resolute strategy and skilful tactics pursued by Dowding and Park. Ironically, their conduct of the battle, in particular their reluctance to employ their fighters in big wings, earned official disapproval, and both were removed from their commands before the year was out. Few battles of comparable importance in world history have been won at such a small cost in human life: between 10 July and 31 October 1940 (the official British dates for the Battle of Britain) Fighter Command's casualties were only 449, though these were nonetheless grievous losses. In the course of the battle Fighter Command lost 915 aircraft, the Luftwaffe 1,733. Tactically the fighting was inconclusive, since neither air force was able to do irreparable harm to the other. At the end of the battle Fighter Command's strength in aircraft was greater than it had been at the beginning. The Luftwaffe took longer to recover, largely because of Germany's low rate of aircraft production, but it had made good its losses both in aircraft and in personnel by the spring of 1941, and its operational efficiency was not noticeably impaired. Its leaders, however, failed to take action to remedy the shortcomings which the Battle of Britain had exposed. Little attempt was made, for example, to step up aircraft production, or to expand the woefully inadequate training programme, or to accelerate the development of a four-engined bomber. It is a remarkable fact that the only major new aircraft type introduced into service in Germany between 1939 and 1944 was the Focke-Wulf 190. In so far as the Luftwaffe never again enjoyed the prestige or the relative striking power that it had possessed in June 1940, the Battle of Britain marked the beginning of its decline.

Dowding's victory in the Battle of Britain was no less significant than Nelson's at Trafalgar, with which, indeed, it has sometimes been compared. Yet in many ways Lord Howard of Effingham's victory over the Spanish Armada in 1588 affords a closer parallel. The defeat of the Spanish Armada was the first great naval battle of modern times, the Battle of Britain the first (and almost certainly the last) great air battle. Like the Battle of Britain, the duel between the English fleet and the Armada was not a setpiece encounter but a string of engagements of varying size and intensity. Both were successful defensive battles, though neither decided the issue of the war. Nor was the disparity in strength between the respective fleets and air forces nearly as wide as was thought at the time: the two battles were more akin to the combat between Hector and Achilles than to that between David and Goliath. Like some of the German generals, notably Field-Marshal von Rundstedt, the Duke of Parma, whose troops were to carry out the landings, was indifferent to the invasion project. The antipathy which existed between Drake and Frobisher finds some echo in the clash between Park and Leigh-Mallory over tactics. Just as Howard was criticized for failing to annihilate the Spanish fleet, so it was argued in some quarters that Dowding and Park could have inflicted greater losses on the Luftwaffe by adopting a more aggressive policy. There, however, the parallel ends, for whereas the defeat of the Armada led to a revival of Spanish naval power, the defeat of the Luftwaffe, as we have seen, was one of the signposts on the road to its ultimate demise.

The failure of the Luftwaffe to destroy Fighter Command in the summer of 1940 had far-reaching strategic consequences. It was the first setback suffered by the Wehrmacht in the Second World War and it dented the myth of German invincibility in much the same way as Napoleon's repulse at Aspern-Essling in 1809 had shown a demoralized Europe that the all-conquering Grand Army could be mastered. Furthermore, it shattered Hitler's hopes of a swift victory and ensured that the struggle would be a protracted one; Germany, whose economy and armed forces were geared to a *Blitzkrieg* strategy, was ill-equipped to fight this kind of war. Hitler realized that in view of Britain's rapidly growing military strength an invasion in 1941 would not be feasible. Germany was thus forced to seek alternative avenues to victory, which involved her in costly campaigns in the Mediterranean. Although the frustration of the German attempt to conquer Britain had nothing to do with the attack on Russia, planning for which had started several weeks before Eagle Day, operations in the East seemed to offer a solution to the stalemate in the West. Hitler was obliged to embark on the invasion of Russia with an unsubdued enemy in his rear. The threat of British intervention on the Continent pinned down more than 35 divisions, thereby reducing the forces available for Operation Barbarossa. Perhaps the last word should be given to von Rundstedt. Shortly after the war he told a group of Russian officers that had the Luftwaffe won the Battle of Britain Germany would have defeated Russia in 1941. The Russians had come to ask him which he considered to be the decisive battle of the war, expecting him to name Stalingrad. When he replied, 'The Battle of Britain', they closed their notebooks and went away.

Keren (1941)

John Strawson

'Am concerned at check developing at Keren. Abyssinia might be left, but had hopes Eritrea would be cleaned up' – read the telegram to Cairo of a worried Winston Churchill on 20 February 1941. The mountainous escarpment of Keren formed a natural fortress barrier shielding the coastal province of Eritrea from the interior of Africa. Italy had annexed Eritrea in 1890 and from there Mussolini's armies had overrun Ethiopia (Abyssinia) in 1935–6. Now, five years later, they had made Keren the bastion of *Il Duce*'s East African Empire against British invasion from the Sudan. Keren was to be a soldier's battle in the grimmest imaginable conditions and terrain and here as nowhere else in the Second World War Italian soldiers of all types were to belie the belief that they were a pushover in battle.

As early as August 1939, General Sir Archibald Wavell, British Commander-in-Chief in the Middle East, concluded that there were four things he must do in the event of Italy going to war alongside Germany. These were to secure the Suez Canal base by acting boldly in the Western Desert; get control of the Eastern Mediterranean; clear the Red Sea; then develop operations in south-east Europe. After Mussolini's entry into the Second World War in June 1940 Wavell wrestled to achieve these objectives. What he had not foreseen was that he would be required to do all four simultaneously with inadequate resources. Yet in spite of some nasty shocks he managed the first of these tasks and was wholly, startlingly, successful in the third. It is of this campaign, the clearing of East Africa and the Red Sea, that Keren formed a part.

Wavell's strategic dilemma is admirably depicted and the one bright spot on an otherwise dark canvas is suitably illuminated by his cable to Winston Churchill in the last week of March 1941, after Keren had been captured. It was in reply to a message from the Prime Minister expressing alarm at Rommel's advance to El Agheila, and it helps to set the battle in its proper context:

> I have to admit taking considerable risks in Cyrenaica after capture of Benghazi in order to provide maximum support for Greece . . . Result is I am weak in Cyrenaica at present and no reinforcements of armoured troops, which are chief requirement, are at present available . . . Have just come back from Keren. Capture was very fine achievement by Indian divisions. Platt will push on towards Asmara as quickly as he can and I have authorised Cunningham to continue towards Addis Ababa from Harrar, which surrendered yesterday.

Wavell had four campaigns on his hands – Cyrenaica, Greece, Eritrea and Ethiopia. It was essential to get the East African battles over and done with. Ethiopia had to be dealt with quickly in order to send the much-needed troops back to the Western Desert where the dangers were so much greater – point which Rommel was shortly to rub home. But before this could be done, before troops and stores could be sent via the Red Sea port of Massawa to Egypt and so on to Libya and Greece, the Asmara–Addis Ababa road had to be captured. And in the way stood the fortress of Keren.

On 19 January 1941, Lieutenant-General William Platt advanced from the Sudan into Eritrea, while a few days later Lieutenant-General Sir Alan Cunningham set out on his march from Kenya with African and South African troops. Platt quickly reached Keren but the battle for it, the most severe of the whole East African campaign, lasted nearly two months. After its capture Platt soon took Asmara and Massawa, thus opening the vital route to the north. Cunningham's successes were equally astonishing in speed and distance. By 25 February he had taken Mogadishu together with a huge petrol dump, and a month later, having advanced 1,000 miles, reached Harrar. By 5 April he had captured Addis Ababa and then the two forces, Platt from the north, Cunningham from the south, converged on Amba Alagi. It was here that the Duke of Aosta, Italian Viceroy of Ethiopia, had concentrated what was left of his armies. By 16 May all was over. The extent and totality of the victory were summed up by Wavell in his despatch: 'The conquest of Italian East Africa had been accomplished in four months . . . in this period a force of 220,000 men had been practically destroyed with the whole of its equipment, and an area of nearly a million square miles had been occupied.'

It was that rare thing – a complete victory, a battle of annihilation since none of the enemy escaped. The fighting was unlike any other in the war. Great mountain barriers had been stormed. In Ethiopia the operations, among which Orde Wingate's Gideon force ranks high, had been largely guerrilla, and had succeeded in tying down large numbers of Italian troops which were thus unable to concentrate against the advancing British columns. Yet these columns had been small and this was their strength, since supply problems, although formidable, had been surmountable. Mobility had been everything, while for the Italians the very size of the huge Empire they tried to protect had paralyzed them. How did the situation appear to the Italian Viceroy?

Despite the Italians' early and relatively insignificant successes of July 1940 when they captured frontier posts in Kenya and Sudan and invaded British Somaliland, Aosta's strategy was essentially defensive. By the beginning of December 1940 he was already expecting British offensives from the Sudan against Eritrea, particularly from Kassala towards Keren, and from Kenya against Italian Somaliland and Ethiopia. Because of fuel and vehicle shortages it was difficult to ensure that his centrally held reserves would be sufficiently agile to reinforce a threatened area rapidly. He therefore decided to send some of these reserves forward, especially in the north towards Eritrea where he rightly thought that the first blow would fall.

In Eritrea itself he ordered the local commanders to organize areas of resistance which were to be firmly held while mobile reserves, mainly colonial brigades, would be prepared to operate between these areas and attack an advancing enemy's flanks. Eritrea contained three colonial divisions and three colonial brigades plus garrison troops. These native troops, *Askaris*, would be peculiarly susceptible to reverses and their loyalty would be unlikely to survive serious setbacks. In the north, where Generale di Corpo d'Armante Luigi Frusci commanded, the Viceroy foresaw grave difficulties in countering the British mechanized forces which would advance across flat country near the Sudan–Eritrea frontier, and on 11 January 1941 he therefore sought Mussolini's agreement to the evacuation of Kassala, Tessenei and Gallabat-Metemma. *Il Duce* agreed. On the other hand, Aosta decreed that there would be no withdrawal from Agordat and Barentu, both south-west of Keren, and that Keren itself would be strengthened by a regiment of the elite *Savoia* Grenadier Division. In this way they would help 'to close the gap absolutely.'

Such was the situation shortly before Platt began his advance. He had two very famous Indian Divisions under his command – the 4th (which Wavell had sent from Libya in January thereby taking the sort of risk he pointed out in his telegram to Churchill) and the 5th stationed in the Sudan since September 1940. These divisions were made up largely of Indian troops, ideally suited to the mountain warfare which they were about to wage, but there were British battalions and other units too. Platt had also formed the 1,000-strong Gazelle Force partly from units in 5th Indian Division, notably the renowned Indian cavalry regiment, Skinner's Horse, and from the Sudan Defence Force. The group included machine-gun, artillery and supporting units and was commanded by the dashing Colonel Frank W. Messervy. While Platt was still on the defensive, Gazelle Force had been used to harass and ambush Italian troops in and near Kassala. So successful were they that the Italians withdrew from Kassala by mid-January.

General Platt's task was clear. He must advance from Kassala into Eritrea and take Massawa, a distance as the crow flies of about 230 miles. There were only two ways of getting there and both routes led through Agordat to Keren. The northern route, a poor and narrow dry-weather road, was via Sabderat and Keru; the southern one was a better road but less direct and went through Tessenei and Barentu to Agordat. A well-surfaced road ran from Agordat to Keren and then on to Asmara and Massawa. The whole country was in one sense ideal for war. Except for the few towns, roads, railways and bridges, there was, as in the desert, little made by man to be destroyed. Yet curiously enough the place was alive with game. For the soldiers themselves it was less hospitable – mountainous, arid and rough. 'The plains and valleys', wrote Lieutena-General Sir Geoffrey Evans, 'were a mixture of jungle or open spaces dotted with outcrops of rock, stunted trees, palms near water and scrub, the mountains, strewn with boulders of immense size, spear grass and thorn bushes, were extremely arduous to climb in the heat, particularly when the troops were loaded with a full pack, ammunition and often an extra supply of water since there was none on the slopes.'

Fifth Indian Division was to advance to Agordat by Tessenei and Barentu, while 4th Indian Division with two of its brigades made for the same objective via Keru. The third brigade of 4th Indian Division was to move to Keren from Port Sudan. The whole advance began with Gazelle Force in the lead on the northern route. There was a certain amount of excitement before they reached Agordat. On 21 January, as a divisional history has recorded,

> while Messervy was engrossed with the situation at Keru, a nearby patch of scrub erupted. With shrill yells a squadron of Eritrean horsemen, 60 in number raced on the gun positions in front of Gazelle Force Headquarters. Kicking their shaggy ponies to a furious gallop, the cavalrymen rose in their stirrups to hurl small percussion grenades ahead of them. With great gallantry they surged on, but the gunners brought their pieces into action in time to blow back the horsemen from the muzzles of the guns.

There could have been few such bizarre actions during six years of war. The intrepid horsemen, led in by an Italian officer on a white horse, left 25 dead and 16 wounded on the field of battle.

More serious business confronted Gazelle Force. The battle for the heights to the south of Keru Gorge required the combined efforts of 4th Battalion, 11th Sikh Regiment, Skinner's Horse and 2nd Cameron Highlanders against firm Italian resistance. Even then it was more the danger of being outflanked and cut off from the south by 10th Brigade of 5th Indian Division than direct frontal pressure which caused the Italians to abandon their positions. By 25 January 4th Indian Division had closed up on Agordat, had cut the Barentu road and faced their first real obstacle. Meanwhile 5th Indian Division was ordered to take Barentu. Italian resistance there was stubborn, and just as 10th Brigade's advance had helped 4th Indian Division to capture the Keru Gorge heights, so 4th Indian Division's subsequent success at Agordat allowed the 5th to overrun the Italians at Barentu on 2 February.

The battle for Agordat resolved itself into a struggle for Mount

Cochen, described by those who saw it as 'a steep and involved ridge system which sprang to a height of 1,500 ft, its rugged barrier extending into the east until it ended above a defile four miles long through which the road to Keren passed.' The Agordat and Mount Cochen position was held by the Italian 4th Colonial Division, which was then attacked by two brigades, the 5th and 11th, of 4th Indian Division. The gallant actions of Indian and British infantry were greatly assisted by four 'I' (Infantry) tanks whose job it was to knock out the Italian armor. Lightweight Bren-gun carriers were used to lure the Italian tanks out of their hides. 'The bait was taken with a vengeance. Eighteen Italian tanks burst from cover and raced to destroy the flimsy intruders. Then the "I" tanks barged into the open, their guns playing on their Italian adversaries at point-blank range. Six medium and five light tanks went up in flames. The survivors scuttled frantically into cover.'

On the crests of Mount Cochen itself the final action had been dramatic and bloody. The Italian commander then had dispatched a company of Eritrean infantry to contain Indian troops advancing on the peak itself so that he could withdraw his main body to new positions. But the Eritreans encountered a covering force of some 40 Rajputana Rifles and Pathan Sappers and Miners who 'fell on the Eritreans like furies, plying the steel and leaving a wake of dead and wounded behind them. The survivors scattered in frantic flight. Over 100 bodies were counted along the slopes after. No further resistance was met as 11th Brigade advanced along the heights and made good the eastern end of the Cochen ridge system overlooking the Keren road.' It seemed at this moment as if the road to Keren itself was open. The cost had not been high. Fewer than 150 casualties had been suffered by Major-General Sir Noel M. Beresford-Peirse's two brigades while the Italian 4th Colonial Division had disintegrated, losing over a thousand prisoners.

Yet the road to Keren was not open. Demolition of the Ponte Mussolini, a great bridge 12 miles east of Agordat on the Via Imperiali autostrada, plus heavy mining of the deviation, bought the Italian rearguards precious time. The retreating enemy were able to pass through the Dongolaas Gorge, 40 miles farther east, and then to prepare another far more formidable demolition. On 2 February the vanguard of 4th Indian Division, advancing along the Ascidera valley, were within two miles of the Gorge's entrance:

From the canyon came dull booms, clouds of smoke and dust curled upwards in the still, hot air. The last Italian rearguards had passed through, and on a stretch of several hundred yards demolition squads were blowing away the retaining walls which pinned the road to the cliffsides. Two tanks crossed the valley to reconnoitre and reported the ravine to be blocked by barricades of huge boulders covered by anti-tank and machine guns. The eastern gateway of the Eritrean fortress was bolted and barred.

The Keren position, to those who first saw it, looked almost impregnable. Fifty-three days were to elapse before the fortress itself was passed by British troops. Either side of the Dongolaas Gorge 11 great peaks rose steeply to a height of more than 2,000 ft above the valley. To the west were Sanchil, Cameron's Ridge, Brig's Peak, Saddle, Hog's Back, Flat Top and Samanna; to the east Fort Dologorodoc, Falestoh, Zeban, Acqua Col and Zelale (the Sphinx), overlooking what was ironically named 'Happy Valley'. Sanchil and Brig's Peak afforded observation of Keren itself and were therefore particularly important. On this naturally powerful position the Italians deployed the best part of 30,000 men, some 40 infantry battalions, supported by 144 guns. Most of the troops were colonial, but the regular Italian battalions included some of their finest fighters – *Savoia* Grenadiers, *Alpini* and *Bersaglieri*.

The two Indian divisions – and because of transport shortages it was impossible to maintain both divisions complete in battle simultaneously – were faced with the disagreeable prospect of a frontal assault. There was simply no other way to open the road through the Dongolaas Gorge and thus achieve the objective of reaching Asmara and then Massawa. The battle can be divided into three phases. The first phase from 3 to 7 February was conducted by Brigadier Reginald A. Savory with his 11th Indian Infantry Brigade. He attempted to capture Brig's Peak and Sanchil. His troops reached both summits, but lost them again to *Savoia* Grenadier counter-attacks, while hanging on to Cameron's Ridge, won by the Scottish regiment of that name. The great difficulty facing the British and Indian infantry was that to reach their objectives at all demanded intensive physical effort. Artillery bombardment could normally reach only the forward slopes and had to be lifted before a final assault. On reaching their objective the exhausted infantry, already depleted in numbers by casualties and by having to use as much as a quarter of each battalion as supply porters, were terribly vulnerable to immediate counter-attack by the protected defenders who were supported by accurate mortar fire.

In the next phase Maj-Gen. Beresford-Peirse used both 5th and 11th Brigades, this time attacking farther east against the Acqua Col where desertions by colonial Italian troops were encouraging, with a view to outflanking the more formidable defenses to the west and pushing straight down the track to Keren. In spite of great efforts by the 4/6 Rajputana Rifles who gained the objective, a counter-attack pushed them off again. Severe fighting by isolated units was the pattern of the battle as this account shows:

> The leading Rajputana Rifle company had reached the haunches of high ground which rose on both sides of the entrance to the gap when heavy mortar and machine-gun fire opened. The company commander fell wounded, but Subedar Richpal Ram sprang to the front and headed the rush which carried the leading platoons over the crest. . . . In the next four hours five counter-attacks were smashed by the bombs, bullets and bayonets of this dauntless handful. An hour before dawn, their last cartridges expended, the gallant Subedar with nine survivors fought back through an enemy block in the rear and rejoined the main body of the battalion, which had dug in under the shelter of a low crest afterwards known as Rajputana Ridge.

Beresford-Peirse abandoned his plan. Next he decided to renew the attack on 10 February in both areas. It was a further story of great gallantry and prizes won only to be lost again. Eleventh Brigade was to capture Brig's Peak and 5th Brigade Acqua Col. Brig's Peak was taken twice, as were Saddle and Hog's Back. None were held. Acqua Col was almost reached – Subedar Richpal Ram of the Rajputana Rifles won a posthumous Victoria Cross in the battle – but his battalion suffered 123 casualties. Such losses could not be sustained. Platt and Beresford-Peirse, while still acknowledging that their main effort must be made at Keren, began to cast about for means of diverting some of the enemy to deal with threats elsewhere.

Thus 7th Indian Infantry Brigade under Brigadier Harold Briggs made its way south from Karora and was supported by the Free

French *Brigade d'Orient* made up of the 14th Foreign Legion Battalion (containing Italians who fought against their own countrymen) and 3rd Battalion of the Chad Regiment. Brigg's force fought a successful engagement against the enemy on 23 February at Cub Cub which was only 45 miles north-east of Keren and began to distract Italian reserves from the Keren front.

Meanwhile, preparations for the next main assault, the third and final phase, went on. They were enormously assisted by British aircraft. Heavy air attacks were made on Italian airfields between mid-February and mid-March and so successful were they that the Italian air force was virtually inactive. By 22 March the *Regia Aeronautica* could only muster 37 serviceable aircraft in the whole of East Africa. Additionally the Italian defenses themselves received repeated attention. By the beginning of March Platt had completed his planning even to the point of briefing his commanders on a sand-model. Fourth Indian Division was to attack to the west of the Dongolaas Gorge taking all the peaks from Sanchil to Samanna, while Major-General Lewis M. Heath's 5th Indian Division, fresh from a mountain warfare refresher course at Tessenei farther east, would capture Fort Dologorodoc and exploit to Falestoh and Zeban. Yet it was still 19 battalions against 42 defending and the attackers were slogging uphill in a temperature of 100°F. Meanwhile Briggs' force, now only about 15 miles distant from Keren to the north-east, would advance.

On 15 March, with maximum air support from some 50 bombers and an artillery bombardment by 96 guns, 4th Indian Division attacked. The 2/5 Mahratta Regiment seized and held Flat Top while 1/6 Rajputana Rifles took Hog's Back for the loss of half their number. But by 1600, after eight hours fighting and climbing, the Cameron's three rifle companies were down to 30 fit men in front of Brig's Peak, having lost 288 men in the effort to capture it. During the night these meager gains were just retained against three Italian counter-attacks. The following night 10th Brigade was thrown in against the two untaken peaks. Its two battalions were so savagely mauled that they were withdrawn to 'Happy Valley'. By the time the attack was called off on the evening of 17 March the division had sustained 1,100 casualties in three days.

On the other flank 5th Indian Division had better luck, taking Fort Dologorodoc on the first night, principally because, unlike the other Italian defenses, it was not overlooked by a high ridge behind.

Its capture proved to be a turning point, for the fort dominated the town and plateau of Keren behind the mountains, thus providing a superb artillery observation post for the British guns. Nevertheless, exploitation of the success to Falestoh and Zeban ended as so often before with the troops pinned down on the forward slopes; this time they even had to be air-supplied before being withdrawn at night.

The two-division offensive had one other positive result – it enabled engineers to examine the original Italian roadblock in the Dongolaas Gorge. They found that the boulders and craters extended back 100 yards, but estimated that a 48-hour clearance would enable tracked vehicles to get through. Furthermore on the west side of the block the railway line to Keren ran under Cameron's Ridge through a barricaded tunnel. Once cleared this offered a covered way approach for armor to get through the Gorge and advance to Keren. No wonder General Heath declared, on receiving this information, that 'Keren is ours!' His division's second effort was fixed for 25 March, giving a week for preparations and the resting of units.

Meanwhile, between 18 and 22 March, the Italians made seven desperate attempts to recapture Fort Dologorodoc during which they suffered many casualties. Among the dead was General Lorenzini, a bold inspiring leader, nicknamed by his men, the Lion of the Sahara. His 4th Italian Division of regular troops had been the mainstay of the defense.

By 20 March Italian units had lost a third of their strength. On 25 March the 9th and 10th Brigades of 5th Indian Division attacked on both sides of the Gorge and seized it, taking some 500 prisoners including many *Bersaglieri* and two batteries of artillery. The following afternoon Sappers and Miners had blasted a way through the road block. This meant that before long the 14 infantry tanks and 50 Bren carriers of Fletcher Force would get behind the main Italian positions. On the night of 26 March the Italians skillfully withdrew leaving only light covering forces. Next morning white flags fluttered from Sanchil and Brig's Peak. Fourth Indian Division advanced and tanks entered Keren by 0800 on 27 March. Asmara, capital of Eritrea, fell on 1 April and Massawa, the Red Sea port, a week later.

The battle was best summed up by General Platt, talking to his officers on 14 March before the final phase started: 'Do not let anybody think this is going to be a walk-over. It is not. It is going to be a bloody battle: a bloody battle against both enemy and ground.

It will be won by the side which lasts longest. I know you will last longer than they do. And I promise you I will last longer than my opposite number.' That Platt was right about the bloodiness of the action needs but statistics and the memory of those present to endorse. The British lost 536 killed and 3,229 wounded. Three thousand Italians, according to their commander, General Frusci, were killed.

Without the determination, devotion to duty and sheer bravery of the regimental soldiers, the battle could not have been won. The magnificent efforts of the logistic planners and producers were also vital, for no troops, however courageous, can win without food, fuel, ammunition and water. The Italians on Mount Sanchil had a piped water-supply – their assailants had to carry two-gallon petrol tins up the heights. Major-General G. Surtees, then a Brigadier in charge of administration for the campaign, did much to win what he called the 'Q' (Quartermaster's) war. He recorded that speed, simplicity, common-sense, improvisation and imagination were the watchwords. But, Surtees continued, none of these would have been any good without the men who carried out the plans – driving the vehicles, humping the stores and evacuating the wounded. 'British, Indian and Sudanese', Surtees wrote, 'grumbling, cursing and laughing, swept by sand storms, soaked in tropical rain, they sweated it out in the heat, they froze in the heights. Unexciting, if not uninteresting, was much of their back area toil, often imposing endurance and struggle against shortage of sleep. At any heroics on devoted service to the fighting men, they would have scoffed and sworn. Yet the urge was there.'

So too was the will to win in the higher commanders. Wavell, despite all his lack of resources and mounting commitments, had had the foresight and boldness to commit the right troops to the right place at the right time. After Keren, 4th Indian Division hastened back to the Western Desert. Eritrea gone, the Duke of Aosta concentrated his dwindling strength in one more great fortress at Amba Alagi. There he was stalked and harried and, eventually, forced to surrender by the converging columns of Platt and Cunningham. Mopping up, interrupted by the rainy season, finished in November 1941. Of all the East African battles Keren was the bloodiest and longest. It had been besieged for nearly eight weeks and was held by nearly four divisions of Italian troops. It was a battle partly won by the skill and perseverance of the British, Indian and French troops and partly lost by the Italians in their reckless but valiant attempts to retake Fort Dologorodoc. The Italians could rightly be proud of their record at Keren, even though, as Brigadier Savory said, 'No enemy but the Italians would ever have allowed us to take the place. It was practically impregnable and even with Italian defenders we suffered heavily and at times began to wonder if we ever would succeed.' For the great 4th and 5th Divisions of the British dominion of India, the battle remains a shining star in their histories.

Kiev (1941)

John Strawson

Hitler hailed it as 'the greatest battle in the history of the world'. For on 16 September 1941 the German *Panzergruppen* of Colonel-Generals Heinz Guderian and Ewald von Kleist had joined hands in the Ukraine at Lokhvitsa, 125 miles east of Kiev. The Soviet commander in the Ukraine, Marshal Semyon Mikhailovich Budenny, had just been sacked by Stalin, but his army group was encircled. Within ten days the Germans captured 655,000 prisoners, 884 tanks, 3,718 guns and 3,500 motor vehicles. Colonel General Franz Halder, Chief of the German General Staff, called Kiev the principal strategic blunder of the Russian campaign. His view seems irreconcilable with Hitler's. How had it all come about?

The answer lies in the planning and aims of Hitler's invasion of Russia. As early as 1924, Hitler's book *Mein Kampf* was explicit: 'We stop the endless German movement to the south and west, and turn our gaze towards the land of the East. If we speak of new territory in Europe today, we can primarily have in mind only Russia and her vassal border states . . . This colossal empire in the East is ripe for dissolution.' Hitler's foreign policy was not just to abolish the Treaty of Versailles and extend the *Reich*'s frontiers to include all Germans. These aims were virtually achieved by 1939 without recourse to war. But *Lebensraum* (living space) demanded far more than what was 'rightly' Germany's. It needed Russia for ideological as well as strategic reasons.

Despite all the campaigns in the west and the south, it can be argued that Hitler concentrated three-quarters of his forces with his prime object clearly in view – the defeat of Russia. Only then could he settle 100 million Germans of pure Aryan stock on lands east of Germany to ensure that the New Order would last for a thousand years.

Hitler knew that the establishment of a German empire in the East, would, sooner or later, mean war with Russia. Even in 1934 he was telling Hermann Rauschning: 'We cannot in any way evade the final battle between German race ideals and pan-Slav mass ideals. Here yawns the eternal abyss which no political interest can bridge . . . We alone can conquer the great continental space, and it will be done by us singly and alone.'

It might be necessary to make arrangements with the Soviet Union along the way, but only the more quickly to erase Russia completely for 'it will open to us the mastery of the world.' In July 1940, with France crushed but England defiant, Hitler turned his arguments inside out when trying to persuade his Commanders-in-Chief about how to defeat England. England's hope lay in Russia and the United States. If Russia dropped out of the picture, America would too, for Russia's elimination would make America think only of Japan's threat to themselves. 'Decision: Russia's destruction must therefore be made part of this struggle. The sooner Russia is crushed the better. The attack will achieve its purpose only if the Russian state can be shattered to its roots with one blow . . . if we start in May 1941, we will have five months in which to finish the job.'

In December 1940 Hitler's War Directive No 21, *Case Barbarossa*, sent a shiver down the spines of those first privileged to read it. 'The German Armed Forces must be prepared, even before the conclusion of the war against England, to crush Soviet Russia in a rapid campaign.' The bulk of the Red Army stationed in Western Russia would be encircled and destroyed by deeply penetrating armored forces. Above all, any Soviet forces still able to fight would be prevented from withdrawing into the depths of Russia. Herein lay the reason for the battle of Kiev. Hitler's directive gave a broad outline of the conduct of operations and the final objective – the creation of a barrier against Asiatic Russia on the general line of the Caspian Sea at Astrakhan to Archangel in the Arctic. It did not say how and where the Soviet armies were to be destroyed. This failure to draw up an absolutely clear and realizable master plan for the Red Army's annihilation ensured that the astonishingly successful Kiev battles made no difference to the final outcome of the war.

Hitler had always maintained that 'we have only to kick the door in and the whole rotten structure will come crashing down.' In order to foment this instant collapse three Army Groups were assembled. Army Group North would strike for Leningrad. Army Group Centre with the two main *Panzergruppen* (1,770 tanks) was aimed at Smolensk. Field Marshal Karl Gerd von Rundstedt's Army Group South was to deal with the enemy west of the Dnieper river in the Ukraine. Throughout planning, Hitler constantly reiterated the need to wipe out, not just put to flight, the main enemy forces. But he consistently failed to lay down any absolute strategic plan or objective to which all operations would contribute and be subordinate.

As *Barbarossa* developed, the Führer constantly chopped and changed, or worse still, vacillated. In spite of rapid advances and huge bags of prisoners, there was little sign of the whole Soviet structure crashing down. Army Group North got to Leningrad, but was repulsed before the city itself and had to be content with investing it. Field Marshal Fedor von Bock's Army Group Centre executed a great pincer movement converging on Minsk and by 10 July, 20 days after the start of the campaign, claimed 300,000 prisoners. The battles around Smolensk started a week later and lasted for three more. They produced a comparable number of prisoners, but took such a toll of von Bock's armies that the advance towards Moscow from Smolensk was not resumed until 2 October. It was this lack of a conclusive decision in the north and center, combined with Hitler's constant change of heart over what constituted decisive objectives, which led to glittering but illusory success in the Ukraine.

On 19 July Hitler issued his War Directive No 33. This directive (and its supplement on the 23rd) caused furious controversy between the Führer and his generals. In the first place Army Group Centre was instructed to keep advancing on Moscow, while its vital *Panzer* formations were hived off. *Panzergruppe 3* was to join in the battle for Leningrad. Guderian's *Panzergruppe 2* would attack the Ukraine in conjunction with von Kleist's *Panzergruppe 1* from Army Group South. Hitler made it clear that the priorities were the capture of Leningrad whose fall, he believed, would lead to the collapse of the regime it politically symbolized, and the Ukraine, an economic objective to be denied to Russia and used by Germany.

Col. Gen. Halder, Chief of the General Staff, argued that the whole campaign was endangered by the lack of a clear aim. Were the Führer's aims military conquest or economic exploitation? Hitler replied that both were equally important. But when Halder supported by von Bock, von Rundstedt, Field Marshal Walther von Brauchitsch (C-in-C of the Army) and Guderian insisted that a final autumn thrust must be made on Moscow, Hitler simply lectured his Commanders on the economic aspects of conducting war. Hitler only conceded Army Group Centre a defensive role after losing its *Panzergruppen*. It would not have to push on to Moscow with infantry alone. A 12 August supplement to Directive No 34 made it plain that the new offensives would be directed north on Leningrad and southwards to the Crimea, Kharkov, the Donets river basin and the Caucasus mountains. Large enemy forces on the flanks of Army Group Centre, especially the Soviet Fifth Army in the Pripet Marshes north of Kiev, were to be destroyed. This was the foundation of the great Kiev battles.

Among those who attempted to dissuade Hitler was the very man who did most to make the Kiev battles a stupendous triumph. In a last-ditch attempt to overturn the decision, Guderian obtained an interview with Hitler in the *Wolfsschanze* ('Wolf's lair' HQ at Rastenburg in E. Prussia) on 23 August. He pointed out that Moscow was the objective which ordinary soldiers understood. It was also a vital communication center, the political solar plexus of the Soviet Union, industrially important and psychologically perhaps conclusively so. He maintained that to capture Moscow first and destroy the Russian forces defending it (half a million men had escaped from the Smolensk encirclement) would make the subsequent overrunning of the Ukraine easy. To go for the Ukraine first would rob the *Wehrmacht* of the chance to take Moscow before winter came.

Guderian heard what was planned for his own *Panzergruppe* – movement to the Ukraine and back involving more than 600 miles – he commented, 'I doubt if the machines will stand it, even if we are unopposed.' But having been told by Hitler that Moscow must wait and the Ukraine offensive go ahead, Guderian assured the Führer that he would do his best. Hitler used Guderian's acquiescence to parry the continued doubts of Halder. He was always dividing and ruling his servants. But whatever the decision-making process, the outcome was that the main striking power of the German Army went north and south, not east to Moscow.

If there was discord among German military leadership about where to continue the offensive, there was just as much discord in STAVKA, the Soviet High Command, about how to stem its seemingly invincible advance. Colonel General M. P. Kirponos's SW Front had been pushed back into the Ukraine, while Hitler's Rumanian satellite armies from the Balkans begun to move into Bessarabia and towards Odessa. The Soviet problem here was the unenviable one of trying to defend a broadening front with disintegrating forces. STAVKA decided to amalgamate Southern and SW Fronts into one SW Theater. Stalin appointed as its Commander his old crony, Marshal Budenny. The Commissar with a main job of evacuating industry was none other than the 47-year-old Lieutenant General Nikita S. Khruschev. The 58-year-old Budenny, having held no real field command for 20 years, had little to recommend him save political 'reliability' against the German professionals, von Rundstedt and von Kleist.

As if choosing so questionable a commander was not enough, Russian strategy itself was soon a matter of violent disagreement. At a meeting in Moscow on 29 July, General Georgi K. Zhukov, Chief of the General Staff, urged that Kirponos's SW Front be withdrawn from the Dnieper river-line, even though this meant giving up Kiev. Stalin angrily rejected such a course, and instantly accepted Zhukov's offer to resign. Zhukov therefore went off to command the Reserve Front. The ailing Marshal Boris M. Shaposhnikov became Chief of the General Staff again. In any event, Stalin's decision to fight on the line of the Dnieper prevailed. Kiev, capital of the second most important Socialist Republic, was to be held at all costs.

Marshal Budenny's army group was positioned in an enormous salient about 150 miles wide, stretching from Trubchevsk in the north to Kremenchug in the south with Kiev as the apex of the salient sticking out to the west. The opportunity for encirclement and annihilation was therefore present from the outset. Budenny had the best part of 1.5 million soldiers in his area, about eight armies, mainly at Uman and Kiev itself.

The German recipe for annihilation was *double* encirclement. The first and *inner* ring would be drawn by three infantry armies; the Second moving SE from Gomel, the Seventeenth striking north from

Kremenchug and the Sixth keeping Russian attention riveted on Kiev itself. Meanwhile the *outer* ring would be closed by Guderian's *Panzergruppe* driving south with some 500 tanks from Trubchevsk to meet von Kleist's 600 tanks striking north from Kremenchug, at a point some 125 miles east of Kiev. It was the strategist's dream, a re-creation of the unique victory won by Hannibal over Rome at Cannae in 216 BC. The Carthaginian military genius had destroyed 70,000 out of 86,000 Romans for a cost of only 5,700. His infantry had lured 16 legions into the heart of their concave formation while the cavalry smashed the Roman wings and enveloped the infantry – to charge into their rear.

While the German plan unfolded, the Russians seemed to be paralysed and incapable of decisive action. Had Budenny had any inkling of the scope of German plans, he might have reversed his troop concentrations to withdraw behind the Dnieper. But having no notion of the kind of battle about to be fought, he reinforced those very areas, like Uman, which were to be engulfed even before the main battle was launched. While Uman was being reinforced, von Kleist's three *Panzer* Corps were dashing eastwards roughly between the two main Soviet concentrations at Uman and Kiev. By the end of July the *Panzers* were more than 100 miles SE of Budenny's main forces. The noose east of Uman was looped by Eleventh Army infantry crossing the river Bug and pushing on to Novo Ukraine where they joined up with 14 *Panzer* Corps from the north. Uman was a foretaste of greater things to come – by 8 August 103,000 prisoners had been taken from 21 divisions of three encircled Russian armies. The week's reduction of the pocket yielded booty totalling 850 field guns, 317 tanks, and 242 AT and AA guns. One German artillery battery pounding these targets fired more ammunition in four days than it had in the entire six-week 1940 campaign in France.

At this point in the Russian campaign – it was still only August – seven weeks after the start, the morale of the *Wehrmacht* was at its peak despite checks at Leningrad. In the south they were advancing fast without too much opposition. When the Russians did counter-attack, they usually signalled their coming by a lot of radio conversation *en clair* and then stuck to their normal pattern of a short artillery bombardment followed by wave after wave of infantry. Sometimes they were supported by tanks or trucks crammed with soldiers which simply drove straight at the German positions until inevitably knocked out. These were halcyon days and it was as well that the Germans enjoyed them for there would not be much more to enjoy after the autumn. This gallop across the Ukraine was recalled by C. Malaparte:

> During the night-time all fighting ceases. Men, animals, weapons rest. Not a rifle shot breaks the damp nocturnal silence. Even the voice of the cannon is hushed. As soon as the sun has set, and the first shadows of evening creep across the corn field, the German columns prepare for their night's halt. Night falls, cold and heavy, on the men curled up in the ditches, in the small slit trenches which they have hastily dug amid the corn, alongside the light and medium assault batteries, the anti-tank cannon, the heavy anti-aircraft machine-guns, the mortars . . . Shielded from sudden attack by the sentries and patrols the men abandon themselves in sleep. There in front of us, concealed amid the corn and with the solid dense mass of the woods – over there beyond the deep, smooth, bleak fold of the valley, the enemy sleeps. We can hear his hoarse breathing. We can discern his smell – a smell of oil, petrol and sweat.

By 7 September German operations were crystallizing. During a visit to von Rundstedt's Army Group South HQ, Halder agreed final details of the plan involving both this army group and Army Group Centre by which all enemy in the Kiev–Dnieper–Desna bend would be destroyed and Kiev itself taken. From Army Group Centre, Guderian would continue his 12-day-old thrust southwards from Starodub to Romny and Priluki with Second Army covering the right flank of the *Panzer* advance. From Army Group South, Seventeenth Army would pin the Soviet forces on the Lower Dnieper below Cherkassy and get a bridgehead over the river at Kremenchug. Then von Kleist could drive northwards from it to link up with Guderian in the general area Romny–Lokhvitsa thus cutting off some six Soviet armies. Field Marshal Walther von Reichenau's Sixth Army would cross the 700-yard wide Dnieper opposite Kiev and attack the encircled Soviet forces there.

Within a few days the German armies had made great strides. Seventeenth Army crossed the Dnieper on 11 September and von Kleist was packing his tanks into the bridgehead. To counter these moves, Budenny's only recourse was a desperate appeal to Stalin on 11 September for permission to withdraw.

It is possible, when we remember that he had given Budenny over a million men, to sympathize even with Stalin's exasperation and his refusal to authorize retreat to the east. Instead the Party slogan was 'Stand fast, hold out, and if need be die.' But by this time it was virtually too late. From the outset Russian leaders just could not believe that Hitler would abandon Moscow as his prior target when it looked as if he could reach it even earlier in the year than Napoleon (14 September 1812) – so while Guderian was seen to be heading south, it was thought that he was only trying to dodge round the strong Soviet forces barring the direct route to Moscow. Russian mobility, despite mechanization tied essentially to the foot soldier, could never hope to match that of the German *Panzer* troops who roamed more or less at will, at least six times as fast.

What is more, after von Kleist's breakthrough, there was nothing to stop them. Indeed with his *Panzers* ranging as far east and south as Dnepropetrovsk, Krivoi Rog and Nikolayev, von Rundstedt's difficulty was not so much that he could not gain his objectives, but to know what these objectives were. All southern European Russia, including the whole of the Donets basin, was his for the taking. There was nothing to stop him swarming on into Asiatic Russia except possibly a shortage of petrol. What should he aim for, what objective was there that would actually finish off the Russians? Their scorched-earth policy, emphasized by the blowing up of the Zaporozhe Dam which supplied power for the Dnieper bend industries, was hardly encouraging or likely to lead to realization of Hitler's prediction that the whole rotten structure would come crashing down. Von Rundstedt, therefore, in keeping with the broad directive of the whole campaign to prevent large bodies of Russian troops from retiring into the hinterland, had switched his *Panzers* back north in order to meet Guderian's drive south and so close the door on the huge prize of Kiev and nearly 750,000 Red Army troops.

Guderian's 24 *Panzer* Corps was being led by two *Panzer* divisional commanders, both wounded in the battle, who subsequently achieved fame. Lieutenant General (later Field Marshal) Walther Model of 3rd *Panzer* Division became known as the Führer's 'Fireman' of 1944 because of a knack for putting out fires, that is, of restoring collapsing fronts both east and west. But now the future 'Lion of the Defence' was displaying the dash and elan of a Rommel. General Ritter von Thoma, the Spanish Civil War tank expert who commanded 17th *Panzer* Division, was later to take over the *Afrika Korps* and be captured by the British at El Alamein. Once Model took the Desna bridges at Novgorod-Severskii, there would be no proper terrain obstacle between Guderian and Kleist. On 26 August Model's division punched into the town on the north bank of the marshy river. The Russians blew the small pedestrian bridge, but a headlong scramble by a special engineer assault detachment secured intact the vital 750-yard wooden road bridge. Lieutenant Störck calmly dealt with the final obstacle – an adapted aerial bomb planted right in the middle of the bridge – by unscrewing the detonator.

Model poured men and equipment along the vital artery to carve out a bridgehead that was to be proof against eight days of Soviet counter-attacks. Thoma's division made a crossing higher up the Desna and led a flank cordon that stretched and stretched to a N–S length of 155 miles but always just held against piecemeal Russian assault. On 9 September, despite late summer torrential rainstorms that churned roads into quagmires and dwindling fuel supplies, 3rd *Panzer* Division captured Romny, the last town before the pincers' rendezvous.

Meanwhile Kleist was about to join up with Guderian. His pincer had been held back so long lest the Russians recognize the threat of double envelopment too soon. On 12 September, the day snow first fell on the Eastern front, 16th *Panzer* division sliced 43 miles north after breaking out of the bridgehead at Kremenchug. The division's infantry needed a day and a half to master Lubny, fiercely defended by workers' militia and NKVD secret police. The closing pincer spearheads were still 60 miles apart. By the 15th, 3rd *Panzer* Division was down to ten battle-ready tanks but under Guderian's stimulus had struggled on beyond Lokhivitsa while the bulk of its units were still mudbound along the road back to Romny. Reconnaissance parties from *Panzergruppen* made contact and on the 16th the greatest encirclement of the entire Russo-German conflict was achieved. Twenty-two days after the opening of the battle 50 Soviet divisions had been trapped. Three days earlier Budenny, specially flown out, had finally been relieved of his command and Marshal Semyon K. Timoshenko, Stalin's indispensable 'rescue' general, appointed in his place.

From 16–19 September the Second and Seventeenth German infantry armies closed in on Yagotin, target of the inner ring of encirclement, while Sixth Army took Kiev on 20 September. For the next week what became known as the Kiev cauldron – originally about 130 miles wide and deep – which for all its efforts outside the Red Army was not able to burst into and meet the belated breakout efforts begun during the night of the 17th–18th, was broken up by the Germans. Some six Soviet armies (5th, 21st, 26th, 27th, 38th and 40th) were either wholly or partially destroyed. One army commander extracted just 500 survivors. Besides having no proper direction, the Russian soldiers simply had not enough ammunition or fuel – two indispensable commodities of modern war – to conduct a co-ordinated battle of any sort. Courage they did have and in a series of fanatical and desperate counter-attacks made by men down to five bullets apiece were simply annihilated.

During the fighting the words of Stalin, magnified to gigantic proportions by the loudspeakers, rain down upon the men kneeling in holes behind the tripods of their machine-guns, din in the ears of the soldiers lying amid the shrubs, of the wounded writhing in agony upon the ground. The loudspeaker imbues that voice with a harsh, brutal, metallic quality. There is something diabolical, and at the same time terribly naive about these soldiers who fight to the death, spurred on by Stalin's speech on the Soviet Constitution. By the slow deliberate recital of the moral, social, political and military precepts of the Commissars, about these soldiers who never surrender; about these dead, scattered all around me; about the final gestures, the stubborn, violent gestures of those men who died so terribly lonely a death on this battlefield, amid the deafening roar of the cannon and the ceaseless blaring of the loudspeaker.

The killing went on for the best part of a week, and then the surrenders began. Once they started they went on and on until over 600,000 Russian soldiers were prisoners. A colossal part of the Red Army, perhaps a third of its June 1941 strength, had been removed from the battle. It was not enough. No matter how many times Hitler might trumpet that 'The Russian is finished,' he obviously was not. The Russian Bear refused to lie down and expire. He insisted on fighting on. And within three months of their fantastic Kiev victory, something like despair was to grip leading German formations as they stumbled to a halt before Moscow and then began to withdraw.

For irony of all ironies, having condemned his generals' notions of capturing Moscow in no moderate terms – 'Only completely ossified brains, absorbed in the ideas of past centuries could see any worthwhile objective in taking the capital' – Hitler insisted Moscow be captured. But he still made the fatal mistake of trying to go for Leningrad and the Caucasus as well. Soon after resuming his advance in the center, *two months* since halting after the Smolensk battle, von Bock had taken another 600,000 prisoners and by 15 October his spearhead was at Mozhaisk, a mere 65 miles from the capital. If even at that point Hitler had gambled all, concentrating the dwindling tank strength of all four *Panzergruppen* on the drive for Moscow, while merely defending the northern and southern fronts, then surely victory – if by that we mean destruction of the Soviet armies defending Moscow and capture of the city itself – would have been within his grasp. Instead he failed to observe the never-to-be-forgotten principles of singleness of purpose and concentration of resources to that end. By the time he had realized it, the chill breath of winter and defeat was breathing down the necks of ordinary soldier and High Command alike.

From the Russian point of view the greatest numerical military catastrophe of their history was caused by Stalin's refusal to give up his regime's tenuous ideological grip on the Ukraine without a fight. Surely in this he may be judged right for to have chucked his hand in there would simply have given the Germans more time and resources to finish off the job in the center. Moscow's loss might well have brought about a total collapse of the Red Army's will to continue as opposed to the willingness of hundreds of thousands of its soldiers to surrender. The same sort of ideological and military question mark had also been half-posed in 1919 during the Russian Civil War when anti-Bolshevik forces were converging on Moscow from all points of the compass. But given that the Ukraine was to be defended in 1941, Budenny's defense ensured that had the Germans been allowed to choose their enemy's response they could not have done better. For the Germans indeed the battle was a brilliantly executed operation of war – the technical and tactical highpoint of the *Blitzkrieg* era.

Yet strategically it was a flop. All the slaughter, all the advances, all the planning and controversy and triumph went for nothing. The magnitude of Russia's resources proved equal to the enormity of the loss. Four million out of her 10 million military casualties occurred in the first six months of almost four years' fighting, but in 1941 alone four million reserves were mobilized. Kiev was a second Cannae – but, as after the first, the losing side would fight on to eventual and total victory.

Leningrad (1941)

Alan Clark

What brought the *Wehrmacht* to a halt at the very gates of Leningrad in 1941? Was it the indomitable spirit of a beleaguered citizen army? Could it have been a breaking from within the German impetus in its thrust forward into Russia's vitals? Or was it the desperation of a population caught frighteningly between a German hammer and the anvil of Communist political oppression?

The three primary objectives for the Germans in their invasion of Russia on 22 June 1941 were the coal and iron fields of the Donet basin in the south, the capital, Moscow, in the center, and the city of Leningrad at the extreme northern point of the front. And to each of these objectives the Germans had assigned a separate army group concentrating their tanks in *Panzer* groups. These were to clear the way and weld the chains of encirclement around the more cumbersome Soviet forces, whose surrender would be forced by the slower moving infantry divisions that followed in the *Panzers'* wake. In their advance, the Luga River was the last major obstacle facing the German army before the city of Leningrad. But on 8 August 1941 the Russian armies collapsed and the 41st *Panzer* Corps, commanded by General Georg-Hans Reinhardt, broke into open country. The German tanks had already travelled nearly 500 miles on their own tracks and the motorized equipment was overdue for servicing after six weeks of continuous use in the dust and summer heat of Northern Russia. The soldiers themselves were exhausted.

They had had only four to six hours sleep a night: but morale was at its height. Now, they felt certain, there would be nothing to stop them capturing Leningrad, the ancient Tsarist capital.

The situation was severe enough for the Russian Chief of Staff, Major General D. N. Nikishev, to report two days later to Marshal Boris M. Shaposhnikov, the Red Army Chief of Staff: 'The difficulty of restoring the situation lies in the fact that neither divisional commanders, army commanders, nor front [army group] commanders have any reserves at all. Every breach down to the tiniest has to be stopped up with scratch sections or units assembled any old how.'

In the city itself, citizens were being conscripted ruthlessly into the *Opolchenye* (militia). But this was little more than an enthusiastic rabble, indifferently armed, without signals or communications equipment, and whose training had been confined to weekends in local Party camps. A contemporary Russian account says that 'in addition to some rifles and machine-guns . . . the workers were armed mainly with Molotov cocktails and hand-grenades; they also had 10,000 shotguns and about 12,000 small calibre and training rifles donated by the city's population.'

Gloomily, and with the threat of a firing squad hanging over him, Lieutenant General M. M. Popov, the Russian Commander in Chief of the Northern Front, reported to his superiors in Moscow: 'To suppose that opposition to the German advance can be resisted by militia units just forming up, or badly organized units taken from the North-Western Front command after they have been pulled out of Lithuania and Latvia . . . is completely unjustified.' And yet even at this moment a plan to storm Leningrad was not part of the German strategy. As early as 8 July Colonel General Franz Halder, the German army's Chief of Staff, had noted that: 'It is the Führer's firm decision to level Moscow and Leningrad and make them uninhabitable, so as to relieve us of the necessity of feeding the population during the winter. The city will be razed by the Air Force. Tanks must not be used for the purpose.' And on 15 July the German Commander of Army Group North, Field Marshal Ritter von Leeb, was given express instructions that 'the immediate mission is not to capture Leningrad but to encircle it.'

It is possible that Gen. Reinhardt's corps could have driven without a halt to the Nevsky Prospect in those early August days; that the SS could have set up their headquarters in the Winter Palace. But the spirit and enforced discipline of the Soviet citizens was so different from that of their Western Allies that it is unlikely the German army's tactics (which succeeded the previous summer in France) would have brought lasting victory in Russia.

Then, between 14 and 18 August, all the Russian forces in the area, at the urgent prompting of Moscow, began to advance. And this counter-offensive – uncoordinated, extravagant, tactically inept, with masses of cavalry and unarmored lorries, with soldiers making costly frontal charges – did, nonetheless, have the effect of diverting General Erich von Manstein's 56th *Panzer* Corps, which should have been reinforcing Gen. Reinhardt's 41st *Panzer* Corps. For three critical weeks Gen. Manstein's corps marched and counter-marched across the dried-out marshes of the upper Illmen river, further exhausting its men and machines. It was not until September that *Panzer* Group IV could again contemplate the problem of Leningrad.

Within the city the activities of the Communist Party became ever more frenzied: 'Comrade Leningraders! Dear friends! Our dearly beloved city is in imminent danger of attack by German Fascist troops. The enemy is striving to penetrate into Leningrad . . . The Red Army is valiantly defending the approaches to the city . . . and repelling his attacks. But the enemy has not yet been crushed, his resources are not yet exhausted . . . and he has not yet abandoned his despicable plan to capture Leningrad.'

Marshal K. E. Voroshilov and Lt. Gen. A. A. Zhdanov organized a 'Military Soviet for the defense of Leningrad' – an independent move which even at this time of acute danger was bitterly resented by Marshal Josef Stalin who expressed his 'extreme dissatisfaction'. Voroshilov's answer was that 'it corresponded to the actual requirements of the situation.' But Stalin brushed this aside and demanded 'an immediate review of the personnel', and both Voroshilov and Zhdanov were dismissed.

In order to assert the Party supremacy over the Army, Foreign Ministers Vyacheslav M. Molotov and Georgi M. Malenkov were sent from the Committee for the Defense of State to replace them. A special order was issued to the troops:

Individual soldiers, commanders, and political workers are forgetting . . . their pledge and are revealing in battle a criminal absent-mindedness, faint-heartedness, and cowardice. Not only are there commanders and political leaders who do not set an example of courage and audacity and do not carry along their soldiers by their example, but there are also loathsome self-seekers who hide in fox-holes and do not lead the fight. Such disgraceful individuals cannot be tolerated in the Red Army. Those who fail to perform their duties have no place in our ranks.

The rattle of firing-squads could stiffen discipline, but Party theorists were of small value in handling men in battle. And at the end of the month Stalin sent General Georgi K. Zhukov, who was given absolute power. In his day, Zhukov was to visit and stabilize in turn every dangerous sector of the Eastern Front. Few commanders, with the possible exception of Montgomery before Alam Halfa in North Africa, can have arrived at their headquarters with so little time to spare.

On the German side, Wilhelm Ritter von Leeb was clear about his personal ambition – to seize Leningrad, the most prestigious prize of the campaign, by force, thus confirming entitlement to his field-marshal's baton. But Hitler had different ideas. His imprecise instructions were: 'to level the town, make it uninhabitable and relieve us of the necessity of having to feed the population through the winter.' The German High Command were against getting involved with the civilian population at all. One of them, Lieutenant General Walther Warlimont, prepared a memorandum. 'Normal' occupation was rejected. It might be acceptable to evacuate the children and the old people 'and let the remainder starve,' but this could lead to 'new problems'. Perhaps the best solution, said Lt. Gen. Warlimont, would be to seal off the whole town, and surround it with an electrically charged wire fence, guarded by machine-guns. But there remained the danger of epidemics spreading to the German front.

In case Warlimont's proposals should be adopted, corps commanders were alerted to the need for using artillery against civilians trying to break out of the city. It was thought 'doubtful whether the infantry will shoot at women and children trying to break out.'

There was also the possibility of the Germans making propaganda capital out of the affair. It was suggested that an approach be made to: 'the philanthropist Roosevelt to send either food supplies to the inhabitants not going into captivity, or to send neutral ships under the supervision of the Red Cross, or to ship them off to his continent.'

Naturally, any response to this which threatened to assume real shape would not have been accepted.

The proper solution was to: 'Seal off Leningrad hermetically, then weaken it by terror [air raids and artillery bombardment] and growing starvation. In the spring we shall occupy the town . . . remove the survivors into captivity in the interior of Russia, and level Leningrad to the ground with high explosives.'

But first the Russian defenders had to be put to rout. Unfortunately for von Leeb's plans, Führer-Directive No 35, issued on 6 September, ordered the diversion of the whole of General Erich Hoepner's *Panzer* Group IV to Army Group Center, where it was to participate in the attack on Moscow. The 8th Air Corps, of close-support dive-bombers, was to co-operate. But Leeb ignored this signal. His plans for a final assault were already complete. By taking advantage of a provision in the Directive that the redeployment be subject to 'first achieving a close encirclement' he staged what was, in effect, a full-scale assault on the city's defenses, with the 1st *Panzer* Division following the left bank of the Neva and 6th *Panzer* straddling the main railway to Leningrad from the south.

Both divisions were soon enmeshed in a net of anti-tank ditches and straggling earthworks which had been thrown up by the construction battalions and *Opolchenye* during the previous weeks. These defenses were often poorly sited and crudely finished, but they were extensive. The Russians were seriously deficient in artillery, and indeed in all arms not produced on the spot at Leningrad and its environs. But they had a large number of medium and heavy mortars whose weight of fire, at the ranges of the first day's battle, was nearly as effective as regular field artillery.

On the coastal sector, between the sea and Krasnoye Seloe, the 12-in guns of the Baltic fleet pounded away at the German rear. Over the battlefield, massive KV tanks roamed singly and in pairs, manned sometimes by civilian testers and mechanics from the Kirov factory where they were still being produced at the rate of about four a day. This was the kind of close in-fighting where Russian courage, obstinacy, cunning in camouflage and ambush more than counterbalanced the deficiencies in command and technique which had crippled them in the open battlefields on the frontier and on the Luga.

The *Panzers*, in contrast, were suffering as armored troops always do when they encounter close defenses after weeks of mobile fighting. Like the British 8th Army when it hit the Tunisian mountains after months in Libya, the tank commanders took fearful punishment as they sought to adapt their tactics in an unfamiliar element. In the first day of the assault four successive commanders of 6th *Panzer* were casualties.

By the evening of 10 September the Germans had penetrated as far as the last line of Russian defenses, which ran along the crest of some shallow eminences known as the Dudergof heights – about six miles to the south-east of Leningrad. During the night many of the tanks of the leading division, 1st *Panzer*, lay out on the battlefield, forward of the main German positions, and fought throughout the hours of darkness to beat off the succession of counter-attacks which the Russians always put in during the night.

By the glare of blazing petrol bottles and sodium flares the Germans broke up one Russian formation after another as they assembled to charge the positions captured during the day. At first light, the *Stuka* dive bombers returned to the battlefield and 41st *Panzer* Corps braced itself for 'one last heave'. The 1st *Panzer* had lost so many tanks that there was only one battalion left with over 50 per cent effective strength, yet they gradually inched their way forward during the day and by 1600 had scaled 'Height 167', a hill 450 ft high, the topmost point in the Dudergof ridge to the south-east of the city.

'In front of the victorious troops stood the city of Leningrad in the sunlight, only 12 kilometres away, with its golden cupolas and towers and its port with warships that tried with their heaviest guns to deny us possession of the heights.'

On the left flank of the *Panzer* corps the infantry were slowly edging their way across the valley, and once the Russian guns and observers had been cleared off Height 167 the Germans were able to make better progress, entering the suburban districts of Slutsk and Pushkin, and, on the evening of 11 September, Krasnoye Seloe.

By 12 September, the fourth day of the assault, it was painfully obvious to the *OKH* that a full-blooded engagement was raging in an area from which they were trying to draw reinforcement. Col. Gen. Halder ordered F. M. Leeb that the city 'was not to be taken, but merely encircled. The attack should not go beyond the Peterfog–Pushkin road.' For another five days close fighting continued although at a diminishing tempo. The German resources were not enough to cope with the dilution of their technical superiority which street fighting imposed.

The only alternative to closing down the operation was massive reinforcement on a scale which, one year later, was to be granted to Field-Marshal Friedrich Paulus at Stalingrad. Halder wrote the epitaph of the battle in the *OKH* diary: 'The ring around Leningrad has not yet been drawn as tightly as might be desired, and further progress after the departure of 1st *Panzer* and 26th Motorized from that front is doubtful. Considering the drain on our forces on the Leningrad front, where the enemy has concentrated large forces and great quantities of material, the situation will remain critical until hunger takes effect as our ally.'

The weight now shifted from the Red Army's soldiers in Leningrad's defenses to the civilian population, although the Communist Party continued for some months to direct its energies at 'stiffening' the army in case a further assault should develop. A 'letter campaign' from schoolchildren mailed every infantryman with a stilted request that 'you at the front must strike harder at the enemy who had the gall to attack our great cities and villages,' and resolutions were constantly sent out from the factory workers to the soldiers in the field:

> With great pain and bitterness we hear that among you there are sometimes cowards and deserters . . . The coward and deserter thinks that he will succeed in hiding from the people's censure and anger. He is mistaken. He will be cursed by his own mother, his wife will turn from him, his name will be spoken with loathing by his own children. With hatred and contempt – that is how his friends and comrades will greet him. A bullet in the head is what such a scoundrel and self-seeker will get.

September passed, and October, and with the leaves stripped from the trees along the Neva came the first frosts, followed by snowfalls. Food was already short, for supplies had not been stockpiled in the town. The German advance to Schlusselburg had occurred so suddenly and the demand for purely military items such as ammunition had been so acute that very little had been brought into the town before the ring of encirclement was sealed.

In two months, and before the ice on Lake Ladoga began to harden, everything that was edible in the city was consumed. Rats were considered a great delicacy. So too was the earth that came from near the Badaev warehouses where the sugar and chocolate had been stored and which had been burned down in one of the *Luftwaffe* raids. As winter tightened its grip, fuel became as scarce as food. One Leningrader remembered:

First, the feeling of being cold. One gets up with it, one walks with it, one goes to bed with it. It seems to wander around somewhere under the skin; it penetrates the bones and sometimes it seems as if it even enters the brain. One can't escape from it. It penetrates under all shirts, sweaters, and jackets, no matter how many one puts on. The second is the feeling of hunger. This feeling has many shadings – from a dull, painful, sharp, unbearable one, which appears as soon as one has eaten one's ration of 125 grammes, to being tortured by fantasies.

Soviet records show that of the 26,600 persons who took the basic civilian military training course (the *Vzevobuch* programme) in the month of November over 6,000 were too ill or weak to finish the course. Of these 800 died of starvation while under training. Another 10,000 were so frail that they could only be given a short course. Trainees were very reluctant to fail as an allocation to the front-line units meant a different and improved ration scale. As fuel ran out so was electricity power confined to military use from emergency generators. In the short days of November and December, Leningrad must have seemed a city of the dead, shrouded in snow and freezing mists from the Baltic, without light or movement. In the factories, starving and frozen workers toiled for 14 hours a day making armaments, many dropping dead at their lathes.

Medical attention for civilians was virtually nil. In hospitals

the absence of electricity, heat, and water made work extremely difficult. The temperature in the wards usually stood between 30° and 35° Fahrenheit. The patients lay fully clothed, with coats and blankets, and sometimes even mattresses, piled on top of them. The walls were covered with frost. During the night water froze in pitchers. The hunger had the effect of causing diarrhea among the patients, many of whom from weakness were unable to use the bedpans. Sheets on the beds were filthy – no water for laundering. The only medicine available was sodium bromide, which the doctors prescribed under various names.

The only hope for Leningrad was to bring supplies across the ice on Lake Ladoga from the harbors of Lednevo and Kabana to Osinovets. The lake was not smooth ice. October gales had made the ice pile up in irregular heaps and there were always some crevasses that never froze. On 18 November, when the ice was only 5 in thick, a small reconnaissance party made the crossing on foot followed by a man on horseback, and for a few days supplies were brought in by ponies drawing sleds with light loads. The first truck column on 24 November lost nine of its vehicles crashing through gaps in the ice into the water. Only two of the drivers survived. But by the end of November there were 500 trucks in use, battling against arctic blizzards, mechanical breakdowns and constant strafing by the *Luftwaffe*.

It was not until January that the ice was thick enough to allow trucks to carry full loads. Few survived more than three journeys on the ice and over 1,000 trucks were lost before the middle of January when the ice was 3 ft thick and could bear almost any load. Yet, in spite of the efforts on the 'ice road', Leningrad never had more than one or two days of food in hand. Even during the previous October the bread ration had been reduced to 400 grammes a day for workers and 200 grammes for other categories and on 20 November these were reduced to 250 and 125 grammes. Under these conditions it was simply a matter of waiting for death by starvation. A schoolgirl, Tania Savich, kept a diary:

Jenia died on 28 December, 1941, at 12.30 a.m.
Grandmother died on 25 January, 1942.
Lena died on 17 March, 1942.
Uncle Lesha died on 10 May, at 4.00 p.m.
13 May, at 7.30 a.m. darling Mama died.

Then Tania herself died.
A Leningrad doctor describes his experiences:

I entered without knocking. My eyes beheld a horrible sight.
A dark room, the wall covered with frost, puddles of water

on the floor. Lying across some chairs was the corpse of a 14-year-old boy. In a baby carriage was a second corpse, that of a tiny infant. On the bed lay the owner of the room, K. K. Vandel – dead. At her side, rubbing her chest with a towel, stood her eldest daughter, Mikkau. . . . In one day Mikkau lost her mother, a son, and a brother who perished from hunger and cold. At the entrance, barely standing on her feet from weakness, was a neighbor, Kizunova, her horrified gaze fixed on the dead. She, too, died the next day.

Had the Germans been as skilled at offensive warfare under winter conditions as the Soviet Army it is possible that a surprise assault in that first bitter winter of 1941–2 might have overcome its emaciated garrison and populace.

The awful winter passed, and during the spring and early summer of 1942 the reinforcement of Leningrad by the sea route across Lake Ladoga gathered momentum. Freight steadily increased from 1,500 tons in May to 3,500 tons in June, and the ships took out wounded and non-combatants instead of returning empty. It gradually became apparent to the Germans that Leningrad was threatening their extreme northern flank, and plans were laid for a full-scale assault.

For this, Manstein's 11th Army, which had by now fought a successful Crimean campaign culminating in the capture of Sevastapol, was given the support, once again, of the 8th Air Corps. In addition, a special siege train of 800 heavy artillery pieces was concentrated round the city. But the German plans were foiled by a series of spoiling attacks which the Russians launched at the end of August. Before Manstein had completed the deployment of his forces most of the German resources were used up in preventing the rupture of their corridor to Lake Ladoga.

At the beginning of 1943 the siege was lifted when the Red Army succeeded in forcing a narrow passage about five miles wide along the southern shore of Lake Ladoga and a rail link was established. From then – although the siege of Leningrad was effectively over – the city's fate was ultimately dependent on the outcome of the great battles that raged in southern Russia.

With hindsight we can see that the Germans might have rushed the city in August of 1941. Had the Germans been able to fight aggressively in the depths of winter their best chance would have been at Christmas 1941 when the citizens and the soldiers' spirits were at their lowest. But the intractable problem remained: highly trained and disciplined troops lose their advantage when dispersed over acres of rubble. Street fighting places a premium on numbers and tenacity. It is unlikely that the Germans could ever have succeeded in storming Leningrad any more than (with much greater resources) they could have been successful at Stalingrad the following year.

But they did come very near to starving the city out. Was it the iron discipline and terror of the Communist Party system that kept it alive?

Pearl Harbor (1941)

Paul Hutchinson

'All hands, general quarters! Air raid! This is no drill!' The alarm sounded for an attack that was to kill 2,403 American citizens as well as cripple her Pacific Fleet. But the Japanese attack on Pearl Harbor on 7 December 1941 was the key that released the unrivalled military might of the US. The eventual fate of the fascist powers – both east and west – was sealed.

Japan's strike at Pearl Harbor is often presented as a surprise attack on the US Navy, yet relations between the two countries were so strained because of Japan's colonizing policies it was practically inevitable that, for Japan to get her expansionist way in Asia, she would have to use force against the US.

In May 1940 the US Pacific Fleet was moved from San Diego to Pearl Harbor. The Fleet had been taking part in maneuvers off Hawaii the previous month and was ordered to stay in Pearl Harbor by Roosevelt when the exercises were finished. This decision did much to spur Japan into signing the Tripartite Pact with Italy and Germany the following September.

By mid-1940 it seemed that the fascist powers were everywhere triumphant. Nazi Germany controlled the better part of Europe and looked menacingly towards Britain from the coast of France. Meanwhile, Imperial Japan was locked in her expansionist war with China – a conflict of almost unsurpassed brutality. America was deeply involved in the fight against the aggressors in both theaters and short of military intervention was giving all possible help.

Public opinion in the US was deeply split over whether or not to go to war, with the majority firmly in the isolationist camp. But President Franklin D. Roosevelt saw clearly enough that unless the dictatorships were defeated the US's own independence would eventually be threatened.

On 27 September 1940 Japan joined the Axis when she entered into a tripartite pact with Germany and Italy. Under the terms of this agreement 'the leadership of Japan in the establishment of a New Order in Greater East Asia' was acknowledged. By this time Britain had been pressured into closing an important life-line to China – the Burma Road. America imposed a partial embargo on exports to Japan. This embargo was later intensified and anything regarded as a strategic war material was included in the restrictions.

It soon became painfully clear in Tokyo that Japan's empire-building conquests in Asia could not possibly continue for much longer without the raw materials of war – especially oil.

Relations between America and Japan continued to deteriorate into 1941 and an armed clash appeared increasingly likely. But US naval strategists did not think an attack on Pearl Harbor at all likely. According to them, such an action would be an impressive but rather pointless piece of sabre rattling – yielding Japan no great benefits. It was for the same reason that the Japanese rejected the idea when it was proposed by Admiral Isoruku Yamamoto in September 1941. Its lack of any military value apart, an attack on Pearl Harbor would snap the already strained relations between the two countries and all-out war would result.

Yamamoto – himself opposed to war with America – kept his faith in the viability of his plan. He had put the finishing touches to this as early as the spring of 1941. But for the attack to succeed, Yamamoto realized that absolute security was essential. There was in existence a cryptographic code which enabled Japanese naval officers to communicate with no risk of American interception reading their messages. Another risk to security in a venture of such importance was the inevitable prolonged argument and counter-argument within the Japanese High Command. The chances of a 'leak' were enormous, so Yamamoto bypassed the High Command altogether and approached Emperor Hirohito's brother Prince Takamatsu, then a navy staff officer based in Tokyo. He was intrigued and told his brother, who gave the go-ahead for the idea to be studied in secret.

As relations between Japan and the US went from bad to worse, Yamamoto trained his men. The harbor at Kagoshima was chosen for dummy dive-bombing and torpedo dropping because the lie of the land was similar to that of Pearl Harbor.

In late July the French were pressured into handing over Southern Indochina to the Japanese. America retaliated promptly. Japanese assets in the US were immediately frozen and the partial embargo already imposed on strategic material was made total. Britain and Holland joined in the economic boycott. The stark choice facing Japan was certain economic collapse or an armed clash. War with the US was no longer a question of 'if' – only 'when'. Unless the flow of oil was swiftly resumed Japan would have to abandon the Chinese mainland – an intolerable loss of face for the military. The absolute deadline for a solution was October.

Talks were held throughout the summer and autumn of 1941. Cordell Hull, American Secretary of State, made his country's position clear – all sanctions would be lifted only if Japan took her forces out of China and Indochina. But the negotiations were nothing but a device for buying time. Hull knew perfectly well that Japan would never accede to such a demand. Despite the pleadings of the Japanese Prime Minister, Prince Fumimaro Konoye, the Emperor and War Minister General Hideki Tojo refused to countenance any compromise. They were convinced of Japanese invincibility against all comers. 'The day after war begins we will have to issue an Imperial Declaration of War. Please see to it, Emperor Hirohito told his Lord Privy Seal, Koichi Kido, on 13 October.

Also in October, the US was warned of a planned strike on Pearl Harbor by an unusual source. Richard Sorge, Moscow's master spy in Tokyo, had passed the information to Josef V. Stalin, who in turn had informed Washington. But American naval strategists still considered an attack on Pearl Harbor unlikely.

Anxious for a peaceful settlement with the US, but outnumbered in the cabinet and overruled by his emperor, Prince Konoye resigned as Prime Minister on 16 October 1941. The extreme hawk Gen. Tojo took his place. At this point the Japanese Ambassador in Washington, Kichisaburu Nomura, asked Tokyo to recall him. His request was refused and the expert diplomat Saburo Kurusu was dispatched to buy time by supervising yet another round of 'negotiations'.

At this point it is worth speculating whether President Roosevelt was really ignorant of Japan's aggressive intentions. Apart from Richard Sorge's warning, the President also had access to *Magic* information – the decoded transcriptions of Japanese secret messages. It has also been suggested that Churchill thought that a Japanese attack on Pearl Harbor would demolish the case of the isolationists and bring America into the war and that Roosevelt agreed.

On 5 November Japan decided to make one more diplomatic approach to Washington before unleashing the now fully rehearsed attack on Pearl Harbor. This approach was sure to fail and was not intended to succeed – merely to give Japan the international veneer of 'peacemaker'. Presuming the breakdown of the talks, the Japanese Supreme Command's operational orders ended with: 'War with the Netherlands, America, England inevitable; general operational preparations to be completed by early December.'

Also on 5 November, the US Chiefs of Staff (Army and Navy) met Roosevelt to discuss the Far East. A month before, Generalissimo Chiang Kai-Shek, the Chinese Nationalist leader, had pleaded with America and Britain for help. US Secretary of State Cordell Hull feared that any further aid to China would provoke Japanese retaliation and General George Crook and Admiral Harold R. Stark urged the President to tread carefully. But it was resolved that if Japan undertook any military action against British, Dutch or US territory, America would intervene militarily.

After this decision the November talks between the two sides had no meaning whatever. Japan demanded a totally unacceptable retreat from America's stated position and tied her diplomats to a deadline of 29 November. This came and went with nothing resolved.

The force destined to attack Pearl Harbor had left Japan almost a fortnight before the 29th and congregated at Tankan Bay in the Kurile Islands. It was a powerful force – six aircraft carriers and nine destroyers, with tankers and supply ships, two cruisers and two battleships in support. Twenty ocean-going submarines acted as an advanced guard. Five of these were equipped with two-man midget subs. This force, commanded by the brilliant Vice Admiral Chuichi Nagumo, was the cream of the Imperial Japanese Navy.

On 26 November, the strong armada left the Kuriles and set

course for Pearl Harbor – adopting a route that would bring them towards the US Pacific Fleet from the north. Japanese met forecasters had told the task force that the weather was expected to be bad in the regions it would pass through. This would make the necessary refuelling tricky, but if they approached from the north there was less chance of being spotted by the Americans.

By 6 December, American naval strategists were still saying an attack on Pearl Harbor was most unlikely. Their grounds for such confidence were the unequivocal reports from US and British reconnaissance planes that Japan was launching a full-scale amphibious operation in the south, and Japanese ships laden with soldiers were reportedly entering the Gulf of Siam. American opinion could not accept the idea that Japan was capable of mounting two naval operations at the same time.

As dawn broke on 7 December, the Japanese carrier force had reached a position 275 miles north of Pearl Harbor. Fifty-one Aichi 'Val' dive-bombers, 43 Mitsubishi Zero-Sens 'Zeke' fighters, 40 Nakajima B5N2 'Kate' bombers with shallow-running torpedoes and 50 high-level 'Kates' left the decks at 0600. Eighty Vals, 54 Kates and 36 Zeros followed up.

The ships lying at anchor at Pearl Harbor were charged to keep a 'Condition 3' state of preparedness. Every fourth gun was supposed to be manned. But as America still regarded herself precariously at peace, none of the main guns was manned and the ammunition for the machine-guns was in locked boxes. The keys were in the charge of officers – some of whom were not even on duty.

A boatswain's mate saw between 20 and 25 aircraft approaching at 0730 but he could not see who they belonged to. All doubt was dispelled when the first bomb dropped just before 0800. Pearl Harbor's naval commander, Admiral Husband E. Kimmel, got the news of the attack three minutes later. Naval air commander, Rear-Admiral Bellinger, broadcast the words that were to smash the isolationist grip on America: 'Air Raid, Pearl Harbor, this is no drill!'

Even the ambitious Yamamoto could scarcely have hoped for a more total surprise attack. The US Pacific Fleet was caught with its pants well and truly down. Blunders and bad luck brought about this American debacle. One certain blunder was when two NCOs, manning a radar station, saw Japanese planes closing in and watched them for 40 minutes. They tried to raise the alarm by telephone, but

failed to contact anybody who believed their report. USS *Ward* gave
another warning at 0645 when she sank a midget submarine at the
mouth of Pearl Harbor. This too was ignored.

'Tora–Tora–Tora!' (Attack, attack, attack!) Commander Mitsuo
Fuchida, in charge of the first wave, signalled to his airmen at 0749.
Six minutes later the bombs began to fall. Their target was Battleship
Row – eight battleships at the SE of Ford Island. Low-flying torpedo
Kates roared in on the hapless ships. Four of them were holed or
damaged in five minutes. While the Kates punished the vessels
below the waterline, Vals were busy smashing decks, bridges and
gun turrets. Other Kates were finishing off the job with high-level
bombing.

The initial attack inflicted shattering losses on the Pacific Fleet.
USS *Arizona* (32,600 tons) blew up and snapped in two. More
than 1,000 men were drowned. The carnage continued when three
torpedoes smashed into *Oklahoma* (29,000 tons). She turned over
– imprisoning what was left of her crew below decks. When holes
were later cut in her bottom only 32 survivors crawled out. A total
of five hits – four torpedo, one bomb – put paid to the 31,800-ton
West Virginia, while the *California* (32,600 tons) blazed for three days
after fires reached her fuel tanks. Then she sank.

USS *Nevada* (29,000 tons) tried to steam out of the harbor, but
Japanese bombers caught her and she finally beached on a mudflat at
the entrance to the harbor. *Maryland* and *Tennessee* escaped relatively
lightly. They were shielded from torpedoes by *Oklahoma* and *West
Virginia*, which were moored on the seaward side. The 33,100-ton
flagship of the US Pacific Fleet, *Pennsylvania*, was in drydock and
was more or less unscathed at the end of the attack.

The old battleship *Utah* had been in use as a target ship for some
time before the Japanese attack. Denuded of her superstructure,
from the air she looked like an aircraft carrier. Japanese pilots
expended valuable torpedoes on this worthless relic.

At the NW shore of the harbor Japanese aircraft damaged the
light cruiser *Helena* and the seaplane tender *Curtiss*, while the light
cruiser *Raleigh* was crippled. The minelayer *Oglala* was sunk. The
destroyers *Shaw*, *Cassin* and *Downes*, the light cruiser *Honolulu* and
the repair ship *Vestal* all suffered damage.

While the Pacific Fleet in the harbor was being pulverized, the
airfields on the mainland were also taking a hammering. At the US
Marine Corps' Ewa Field were 49 airworthy planes. By the time the

Japanese were through with them only 16 remained intact. Kaneohe was a flying-boat base equipped with 36 Catalinas. After the attack an incredible 27 were complete write-offs while six others were severely damaged. This was one of the most punishing attacks on air bases in the Second World War. Of 148 first-line naval aircraft, at least 112 were destroyed, as were 52 out of the 129 Army planes. Thirty-eight American planes did take off. Ten of them were shot down.

The first Japanese wave then departed. Its attack had lasted 25 minutes. In that time thousands of American lives had been lost and millions of dollars worth of strategic weaponry destroyed. But there was more to come.

At 0845, 36 Zekes, 54 torpedo Kates and 80 high-level Kates provided Japan's second wave. But now the Americans had woken up and were a little more prepared. Shore batteries opened up as did still-serviceable ships' guns. Japan lost only nine planes in the first wave. In the second the score rose to 20 in return for little effect – its value being confined to finishing off already crippled installations. The submarine base escaped unscathed as did the fuel depot. Here was stockpiled almost as much oil as Japan had in her entire reserves.

President Roosevelt spoke of the 'day that shall live in infamy.' If it was, it was also a day of appalling military cost to the United States. The Japanese had lost 29 aircraft and 55 men. For this meager expenditure 2,403 soldiers, sailors, airmen and civilians had been killed, 164 planes destroyed and six battleships and three destroyers sunk, while a number of others had been badly damaged. Apart from the dead, the Japanese left 1,178 wounded Americans in Pearl Harbor. The only section of the US Pacific Fleet to escape damage was its carrier force. It was not at Pearl Harbor at the time of the attack.

If the Japanese had sent in a third wave – as Cdr Fuchida wanted – there is little doubt that they could have totally devastated Pearl Harbor. But Fuchida did not have his way. Vice-Adm. Nagumo, the task force commander, believed that he and his men had done more than a good day's work and the effectiveness of the strike had certainly surpassed all expectation. His force turned tail and settled down to a quiet journey home to Japan.

At 1347 Washington time, news of the attack reached Cordell Hull. Abruptly breaking off the now pointless diplomatic wrangle he unceremoniously dismissed Nomura from his presence.

The isolationist grip on America was at last smashed and she was now at war with Japan. The attack on Pearl Harbor, while brilliantly successful in itself, unleashed the might of the US military machine against Japan, as well as her German and Italian partners. For Japan the end would not come until she was utterly demoralized and Hiroshima and Nagasaki had been flattened by the atom-bomb. The entry of America into the war ensured the eventual defeat of fascism in both theaters.

Singapore (1942)

C. C. M. Macleod-Carey

It was Friday 13, February 1942 and I was watching the sun rise from my Command Post on top of Mount Faber, Singapore. The rays from the red orb of the sun radiated in ever widening shafts of red; just like the old 'Rising Sun' flag of Japan used to be.

I remember that I was feeling pretty gloomy at the time but this evil omen gave me an uncomfortable sense of impending doom. Singapore at that time was obviously in its death throes and there seemed to be very little future in it. The Japanese Army had driven right down the length of Malaya and the city was closely besieged by a ruthless and efficient enemy.

About midnight the following night, a signal came from HQ at Fort Canning saying an unidentified ship had been located just outside the minefield covering the entrances to Keppel Harbour and that no British ship was in the area. I was at that time second-in-command of the 7th Coast Artillery Regiment covering Keppel Harbour with its powerful armament of 15-in, 9.2-in, 6-in and a host of other smaller weapons. There was another similarly equipped regiment defending the Naval Base at Changi. I rang up the Port War Signal Station, our line with the Navy, which was manned by sailors. There was no reply and we discovered later that it had been evacuated but for some reason no one had informed us. I then ordered the 6-in batteries at Serapong, Siloso and Labrador to sweep the area with their searchlights. Almost immediately a ship which seemed to be of 8,000 tons was illuminated at a range of 7,000 yards, just outside the minefield. We challenged the ship by Aldis lamp but the reply, also by lamp, was incorrect.

Fortunately, in order to assist in this sort of situation, the Navy had posted an excellent rating who was standing by my side. We had a copy of *Jane's Fighting Ships* and the rating pointed to a photograph of a Japanese landing craft carrier and said, 'I reckon that's it, sir.' I gave the order 'Shoot' and within seconds all six 6-in guns opened up with a roar. The guns had been permanently sited, and even without radar, which had not been installed, their instruments and range-finding gear were so accurate that preliminary ranging was unnecessary. Direct hits were scored at once. Flames, sparks and debris started flying in all directions. The crew could be seen frantically trying to lower boats but it was all over in a matter of minutes, after which the ship just disappeared into the sea.

This action was reported to Fort Canning but it is strange that it has never, so far as I know, been mentioned in an official account. Most likely the record was lost together with a good many other documents in the subsequent events after the surrender of Singapore.

Next morning we were ordered to fire the guns at the very large number of oil tanks situated on the islands around Pulau Bukum about 3.5 miles from Keppel. Something like 200,000 tons of oil were set on fire. After that we were ordered to blow up all the guns. This was achieved by placing a charge of gelignite in the breech of each gun and another in their magazines. Time fuses were lit and the resulting explosions were pretty impressive.

Singapore in its death throes has been described in all its harrowing details by a good many writers. It is not a pretty story but the overriding factor of which everyone was painfully conscious was that the supply of water had just about dried up. In fact, troops were having to break into houses to get at the water remaining in the cisterns.

On the evening of 15 February, the gunners manning the Command Post on Mount Faber had been joined by a small Indian Commando unit and were holding a line across the main road near Keppel Golf Course below Mount Faber. At about sunset we distinctly heard Japanese troops farther up the road shouting 'Banzai!' 'Banzai!' 'Banzai!' Shortly afterwards orders were received from Fort Canning that we were to cease fire and we were informed that the great fortress of Singapore had surrendered. The Coast

Artillery had done its best and the fact is that the power and efficiency of its armament had the effect which it was designed for. It was exceedingly unlikely that the Japanese naval forces would be so rash as to make a frontal attack on Singapore because it is doubtful if they would have survived the encounter.

The plans for countering the expected invasion of Malaya by the Japanese were based on this factor and they were well conceived. The 11th Indian Division was poised on the frontier of Malaya and Thailand in December 1941, and Operation Matador was to send 11th Indian Division into Thailand and occupy the beaches at Singora and Sungei Patanie before the Japanese landed. British officers dressed in plain clothes and riding bicycles had been sent into Thailand to reconnoiter the area, where they met Japanese officers doing precisely the same thing. Air reconnaissance had reported large numbers of Japanese transports heavily escorted by warships and yet Operation Matador was called off for political reasons. So we got off to a bad start and our troops were caught on the 'wrong foot'. It soon became apparent that Japanese methods of warfare were totally different from ours and we had an awful lot to learn.

Part of my job was to direct the fire of the coast guns on to landward targets. It was mostly harassing fire, sometimes at the request of the Army and sometimes at targets picked at random, such as likely landing places on the north and west side of Singapore Island. There was no possible means of observing and correcting the fall of shot at 27,000 yards (15.3 miles) or more, so what the results were, goodness only knows. The only live Japanese I saw was a little perisher perched on top of a telescopic mast where he was probably spotting for his own guns. He was about three miles from where I was watching with my binoculars and just behind the grandstand of the racecourse near Burkit Timah. I turned the Connaught 9.2-in battery on to him and fired about 30 rounds. The little man disappeared in a cloud of smoke, dust and debris most of which came from the grandstand. Coast Artillery was not designed for this job but it certainly made a lot of noise, particularly the 15-in guns, whose flashes at night were quite spectacular. It was all a matter of firing at map references and hoping for the best.

I am anxious to dispel the myth that the Coast Artillery did not turn round and shoot at the enemy, so I propose to deal with each of the main batteries in turn.

The searchlights were manned by locally enlisted Malays who

deserted overnight the day before the surrender. They just vanished – with one exception. He was a half-caste whom we promoted to Bombardier because he spoke English and Malay fluently and was very useful. He stayed and the curious thing is that he reported to me a month later in Colombo (Ceylon) and asked me if he could be sent back to Malaya. Intelligence grabbed him, gave him a course of training and, eventually landed him with a wireless set on the coast of Malaya. I hope he survived.

The following is an account of the actions of the Coast Artillery batteries.

Faber Fire Command

Pasir Laba Bty.   Fired at the Japanese crossing Johore Strait in boats but the battery was a sitting duck for the Japanese who brought up mortars and lobbed bombs from concealed positions until the battery was put out of action. The guns were blown up and the detachments withdrew.

Buona Vista Bty.   When Vickers installed the two 15-in guns in 1938 they fitted Magslip cables that were too short for all-round traverse. These cables carried an electric impulse from the Plotting Room to actuate the dials on the guns. The result was that stops were put on the traversing arcs of the guns which prevented them from pointing inland. The Japanese broke into the battery area but were driven out by the gunners and Australian infantry. The guns were then blown up and the personnel marched to Mount Faber and next day were attached to an infantry battalion with their battery CO Major Phillip Jackson.

Siloso and Labrador Btys.   Both batteries fired a good deal of HE at Japanese troops advancing along the coast road through Pasir Panjang. It was reported to me by an infantry sergeant that the guns had caused a lot of Japanese casualties.

Serapong and Silingsing Btys.   Owing to hills and buildings, they were not well sited to fire inland and I do not know whether they actually fired or not. It is possible that they fired counter-battery programs.

Connaught Bty.   The three 9.2-in guns fired a considerable amount of ammunition including all their 90 HE rounds. Targets which I know were engaged included Johore Bahru, right across Singapore Island, where the Japanese had their HQ, possible landing places on the south bank of Johore Strait, a tank attack on the Bukit Timah road, Tengah Airfield, Jurong road and the Japanese artillery spotter already mentioned. Also counter-battery programs.

Changi Fire Command

Most of the action took place on the western side of the island. It is difficult to obtain accurate information on this Fire Command but it is obvious that the guns could only in many cases have been fired at extreme range.

Johore Bty. I do know that the three 15-in guns fired a great deal of their AP ammunition, notably at Johore Bahru and the reservoir area. They had all-round traverse but they had to knock down some of the concrete emplacements in order to get the shields round. Colonel Masanobu Tsuji, Chief of Staff Japanese Twenty-Fifth Army (Lieutenant General Tomoyuki Yamashita), records coming under their fire on the newly captured Tengah Airfield (11 February). Abandoning his car, he was blown into a ditch and watched the 50-ft-wide shell-holes appear around the drainage pipe he crawled into.

Tekong Bty. The three 9.2-in guns fired at several targets including the 400 Japanese landing on Pulau Ubin island.

Counter Battery An organization was hastily set up with OPs (observation posts) on the tops of high buildings such as the Kathay Building and other places. Bearings of enemy gun flashes were fed into an operation room, probably in Fort Canning.

There must have been plenty of enemy batteries to neutralize. The Japanese did not make great use of their artillery in their advance through Malaya, relying mostly on their infantry guns and mortars which they were very expert at handling. For the final assault on Singapore Island they deployed a very large concentration of artillery which they managed somehow to transport all the way down the peninsula. Japanese Army engineers excelled in repairing broken bridges. They brought up a considerable amount of heavy artillery which, judging by the effect of their shells, must have been up to 6-in caliber. Their preparatory bombardment (from 440 guns) before crossing Johore Strait was almost of First World War proportions.

One was constantly aware that once the small supply of HE was used up the guns could only fire armor-piercing (AP) projectiles.

These are made with very thick, hard steel walls and nose, designed to penetrate the thick armor-plate of a warship without collapsing. They have a delay-action fuse fitted to the base of the shell. The effect is that the shell detonates inside the ship and, as the quantity of ammatol or lyddite explosive is comparatively small, due to the thickness of the walls, the shell casing breaks up into very large chunks of steel. These smash up boilers, steam pipes, electric cables and machinery and generally create havoc inside the ship. As a man-killing instrument of warfare AP ammunition is not very effective. I expect the shells with a high angle of descent drilled a hole about 20 ft deep and there was none of the fragmentation which is essential for antipersonnel requirements.

It is interesting to indulge in that well-known pastime of hindsight and wisdom after the event. The lessons of Singapore were learnt and applied with considerable urgency in Ceylon. Colombo and Trincomalee were the last remaining bases for the Royal Navy in the Far East and were vitally important. The following measures were taken and, had they been applied in Singapore, it is reasonable to suppose that the Coast Artillery could have been more effective.

1 The post of C-in-C and Governor-General was created and ably carried out by Admiral Sir Geoffrey Layton. This ensured there was little likelihood of politics rearing its ugly head and cramping the style of the Service Chiefs in the way that it did in Malaya. The atmosphere in Ceylon was electric – 'There is not going to be another Singapore here.'

2 Both Colombo and Trincomalee had quite powerful Coast Artillery of modern 9.2-in and 6-in guns. All guns were given all-round traverse and overhead cover against air attack.

3 Each Fire Command was given an armored, tracked vehicle which was fitted with a No. 19 wireless set, to act as a mobile OP for co-operation with the field army.

4 Permanent OPs were established round the perimeter of each port. These OPs had a permanent telephone line to an operation room.

5 Each coast bty had its own 40 mm Bofors AA gun manned by coast gunners.

6 Each Fire Command had on its establishment a fully equipped eight-gun 25-pounder field battery. This had the good psychological effect of identifying the coast gunners

with the field army instead of being out on a limb as they were in Singapore.

7 An expert in counter-battery work was sent down from India who organized a workable counter-battery organization. He also instructed the officers in that important aspect of artillery work.

8 The proportion of HE ammunition was augmented.

In conclusion it can be stated that the coast artillery did its job just by being there. Singapore was one of the most heavily defended ports anywhere and the existence of its enormously powerful artillery dictated the strategy of the war in those parts. The Japanese were fully aware of this and we knew that they knew, so the campaign started more or less exactly as it was expected it would. The Coast Artillery locked the front door and it was up to the field army to bolt the back door.

Santa Cruz (1942)

Michael Orr

In 1942, the seemingly unstoppable expansion of Japanese imperialism threatened to engulf the whole of SE Asia and even Australia. American forces in the Pacific fought desperately to stem the tide. The Battle of the Santa Cruz Islands was of vital importance. There was no clear victor at the time but it was to significantly affect the war in the Pacific. Why?

Between May and October 1942 a series of four naval/air battles in the western Pacific established that the aircraft carrier had replaced the battleship's supremacy in the world's fleets. The battleship era was by no means completely finished and a number of vital battleship actions were still to be fought, but the aircraft carrier had become the linchpin of the fleet. The battleship and every other type of warship were now its subordinates. This change vastly increased the potential of seapower. The ability of the battleship to influence a war directly was limited to a score of miles – the range of its guns. But the carrier was a far more flexible weapon – able to strike over hundreds of miles and influence events over huge areas.

The strategic problems which the two sides faced were very similar. Guadalcanal lay at the end of a long and difficult line of communication and competed with other areas for scarce resources. The Japanese were very slow to realize the island's importance, giving more priority to the war in China and the threat of a war with Russia. The Imperial Navy therefore was forced to make do with the troops already in the SW Pacific. On the American side, Guadalcanal had to compete with the Battle of the Atlantic and the need to supply Russia. And preparations were reaching a climax for the Operation Torch landings in North Africa. It was not surprising that the Marines on Guadalcanal were soon thinking of themselves as a forgotten army.

After several months of fierce fighting neither side wanted to risk their depleted fleets without the certainty of decisive victory. The Japanese chose to wear their enemy down until they could re-establish an effective superiority. The waters between the American base at Espiritu Santo, in the New Hebrides islands, and the Solomons were so heavily patrolled by Japanese submarines that the area was dubbed 'Torpedo Junction'. Henderson Field, near Lunga Point, was in the possession of the Americans. They took advantage of this to control the waters around Guadalcanal during daylight.

A pattern of operations was soon established. American convoys delivered supplies from Espiritu Santo to their garrison while day lasted, but withdrew at nightfall. Under the cover of darkness the 'Tokyo Express' of Japanese troop-carrying destroyers and cruisers would rush down 'the Slot' to land stores and reinforcements or bombard the American positions. But they would have to leave in a hurry in order to be out of range of avenging aircraft from Henderson Field before daybreak. Thus neither side was able to achieve a superiority in ground forces on the island. The Japanese were particularly short of supplies, rather than men. They had few landing craft and had to rely on fast destroyers and small boats. The Americans found fuel for Henderson's aircraft their greatest problem.

A series of skirmishes and minor battles established the Japanese superiority in night fighting and turned the water north of Guadalcanal into a wreck-strewn 'Ironbottom Sound'. An attempt by the Japanese to force through a larger convoy than usual resulted in another carrier battle on 24 August.

The honors of the Battle of the Eastern Solomons were fairly evenly shared. A Japanese light carrier, the *Ryujo*, was lost. The American carrier *Enterprise* was damaged and had to return to Pearl Harbor. The next weeks saw several successes for the Japanese policy of attrition. The carrier *Wasp* was sunk, and the carrier *Saratoga* and the battleship *North Carolina* damaged. At one time the Americans had only one carrier in the Guadalcanal area. Better news for the Americans came with the Battle of Cape Esperance on 11 October when a Japanese cruiser force was severely damaged in a night action.

By this time the Japanese had decided to break the stalemate on Guadalcanal, which was also delaying the progress of the New Guinea campaign. In mid-September Imperial Army and Navy Staffs agreed that: 'After reinforcement of Army forces has been completed, Army and Navy forces will combine and in one action attack and retake Guadalcanal Island airfield. During this operation the Navy will take all necessary action to halt the efforts of the enemy to augment his forces in the Solomons area.' The capture of the airfield was left to the Army. After its experience at Midway, the Navy was apparently chary of risking a major battle while the enemy had the use of an 'unsinkable aircraft carrier' – Henderson Field. During October the 'Tokyo Express' increased its work, with heavy bombardments of Henderson Field and other American positions. It brought the Japanese strength on the island up to 20,000 men.

The Americans were fully aware of their own danger. On 15 October Admiral Chester W. Nimitz, C-in-C in the Pacific, considered that his forces could not control the sea. Supplying American positions could be done, but only at great military cost. By 18 October Vice Admiral William F. Halsey had been appointed to succeed Vice Admiral Robert L. Ghormley as Comsopac (Commander, South Pacific Area). Halsey's reputation in the Pacific was second to none. He had commanded the carrier task forces which had first struck back at the all-conquering Japanese and in particular had commanded the group from which the Doolittle Raid on Tokyo was launched. His strategy was 'Kill Japs! Kill more Japs!' At last, with the Torch convoy on its way, Washington was prepared to increase its support of the South Pacific operations.

The Japanese had planned to capture Henderson Field on 21 October, but the unexpected strength of the American garrison (which rose to over 23,000 Marines and GIs) caused them to postpone the attack until 23 October. The delay did not do them much good. They lost over 2,000 men and all their tanks. However, on the 24th Admiral Isokuru Yamamoto, the Japanese naval C-in-C, warned his military colleagues that the fleet, which had been at sea since 11 October, was running dangerously short of fuel and would soon have to withdraw. The attacks on Henderson Field therefore continued and a false report of victory in the early hours of 25 October brought the Japanese fleet hurrying south, only to reverse their course as soon as the report was denied. At 1200, two Japanese carriers were spotted by a Catalina flying boat but they immediately turned away and so avoided the search aircraft of the American carriers.

Another night of doubt and indecision followed for both fleets. On land the Japanese mounted another attack, but were eventually forced to admit defeat. The first part of the Japanese plan had failed. The outcome of the land attack was so uncertain that the units of their fleet had been drawn much farther south than intended. On the night of 25/26 October elements of the Japanese navy were twice sighted and attacked by Catalinas. In his headquarters at Noumea, in New Caledonia, Admiral Halsey was in no doubt what his orders to his commanders at sea should be: 'Attack – Repeat – Attack!'

Task Force 64, led by Rear Admiral Willis A. Lee, in *Washington*, was responsible for protecting Guadalcanal from night bombardments and operated independently throughout the battle. During the night of 25/26 October, the battleship *Washington* was patrolling west of Savo Island. Task Force 16, under Rear Admiral Thomas C. Kinkaid, was based on the carrier *Enterprise*. Rear Admiral George D. Murray commanded Task Force 17 from the carrier *Hornet*.

Enterprise and *Hornet* were sister-ships, completed in 1938 and 1941 respectively. In October 1942 they were the last word in carrier design and represented the fruits of the USN's inter-war experience of aircraft carriers. With a displacement of 19,000 tons (*Enterprise*) and 20,000 tons (*Hornet*) they were capable of speeds up to 34 knots and could operate between 80 and 100 planes. Both ships were veterans of the Pacific war, having worked together on the Doolittle Raid to Tokyo and at Midway.

The battleship *South Dakota* of Task Force 16 was one of a new generation of fast ships. With a displacement of 35,000 tons, she was capable of 28 knots and had a main armament of nine 16-in guns. She was fresh from Pearl Harbor where her AA guns had been increased to include 68 of the new 40 mms in quadruple mounts and 78 20 mm guns. Captain Thomas L. Gatch, her commander, neglecting the conventional 'bull', had concentrated on gunnery practice. The battle that followed proved that he had made a trained and efficient fighting team of his inexperienced ship's company.

The Japanese divided their fleet into a number of smaller units as well, but on principles which differed significantly from those of the Americans. The two main elements were the Advance Force, under Vice Admiral Nobutake Kondo, in *Atago*, and the Striking Force under Vice Admiral Chuichi Nagumo. The Advance Force was intended for the close support of the troops on Guadalcanal and had been responsible for most of the night bombardments of the American positions during October. On 26 October it consisted of two battleships, four heavy cruisers and a destroyer screen. Originally two carriers had provided air cover, but *Hiyo* had developed engine trouble and had been forced to return to Truk on 22 October. This left only her sister ship *Junyo*, completed as recently as May. Both ships were converted passenger liner hulls. For their size, 24,000 tons, they carried a small complement of aircraft, just over 50, and were underpowered, being capable of only 25.5 knots.

The Striking Force to deal with any major interference by the American fleet, was sub-divided into a Carrier Group, under Nagumo, of three aircraft carriers and their screen, and a Vanguard Force, under Rear Admiral Hiroaki Abe, of two battleships, three heavy cruisers and a destroyer screen. The carriers *Shokaku* and *Zuikaku* were sister-ships, designed as fleet carriers to work with the *Yamato*-class super-battleships. They displaced 25,000 tons, but with engines capable of 160,000 SHP they had a speed of 34 knots. Able to handle air groups of over 80 planes, they had operated together at Pearl Harbor and the Coral Sea. Damage in the latter battle ensured that they missed Midway. *Zuiho* was a light carrier, originally designed as a submarine tender. Displacing 11,000 tons, she could reach 28 knots with up to 30 aircraft.

The Japanese practice of dividing their fleets into sections has been criticized. The fault lay not so much in the division itself but the way in which it was done. By separating the individual parts too much and dividing their carriers between the parts they generally ensured that only a fraction of their available carrier strength would be able to intervene in any battle. This happened at Midway and, to a lesser extent, at Santa Cruz. Within the main divisions of the fleet, the carriers operated as a unit, but without the support of other types of ship, save destroyers. Although this made it easier to co-ordinate aircraft operations, it meant that the carriers were exposed to air attack.

Once their carriers were sighted, all the Japanese eggs were in one basket. And they lacked the fearsome AA fire of the Americans.

At Midway four Japanese carriers were caught together and three were sunk. The fourth escaped temporarily because of a fortuitous rainstorm. On the other hand the Japanese, although they sighted one American carrier group at Midway, remained ignorant for a long time of the presence of another, stronger, group. A further Japanese disadvantage was that their carriers had restricted bridges and limited radio facilities. This made them unsuitable as flagships, yet they had to be used as such.

First light on 26 October came shortly after 0500, revealing a fine day, with just enough cloud in the sky to conceal a dive-bomber attack. The American carriers were by then north of the Santa Cruz Islands. They chose to approach Guadalcanal from that direction rather than risk encountering Japanese submarine patrols in Torpedo Junction. Their course was north-westerly and less than 200 miles ahead of them were the Japanese forces in a triangular formation. The Vanguard Group of the Japanese Striking Force was leading the carriers by 60 miles. One hundred miles to the west was the Advanced Force, with the carrier *Junyo* maneuvering independently even farther west. The Japanese forces were all steering northwards. Both sides were aware that the enemy's carriers were at sea, but neither knew the other's exact location. Delays in transmission meant that Kinkaid had not received the report of the Catalina which had attacked *Zuikaku* during the night. This was unfortunate because the overwhelming advantage in carrier battles went to the side which struck first. Kinkaid ordered an aircraft search from *Enterprise*. Sixteen Dauntless dive-bombers took off. Each was armed with a 500-lb bomb. They fanned in pairs to the north and west. One group saw a 'Kate' torpedo bomber on a similar mission and at 0617 the Vanguard Group, led by Admiral Abe, was sighted. There was no sign of the carriers until 0650. The first pair of scouts could not break through the fighter patrols. Then at 0740 another pair, having heard the sighting report and altered course, made an unobserved approach. They attacked the light carrier *Zuiho* and both scored a hit. A 50 ft hole in the flight deck made the carrier useless. But it was too late to prevent a strike taking off.

The 'Kate' spotted by *Enterprise*'s aircraft had identified a carrier task force at 0658. At 0700 a 65-strong force of 'Zekes', 'Kates' and 'Vals' flew off and another group was soon being ranged. The American carriers did nothing about their sighting reports until 0720. Even then, the attack was not co-ordinated. At 0730, 15 Dauntless, six Avenger torpedo bombers and eight Wildcat fighters left *Hornet*. *Enterprise*'s first strike consisted of eight Avengers and eight Wildcats and only three Dauntlesses. The carrier was by now critically short of dive-bombers. Six had not returned from the previous evening's attempt to find the Japanese carriers, six more were on anti-submarine patrol, and the 16 scouts had not yet come back. The *Enterprise*'s strike flew off at 0800 and was followed at 0815 by *Hornet*'s second strike – nine Dauntlesses, nine Avengers and seven Wildcats. With their targets nearly 200 miles away there was neither time nor fuel for the aircraft to circle the carriers until a concentrated strike could be built up. Squadrons flew in a long-drawn-out gaggle. As they flew they passed the incoming Japanese strike. Some Japanese fighters left their convoy to attack the *Enterprise* group. Four Wildcats and four Avengers were either shot down or severely damaged and forced back to the carrier. The size of the *Enterprise*'s strike had been halved at a cost of only three 'Zekes'.

The American fleet was expecting the Japanese strike. Every possible step was taken to avoid a disastrous carrier fire, such as that which had destroyed the *Lexington* at the Coral Sea. Aircraft were secured in the hangar deck, aviation fuel lines were filled with carbon dioxide, and damage control parties were on constant alert. Speed was maintained at 28 knots and around the carriers their escorts were poised to provide massive AA fire.

The first line of defense was the 38 Wildcats of the combat air patrol (CAP). This was directed from the *Enterprise*. But the officer in charge was new to his job, having recently replaced a Midway veteran whom Halsey had taken to Noumea. For some time the fighter-direction team could not distinguish between the American and Japanese air groups on their cluttered radar screens. It was 0857 before a clear picture emerged. The CAP was too near the fleet, and too late – only 10 miles out at 0906. Although the Wildcats claimed some victims, neither they nor the American gunners could break the co-ordination of the Japanese attack.

At about 0900 *Enterprise*'s group was hidden by a rain squall. This left *Hornet* – lacking the close support of a battleship like *South Dakota* – to face the full might of the Japanese attack alone. 'Val' dive-bombers began the assault, scoring one hit and two near-misses. The squadron commander, his plane having been hit, made no attempt to drop his bombs but kept on diving. The 'Val' bounced off the carrier's funnel and burnt through the flight deck. The dive-bombers suffered heavily, but their attack covered the approach of a squadron of 'Kate' torpedo bombers from astern. Two torpedoes crashed into *Hornet*'s engine-rooms and she slowed to a halt under a pall of black smoke. A sitting target, *Hornet* was hit by three more bombs and then a burning 'Kate' made a suicide run into the ship's port side. It was all over in 10 minutes. The Japanese had lost 25 planes, but the once-formidable *Hornet* was a listing, blazing wreck.

Meanwhile the American air groups were approaching the Japanese fleet. But their straggling formation had been disturbed by the fighters. They were unable to deliver a united attack, or even find the same target. Fifteen Dauntlesses from *Hornet* led the attack. The first wave of defending fighters was kept at bay by their escorting Wildcats but the Dauntlesses were then left without protection. At 0930 *Shokaku* and *Zuiho* appeared below and the main Japanese CAP above. Even so, 11 bombers got through and scored between three and six hits on *Shokaku*. The 1,000 lb bombs tore her flight deck apart and started a tremendous blaze in the hangar. But there were no torpedo bombers to finish the job. *Hornet*'s Avengers had lost touch with the rest of the strike and so *Shokaku* and *Zuiho* went unmolested as they limped towards Truk. The Avengers made contact with Abe's Vanguard Group, but they were so short of fuel that they could not continue to search for the carriers. At 0930 they made an unsuccessful attack on the cruiser *Suzuya*. The rest of the American aircraft also missed the carriers and attacked Abe's group. *Hornet*'s second wave damaged the cruiser *Chikuma* but *Enterprise*'s aircraft had no luck at all.

As the American aircraft turned for home the result of the battle was still very much in the balance. Two Japanese carriers were out of action, but the second strike from *Shokaku* and *Zuikaku* had not yet attacked. *Zuikaku* was ready to gather up the survivors of all three carriers and prepare another strike. *Junyo* was hurrying westwards and, as Nagumo's flagship *Shokaku* was out of action, he transferred command of flying operations to Rear Admiral Kakuji Kakuta on board *Junyo*. She was still more than 300 miles from the American task forces. Even so, Kakuta ordered a strike to commence. Her aircraft were to land on *Zuikaku* or *Shokaku* after the attack.

On the American side, *Hornet*'s fires had been brought under control, although at one stage the order to abandon ship had been given. By 1005 the 9,050-ton cruiser *Northampton* was ready to begin towing the carrier when an unsuccessful attack by a stray 'Val' disrupted operations.

Although Task Force 16 had not yet been attacked, it was the scene of increasing confusion. Overhead were stacked the surviving aircraft from both carriers. They were by now nearing the end of their fuel. At 1002 the destroyer *Porter* was torpedoed by a Japanese submarine while picking up the crew of a crashed aircraft. The *Porter* was so badly damaged that she had to be sunk by gunfire, her crew transferring to another destroyer, *Shaw*. A submarine was the last thing which any carrier wanted to encounter while forced to keep a straight course for aircraft to land.

Then (almost as soon as the landings started) the second Japanese strike was detected on the *South Dakota*'s radar. *Enterprise* suspended operations and prepared to defend herself. Fortunately this attack was not so well co-ordinated as that on *Hornet*. The dive-bombers arrived 20 minutes before the torpedo-bombers and were met by the heaviest AA fire yet seen in the Pacific War. *South Dakota*, only 1,000 yards from *Enterprise*, showed to perfection her crew's gunnery skills. She shot down 26 'Vals', *Enterprise* claimed another seven. But two bombs found their mark, damaging the flight deck and starting fresh fires in the hangar. But the torpedo-bombers were too far behind to deliver the final blow.

When they finally arrived they were attacked by the combat air patrol. One Wildcat pilot, Lieutenant Vejtasa, shot down six before he ran out of ammunition. About 14 'Kates' got through to the Task Force. Five of these were destroyed by AA fire. Then the surviving Japanese moved in on the luckless *Enterprise*, attacking on both sides. Full-speed maneuvering by her captain once more saved the carrier. One 'Kate' did not even try to launch its torpedo, but dived straight onto the forecastle of the destroyer *Smith*. The blazing ship used *South Dakota*'s wake to douse her fires and so survived the battle.

On board *Enterprise*, the ship's company worked with disciplined but feverish haste to clear the flight deck and complete the recovery of the circling aircraft before they ran out of fuel. The appearance of a submarine periscope made things more difficult. Then at 1101 *Junyo*'s aircraft appeared on *South Dakota*'s radar screen. Alerted by this, her gunners opened fire on six unidentified aircraft at 1110. These proved to be returning Dauntlesses. By the time that this mistake had been sorted out *Junyo*'s aircraft were hidden in the cloud over the Task Force. Twenty attacked in a two-minute flurry, but achieved only one near-miss on *Enterprise* and lost eight planes. At 1127 two isolated 'Vals' dived on *South Dakota* and the AA cruiser *San Juan*. One bomb exploded on *South Dakota*'s foremost turret, without penetrating the armor. But Captain Gatch was wounded by splinters and for a moment the battleship was not under command.

As *South Dakota* headed towards *Enterprise*, *San Juan* was hit astern and her rudder jammed. The tight formation of Task Force 16 was shattered as the ships maneuvered out of the way of their careering consorts. Both ships were soon under control and *Enterprise* was able to land aircraft again. But with her forward elevator out of action the carrier was slow in getting aircraft below and several planes were forced to ditch before their turn came. *Enterprise* launched a CAP, but did not attempt to renew the battle. All morning the carrier had been steering south-eastwards into the wind, but at 1400 she turned east. Admiral Kinkaid had decided that with only *Enterprise*'s limited capacity to operate aircraft he could not risk an offensive against an unknown number of Japanese carriers.

The Japanese still had two carriers left in the battle, but had lost over 100 aircraft. *Zuikaku* and *Junyo* collected the mixed assortment of aircraft and sent them off in penny packets. Kondo and Abe also increased the speed of their battleship squadrons, hoping to finish off the crippled American ships after nightfall.

The cruiser *Northampton* was inching *Hornet* to safety when they were spotted at 1515 by Japanese aircraft. *Northampton* cut her tow, leaving the stationary carrier an easy target for the approaching torpedo planes. One hit was enough to seal her fate. The order to abandon ship was given, but three more Japanese formations attacked before all the survivors had been taken off. Then *Hornet* showed the same endurance as her sister-ship *Yorktown* at Midway. Destroyers fired nine torpedoes into her and over 400 5-in shells.

But *Hornet*, burning from stern to stern, was still afloat when she was sighted by Abe's ships at 2120. The Japanese at least had the satisfaction of avenging the Doolittle Raid by giving the *coup de grâce* to the ship which launched it.

During the night, the Japanese carriers were once again attacked by Catalinas. It was not until the afternoon of the 27th that the Combined Fleet began its withdrawal to Truk.

At the end of the battle neither side had suffered decisive losses. The Americans had lost *Hornet* and a destroyer. *Enterprise, South Dakota, San Juan* and a destroyer had been damaged. No major Japanese unit had been sunk, but two carriers and a destroyer had been damaged. *Shokaku* was out of action for nine months. The Japanese also lost 100 aircraft, against American casualties of 20 planes destroyed in action and another 54 missing or damaged.

What was the final result of the battle? Admiral Samuel E. Morison claims in the Official History of the battle, 'The Struggle for Guadalcanal', that 'Measured in combat tonnage sunk, the Japanese had won a tactical victory; but other losses forced them back to the Truk hideout.' This is less than fair to the Japanese. Truk was no more a 'hideout' than Noumea, and the American fleet turned for home first. The real reason for the retirement of the Japanese fleet was the failure of their army to capture Henderson Field. The struggle for Guadalcanal reverted to its former pattern: supply runs by day and night and a long, hard fight on land. Eventually the Americans won the reinforcement battle and in February 1943 Japan evacuated the survivors of her garrison.

With the advantage of hindsight it would be easy to argue that the Battle of Santa Cruz made little difference to the final result. But this is to ignore the question of what might have been. After Santa Cruz the Japanese had four undamaged carriers and the Americans had only the damaged *Enterprise* and the escort carrier *Long Island* in the Pacific. Japan had the opportunity to exploit her carrier superiority and win the decisive victory which had escaped both sides. She failed to do so because, although she had the carriers, both aircraft and pilots were lacking.

The Japanese fleet, lacking both air cover and the striking power of the carrier, could not check the American daylight convoys. By the time the Japanese carrier fleet had been repaired and re-equipped it was too late to save Guadalcanal. When the two fleets next met, in the Philippine Sea in June 1944, Japan

could send only nine carriers and 430 aircraft against 15 carriers and 891 aircraft. Whether or not Santa Cruz was a setback
for the Americans it bought them enough time to ensure final
victory.

Kokoda Trail (1942)

John Laffin

One of the least known of all the campaigns of the Second World War is that of the Kokoda Trail over the Owen Stanley Mountains in Papua New Guinea. But among land battles it ranks with Stalingrad and the Burma Campaigns for sheer toughness, and with Stalingrad, Alamein and the Normandy landings in importance.

A no-holds-barred fight between the Australians and Japanese, the Kokoda Trail campaign – sometimes called the Battle of the Ranges – lasted seven months and put an end to the myth of Japanese infantry invincibility. It also saved Australia from invasion – with the naval battle of the Coral Sea – and gave Australian military history a name to place alongside Gallipoli and Tobruk.

After their attack on Pearl Harbor in December 1941 and their steam-roller successes in the Pacific and SE Asia, the Japanese turned their eyes to Australia. No matter how successful a landing on the Australian mainland might be, they first had to capture the islands to Australia's north. Lightly defended, New Britain and New Ireland quickly fell. Next on the list was New Guinea, whose northern part was Australian mandated territory, while the southern part, Papua, was Australian soil.

The capital, Port Moresby, was the Japanese target. On the southern coast of the island, it was the most vital supply link with Australia. A second force would take Milne Bay at the eastern end of

New Guinea and a third would menace the Bulolo Valley and another key settlement, Wau, in the north.

The first people to know of the Japanese arrival off the north coast, 63 air-miles from Moresby, were a lieutenant and a sergeant at Buna Government Station, who, on 21 July 1942, watched an enemy cruiser shell shore targets. The sergeant ran to the radio hut and on emergency frequency sent off his report:

A JAPANESE WARSHIP IS SHELLING OFF BUNA, APPARENTLY TO COVER A LANDING AT GONA OR SANANANDA. ACKNOWLEDGE, MORESBY. OVER . . .

Over and over again, the message was repeated, but Moresby did not acknowledge.

Soon it was too late to matter. The Japanese had landed their vanguard of 2,000 troops to begin a thrust across the forbidding mountains. There was little that generals in Port Moresby or their leaders in Australia could do.

The elite divisions of the volunteer Australian Imperial Force were not available at the time. The 6th and 7th were either on their way back from fighting German, Italian and Vichy French troops in the Middle East or regrouping in Australia, the 8th had been lost in the lightning Japanese conquest of Malaya and the 9th was Eighth Army's trump card in the first Battle of Alamein. Until the 6th and 7th Divisions could be brought in, the defense of Papua depended on militia battalions. The militiamen had not volunteered for service outside Australia, most were city conscripts and many considered they had been 'shanghaied' to Port Moresby without being told where they were going.

The men of the Australian Imperial Force (AIF) – volunteers to a man – despised the militiamen as 'chokos', chocolate soldiers. With some outstanding exceptions, morale was low in the militia units. In Moresby many were unloading stores from ships, digging slit trenches for air-raid defense and guarding airfields. Virtually untrained in jungle warfare, the most arduous of fighting, they rotted in tropical heat.

Meanwhile a formation known as 'Maroubra Force' (after a famous Sydney beach) commanded by Lieutenant-Colonel W. T. Owen was trying to stem the Japanese advance. The striking unit of this 'force' consisted of one grossly understrength battalion – the 39th – formed of a few hundred militiamen and stiffened by AIF reinforcements. Their average age was 18. If the Japanese could defeat them and take Kokoda airfield – the only way the defenders could receive adequate reinforcements and supplies – they might well be in Port Moresby before the AIF veterans could arrive.

The battle developing was to be fought in a terrible climate in jungles, swamps and mountains. The Owen Stanley range, which reaches a height of 13,000 ft, is a maze of ridges, spurs, valleys and rivers. Each big river is laced like a shoe with numerous small ones. The northern coast has flat and perpetually swampy ground, blanketed with dense and smelly rain forest which the sun never penetrates. The mountain jungles drip water continuously. Such tracks as exist are steep, muddy and treacherous. In places the jungle is thick with vines and creepers armed with spikes the size of fingers. Paths had to be hacked with machetes.

Vast areas are infested with malarial mosquitoes, leeches and other insects which burrow into the flesh and cause painful, itchy swellings. Here and there the jungle is broken by clearings of *kunai* – elephant grass. But because these were ideal for ambush, troops learned to avoid them.

Much fighting took place on a one-man front – the width of the track. Many Australians were killed or wounded by Japanese snipers, tied into position high up in the trees. They would allow perhaps a hundred troops to pass while they waited to pick off an officer or NCO. As a precaution the Australians abandoned badges of status and nobody was addressed by rank. Even senior officers were known by a makeshift codename. A CO might be 'Dick' or 'Curly' to his troops. The Japanese sniper who waited so patiently for a target was nearly always killed – as he knew he would be – by the troops he had allowed to pass.

The Japanese who landed at Gona and Buna trapped many Europeans at the plantations, missions and hospitals. Only a few escaped and crossed the mountains to safety. Most of those captured were murdered. In front of terrified natives, an Anglican mission party – two ministers, two women, two half-caste mission workers, a six-year-old boy and an army officer – were beheaded one by one with a sword – the boy last of all.

After several aggressive rearguard actions Col. Owen's battered battalion was forced back. When the forward Japanese troops met opposition they deployed and engaged while support moved in with machine-guns and mortars. With probing attacks the Japanese found out the width and depth of the defenses by drawing Australian fire. Stronger support units would then move around the Australian flanks to force a withdrawal or to wipe out the enemy by a rear attack. The Japanese often shouted, fired furiously, blew whistles and pulled noisily at the jungle in attempts to frighten the Australians into withdrawal. They sometimes shouted orders or requests in English to lure them into ambush, but without mastery of the Australian accent or slang this rarely worked.

The administration post of Kokoda – 1,200 ft above sea level and 45 miles from Port Moresby – possessed the only airfield between Port Moresby and the northern coast. To defend this vital place Col. Owen had about 80 men in all – 60 young soldiers and a handful of Papuans from the Papuan Infantry Battalion under Major Watson. This small exhausted force cheered mightily when they saw aircraft approaching with reinforcements. Then the planes sheered off, climbed steeply and vanished. Word had been flashed to them from Army HQ in Melbourne, 2,000 miles away on the mainland, that Kokoda had fallen. Had those planes landed the epic of the Kokoda Trail might never have happened.

That night 500 Japanese attacked Kokoda. In this first pitched battle on Papuan soil, attackers and defenders became mingled in the confused fighting. Col. Owen was mortally wounded. Maj. Watson, assuming command, extricated the survivors and withdrew to the native village of Deniki.

For several days the 39th, under Major Alan Cameron, fought a savage rearguard action. With malaria and dysentery adding to their casualties, the battalion was in poor shape by the time it reached Isurava. Here on 16 August, what was left of Maroubra Force was taken over by an AIF veteran officer, Lieutenant-Colonel Ralph Honner, who had been ordered hurriedly to the crumbling front.

Honner, with service in Libya, Greece and Crete, looked at his thin, gaunt and tattered men. They had been unable to change their clothing for weeks. Their boots were rotting on their feet. Despite great care, their Bren light machine-guns and Lee-Enfield rifles were rusting. When it got through, their food was bully beef and biscuits. They lived in continual rain without shelters or groundsheets. At night they shivered, blanketless, in the cold. Supplies were dropped from aircraft but much was lost in the jungle. Yet these men could still fight and Honner decided on a stand at Isurava. He had a few hundred men and his largest weapons were 3-in mortars firing a 10 lb shell. Against this puny force were three battalions of the Japanese 144th Regiment, with another full regiment, the 41st, coming up fast. Supporting them were a mountain artillery battalion and two engineer units – about 4,000 men in all.

Despite these odds, the Australians fought the Japanese hand-to-hand in a series of ambushes and raids for two weeks. One group of 39th sick and wounded were on their way down the trail to Moresby. Upon hearing that their battalion was fighting for its life they disobeyed orders, turned round and hurried back into action.

Another battalion placed under Honner's command, the 53rd, was not so valiant. Slow to move forward and reluctant to fight, it was removed from an offensive role after its CO was killed. Its men were made carriers and porters on the Kokoda Trail.

On 25 and 26 August, Major General Horii, the Japanese commander, launched a full-scale offensive. On the 28th the Japanese, shouting 'Banzai!' made frontal attacks on Australian positions. Violent hand-to-hand fighting followed. Horii did not know it then but he was too late to win the campaign.

The AIF had arrived at Isurava.

The 150 survivors of the 39th had left Isurava the day before the battle, fighting their way out down the trail. They were young, tired veterans who had held on for as long as they had been asked. The Japanese now faced men of the first AIF battalion to reach the battle – the 2/14th, soon joined by part of the 2/16th, both part of the 21st Brigade. On 29 August, Gen. Horii concentrated five battalions in a narrow valley for a decisive blow against the still heavily outnumbered Australians. Along the entire 350-yard Australian front he unleashed a storm of artillery shells, mortar bombs and continuous machine-gun fire; then wave after wave of infantry went in. The Australian veterans fought off every attack. One platoon repulsed 11 attacks of 100 or more men. It lost its commander and every NCO. A private soldier took command, with other privates acting as NCOs.

During the fighting on this day Sergeant R. N. Thompson led a fighting patrol of seven men to push the enemy back along the track. One of his men was 24-year-old Private Bruce S. Kingsbury, armed with a Bren and grenades. Seeing that the Japanese were getting ready for a fresh assault, Kingsbury charged them. Japanese machine-gunners opened fire on him from farther back but Kingsbury ran on, sweeping the enemy positions. The patrol finished what Kingsbury had begun and regained 100 yards of track – considerable in jungle warfare. While Thompson was preparing a holding position a Japanese sniper killed Kingsbury. He was awarded a posthumous VC. At another point Acting Corporal Charles McCallum – wounded three times – killed 40 Japanese in a brief, furious action while extricating the survivors of a forward platoon from a dangerous position. He won the Distinguished Conduct Medal.

The Australians held Isurava for four days before Japanese pressure became too great. The Australian commander, Brigadier A. W. Potts, could not challenge Horii's control of the upper spurs and ridges without weakening the defense of the main track, the Australians' lifeline route to Moresby. The 2/14 and 2/16th Battalions made a slow, deliberate withdrawal. A bloody bayonet charge checked the Japanese but their outflanking movements isolated parties of Australians. Those captured were killed on the spot.

Others finally reached safety after such privations that only a tropical, mountainous jungle can inflict. One badly wounded soldier crawled for three weeks on his hands and knees. Most wounded men were luckier, being carried to medical help by native porters – lauded by the Australian public as 'the Fuzzy-Wuzzy Angels'.

At Iora Creek an ever-thinning line of Australians killed 170 Japanese and kept their line intact before withdrawing to Imita Ridge, the last defensible point of the Owen Stanleys. Here they held while the Japanese dug in on the facing ridge – Iorabaiwa. Horii had a chance to smash through but again he was too late. The three battalions of a fresh AIF Brigade, the 25th under Brigadier K. W. Eather, relieved the exhausted 21st Brigade.

While the Japanese were striking for Port Moresby over the mountains a linked action was developing at Milne Bay, 200 miles to the east. The Royal Australian Air Force (RAAF) had established Kittyhawk fighter-squadrons there in July 1942 and the 7th Infantry Brigade (militia) and 18th Infantry Brigade, AIF – both under Major-General C. A. Clowes – were moved in to defend them. A few hundred Americans had also arrived. On 24 August a Japanese invasion got under way and troops and tanks landed from barges the following day.

On 4 September the first VC of the New Guinea campaigns was earned at Milne Bay by Corporal John Alexander French. When

Japanese machine-guns held up the advance, Corporal French ordered his section to take cover and with grenades rushed the first of a group of three machine-guns. He silenced the first, returned for more grenades and put paid to a second. Firing a Thompson sub-machine-gun he rushed the third gun and killed its crew. He died from wounds on the edge of the gunpit.

By 7 September, after much patrol fighting, Japanese naval attacks and RAAF strikes on enemy troop barges, the Japanese had lost the battle and at least 1,000 dead – mostly elite marine assault troops. Fighting was invariably savage. One Australian was found dead with 30 Japanese corpses around him. The heads of two had been smashed in with the butt of the Australian's sub-machine-gun.

Crackers with a slow-burning wick led a few Australians to their deaths. A Japanese would creep through the long grass, place a lighted cracker and then steal away and position himself. When the cracker exploded, an Australian would turn towards the sound and perhaps advance towards it. The Japanese sniper would see the sudden movement and have time to aim and fire. Here, as elsewhere in New Guinea, men often died without ever seeing the enemy in the impenetrable jungle darkness.

Milne Bay was the first clear-cut land victory over the Japanese anywhere in the war. Strategically it confined the main Japanese operations in Papua to the Buna–Kokoda area and spelt failure for the Japanese plans to capture Port Moresby.

This was not clear at the time and in the Owen Stanleys the Australian 25th Brigade was preparing for the counter-attack which would push the enemy out of the mountains. These men had already beaten the Foreign Legion in Vichy French Syria.

Using the Australian-made Owen gun, a 9 mm light sub-machine-gun for close quarter fighting, the Australian infantry soon dominated the valley between the Imita and Iorabaiwa ridges. For the first time the Australians had artillery – two 25-pounders painfully dragged up the tracks. Australian aircraft, for the first time able to help their infantry, destroyed the bridge over the wide, treacherous Kumusi River – cutting Horii's supply lines. On 26 September Horii, obeying an order from his HQ at Rabaul, began a withdrawal. Men too sick or weak to keep pace were simply left to die.

The Australian pursuit was governed by the ability of the RAAF to drop supplies. Ground troops rarely recovered more than 30 per cent of a drop. The track was so bad that, even without enemy opposition, a battalion would sometimes cover only a mile a day. Every day at noon, rain fell in solid sheets over the mountains, turning the tracks into narrow streams of black and yellow mud. Hidden in this mud were countless tree roots to catch the boots of tired soldiers. Steps cut into the track deteriorated into mudpools.

On one spur of Imita Ridge engineers cut and blocked with logs 2,000 steps – ironically nick-named the Golden Stairway. This was not the record number; Maguli Ridge had 3,400 steps.

The track was disheartening. For every 1,000 ft of altitude the troops climbed they dropped 600 ft to the start of the next ascent. Between Uberi and the crest of the Owen Stanley range the track climbed more than 20,000 ft in this switchback fashion. It crossed many rivers by log or vine bridges. At times it climbed or skirted precipices.

The temperature lurched from humid, oppressive heat to bitter cold. When not rain-drenched the soldiers were sweat-soaked. In these conditions a man was too old for jungle warfare at 30. The Japanese were so hungry that they frequently ate flesh cut from Australian or their own dead. But they often turned and fought back – on one occasion holding the Australians for eight days. Beheading or bayoneting captives, the Japanese remained a disciplined and formidable foe. Cleverly concealing their weapon pits which they made proof against mortar fire, they had to be prised out of every position.

Their food supply improved as they fell back to their bases. They could also use artillery, which the Australians were denied. The guns could not be taken across the ranges. But the Australian advance was irresistible and, on 3 November, they re-entered Kokoda.

To commemorate the recapture the Australian commander, Major-General G. A. Vasey, raised the Australian flag and presented medals to five natives for loyal and meritorious service. A great crowd of carriers assembled for the ceremony – the first of its kind in the campaign. 'Without your help', Vasey told the natives through an interpreter, 'we would not have been able to cross the Owen Stanleys.' All the carriers received gifts of knives and rami – the native kilt-skirt.

Vasey might have added that without Dr G. H. Vernon and Captain Herbert Kienzle the natives would not have been an effective force. Vernon had fought in the First World War as Regimental Medical Officer to the 11th Light Horse Regiment and had returned to Australia with the Military Cross. Stone deaf – from a bursting shell at Gallipoli in 1915 – he was working in Papua as a government medical officer when the war with Japan broke out. The Australian Government evacuated the women, children and older men. Although Vernon was 60, he refused to leave, even when threatened with arrest. Instead, he took upon himself the medical care and much of the organization of the native carriers between Owen's Corner – at the end of the motor road from Port Moresby – and on to Kokoda. His first dramatic act was to post himself to the 39th Battalion when he heard that the unit was temporarily without its medical officer. In this way he served through the first battle of Kokoda, patching up many wounded and treating the dying Col. Owen. He was one of the last four men out of Kokoda.

Resuming his work with the natives, Vernon – himself a strong mountain walker – kept the carrier line working. Everything that went up to the troops was carried on the backs of these natives. Unavoidably loaded and worked to the limit they came to love Dr Vernon. He saw to it that they had proper rest periods and treatment. Having taken supplies up, the natives became stretcher bearers and brought out many badly wounded men. On those tortuous tracks and crossing rushing rock-strewn rivers, eight men were needed for each human load. Carrying a stretcher in these conditions was an appalling task. Sometimes it had to be held at arm's length above the head. Yet the bearers always managed to be gentle and careful.

Herbert Kienzle – a rubber planter when war came – was also responsible for organizing and maintaining much of the native line of communication across the Owen Stanleys.

Strangely, Vernon got no official recognition for his extraordinary labors, which contributed in no small measure to his death in 1946, aged 64. Kienzle received an MBE, the lowest class of the Order of the British Empire.

From Kokoda, the Australian infantry pushed on steadily. At Gorari on 11 November two battalions of the 25th Brigade – 2/25th and 2/31 st – made fierce bayonet charges, killing 580 Japanese in fighting that lasted five days.

This action – by jungle warfare standards a major battle with serious casualties – demonstrated Gen. Vasey's tactical skill. By clever maneuvering he had caught the rarely surprised Japanese off guard. The victory precipitated the collapse of organized resistance outside the Buna–Gona beach-head. The able, determined Gen. Horii, in an effort to evade capture, tried to cross the white-water Kumusi River on a raft and was drowned when it overturned.

The last bitter phase of the fighting was fought at Buna, Sanananda and Gona in a vast morass of swamp, mud and battle-torn jungle. Many Australians, exhausted by combat, fever, lack of sleep and poor food went out on patrols with high temperatures. In November 1942 alone the evacuations numbered 1,500, but by now American troops were reinforcing the Australians. Their numbers and weight of firepower were decisive. In other parts of northern New Guinea fighting would go on until 1944 but the Battle of the Ranges was over.

The 39th Battalion, which had begun the Battle of the Kokoda Trail, was in at the end. Colonel Honner led it back over the mountains to victory in action at Gona.

On 23 January 1943, the Kokoda Trail campaign completed, the battalion held a roll call. Its strength amounted to seven officers and 25 men – out of a normal 800.

Stalingrad (1942)

Peter Young

By the end of 1941 the Russians, it is estimated, had already suffered about 4,500,000 casualties. It is idle to pretend that their long retreat was part of a subtle master-plan, though this myth was an article of faith to all good Bolsheviks while Stalin lived. Even so their heavy sacrifices had won the Russians time to organize new armies and by December 1941 the Germans had identified 280 rifle and cavalry divisions and 44 tank or mechanized brigades.

The great Russian winter offensive, designed to encircle the German Army Group Centre, had lost its momentum by mid-February. Fresh German divisions arrived to fill the gap torn by the Russians between Army Groups Centre and North, and the Germans, clad in the furs and winter clothing produced by Goebbels' appeal, made a gradual recovery. Then came the spring rains, and, both sides being stuck in the mud, there was a temporary halt.

On the ground the great Russian offensive had been indecisive, but in people's minds it had a tremendous importance. The veteran Russian generals, January and February, had lost none of their old skill; the new ones Zhukov and Koniev had also proved their worth. The myth of Teuton invincibility was exploded. Everywhere the men who were to face the German armies in the years ahead took heart. But despite all this Hitler himself had strengthened his personal position. His will-power, he could boast, had saved the day, when his staff-trained generals had wanted to take refuge in retreat. The

Führer was now his own Commander-in-Chief. General Halder, chief of the OKH, was no more than his personal chief of staff. By remote control this semi-educated former corporal conducted the operations involving millions of men, from his Headquarters, the *Wolfschanze*, at Rastenburg in East Prussia. On 5 April 1942 he issued Directive No 41 in which he outlined his plans for his summer offensive. His aim was 'to wipe out the entire defence potential remaining to the Soviets, and to cut them off, as far as possible, from their most important centres of industry.' All available German and allied forces were to take part in this task, but the security of occupied territories in western and northern Europe, *especially along the coast*, was to be ensured in all circumstances.

The plan was for Army Group Centre to stand fast while the armies in the north were to capture Leningrad and link up with the Finns, while those in the south were to break through into the Caucasus. Hitler considered that these aims could only be achieved one at a time and therefore meant to begin in the southern sector by 'destroying the enemy before the Don'.

The Russians too were thinking in terms of the offensive and, as preliminary operations, meant to launch local attacks at Leningrad, Demyansk, Orel, Kharkov, in the Donetz bend, and in the Crimea. On 12 May Marshal Timoshenko (South-West Front) began with a thrust near Kharkov, only to find that he had run into the main German striking force. With the concurrence of his political commissar, Nikita S. Krushchev, he asked Stalin to let him call off the offensive. This permission was refused, and when on 17 May the Germans struck back, his force in the Izyum bridgehead south of Kharkov was seriously compromised. On 19 May Stalin gave Timoshenko his belated permission to extricate his men, but the trap had sprung. In the fighting that followed 240,000 Russians were taken. And that was the end of Stalin's summer offensive.

For the Germans this was a great start to the campaigning season, but there was now a delay of two months while they overran the Crimea. Sevastopol, which had held out for eight months, fell to the Eleventh Army on 1 July.

It was not until 28 June that the main German summer offensive was begun by Army Group B. By 6 July the Second and Fourth Panzer Armies had taken Voronezh. Meanwhile, on 30 June the Sixth Army had pushed eastward from Kharkov to act as the southern jaw of a giant pincer movement. The bag produced by this encirclement fell short of 100,000 prisoners, and Hitler, so far from being grateful for a respectable victory, sacked von Bock and on 13 July gave command of Army Group B to Field-Marshal von Weichs. On the same day Hitler ordered Army Group A, with Fourth Panzer Army attached, to turn south, cross the lower Don and drive the Russians into a pocket round Rostov. The town fell on 23 July, but once again the Führer got less prisoners than he had bargained for. It was at this juncture that, most unwisely, he removed about half of the Eleventh Army for his Leningrad offensive. As in 1941 he was flouting the principle of concentration of force.

The early summer of 1942 had seen some revival of the old German successes – the rapid overrunning of the Crimea; the capture of Tobruk (21 June); the air offensive which seemed to be starving Malta into submission. Certainly Hitler had reason to be pleased with these successes, but they deluded him into believing that his strategic situation was rather better than was actually the case. On 21 July, in Directive No 44, Operations in Northern Finland, he stated his view that:

> The unexpectedly rapid and favourable development of the *operations against the Timoshenko Army Group* entitle us to assume that we may soon succeed in depriving Soviet Russia of the Caucasus, with her most important source of oil, and of a valuable line of communication for the delivery of English and American supplies.
>
> This, coupled with the loss of the entire Donetz industrial area, will strike a blow at the Soviet Union which would have immeasurable consequence.

He went on to say that the time had come to cut the northern supply route, the Murmansk railway, by which the Anglo-Saxon powers were supplying Russia. He assumed that Leningrad would be captured 'in September at the latest'.

In his next Directive (No 45), which dealt with the Caucasus offensive, he alleged that only weak forces from Timoshenko's Army Group had got back across the Don. 'We must expect them to be reinforced from the Caucasus.' In a perceptive moment he added: 'A further concentration of enemy forces is taking place in the Stalingrad area, which the enemy will probably defend tenaciously.'

The German successes continued in August, but already the troops were showing signs of tiredness and their tactics were becoming stereotyped. Marshal Chuikov (64th Army), who had his Second World War 'baptism of fire' on the Don Front in July, has some comments on their performance.

Observing how the Germans carried out their artillery preparation against the 229th Infantry Division's sector, I saw the weak points in their tactics. In strength and organization this artillery preparation was weak. Artillery and mortar attacks were not coordinated or in depth, but only against the main line of defence. I saw no broad manoeuvre with artillery cover in the dynamic of battle.

He goes on to say:

I was expecting close combined operations between the enemy's artillery and ground forces, a precise organization of the artillery barrage, a lightning-fast manoeuvre of shell and wheel. But this was not the case. I encountered the far from new method of slow wearing down, trench by trench . . .

The German tanks did not go into action without infantry and air support. On the battlefield there was no evidence of the 'prowess' of German tank crews, their courage and speed in action, about which foreign newspapers had written. The reverse was true, in fact – they operated sluggishly, extremely cautiously and indecisively.

The German infantry was strong in automatic fire, but I saw no rapid movement or resolute attack on the battlefield. When advancing, the German infantry did not spare their bullets, but frequently fired into thin air.

On the other hand the thoroughly efficient co-operation of the *Luftwaffe* showed the familiarity of the pilots with the tactics of both sides.

In modern warfare victory is impossible without combined action by all types of forces and without good administration. The Germans had this kind of polished, co-ordinated action. In battle the different arms of their forces never hurried, did not push ahead alone, but fought with the whole mass of men and technical backing. A few minutes before a general attack, their aircraft would fly in, bomb and strafe the object under attack, pinning the defending troops to the ground, and then infantry and tanks with supporting artillery and mortar fire would cut into our military formations almost with impunity.

Meanwhile, on the Leningrad front the Russians had made an unsuccessful attempt to break the German siege, but had at least forestalled the German attempt to capture the city.

In the south Army Group A (Field-Marshal von Kleist) had taken Maikop, but too late to prevent the complete destruction of the oilfield. German Jäger planted the Swastika on Mount Elbrus, but the Russians still held out in the passes of the Caucasus. By 21 August the Führer was already 'very agitated' by the lack of progress on that front. The Sixth and Fourth Panzer armies closed in on Stalingrad, but being compelled to detach troops to guard their flanks, were gradually brought to a halt by 6 September. At last the Russians seemed to be getting the measure of the invaders. Their losses in men and territory, though grievous, had been far less serious in 1942 than in the previous year. In terms of attrition the German position was by no means brilliant. Hitler's armies on the Eastern Front numbered some 3,138,000, excluding the Finns, while Stalin had 4,255,000 men in the field. Behind the German front the partisans were active, as Hitler tells us in Directive No 46 of 18 August.

In recent months *banditry in the East* has assumed intolerable proportions, and threatens to become a serious danger to supplies for the front and to the economic exploitation of the country.

By this time he had evidently resigned himself to the thought that the war was not going to be won that year:

By the beginning of winter these bandit gangs must be substantially exterminated, so that order may be restored behind the Eastern front and severe disadvantages to our winter operations avoided.

He expressed the pious hope that the confidence of the local population in German authority could be gained by handling them strictly but justly – a notion that would probably not have worked in the summer of 1941, and was certainly unrealistic in the autumn of 1942.

As the situation worsened, Hitler resorted to his old remedy of sacking generals. List was the first to go (9 September), and for two and a half months the Dictator actually commanded Army Group A in person: an extraordinary arrangement. The fact that his HQ, Vinnitsa in the Ukraine, was 700 miles in the rear of his front might have daunted a more professional soldier, but in Hitler's fantasy world such considerations went for little. On 24 September, after a series of fearful scenes, Halder was relieved as chief of OKH by General Zeitzler. Warlimont, whose position as Deputy Chief of the OKH staff gives his evidence considerable weight, assesses the Führer's state of mind at this period. He tells us of a briefing conference:

> Hitler fixed me with a malevolent stare and suddenly I thought: the man's confidence has gone; he has realized that his deadly game is moving to its appointed end, that Soviet Russia is not going to be overthrown at the second attempt and that now the war on two fronts, which he has unleashed by his wanton arbitrary actions, will grind the Reich to powder. My thoughts ran on: that is why he can no longer bear to have around him the generals who have too often been witnesses of his faults, his errors, his illusions and his day dreams; that is why he wishes to get away from them, why he wishes to see people around him who he feels have unlimited and unshakeable confidence in him.

Colonel-General Halder was a typical German General Staff officer of the old school, a thorough professional soldier. Dismissed by Hitler he wrote in his diary 'My nervous energy is used up and his is not as good as it was. We must part.' No doubt it was a relief to go. Hitler now prepared to run the army on his own lines. It was 'necessary to educate the General Staff in fanatical belief in an ideal.' The Army 'rather than relying on technical competence . . . must be inspired by the fervour of belief in National-Socialism.'

For a time the new chief of staff, Zeitzler, enjoyed great popularity with Göring and the rest of Hitler's courtiers. He certainly began well, with an address to the officers of OKH in which he said:

I require the following from every Staff Officer: he must believe in the Führer and in his method of command. He must on every occasion radiate this confidence to his subordinates and those around him. I have no use for anybody on the General Staff who cannot meet these requirements.

This was to be the atmosphere at HQ during the siege of Stalingrad, in that winter when the tide of war had at last reached the turn.

November was a black month for Hitler. The news of El Alamein, followed by that of Torch, made it clear that sooner or later the Axis forces in North Africa were going to be crushed. This news came when Hitler was on his way to address the 'old comrades' of the Nazi party in the Munich Beer Cellar. By way of offsetting the bad tidings he could think of nothing better than to assure the veterans that he was now master of Stalingrad, where the doubtful battle had been raging since early September. On 19 November the Russian Fifth Tank Army broke through the Roumanian Third Army North of that city. By the 22nd the Sixth German Army and about half of General Hoth's Fourth Panzer Army were encircled; 280,000 men were in mortal peril.

This was indeed a reversal of fortune, for in the September days there had been desperate fighting at Stalingrad, and the Russians had barely clung to the west bank of the Volga. Marshal Chuikov, who bore much of the responsibility, had decided, as a result of his experiences against 'the Whites' in the Civil War and his study of enemy tactics,

that the best method of fighting Germans would be close battle, applied night and day in different forms. We should get as close to the enemy as possible, so that his air force could not bomb our forward units or trenches. Every German soldier must be made to feel that he was living under the muzzle of a Russian gun, always ready to treat him to a fatal dose of lead.

They reduced No Man's Land to the throw of a grenade. Strongpoints were fortified in the centre of the city and garrisoned by 50 or 100 men. Buildings changed hands not once but many times. From 17–20 September, for example, there was a fierce struggle for an enormous building on the southern outskirts of the town, the grain elevator. Colonel Dubyanski (OC Guards Infantry Division) reported by telephone to Chuikov: 'The situation has changed. Before, we occupied the upper part of the elevator and the Germans the lower part. Now we have driven them out of the lower part, but German troops have penetrated upstairs and fighting is now going on in the upper part.'

Stubborn fighting marked the resistance of improvised fortresses without number. Archetype of these was the defence of 'Pavlov's House', a key strongpoint in the central district held by a handful of men belonging to Rodimtsev's 13th Guards Infantry Division. Sergeant Jacob Pavlov and two of his men, Alexandrov and Afanasiev, were Russians. The rest of his garrison were Subgayda and Gluschenko from the Ukraine; Mosiyashvili, and Stephanashvili, both Georgians; Turganov, an Uzbek; Murzayev, a Kazakh; Sukba, an Abkhazian; Turdiev, a Tajik; and Ramazanov, the Tartar. It was a roll call of the nationalities of the USSR! Chuikov tells us that the Germans 'unleashed a torrent of bombs and shells on to the house', which was held for more than 50 days, without sleep and rest, and remained impregnable to the end. For his dogged defence Pavlov became a Hero of the Soviet Union.

All through October the struggle went on. Those were the darkest days. But somehow the Russians hung on. Reserves were fed in across the Volga as they reached the front and eventually Paulus' seemingly inexhaustible reserves could do no more. On 29 October the battle began to die down, and the next day, apart from exchanges of firing, there was no action. On the 31st the 62nd Army counter-attacked from its narrow strip of land along the banks of the Volga. Advances were measured in yards, but the attack was a great success and retook part of the Krasny Oktyabr factory.

Early in November the temperature dropped sharply and ice began to appear on the river. On 11 November Paulus launched a new attack, but this too was held in two days of stubborn fighting. The *Luftwaffe*, which in October had been flying as many as 3,000 sorties a day, could no longer manage more than 1,000.

And thus it came about that when on 19 November the Russians counter-attacked on three fronts at once a trap closed behind the Germans which cost them 22 divisions.

Hitler entrusted to Field-Marshal von Manstein the task of rescuing Sixth Army, but he refused Paulus permission to try and break out. The supply difficulty became acute. Petrol, shells, and firewood were hard to come by. After Christmas the bread ration was cut by half to 50 grammes a day. Many of the men existed on watery soup fortified with the bones of horses they dug up. Colonel Dingler tells us that 'As a Christmas treat the Army allowed the slaughtering of 4,000 of the available horses.' This was no help to the armoured and motorized Divisions.

The cold was bitter in December and the ground was too hard to dig. Aeroplane tyres stuck to the runways. If a position was abandoned the soldiers found themselves without dugouts or trenches when they got back to their new line. Without petrol the armour could not manoeuvre to repulse the Russian attacks. The apertures of tanks became blocked with ice. Men froze to death in their vehicles.

But all hope was not yet gone. On 9 December it was announced that Fourth Panzer Army, which had been reinforced, would start its relieving attack next day, and by 16 December distant gunfire could be heard. Plans were made to break out as soon as Colonel-General Hoth's spearhead should be within 20 miles.

The plans for the relief were carefully examined by Field-Marshal von Manstein. It was decided that Hoth, himself 'an officer with an excellent reputation', should make his thrust from the direction of Kotelnikovski some 60 miles SE of Stalingrad. At Nizhna Chirskaya on the Chir the Germans were only 25 miles away, but an attack from this direction would involve a crossing of the Don, which von Manstein rightly rejected as too hazardous an operation.

From the first Hoth met with furious opposition from strong Russian forces of armour and infantry under General Vatutin. It took the Germans a week to fight their way forward 30 miles, but at the end of it they succeeded in capturing two crossings over the river Aksay by a *coup de main*. They were still 45 miles short of the beleaguered army.

At this moment Marshal Zhukov launched a massive offensive on the middle Don, tore a 60-mile gap in the front of the Italian Eighth Army, and thrust southwards towards Rostov, threatening the communications of Field-Marshal von Kleist's Army Group in the Caucasus. Von Manstein had nothing up his sleeve. To check the Russian flood he was compelled to take 6th Panzer Division from Hoth's army. On paper the latter still had two panzer divisions, though their tank strength was now down to 35. Desperate fighting during the next week brought no real progress, partly perhaps because Paulus himself remained inactive. Had he also attacked, the Russians might not have been able to concentrate against 57th Panzer Corps, Hoth's spearhead. Again lack of petrol may have been the key to the tactical situation.

On Christmas Eve the Russians counter-attacked the Aksay bridgehead in great force, and, keeping up the pressure night and day, had retaken both bridges by the 26th. The decimated Germans withdrew southwards.

> The characteristic features of this dramatic battle were mobility, quick reaction and utter perseverance on both sides. Tanks were the main weapon used and both sides realized that the main task of the armour was to destroy the opposing tanks.
>
> The Russians did not stop their attacks when darkness fell, and they exploited every success immediately and without hesitation. Some of the Russian attacks were made by tanks moving in at top speed: indeed speed, momentum and concentration were the causes of their success. The main effort of the attacking Russian armour was speedily switched from one point to another as the situation demanded.

Von Mellenthin concedes that 'the tactical conduct of the battle by the Russians was on a high level.' By 26 December, 57th Panzer Corps had 'literally died on its feet'.

No power on earth could now save the Sixth Army, least of all the *Luftwaffe*, which Göring had promised would keep Paulus supplied. On 15 January the Hungarian Second Army disintegrated, and far away in the north on that same day the German siege of Leningrad was broken. On the 22nd General Zeitzler, urged on by von Manstein, plucked up his courage to ask Hitler whether Sixth Army should now be authorized to capitulate, only to be told that the army should fight to the last man. But Sixth Army had reached the end of its tether. On 31 January Paulus, who had been promoted Field-Marshal only the previous day, surrendered. Hitler had lost 20 German divisions, of which three were armoured and another three motorized, besides two Roumanian divisions – whom their allies had struck off the ration strength a fortnight before the end!

The Germans lost 60,000 vehicles, 1,500 tanks and 6,000 guns. Of the 280,000 men encircled 42,000 wounded, sick and specialists were evacuated by air; 91,000 surrendered. Of these, it is thought only 6,000 lived to see their homes once more.

It has often been suggested that Hitler should have given Paulus permission to break out. But had this been attempted it is difficult to imagine it being successful. We know that petrol for the six mobile divisions was lacking. The remaining 16, with the possible exception of the Roumanian cavalry division, were comparatively slow-moving and had eaten most of their horses by the end of December. If Hitler and his entourage had withdrawn Sixth Army at the end of October, when it was clearly stuck, a large part of it might have made a reasonably orderly retreat. By the time von Manstein tried to break through, there was really very little hope of pulling Paulus back, even had Hitler consented to such an attempt. Mussolini, more clear-sighted about other people's troubles than his own, commented that Stalingrad 'makes clear to the minds of the masses the great attachment of the Russian people to the regime – a thing proved by the exceptional resistance and the spirit of sacrifice.'

No disaster suffered by the Allies in a war where disasters had not been lacking could be compared with the blow Hitler received at Stalingrad. And he was soon (13 May) to receive another at least as costly in Tunisia. Truly the tide had turned in those November days of 1942 when Montgomery emerged victorious from the field of El Alamein; when Eisenhower's host set foot on the shores of North Africa; and when, after an epic defence, the Russians encircled their besiegers on the banks of the Volga.

El Alamein (1942)

J. F. C. Fuller

The first three weeks of July, 1942, on the El Alamein line [in North Africa] were devoted to attack and counter-attack. Rommel's one aim was that the front should not become static, and Auchinleck's aim was to make it so. The latter won the tussle and the outcome of the campaign became a question of reinforcements and supplies.

Faced with this situation, Rommel calculated that up to mid-September the advantage would be his; but in this he was badly deceived, because from the end of July on Auchinleck switched the main weight of his air offensive from the forward positions to the ports of Mersa Matruh, Bardia, and Tobruk, which left Rommel with Benghazi – 680 miles away – as his nearest secure base of supply. The results were that by the middle of August he was still short on establishments of 16,000 men, 210 tanks, 175 troop carriers and armoured cars and 1,500 vehicles; his army consumed double the amount of supplies that crossed the Mediterranean, and had it not been for the vast enemy dumps captured in Marmarica and western Egypt, 'it would', as he says, 'never have been able to exist at all.'

Rommel was severely criticized for not halting on the Egyptian frontier after he had taken Tobruk. True enough, had he done so he would have curtailed considerably his communications, but this in itself would not have solved his supply problem, because, as long as Malta remained in British hands in the long run it was impossible for him to out-stockpile his enemy. Further, once his attempt to rush the Alamein position failed, he could not fall back on a rear position because he had not sufficient transport simultaneously to supply his forward position and build up a position in rear. Since to remain where he was could not solve the problem of driving his enemy out of Egypt, he realized that he would have to attack, not when he was fully ready – that he could never hope for – but before his enemy's deficiencies had been made good.

It should be remembered that because Rommel was nominally subordinated to Marshal Bastico, Marshal Cavallero, the Italian Chief of Staff, whom Ciano calls 'that crook' and 'this charlatan,' was responsible for the supply of Rommel's army. In order to clarify the supply situation, Rommel asked Cavallero and Field-Marshal Kesselring to meet him in Egypt. This they did on 27 August, and when they guaranteed to supply him with 6,000 tons of petrol, one-sixth of which Kesselring promised to deliver by air, Rommel decided to attack. But to be doubly assured, he turned to Cavallero and said that the outcome of the battle would entirely depend on its receipt, to which the latter replied: 'You can go on with the battle, it is on its way.' Unfortunately for Rommel, Kesselring failed to mention the recent arrival in Malta of Spitfire aircraft, which profoundly altered the situation.

When Rommel was thus engaged, General Alexander arrived at Cairo on 8 August, and four days later he was joined by General Montgomery, who at once assumed command of the Eighth Army.

Montgomery was a man of dynamic personality and of supreme self-confidence. Known to his officers and men as 'Monty', he was a past-master in showmanship and publicity; audacious in his utterances and cautious in his actions. Though at times smiled at by his officers, his neo-Napoleonic personal messages – 'I am proud to be with you' . . . 'YOU have made this Army what it is. YOU have made its name a household word' . . . '*YOU* and I together will see this thing through,' etc., etc., interlarded with 'The Lord Mighty in Battle' and 'hitting the enemy for six,' electrified his men. He was the right man in the right place at the right moment; for after its severe defeat the Eighth Army needed a new dynamo and Montgomery supplied it.

As soon as he arrived at his headquarters he summoned a meeting of his staff and said that his mandate was to destroy the Axis forces in North Africa, and if anyone doubted this he had better clear out. He added that he had ordered all withdrawal plans to be burnt; that the defence of the Delta meant nothing to him; and that in a fortnight he would welcome attack, but he did not intend to assume the offensive until he was ready to do so. In order to carry it out, it was essential to have a *corps d'élite*, like the Afrika Korps; therefore he would at once create one out of two armoured and one motorized divisions. Further, it was also essential that Army and RAF headquarters should live in close proximity, so that the planning of the great offensive he had in mind might be a joint effort from the start.

Except for the Wadi Akarit position north of Gabes, the El Alamein Line was the only one in North Africa that offered no flank that could be turned from the south. Rommel's tactical problem was how to penetrate this position, and because of his enemy's minefields and the tactical features in rear of them, it was by no means easy to solve. The former ran from Tel el Eisa, close by the Mediterranean, to Hunter's Plateau, which fringed the Qattara Depression, the northern border of which was girt with precipitous cliffs; and the latter comprised two ridges, the Ruweisat, about 200 ft above sea level, which ran from the centre of the front eastward, and the Alam el Halfa, to its south-east, which at its highest point was a little over twice the height of the former, and which extended in a north-easterly direction towards El Hamman on the Alexandria–Mersa Matruh railway.

Auchinleck's plan, which Alexander and Montgomery accepted as the basis of their own, was to hold as strongly as possible the area between the coast and the Ruweisat Ridge; lightly to hold but heavily to mine the area south of it to Hunter's Plateau; and to hold in strength the Alam el Halfa Ridge so that, should the enemy's mobile forces penetrate the front either north or south of the Ruweisat Ridge, they could be counter-attacked in flank, and should they break through along the ridge itself, then they could be met frontally.

When Montgomery assumed command of the Eighth Army he found the front held by the XXXth and XIIIth Corps, the former north of the Ruweisat Ridge and the latter south of it. The former consisted of the 9th Australian, 1st South African and 5th Indian Divisions and the 23rd Armoured Brigade; the latter of the 2nd New Zealand and 7th Armoured Divisions. Alexander had in reserve the 8th and 10th Armoured and the 44th and 51st Infantry Divisions, also the 1st Armoured and 50th Infantry Divisions, both refitting. At once Montgomery asked for the 44th and 10th Armoured Divisions, the one to hold the Alam el Halfa Ridge and the other to occupy its western extremity as a mobile striking force.

Rommel's army was disposed as follows: In the north the German 164th Infantry Division, then the Italian XXIst Corps, which consisted of the Trento and Bologna Divisions and Ramcke's German Parachute Brigade, and lastly the Brescia Division of the Italian Xth Corps; all these formations were in front line. As his striking force Rommel had the Afrika Korps, which consisted of the 15th and 21st Panzer Divisions; the German 90th Light Division (motorized infantry); and the Italian XXth Mobile Corps, which comprised the Ariete and Littorio Armoured Divisions and the Trieste Division. In rear, at Mersa Matruh and Bardia, were the Italian Pavia, Folgore, and Pistola Divisions in reserve.

Rommel's plan was to make a feint attack in the north, a holding attack in the centre, and the main attack in the south. On the night of August 30–31, lanes through the southernmost sector of his enemy's minefields – which he believed to be weak, but which were strong – were to be cleared by German and Italian infantry. Next, at dawn on the 31st, the Afrika Korps was to follow through, take the Alam el Halfa Ridge and make for the area south-west of El Hamman. In the meantime the 90th Light Division and the Ariete and Littorio Armoured Divisions were to break through to the north of the Afrika Korps and cover the left flank of its advance. His idea was to cut off his enemy from his supply depots, while the 90th Light Division and XXth Mobile Corps held the enemy, and then annihilate him. He sought a decisive battle, and for its success it was imperative that the Alam el Halfa Ridge should be overrun early on the 31st.

According to General Alexander, the opposing forces were evenly matched on the southern half of the front. Both had about 300 field and medium guns and 400 anti-tank guns; Rommel had 500 medium and light tanks, and the XIIIth Corps 300 medium and 80 light tanks and 230 armoured cars. Besides these, 100 tanks with the 23rd Armoured Brigade constituted a reserve. Though numerically evenly matched, Rommel was badly outclassed, because half his tanks were Italian and they were very indifferent machines.

For Rommel, the battle of Alam el Halfa was a desperate gamble because the plan on which it was based was the only one feasible with the means at his disposal, and precisely because of this Montgomery expected Rommel to adopt it. For Montgomery, whose intention it was to maintain a firm defensive until he was fully prepared to attack, it was a heaven-sent opportunity; not only did it enable him to rebuild the morale of his army, but at the same time it enabled him to weaken that of his opponent and thereby doubly assure the success of his eventual offensive. In order to impede an attack on the southern sector of his front Montgomery considerably added to its minefields that on the night of August 30–31 when the Germans and Italians began to clear lanes through them, they were greatly delayed. To add to this difficulty, General von Bismarck, commander of the 21st Panzer Division, was killed by a mine, and the commander of the Afrika Korps, General Nehring, was severely wounded. Further, Rommel was so sick that he was unable to leave his truck. This, Desmond Young considers, was 'perhaps the greatest handicap of all', because Rommel – like Charles XII – 'relied much more on his personal observation and judgement during the progress of a battle than on a preconceived plan.'

The results of these misfortunes were that there was no surprise; the advance of the Afrika Korps was delayed; that of the 90th Light Division still more so; and the Ariete and Littorio Divisions could not penetrate the minefields. Rommel, bereft of half his striking force, was compelled to abandon his sweep to the north-east and restrict the attack of the Afrika Korps to the western end of the Alam el Halfa Ridge. But its advance was so impeded by soft sand and by air attacks that at 4 p.m. it had to be called off.

During the night of 31 August – 1 September the Italo-German forces were so pounded by the RAF that, on 1 September, Rommel was compelled to abandon any attempt to carry out a major operation, and only desultory fighting on the Alam el Halfa Ridge followed. In the meantime Montgomery, when he saw that the battle was in his hands, switched the 10th Armoured Division from the south to the west of the ridge preparatory to carrying out a counter-attack southward with the 2nd New Zealand Division directly he had exhausted his enemy's offensive.

On 2 September, still under constant air attack and desperately short of petrol, Rommel renewed his offensive, but with so little success that he ordered a withdrawal for the morning of the 3rd. Montgomery then launched his counter-attack, and at the same time ordered his 7th Armoured Division to harass the enemy's southern flank. After stiff fighting he drove him back to the minefields, and at 7 a.m. on 7 September called off the battle. Rommel's losses were nearly 3,000 men killed, wounded and missing, 50 tanks, 15 guns, 35 anti-tank guns and 400 lorries lost; and Montgomery's losses were 1,640 killed, wounded and missing, and 68 tanks and 18 anti-tank guns put out of action.

Kesselring's opinion is that if Rommel had not been sick he would never have pulled out of the battle because he had 'completely encircled his enemy.' This is a fantastic statement, and more especially as it is made by a highly experienced soldier. There was no encirclement, and once the battle had opened Rommel was under no illusion that his enemy's command of the air predoomed his defeat. He has much to say on this question, and among other things that,

> Whoever enjoys command of the air is in a position to inflict such heavy damage on the opponent's supply columns that serious shortages must soon make themselves felt. By maintaining a constant watch on the roads leading to the front he can put a complete stop to daylight supply traffic and force his enemy to drive only by night, thus causing him to lose irreplaceable time. But an assured flow of supplies is essential; without it an army becomes immobilized and incapable of action.

This should be remembered when we come to the part played by Rommel in the Normandy campaign of 1944.

'With the failure of this offensive,' writes Rommel, 'our last chance of gaining the Suez Canal had gone.' He knew that the battle for supplies was irretrievably lost, if only because the large convoy of 'well over 100,000 tons, laden with the very latest weapons and war material for the Eighth Army', which he expected 'would arrive at Suez at the beginning of September,' arrived there on 3 September with Roosevelt's gift of 300 Sherman tanks. He knew that his enemy would attack, and in all probability under a full moon. Kesselring remarks: 'Was it right under these circumstances to wait for the British offensive?' and adds that neither OKW nor the Comando Supremo would have objected to a withdrawal. Although this assumption is highly improbable, possibly the reason why Rommel stayed where he did was that either a voluntary withdrawal was repugnant to him, or that he had not the petrol and vehicles to carry it out. This latter reason is supported by Ciano, who, on 2 September, entered in his diary: 'Three of our tankers have been sunk in two days,' and on the 3rd, 'Rommel's pause continues, and, what is worse, the sinking of our ships continues.' But had Rommel fallen back shortly before the next full moon, he would have disrupted his enemy's plans.

Whatever his reasons, he decided to stand and accept battle. His plan was to hold with outposts only his forward belt of minefields, in which some 500,000 mines and vast numbers of captured British bombs and shells had been sunk, and to fight his defensive battle in a mined zone 1,000 to 2,000 yards behind. On his northern flank he posted the German 164th and 90th Light Divisions in depth; allotted to the Italians the defence of the front south of them; and divided his armoured divisions into two groups, the 15th Panzer and Littorio Divisions in the north, and the 21st Panzer and Ariete Divisions in the south. Tactically this was a faulty distribution and unlike any Rommel had hitherto adopted; possibly it was forced upon him through lack of petrol. In all he had 300 Italian tanks of little fighting value and barely fit for action, and 210 German tanks, of which 30 were Panzer IVs armed with 75 mm guns, and the remainder Panzer IIIs with 50 mm guns.

As he was then a very sick man he decided to return to Germany, and on 22 September he handed his command over to General Stumme, an experienced tank officer, and informed him that should the enemy attack he would at once return. This was not a very satisfactory arrangement. Back in Germany, on 10 October he was presented with his Field-Marshal's baton, which had been awarded to him immediately after the fall of Tobruk.

While Rommel was engaged on his unenviable task, his opponent, General Alexander, prepared for an all-out offensive. On 10 August Mr Churchill had handed to him a directive to annihilate the German–Italian Army 'at the earliest opportunity', but the date was governed by certain factors. Firstly, Operation Torch had been scheduled for 8 November; and it was considered of vital political importance, in order to win over the French in Morocco and Algeria, that the Axis forces in Egypt should be decisively defeated before the invasion was launched. Secondly, because the 300 Sherman tanks would not arrive until early in September, and when they did several weeks' training with them was imperative, as well as a full moon under which to attack, the date fixed upon was the night of 23–24 October.

The next problem was one of grand tactics: where should the

decisive blow be struck on the 40-mile front? Although in the front's southern sector the minefields were less extensive than in the northern, because a successful penetration in the south would drive the enemy northward towards his communications – the coastal road – it was decided to deliver the main blow in the north, to gain an outlet on to the coastal road, and to cut off the bulk of the enemy forces south of it. This settled, the next problem was one of minor tactics.

Because minefields can no more be rushed by tanks than wire entanglements can be rushed by infantry – and in the northern sector they were from 5,000 to 9,000 yards in depth – it was agreed that the initial advance would assume the form of an old-fashioned infantry attack accompanied by mine clearing parties and covered by artillery and bomber aircraft, with tanks in rear.

On 6 October, Montgomery issued his plan. The main attack was allotted to the XXXth Corps (Lieutenant-General Sir Oliver Leese) on a four divisional front of six to seven miles in width. Its task was to cut two corridors through the minefields; the northern south of Tel El Eisa, and the southern across the northern end of the Miteiriya Ridge. Once this had been done, the Xth Corps (Lieutenant-General Sir Herbert Lumsden) which comprised the 1st and 10th Armoured Divisions, was to pass through and engage the enemy's armour. In the meantime, to mislead the enemy and pin down the 21st Panzer Division in the extreme south, the XIIIth Corps (Lieutenant-General Sir B. C. Horrocks) and the 7th Armoured Division were to carry out two subsidiary attacks against the enemy's right flank. In all Montgomery had seven infantry divisions, a formation of Free French, a Greek brigade, three armoured divisions and seven armoured brigades; a total of 150,000 men and 1,114 tanks, of which 128 were Grants and 267 Shermans, both armed with 75 mm guns, and 2,182 pieces of artillery, of which 1,274 were anti-tank guns of various types. The battle was to be opened by a short intense counter-battery bombardment, to be followed, once the infantry advanced, by a bombardment of the enemy's defences. From 6 October to the night of the 23rd the RAF (500 fighters and 200 bombers) was to intensify its attack on the enemy's communications and transport, next, to support the artillery bombardments, and finally to concentrate on the areas in which the enemy's armour was located.

In addition, there was an elaborate cover plan, the aim of which was to make good lack of strategical surprise by deceiving the enemy. The first task was to conceal the various concentrations as much as possible, and the second, by means of dummy hutments, dumps, tanks, vehicles, gun emplacements, water installations and a pipeline, to mislead the enemy about the probable date, and direction, of the attack. Until the invasion of Normandy, it was the most elaborate fake undertaken, and its principle was – hide what you have and reveal what you haven't.

At 9.40 p.m. on 23 October, under a brilliant moon, the whole of the artillery of the Eighth Army, nearly 1,000 guns, simultaneously opened fire on the enemy battery positions. Twenty minutes later the infantry advanced, and on the XXXth Corps front by 1 a.m. on the 24th the enemy forward defences were captured without serious loss. Half an hour's halt was then made in order to reorganize, after which the advance was resumed and met with stern opposition. Nevertheless, by 5.30 a.m. the Australians had secured most of their final objective, and the New Zealanders the whole of theirs; but in the centre the 51st Division was held up by strongpoints in the middle of the northern corridor some 1,500 yards from its final objective, and in the south the 1st South African Division was held up for several hours.

The Xth Corps crossed its starting line at 2 a.m., but the engineers, who worked behind the infantry, were so greatly delayed in lifting the mines that it was not until 6.30 a.m. that the southern corridor was sufficiently cleared to permit the 9th Armoured Brigade, followed by the 10th Armoured Division, to move forward. When the latter did go ahead it gained a footing on the eastern slope of the Miteiriya Ridge, but came under such heavy fire that it could proceed no farther. In the meantime, the 2nd Armoured Brigade and the 1st Armoured Division had been seriously delayed by mines and artillery fire in the northern corridor, and it was not until 3 p.m., after an intense artillery bombardment and a combined attack by the 51st Division and the 1st Armoured Division, that the corridor was finally established. These delays put back the timetable and prohibited a break-out on the 24th.

In the south the operations of the XIIIth Corps met with so limited a success that Montgomery instructed Horrocks to press the attack no farther, but to resort to 'crumbling' action – local attacks of attrition – without the 7th Armoured Division being involved.

On the Axis front the situation rapidly deteriorated, for although the outposts had fought staunchly, the terrific enemy bombardment so smashed the network of communications that command was paralysed. General Stumme went forward at dawn on the 24th to find out what was happening, and shortly after had a heart attack and died. When this became known hours later, General von Thoma, Commander of the Afrika Korps, assumed the chief command.'

When the battle opened, Rommel was in hospital at Semmering, and on the afternoon of the 24th he was telephoned by Field-Marshal Keitel, who inquired whether he would be well enough to return to Africa. He replied that he was, and at 7 a.m. on the 25th took off for Rome. When he arrived there at 11 a.m. he was met by General von Rintelen, the German military attaché, who informed him that only 'three issues of petrol remained in the African theatre,' which was equivalent to '300 kilometres worth of petrol per vehicle between Tripoli and the front'. As experience had shown that one issue of petrol was required for each day of battle, it was obvious to Rommel that the battle was as good as lost, for without petrol the army could no longer react to the enemy's movements.

That evening Rommel learnt from von Thoma that ammunition was so short that Stumme had forbidden the bombardment of the enemy's assembly positions on the night of 23–24 October, and that on the 24th and 25th the petrol situation had so deteriorated that major movements were no longer possible, and that only groups of the 15th Panzer Division had been able to attack; that they had suffered frightful casualties; and that the division was now reduced to 31 effective tanks.

In spite of this crippling shortage of means, the Axis forces put up so determined a defence that Montgomery realized that his 'crumbling' attacks were too costly. He decided to switch the axis of the offensive more to the north, and instructed the XXXth Corps to order the 9th Australian Division to direct its offensive toward the coast, to cut off the enemy in the salient which had been created north of the Tel el Eisa Ridge. At the same time the 1st Armoured Division was ordered to fight its way westward toward what the British called Kidney Ridge and the Germans Hill 28. These attacks resulted in the most savage fighting of the battle. The Australian advance was successful, but the 1st Armoured Division made no appreciable progress until nightfall, because Rommel brought forward the 90th Light Division, elements of the 15th Panzer and Littorio Divisions, and a battalion of Bersaglieri. He writes: 'Rivers of blood were poured out over miserable strips of land,' and after it had grown dark: 'Never before in Africa had we seen such a density of anti-aircraft fire. Hundreds of British tracer shells criss-crossed the sky and the air became an absolute inferno of fire.' At length, during the night, the 1st South African and 2nd New Zealand Divisions gained 1,000 yards more depth on the Miteiriya Ridge, and the 7th Motor Brigade of the 1st Armoured Division established itself on Kidney Ridge.

On 26 October it became apparent to Montgomery that the momentum of his attack was on the wane, and that his break-in area was still hedged in by a strong anti-tank screen. He decided to assume a temporary defensive, and to regroup his forces and build up fresh reserves for a renewal of the offensive in the north. He ordered the 2nd New Zealand Division to be relieved by the 1st South African Division and brought into reserve, and the front of the latter to be taken over by the 4th Indian Division, which was placed under the command of the XIIIth Corps. Further, he instructed the XIIIth Corps to send north the 7th Armoured Division and three brigades of infantry.

While these moves were under way, on the night of 26–27 October Rommel moved the 21st Panzer Division north, and on the 27th violently attacked Kidney Ridge, but was repulsed at such heavy cost that Montgomery was able to withdraw the 1st Armoured Division and the 24th Armoured Brigade into reserve. At the same time he ordered the 9th Australian Division to attack the enemy in the coastal sector on the night of the 28th–29th. Apparently Rommel expected this attack, and in order to reinforce his left he was compelled to denude his southern front of practically all heavy weapons and German units and to replace them by part of the Ariete Division which had been engaged in the north.

The Australian attack was launched under cover of an intense bombardment at 10 p.m. on the 29th in the direction of the coastal road between Sidi Abd el Rahman and Tel el Eisa. For six hours the battle raged furiously, and 'again and again', writes Rommel, 'British bomber formations flew up and tipped their death-dealing loads on my troops, or bathed the country in the brilliant light of parachute flares.' So intense was the fighting that, on the morning of the 30th, Rommel began to consider a withdrawal to the Fuka position, which ran from the coast 50 miles west of El Alamein southward to the Qattara Depression. This is the first intimation of a contemplated retreat which, irrespective of the severity of the fighting, was being pressed to the fore by petrol shortage. On 27 October only 70 tons had been delivered by the *Luftwaffe*, and on the 29th Ciano entered in his diary: 'Another oil tanker was sunk this evening . . . Bismarck has learned from Rintelen that Rommel is optimistic about the military quality of the troops, but that he is literally terrified by the supply situation. Just now not only is fuel lacking but also munitions and food.'

During the morning of 29 October Montgomery became aware that the 90th Light Division had been moved into the Sidi Abd el Rahman area, and as this indicated that Rommel had reacted to his intent to break out along the coastal road, he decided to shift the axis of his break-through attack southward so that it would fall mainly on the Italians. In order to cover this operation and pin down the 90th Light Division, he ordered the 9th Australian Division to resume its attack on the night of the 30th–31st. In the meantime the 2nd New Zealand Division was to be brought up in readiness to force a gap through the enemy's front a little to the north of the existing northern corridor, and once it had been made the Xth Corps with the 1st, 7th, and 10th Armoured Divisions was to pass through it into the open desert. This operation was code-named 'Supercharge'. Montgomery writes: The operation

> was to get us out into the open country and to lead to the disintegration of Rommel's forces in Egypt. We had got to bring the enemy's armour to battle and get astride his lines of communication. Second New Zealand Division's tasks involved a penetration of some 6,000 yards on a 4,000 yards front. I made it clear that should 30 Corps fail to reach its final objectives, *the armoured divisions of the 10th Corps were to fight their way through*.

On 30 October, Rommel had the Fuka position reconnoitred, and although he realized that because the Italian infantry had practically no transport they would be no more than a dead weight in the open desert, he nevertheless planned to load as many of them as he could on his transport columns and withdraw them under cover of night, after which his remaining motorized forces were, on a wide front, to beat a fighting retreat to the west. 'But first,' he writes, 'we had to wait for the British move, to ensure that they would be engaged in battle and could not suddenly throw their strength into a gap in our front and then force a break-through.'

It came that night, when the Australians resumed their attack toward the coast and, after they had reached it, they turned eastward and cut off the Panzer Grenadiers of the 164th Division in the northern salient. But most of the grenadiers, helped by counter-attacks delivered by elements of the 21st Panzer Division and the 90th Light Division, effected their escape.

Montgomery's original intention had been to launch 'Supercharge' on the night following this attack, but the situation compelled him to postpone it for 24 hours, and it was not made until 1 a.m. on 2 November, after an intense artillery bombardment, reinforced by relays of bombers. Under cover of a creeping barrage two brigades of the 2nd New Zealand Division, supported by the 23rd Armoured Brigade, moved forward on a 4,000-yard front; their task was to drive a lane 4,000 yards in length through the enemy's position, clear it of mines and open a path for the 9th Armoured Brigade, which before dawn was to push forward another 2,000 yards to the track which ran south from Sidi Abd el Rahman, and establish a bridgehead from which the 1st, 7th, and 10th Armoured Divisions could debouch into the open desert and bring on a decisive armoured battle.

The lane was successfully cleared, but when a little before daylight the 9th Armoured Brigade reached the track, it ran into a formidable anti-tank gun screen and suffered a loss of 87 tanks – over 75 per cent of its strength. In the meantime the 1st Armoured Division debouched and was at once engaged by the Afrika Korps. A fierce tank battle followed around Tel el Aqqaqir. Although Rommel's tanks were outclassed by his enemy's, and their 50 mm and 49 mm (Italian) guns could make little impression on the British Grant and Sherman machines, the attackers were brought to a halt and the penetration sealed off. Nevertheless, Rommel was under no illusions; he realized that the battle was lost. Not only were there signs of disintegration – units of the Littorio and Trieste Divisions streamed to the rear – but the supply situation, he writes, was 'absolutely desperate'. During the day his army had expended 450 tons of ammunition, and only 190 tons had been brought to Tobruk by three destroyers. He also states: 'The Afrika Korps had only 35 serviceable tanks left.'

'This then', writes Rommel, 'was the moment to get back to the Fuka line,' and especially as 'the British had so far been following up hesitantly and that their operations had always been marked by an extreme, often incomprehensible caution.' He then made what he acknowledges was a crucial blunder. Early on the morning of 3 November he sent his ADC, Lieutenant Berndt, to report direct to Hitler and to ask him for full freedom of action. He did not doubt that it would be given and ordered part of the Italian formations to retreat. At 1.30 p.m. he received Hitler's answer: stand fast and yield not a yard of ground. 'As to your troops,' it read, 'you can show them no other road than that to victory or death.' Rommel then halted the withdrawal, and in the evening sent Berndt back to Hitler with a message to inform him that to stand fast meant annihilation.

Early on 4 November Kesselring arrived at Rommel's head-quarters and, according to Rommel, said to him, 'that the Führer had learnt from his experiences in the East that, in circumstances like these, the front must be held at all costs.' In his *Memoirs* Kesselring contradicts this, and writes that he told Rommel, 'there could be no question of any such folly, that Hitler's order must be ignored,' and that he would accept full responsibility for ignoring it.

When on the morning of 3 November Montgomery learnt of his enemy's withdrawal westward, he asked the Desert Air Force to switch the whole of its weight to the retreating Axis columns. But it was not until nightfall that he ordered the 51st Division and a brigade of the 4th Indian Division to move forward on a four-mile front and to break through the southern sector of the enemy's anti-tank screen and win a gap through which he could pass his three armoured divisions. This was successfully done by the morning of the 4th.

Of this, the final action of the battle, Rommel supplies the following dramatic description:

> Enormous dust-clouds could be seen south and south-east of headquarters, where the desperate struggle of the small and inefficient Italian tanks of XX Corps was being played out against the hundred or so British heavy tanks which had come round their open right flank. I was later told by Major von Luck, whose battalion I had sent to close the gap between the Italians and the Afrika Korps, that the Italians, who at that time represented our strongest motorized force, fought with exemplary courage. Von Luck gave what assistance he could with his guns, but was unable to avert the fate of the Italian Armoured Corps. Tank after tank split asunder or burned out,

while all the time a tremendous British barrage lay over the Italian infantry and artillery positions. The last signal came from the Ariete at about 15.30 hours: 'Enemy tanks penetrated south of Ariete. Ariete now encircled.'

By nightfall the XXth Italian Corps had been destroyed; the Afrika Korps on its left had been broken through and its commander, General von Thoma, captured; a 12-mile gap had been driven through the Axis front; and Rommel had no reserves and no petrol. In spite of Hitler's insane order, retreat became compulsory, and Rommel tried to save what he could of his army. Next morning a message arrived from Hitler's headquarters to authorize the withdrawal.

That Rommel was ever able to withdraw even his motorized units was firstly because of Montgomery's instinctive cautiousness, and secondly because of the reluctance of the RAF to engage in low flying attack, as it had done so successfully after the battle of Vittorio-Veneto. According to General Alexander, the Eighth Army could still muster 'very nearly six hundred tanks against eighty German'; it needed only a modicum of audacity by Montgomery to turn his enemy's retreat into a rout. On the second point, de Guingand writes:

> With the virtual air superiority we possessed, and the state of disorganization of the enemy, it looked to us in the Army that here was the 'dream target' for the RAF. In the event, the results appeared very disappointing. When setting out along the road between Alamein battlefield and Daba, I had expected to see a trail of devastation, but the visible signs of destroyed vehicles were few and far between. After Daba much better results had been obtained but even here a lot of the vehicles we found had stopped through shortage of petrol.

This he rightly attributes to the RAF's trust in high-level bombing instead of low-level machine-gunning, with the consequence that training in low flying attack had been neglected. Had it not been for this, his opinion is that Rommel's withdrawal would have been paralysed.

The crux of Rommel's retreat was the pull-out on the night of 4–5 November, when chaos reigned, but fortunately for him his methodical opponent, fearful of the difficulties of a night pursuit, halted his forces. 'On 5 November', Montgomery informs us, 'I regrouped for the pursuit.' Thus he lost some 18 invaluable hours. When he had regrouped he decided that the Xth Corps (1st, 7th Armoured and 2nd New Zealand Divisions) were to lead the chase; the XXXth Corps was to come into reserve between El Alamein and Mersa Matruh; and the XIIIth was to clear up the battlefield. In spite of this delay, by an outflanking movement through the desert he nearly cut off his enemy at Mersa Matruh. But on 6 November the van of the 1st Armoured Division was brought to a halt through lack of petrol and Rommel succeeded, as he says, 'in forming a fairly firm front and beat off all enemy attacks.' He adds that his enemy 'still continued to operate with great caution.'

It is also stated that 'conditions on the road were indescribable. Columns in complete disorder – partly of German, partly of Italian vehicles – choked the road between the minefields [south of Mersa Matruh]. Rarely was there any movement forward and then everything soon jammed up again. Many vehicles were on tow and there was an acute shortage of petrol, for the retreat had considerably increased consumption.'

To add to the difficulties of both sides, and more particularly to the pursuers, on the 6th torrential rain made the desert tracks impassable. For 24 hours the pursuit was bogged down. According to Montgomery the rain saved Rommel 'from complete annihilation.'

Bou Arada (1943)

Donald Gurrey

When the Allies landed in Algeria in November 1942 it was hoped that a quick dash up the 400-mile road to Tunis might enable the latter to be seized and Rommel's line of retreat from Libya cut off. The speed with which the German High Command rushed *ad hoc* formations over from Italy and Sicily thwarted this pious hope. A set-piece drive up the Medjerda valley from Medjez-el-Bab on Christmas Day 1942 had to be abandoned when torrential rains made the going impassable. With stalemate at Medjez and in the broken mountainous terrain to the north the German forces were quick to probe the open flank to the south, up till then only guarded by long-range patrols of 1st Derbyshire Yeomanry, the British 6th Armoured Division's armored reconnaissance unit. German pressure along the Pont-du-Fahs/El Aroussa road, 20 miles to the south, began to mount.

Leaving 78th Infantry Division to hold the Medjez sector, the British First Army's only other division, 6th Armoured, accordingly moved down in early January to the Bou Arada area. The aim was both to block any German advance and to see if a drive towards Tunis might be forced up this axis. From this time until late in February the Bou Arada–Goubellat plain area became the division's main 'stamping ground'.

The 6th Armoured, under 41-year-old Major-General Charles F. Keightley, was short in experience but high in training and morale;

its formation sign was a mailed fist (referred to in later months by nurses from a neighboring field hospital as 'the sign of the disengaged hand'). The division's tanks were in 26th Armoured Brigade (16th/5th Lancers, 17th/21st Lancers, 2nd Lothian and Border Horse with 10th Rifle Brigade as their battalion of infantry). The Derbyshire Yeomanry had armored cars for scouting. The 38th (Irish) Infantry Brigade (6th Royal Inniskilling Fusiliers, 1st Royal Irish Fusiliers, 2nd London Irish Rifles) provided the main infantry element (to be replaced, later in the campaign, by 1st Guards Brigade, which had come out to North Africa as an independent brigade). The artillery support was provided by 12th Royal Horse Artillery Regiment (RHA), 152nd Field Regiment (The Ayrshire Yeomanry), both with 24 25-pounder field guns; 72nd Anti-Tank Regiment (48 6-pounders) and 51st Lt AA Regiment (54 Bofors 40 mm). Extra artillery was borrowed from 5th Corps to 'thicken up'; 17th Field Regiment and one troop of 14th/16th Medium Regiment with four 5.5-in guns.

Bou Arada itself and the foothills south of it were held by a motley but enthusiastic French force designated Groupement Tremeau: 4ème Chasseurs d'Afrique, three companies of Algerian *tirailleurs*, 1ère Bataillon, 1ère Régiment Etrangère (French Foreign Legion), two companies of colonial infantry and a squadron of mounted *Spahis*. For artillery support they had 12 75 mm guns – the famous *soixante-quinze* of 1914–18 vintage. To the SE, British 1st Parachute Brigade fought a difficult running battle in the broken scrub-covered hills between Bou Arada and the Djebel Mansour, a critical feature which dominated a mountain road giving access to Bou Arada from the south.

The terrain presented interesting tactical problems. The Plain of Goubellat, halfway between Medjez and Bou Arada, was flattish rolling farmland, intersected by occasional wadis; it was dominated by higher ground on all sides and was therefore untenable (even if sufficient troops had been available). The high ground to the NE of it, close to Medjez, was held by units of 78th Division; but to the west and SW of it ran a high ridge, the Djebel Rihane, rising to 2,500 ft at its maximum and running southwards to within a mile or so of the El Aroussa–Bou Arada road. This ridge was covered with dense *maquis* scrub, making it impossible to defend, since there was no field of fire in any direction. In consequence the whole ridge was unoccupied for some 10 miles of its length except for some Derbyshire Yeomanry posts on the main tracks and for a standing patrol of 24 *Spahi* cavalry. Yet immediately to the west of it ran the main Medjez–El Aroussa road, carrying heavy military traffic.

By day, the Goubellat plain slumbered in apparent peace, empty of life; but at night there was heavy patrolling by both sides, and Royal Engineer (RE) detachments from 6th Armoured Division's 5th Field Squadron were quickly active in setting a colorful selection of booby traps in and around Goubellat village. One variety was sunk into the earth surface of paths and tracks, and fired a bullet into the foot of anyone unlucky enough to step on it. The main struggle quickly concentrated, however, on a long bare stony ridge which ran along the south side of the plain, some four miles north of the little village of Bou Arada. The Germans, with their experienced military eye, had quickly identified this as the key to this sector, just as Longstop Hill was to the Medjez–Tunis axis. In the fighting of early January 1943 the Irish Brigade managed to grab a feature on this ridge, lying just on the west side of the Bou Arada–Goubellat–Medjez road and christened 'Grandstand Hill'. The Germans held onto a rather high 'pimple' known, for self-evident reasons, as 'Two-Tree Hill'. Between these two features, 1.5 miles apart, a First World War-style trench system quickly developed, wired-in and with only a few hundred yards separating the two front lines.

Between this ridge and Bou Arada village stretched flat open wheatfields, the main road through them being fully visible to the Germans on Two-Tree Hill. A couple of small woods on the east side of the road gave admirable cover for 72nd AT Regiment's 6-pounders in enfilade positions, but by day there were no infantry positions along some two miles of this road, although 38th Brigade were responsible for providing standing patrols at night to protect the guns. The main 25-pounder gun positions lay in masked ground to the west of the road. On the German side, 75 mm PAK 40 AT guns concealed in wadis along the south flank of the ridge, together with deep minefield belts among the wheatfields, foiled any easy British tank attack eastwards across the open ground.

Overall, the British and German forces facing each other were virtually equal in the early weeks. The British infantry were more numerous, but the Germans opposite them had vastly more battle experience and, with 54 MG42s per battalion, far more firepower. The British had many more tanks, but the 6-pounders and the 2-pounders of their Crusaders and Valentines were well outgunned by the fewer *PzKpfw III*s and *IV*s, especially over the long ranges of this open terrain. Only in artillery were the British greatly superior. Time and again in the Tunisian campaign it was the concentrated fire of well-drilled 25-pounder and 5.5-in guns, controlled by Forward Observation Officers with a clear view of the enemy over the open ground, which brought menacing German attacks to a standstill.

But in the air, through January and February, the *Luftwaffe* held the whip hand. Their airfields were only 35 miles away, with concrete runways, permanent hangars and workshops, whereas the RAF were 80 miles back at Souk-el-Arba, flying off PSP (Pierced Steel Planking) runways laid on a sea of mud, the aircrews and fitters living in tents, cold and wet. For the 10-mile road from El Aroussa to Bou Arada the term 'dead straight' had a nasty ambiguity to it unless one kept a nervous eye open for 'Gert and Daisy' the pair of Me109s which would swing suddenly over the crest of nearby hills. A squadron of Ju87s put in frequent appearances, travelling majestically in tight formation just out of Bofors range, to peel off and swoop down on forward positions or on supply dumps in El Aroussa.

We have already listed the Allied troops engaged, who were they up against? Facing Medjez itself was 86th *Panzergrenadier* Regiment, of 10th *Panzer* Division. The principal infantry force south of this, manning positions down the east edge of the Goubellat plain, on the Two-Tree ridge and covering the Pont Du Fahs axis, were three battalions of the *Hermann Goering Jäger* Regiment. This was a crack formation, originally airborne, often referred to as 'Division Koch' after its paratrooper CO, a 29-year-old *oberstleutnant* (Lieutenant Colonel) with the Knight's Cross. Also on this sector was one of the several improvised infantry units quickly assembled by the Germans to meet the sudden Tunisia crisis, a *Marschbataillon* designated A/24, under *Oberleutnant* (First Lieutenant) Helmcke. This had been formed in Hamburg in November from men wounded on the Russian Front; it had left by train on 9 December for Naples and Palermo, arriving in Tunis on Christmas Day aboard two Italian destroyers. Its unusual organization consisted of four companies of four platoons, the fourth platoon in each company being a heavy platoon with six heavy machine-guns and two 81 mm mortars.

Armored support was provided by 1st and 2nd Battalions of 7th *Panzer* Regiment; each battalion consisted of three companies of 12 tanks with an HQ of five, giving a battalion total of 17 *PzKpfw II*s and 24 *PzKpfw III*s or *IV*s (1st Battalion for example had 21 Mark IIIs and 3 Mk IVs). The 2nd Battalion had suffered badly on the way over; both 5th and 8th Companies lost all their tanks and drivers when the MV *Menes* was sunk off Bizerta on 3 December. The survivors benefited to some extent, since 8th Company was subsequently re-equipped with 12 brand-new *PzKpfw IV Ausf F2*s with the more powerful long-barreled 75 mm gun. Artillery support was scant; 90th Artillery Regiment, of 10th *Panzer* Division, had to spread itself widely over the whole sector and suffered badly from lack of ammunition. It had 24 105 mm guns and 12 150 mm howitzers, plus one battery of 88 mm AA guns and one of self-propelled 75 mm *Sturmkanone*.

The *Hermann Goering (HG) Jägers* were 6th Armoured's principal adversary. The 1st Battalion was commanded by *Hauptmann* (Captain) Jungwirth, 2nd Battalion by *Hauptmann* Becker; a third battalion was created, early in December, by *Hauptmann* Schirmer withdrawing companies from the other two battalions. These battalions had three companies apiece, armed with 18 MG42s (double the normal establishment) and three 50 mm mortars, plus a heavy company of 12 HMGs of 4–6 81 mm mortars. The 2nd Battalion had some 4–6 75 mm AT guns under command; doubtless the other battalions were similarly supported. An illustration of the stop-gap arrangements forced on the German High Command by the Allied landings is that 14th Company of 104th *Panzergrenadier* Regiment, nominally a unit of 21st *Panzer* Division and about to join it in Libya, was diverted from Italy to Tunisia on 11 November and operated from the outset as a unit of the *HG Jägers*.

By any standards these were first-class troops; most of them had considerable battle experience and were adept at holding defensive positions. Their officers were good leaders and courageous; by 20 March, for example, no company of 3rd Battalion had any officers left alive apart from the company commander.

After the initial clash with 38th Infantry Brigade early in January all further attempts by British infantry to capture Two-Tree Hill and advance east along the ridge were beaten off. Two-Tree Hill remained a real thorn in the flesh; it dominated the British forward defense lines both by observation and by the fire of well dug-in machine-guns. Already by 13 January the *HG Jägers* were demonstrating their aggressiveness when they struck across the Bou Arada–Grandstand road with two night raiding parties of 12 men each. These surprised 'D' Troop 12th RHA, which had just moved in that night, taking prisoners and blowing up guns and tractors with satchel charges. A couple of weeks later they again showed initiative when a gunner observation post, established high up on the Djebel Rihane with a clear, if distant, view of the whole Two-Tree ridge, was taken out by a patrol which crept up the mountainside at night and killed the subaltern and sergeant sleeping there.

By mid-January, however, 6th Armoured Division were firmly installed; 38th Brigade holding the Grandstand Hill feature, 26th Armoured Brigade just behind them on the plain, ready to block any breakthrough by the German armor. It was just in time. On 18 January *Generaloberst* (Colonel General) Jürgen von Arnim (commanding Fifth *Panzer* Army in Tunisia since 9 December) launched Operation *Eilbote I* (special messenger), an operation aimed at driving back the French (who had been advancing from Robaa towards Pont du Fahs) while holding back 6th Armoured by a diversionary attack. The latter was so fierce that many considered it at the time to be the main attack.

The *Jägers* had taken the brunt of the early fighting for Grandstand Hill on 11–12 January; so this time it was *Marschbataillon A/24* that led the attack, with 1st and 3rd Companies moving at first light against the British positions in front of Grandstand, supported below the hill by 2nd Battalion, 7th *Panzer* Regiment. The positions attacked were held by the Royal Irish Fusiliers and the Inniskillings, and although A/24 once gained a footing on Grandstand Hill, it was forced eventually to withdraw, suffering heavy casualties from artillery fire. By nightfall it was back to its start lines. During the morning a dive-bombing attack was made by 12 Ju87s on El Aroussa, repeated at 1600 against Bou Arada.

More unusual was the first attack, outside Russia, by the new

Henschel 129B 'tank-buster' aircraft, armed with one 30 mm and two 20 mm cannon as well as machine-guns (8 *Staffel*, II *Gruppe*, *Schlachtgeschwader* 2 operated seven Hs129s from El Aouina airfield, north of Tunis, at this stage). Three of these attacked Bou Arada during the morning, probably believing it to be infested by British armor. One was shot down by 51st Light AA's Bofors, crashing close to the crossroads and yielding valuable technical intelligence; both the others were hit and damaged, one possibly crashing behind the German lines.

During this time 7th *Panzer*'s 2nd Battalion, under *Hauptmann* Burk, attacked west astride the Pont du Fahs–Bou Arada road at first light, using some 25 tanks, including four *PzKwpf IV*s and 17 *PzKwpf III*s from 7th and 8th Companies. Three miles from Bou Arada they swung half right and made across the wheatfields for the Bou Arada–Grandstand road, apparently not suspecting the presence of 17th Field and 72nd AT Regiments, the latter hidden in the outskirts of Bou Arada and in the woods east of the road. Fire was opened at 800 yards and three Mark IIIs and four Mark IVs were quickly put out of action. Half of the remaining tanks swung north behind a feature called Mehalla, while the rest withdrew behind a farm a mile to the east, whence they engaged our guns with direct fire, using HE. Both these groups of tanks were pounded repeatedly by the divisional artillery, immobilizing another Mark III. By 1400 the *Panzers* were withdrawing under continuous shellfire, followed up at dusk by two squadrons of Lothians and Border Horse, who harbored as night fell some 4 miles farther east, in an area held by 10th Rifle Brigade. During the night Royal Engineers went out and blew up the eight immobilized German tanks to prevent their removal and repair.

The next morning, 19 January, started quietly, disturbed only by a low-level attack on Bou Arada at 1100 by three Focke-Wulf 190 fighter-bombers, but during the afternoon 6th Inniskillings carried out a sweep of the Point 286 feature and prisoners were taken. While this was in progress the usual dozen Stukas bombed Royal Irish Fusilier positions just east of Grandstand, and there was unusually heavy shelling of the area by the German 90th Artillery. There was welcome support for the hard-pressed Irish Brigade that evening when 3rd Grenadier Guards Battalion, detached from 1st Guards Brigade, arrived to relieve 2nd London Irish of its position just south of Bou Arada, thus allowing them to reinforce their brigade up at Grandstand.

January 20 saw a renewed Stuka attack on 12th RHA and 152nd Field gun positions, but this time two were shot down by Bofors fire, which was improving with so much practice. When the attack was repeated at 1315 a timely radio intercept was received to the effect that the Stukas were expecting to have their targets indicated for them by smoke shells. The smoke which the German mortars fired shortly afterwards onto the British positions was puny compared with that which 12th RHA quickly fired onto the German infantry positions, so that it was these latter which received the full weight of the Stuka attack, to the delight of the British forward troops.

That night an assault was launched in the moonlight by 38th Infantry Brigade to secure Points 279 and 286; in spite of a sharp counter-attack by A/24 the next morning the positions ended up in the hands of the London Irish. Two out of the four German tanks which attempted to intervene were destroyed by indirect artillery fire, together with two SP guns. Prisoners from A/24 said that they had never experienced artillery fire like this before, even in Russia; at least two of their companies had been halved in size during the previous 72 hours.

There was then a lull in the sector, broken only by an unusual night tank attack by 7th *Panzers*. This broke through across the Bou Arada–Grandstand road, causing some of the Irish to abandon their positions; the 6-pounder AT gunners stood firm, but were unable to fire for lack of any target illumination. After milling around somewhat inconclusively in the darkness, on the edge of the field gun positions, the *Panzers* withdrew before dawn, having caused little damage but a good deal of alarm.

In mid-February, 26th Armoured Brigade, 12th RHA and 1st Guards Brigade were all withdrawn from the sector in order to rush back to block Rommel's Kasserine Pass attack, leaving the Bou Arada valley only thinly held. This led to some excitement on 26 February, when von Arnim launched Operation *Ochsenkopf* (oxhead) to aid Rommel in the south. The main weight of *Ochsenkopf* was directed against 46th (North Midlands) Infantry Division at Sidi Nsir, north of Medjez; but pressure was exerted all along the front and included a well-executed raid in force right across the Djebel Rihane, to cut the El Aroussa–Medjez road at a point known as 'Steamroller Farm'.

Two battalions of *HG Jägers*, with seven tanks under *Leutnant* Beisbarth from 6th Company, 7th *Panzer*, four armored cars and ten lorries, moved by night south of the Mahmoud Gap – the shallower part of the Djebel Rihane – and set up road blocks with tanks and machine-guns. The raid was commanded by *Hauptmann* Schirmer himself, and had been begun on 24 February by advance parties of the German battalions 'lying up' just short of the main road and observing British movements. The Intelligence Officer (IO) of 'Y' Division – a special force consisting of little more than the bulk of 38th Irish Brigade and half the 6th Armoured's divisional artillery, left to hold the Bou Arada sector – had already learnt of this, both from interrogation of prisoners and from an Arab who had been bribed by the Germans to lead them across the Djebel Rihane by a little-known track, but who had thereafter reported in to the nearest French troops.

An SOS to First Army for extra troops resulted in the only reserve available – No. 6 Commando, withdrawn only the day before after some vicious fighting on Green Hill, near Beja – being sent forward on 25 February, bivouacking just north of Steamroller Farm. The 'Y' Division IO, Captain Noel H. Burdett, went up that night to brief them of the danger of their situation, and recommended an immediate offensive patrol. Lieutenant-Colonel Mills-Roberts, the 500-strong Commando's CO, was sympathetic but considered, perhaps understandably, that his men needed a night's rest first. By dawn on 26th it was too late: the *Jägers* had seen the Commando arrive, surrounded it during the night and opened fire from higher ground and Steamroller Farm at first light. A sharp battle developed, but when the first *Panzers* appeared towards midday the Commando, having no AT weapons, could only run for it. They lost a number of killed and badly wounded, and over 50 prisoners, including six officers – one being the unfortunate Capt. Burdett (who later, however, escaped from POW camp and got away safely to Switzerland).

Next day a squadron of Churchill tanks – its first action in Tunisia – arrived in El Aroussa via Teboursouk and moved up towards Steamroller Farm. The unit was shelled with fearsome accuracy by an 88 mm gun brought across the Rihane by the Germans, who seemed content to hold their position without ranging further afield. The British artillery now set to work, both from the El Aroussa and Medjez sides, and began to plaster the farm with shellfire. By dawn on 28 February the Germans had evacuated it for more discreet cover on the hillsides, but many of their vehicles were hit and 'brewed up' across the landscape. *Hauptmann* Schirmer was soon calling up on the radio for Stuka attacks to be made on the British troops now closing in on him. In this wild country, with no front line easily identifiable, some of the bombing almost inevitably fell on the German troops themselves. By the next night a German withdrawal back to the far side of the Goubellat plain was in full swing (after an epic Churchill tank attack), and the crisis was over; the sector was to remain thereafter relatively quiet until the final attacks towards Tunis were launched from here some six weeks later.

Kursk (1943)

Alan Wykes

The German armies in Russia were prepared for a massive offensive to reverse the disaster of Stalingrad. The finest divisions of both the *Wehrmacht* and the *Waffen SS* were gathered in an enormous concentration of men and armor. Armed with the latest tanks, their morale high, they expected to be unstoppable, even if the Russians were ready. But 'Whenever I think of this attack', said Hitler, 'my stomach turns over' – and his queasiness was understandable. For now, in the spring of 1943, both he and his generals knew that only a decisive victory over the Red Army could ease the relentless, threatening pressure on the Eastern Front.

The cracks in the wall of Axis domination were becoming ever more numerous and more apparent. The Allies were beginning to overcome the efforts of the U-boats. Italy was in a more parlous state than ever before. Japan's advances in Burma and the south-west Pacific had been stopped, and were going into reverse. The bombing of German industrial centers was disrupting essential war supplies. The hit-and-miss methods of the Red Air Force were being offset by increasing numbers of planes and the increasing skill of the Russian air crews. And the threat of a Second Front kept many German divisions tied up in Europe, reducing the possibility of any major effort on the Russian front.

Then, in March, came Field Marshal von Manstein's great victory at Kharkov for Army Group South and it seemed for a moment as if the tide was turning. But it was a short-lived hope. The victory, so far as the restoration of the German initiative was concerned, was incomplete. A great Russian-held salient remained – a bulge roughly semi-circular in shape, driven some 75 miles westward into the German lines at Kursk, with its base measuring more than 100 miles from north to south. Within the salient were said to be a million men, and armaments in proportion. Clearly, a pincer movement thrown across the base of the salient would cut off and destroy the forces contained in it and considerably weaken the total power of the Soviet army, and von Manstein planned such a movement to clinch his victory.

As so often before, however, the weather took a hand. The spring thaw turned vast tracts of frozen ground to mud, rivers rose, swamps appeared, ruined villages were mirrored in the desolation of floods. There was nothing von Manstein could do but withdraw his armor to save it from getting bogged down, and leave the infantry in possession while a plan was worked out. But there was a catch: the longer the Germans remained purely on the defensive, the sooner there would be an attempt by the Russians to widen the salient and breach the German front completely.

At a time when speed and decisiveness of action could have produced results, the Germans vacillated. Hitler changed his mind. His generals feuded among themselves. And there were conflicting interpretations of the demands of the situation in Europe. Even the promise of a new assault on the Don and an advance towards Moscow after the salient had been pinched out could not bring the Führer to decide. Tanks and other heavy assault weapons – particularly the Tigers and Panthers – were not reaching the army in the expected numbers. It was 11 April before the semblance of a design was arrived at, and it was in essence the same design that von Manstein had been unable to fulfill after Kharkov. It was indeed the obvious plan – and its obviousness was now appreciated equally by the Russians, who made haste to improve their defenses round Kursk. Any chance of surprise had been lost. Now, the only possibility lay in an assault so tremendous that no defenders could resist it.

Such an attack meant risking far more armor than the Germans could afford to lose, and if infantry support was to be forthcoming for the tanks it also meant imprudently weakening the front both north and south of the salient.

Hitler was himself caught in a pincer movement of commitment.

On the one hand he had the conflicting views of his advisers as to the possibility of success. Field Marshal von Kluge, the Army Group Center commander, and Generals Keitel and Zeitzler of the Army General Staff were in favor; Colonel-General Guderian, the Inspector-General of Armored Troops and, by this time, von Manstein himself were equally strongly against. On the other hand, there was the assurance of Speer, Minister of Production, that the necessary tanks would be available, and the certainty that without a German offensive the whole weight of the Soviet forces would come crashing against the over-stretched *Wehrmacht*.

While Hitler hesitated, General Vatutin and the Red Army went ahead – not merely with defenses as impenetrable as they could be made, but also with the preparation of a large-scale counter-attack. The news filtered back to Hitler intelligence reports and alarming air photographs that indicated the withdrawal of the Russian mobile forces from the area west of Kursk in obvious preparation for a counter-attack. But at last, on 10 May, Hitler gave his consent to the plan – it was to be called Operation Zitadelle – emphasizing his underlying reluctance with the words 'It must not fail.'

The forces were decided. Colonel-General Model's Ninth Army, with seven *Panzer*, two *Panzergrenadier*, and nine infantry divisions was to attack from the north. Colonel-General Hoth's Fourth *Panzer* Army, with ten *Panzer*, one *Panzergrenadier* and seven infantry divisions would sweep up from the south. The two arms of the pincer would meet east of Kursk, thus enclosing the salient and cutting off huge Russian forces. But, although the plan and deployment were decided, Hitler continued to hesitate.

Knowing that the Russians were building up their defenses, he postponed the first mooted date for the start of Zitadelle from 13 June until the beginning of July so that an extra couple of battalions of Panthers could be sped off the production line and allotted to Model's northern pincer. The opening of what was to become known – justifiably – as the greatest tank battle in history was finally fixed for 1500 on 4 July, despite continued proposals for abandonment from von Kluge, von Manstein and Guderian.

Opposing the 36 German divisions was a force of 11 Russian Armies, including the crack Sixth and Seventh Guards Armies that had fought so well at Stalingrad and the First Tank Army. Each Russian 'army' corresponded approximately with a German corps in size. In terms of manpower there was little to choose between the conflicting forces, but the Russians had reinforced the north corner of the salient, which would bear the brunt of Model's attack, with thickly sown minefields – so dense that, according to Marshal Rokossovski, who was the joint commander on the Kursk front with Vatutin, 'you could not have put one of Goering's medals between them.' There were 2,200 anti-tank and 2,500 anti-personnel mines per mile of the defensive front, four times the density at Stalingrad. In addition there were no fewer than 20,000 guns of various kinds, including 6,000 76.2 mm anti-tank guns and more than 900 *Katyusha* rocket guns. For attack they had the famous T34 tank – one of the best armored vehicles to be produced during the war – with its long-range 76 mm gun and great reliability.

The German attacking force was largely based on the new Panther D, a fine tank in many ways but with numerous technical faults caused by hasty production. But the Germans still had considerable superiority in the air, as was to be proved by the squadrons of Stuka dive-bombers.

But if the opposing forces were fairly matched there were other factors that would determine the course of the battle – not least the lost element of surprise, which had been frittered away in argument and indecision.

The ground over which the battle was to be fought was reasonably good for tank warfare. Kursk lies in the basins of the Don and Dneiper and the countryside which surrounds it and formed the salient is characterized by low hills and wide-ranging plains of fertile arable land. The ground is watered by numerous brooks and tributary rivers – one of them, the Pena, being a swift stream running between steep banks. Cornfields stretch for unbroken miles across the landscape. Such roads as there are are for the most part sandy cart-tracks that become unusable by wheeled traffic during heavy rain. Numerous scattered villages lie in the shallow valleys and small thickets bristle on the low hills. To the north of the village of Beresowka there is a thickly wooded area, roughly circular in shape and some four miles in diameter.

Along the southern front of the salient, Hoth's Fourth *Panzer* Army was lined up along a slight curve extending some 30 miles from west to east. First the 3rd and 11th *Panzer* divisions and the *Gross Deutschland* division (a *Panzergrenadier* unit with a high complement of tanks under 48 *Panzer* Corps); then the three SS divisions, *Leibstandarte Adolf Hitler*, *Totenkopf* (Death's Head) and

Das Reich in the SS *Panzer* Corps; and on the right wing the 6th, 19th and 7th *Panzer* divisions of 3 *Panzer* Corps. There had been the closest co-operation between ground and air forces and the utmost care had been taken to get the huge force of tanks into position under cover of darkness. 'Morale', according to Model, 'was high' – and was raised even higher by a message from the Führer:

> Soldiers of the Reich! This day you are to take part in an offensive of such importance that the whole future of the war may depend on its outcome. More than anything else, your victory will show the whole world that resistance to the power of the German army is hopeless.

Unfortunately the message arrived during a four-hour intense artillery bombardment from the Russians which confirmed that the defenders were well aware that the attack was about to be launched. The intensity of the bombardment inevitably had its effect on the striking power of the attackers, but the attack began as planned at 1500 after a return bombardment by German artillery and some devastating strikes on the forward Russian lines by dive-bombing Stukas.

By 1900 advance infantry and grenadiers of the three divisions on the German left flank of the southern pincer had thrust into the Russian forward line at Luchanino, Alexejewka and Sawidowka – three villages only lightly held by the defenders. The ease with which they were taken was characteristic of the tactic, much used by the Russians throughout the battle of Kursk, of luring the attackers into a position that subsequently proved to be untenable.

Model's northern pincer managed to break into the salient on a 15-mile front and 47 *Panzer* Corps pushed forward about five miles during the next 30 hours, but at great cost in huge Porsche Ferdinand (or *Elefant*) assault tanks. These lacked machine-guns and, as Guderian had warned long before, quickly proved vulnerable. As their escorting light tanks were knocked out, they found themselves at the mercy of infantry who dashed out from slit trenches and directed flame-throwers into the engine louvres, thus setting the fuel systems alight and forcing the crews to either be roasted alive or to bale out into captivity. The Model thrust was to gain only five more miles to south and west during the next week. Engineers who tried, under covering fire, to clear lanes through the minefields found that this only aided the Russians, who deftly scored many hits with rockets and 76 mm guns as the tanks passed through.

'For all our bitter struggling in the north', one young officer wrote subsequently, 'we moved virtually nowhere – we stood still. It was like Verdun in 1916. There was a little village called Teploye. We saw it first on the second day and we never saw it more clearly than then. Thick black smoke from brewed-up tanks blew about and each time the smoke cleared away we saw Teploye again, but it was like a mirage. We never got any nearer.'

In the south, Hoth's forces gained ground by advance detachments of infantry and grenadiers, but only at great cost. During the night the defenders withdrew and the front line was shelled throughout its length. Paul Hausser, commander of the three SS divisions *Leibstandarte*, *Totenkopf* and *Das Reich*, wrote afterwards: 'Again and again we showed this weakness of tactics that made us insist on holding ground that had been too easily gained. Having chased Ivan out, we should have withdrawn ourselves and let him bombard the place out of existence. Then we could have moved the armor forward relatively safely.'

This lack of imagination, which was characteristic of German planning, in this particular case won an undeserved reward. During the night a cloudburst caused an immediate overflowing of the Pena and its tributary streams and turned the ground into an impassable morass. But for this, all the tanks would have been moved up into the line of bombardment. Even as it was, the losses were considerable because of the difficulty of taking up camouflaged positions, so that when daylight illuminated the swamped valleys the Red Air Force easily picked out the stranded tanks and attacked.

Luftwaffe Stukas attacked too and had considerable success in demolishing Russian artillery batteries, but as one pilot, Hans Rudel, has recorded, 'The Russian guns were almost as numerous as their mines, and the camouflage was masterly . . . you had to assume that every copse was a gun battery and dive down to treetop level . . . four times out of five you found you scored a hit on a 76 . . . if it didn't get you first.'

This success, however, did little to neutralize the trouble that faced the tanks on the morning of 5 July. The whole of 48 *Panzer* Corps – 3rd and 11th *Panzer* divisions and *Gross Deutschland* – were ordered to move up from the bombarded villages to the next Russian line of defense and capture Ssyrzew and Ssyrzewo, which lay beyond the

Pena river, and wheel round to the north-west to capture the wood at Beresowka and the three small hills that lay beyond it. The floods from the cloudburst, however, made this impossible without the aid of engineers to bridge the river and the flooded cornfields on either side of it, and the engineers were continually harassed by snipers and Soviet planes. As the grey day advanced, the dense formation of tanks along 48 Corps' entire front was seen to be extremely vulnerable – many of them bogged down because they had approached too near the swamped ground round the Pena, and all of them on open ground that made them easy prey for aerial attack.

The three SS divisions on 48 Corps' right were more fortunate. The ground over which they attacked was slightly higher and much of it was outside the cloudburst area, so that the hazard of swampy ground was considerably reduced. Sepp Dietrich of SS *Leibstandarte*, a commander of great skill and daring, forced his tanks forwards some seven miles during the day, knocking out 27 T34s in his advance. By late afternoon his patrols reported the village of Gremutshy clear of enemy, but Dietrich was not to be caught in the lure of a deserted objective. He halted his tanks, got them hull down in folds in the ground and saw that they were well camouflaged. His cunning was rewarded. At sunset the bombardment of Gremutshy began and continued till midnight. Then the whole of the *Leibstandarte* moved forward – without having lost a single tank in the baited trap. Gremutshy had been reduced to a smoking ruin by shelling. Its thatched cottages still blazed fiercely and dust rose in clouds from the rubble as, in the moonlight, Dietrich's tanks skirted the razed village and got into position for a dawn attack.

Dietrich supposed, rightly, that the Russians believed their bombardments had disabled or destroyed many German tanks and that they were therefore unprepared for the attack. But, since surprise was of the essence, there was no time for such refinements as the clearing of minefields, and there were a good many casualties as SS *Leibstandarte* pressed on. But by midday the huge Panthers, which were impervious to 76 mm fire except at point-blank range, had penetrated the Russian defensive positions south of Werchopenje and were making for Hill 260 a mile south of Nowosselowka – one of the objectives that had been unattained by 48 Corps. Their losses had been heavy, however – as much from breakdowns as from Russian attacks. The day ended with stalemate on that middle section of Fourth *Panzer* Army's front.

It was in fact only on the third day, 7 July, that any real success was achieved by the southern pincer. By that time the sun had dried out the swampy ground and the battlefield presented a different, though equally desolate, appearance: miles of devastated cornfields, hundreds of burnt-out tanks of both sides, and the bodies of the dead already swelling obscenely in the heat. A soldier's diary records, 'One man had been caught by bomb blast while squatting in a ditch with his trousers down. It seemed the ultimate in humiliation.'

The minefields had created great devastation and the blackened flesh and bones of those who had been blown up were strewn grotesquely over the battlefield:

> Coming stealthily upon a small copse I looked warily up to meet the face of a sniper poised in a tree. Panic-stricken I fired my pistol up at him before he could get me; but it was just a head, a blown-off bodiless head, still – it seemed to me – smiling craftily, that had lodged in the branches there. When I climbed up I dislodged it and it fell to the ground with a thud, the crafty smile undisturbed.

By this time, the Russians had moved back into the ruins of Gremutshy in preparation for a counter-attack. While they were forming up for this, 48 *Panzer* Corps launched their delayed attempt to make their two-pronged wheel to the north-west. They caught the enemy by surprise, broke through on both sides of Ssyrzew in great force and caused havoc among the assembling Seventh Guards Army, which fled in disorder to shelter behind Hill 243 beyond Werchopenje, losing 70 tanks and artillery pieces in the carefully timed and aimed German barrage.

With the ground clear before them, *Gross Deutschland* now gained momentum and wheeled round to Ssyrzewo with only the most minor casualties. The Russians seemed for the moment nonplussed. But by afternoon they had recovered and launched their counter-attack on Ssyrzewo. It resulted in a head-on collision in which 500 tanks simply faced each other and went on firing until, after several hours, the reverberation of guns along the steep banks of the Pena diminished and night fell on the still-blazing hulks.

No ground had been gained by either side, and it became clearer

than ever that the chief characteristic of the Battle of Kursk –
which town, though less than 40 miles to the north, remained to
the Germans as remote as the moon – was the huge wastage of men
and arms in a fight that lacked any subtlety of direction. Mass was
posed against mass in a conflict that, in theory, should have been brief
and sharply decisive, but in five days showed no sign of reaching a
climax.

Dietrich, one of Hitler's oldest friends, said in one of his rare
criticisms of the Führer:

> Perhaps the feeling of failure had permeated the troops on the
> Russian front since Kharkov. Not to be able to clinch the
> victory then was a bad thing. Then Hitler's uncertainty was
> a sign. The conflict between the top commanders was another.
> There were personal feuds. Kluge and Guderian hated each
> other; they nearly came to blows once. Hitler's intuition was
> always right, and he should have allowed it to overcome the
> pressure of the generals who wanted Zitadelle to go on for
> their share of the glory. Also, the way the Russians poured
> men and machines into the fray was absolutely unlimited. They
> simply had a disregard for numbers. It didn't matter to them
> that they were losing a million. Another million were packed
> behind them ready to be fed into the battle machine.

It was true, although it could hardly be said that Hitler was sparing
in his expenditure of men and machines either. But his was the
expenditure of desperation, and the Russian High Command knew
this very well. Viewing the battle in retrospect Stalin declared to the
Supreme Soviet: 'We were an immovable mass against which the
Fascists tried to pitch an irresistible force. A scientific impossibility
in any case. But they were out-maneuvered by our generals also.
They never had a chance.'

That was untrue. There were a number of occasions when Russian
tactics were as unimaginative as the Germans', and many more when
the jaws of the pincer seemed to be closing. But it was always a
piecemeal closure by isolated units, never a concerted forward
movement. The shoulder-to-shoulder positioning of Hoth's entire
Fourth *Panzer* Army within a 30-mile front had packed a punch
that could hardly have failed. Yet it was a punch that was weakened
by circumstances that should have been anticipated. Such simple

devices as the lure of the abandoned village were overlooked, and the enemy's ability to contain Model's northern force in, so to speak, a salient within a salient was not appreciated. This last factor dealt the death blow to the whole operation. With every abortive attempt Model made to press southward it became increasingly difficult for Hoth to link up with him. 'The Russians have learnt a lot since 1941,' he told Manstein, 'They are no longer peasants with simple minds. They have leant the art of warfare from us.'

Wherever they had learnt it, their knowledge was nowhere more apparent than in the intense fighting that took place around the railway junction of Orel, north of the salient. The Russian Third Army had forced its way forward with the object of encircling Model's Ninth Army in a sweep to the south-west. In that objective it failed, but it did keep most of Model's infantry and artillery engaged in defense instead of attack. The German infantry were thus unable to lend support to the southward armored thrusts that were meant to link up with the Fourth *Panzer* Army on the heights east of Kursk. For three continuous days and nights from 9 to 11 July, Orel in the north and Belgorod in the south – where the Seventh Guards Army was attempting a similar tactic to split the SS divisions from their supporting battle group in 48 *Panzer* Corps – were subjected to bombardment after bombardment. 'It was a continual earthquake,' one eye-witness put it, 'The ground just split asunder and any tank on the move would tip into the fissure.'

Yet another blow was delivered by the Red Air Force, which succeeded in bombing the German supply base at Poltava and destroying the railway line to Kharkov, making lengthy and delaying engineering work necessary. There was no doubt that, whether newly learnt or not, the art of warfare was much in evidence in the Russian designs.

By the time both German pincers had been fighting uninterruptedly for a week, they were showing signs of exhaustion. A shortage of supplies and ammunition, abetted by the cutting off of the railhead, was also making itself felt. But on the left flank of the southern pincer they managed to drive the enemy off the main road from Rakowo to Kruglik and head for the Beresowka forest. Once that objective was attained there was a good chance of capturing Hill 247 with the help of the north-west sweep of the SS division on the right flank, which was intended to wheel round from Hill 260 south of Nowosselowka and make a synchronized attack on Hill 247 from the east.

During the night of 9 July the 3rd *Panzer* Division entered the village of Beresowka from the west, much reduced in numbers – at least a third of its heavy tanks lay burnt out on the battlefield – but tenaciously holding on to every inch of ground it had fought for up the Kruglik road. Help was on its way in the form of one regiment of SS *Leibstandarte* that was making its way unopposed across open country from Werchopenje. Rudolf von Ribbentrop, son of the German Minister, was in command and reported later that he had got to within half a mile of the woods north of the village when a strong Russian counter-attack met them. 'Russian tanks of all sizes came streaming out of the forest and fanned out to meet us,' he said, 'Visibility was bad because of the cornfields, but there was a battle royal and we shot up two of their big mobile guns before the *Luftwaffe* came in to help.'

As one of the pilots described it: 'In the first attack four tanks explode under the hammer blows of my cannon; by evening, after four more sorties, the total rises to 12. The evil spell is broken, and in the Stuka we possess a weapon which can speedily be employed everywhere and is capable of dealing successfully with the formidable numbers of Soviet tanks.'

This was wishful thinking on his part, however. Nothing could deal wholly successfully with the huge number of Soviet tanks. On every section of the battlefield those that were destroyed or immobilized were replaced with seeming magical rapidity. Supplies were endless 'and appeared from nowhere,' as Manstein told Hitler at a conference at the Führer's headquarters on 12 July. By that time the railhead at Poltava was operating again, but there were no endless supplies coming from Germany. The enormous force of fighting vehicles with which Manstein and Kluge had opened the battle to close the Kursk salient had been depleted by more than half. There was continual activity at the repair shops to get into some sort of fighting order those tanks – especially Panthers and Tigers – that had been retrieved from the battlefield. An equally continual effort was made to overcome the successes of the Soviet aircraft in attacking the ammunition trains for which every German tank still left in the field was desperately waiting.

It was now being proved only too clearly that Hitler had indeed put in hazard far more armor than he could afford to lose. Although no resolution of the Kursk conflict could yet be seen, developments in Europe were calling for a speedy conclusion of the offensive and the transfer of forces to the western theater. For, by 12 July, the Allies had landed in Sicily.

The climax to the battle of Kursk was reached during the two days 12 to 14 July, although it amounted to only the fadeaway ending of a battle of attrition. For nine days the two contestants had been slugging at one another like heavyweights swinging giant blows that consistently failed to achieve the knockout.

Early on the morning of 12 July, Hoth summoned his corps commanders and planned for a breakthrough before the Russians could intensify their defenses between Kruglik and Nowosselowka and build up their forces for a big push southward. He had received intelligence reports indicating that the extreme southern tip of Army Group South's fortified line along the Donetz and Mius rivers, between Taganrog and Stalino, was under the threat of a Russian attack. 'We shall be needed there,' he told Hausser, commander of the SS Corps. 'Let us finish the issue of Kursk once and for all.'

Brave words. His armored strength consisted now of only 600 operative tanks to spearhead the attack. Every man in Fourth Army was suffering from battle exhaustion, and ammunition was at a premium. In contrast, Vatutin had new machines, including the new 85 mm SU85 self-propelled gun, and men fresh to the front. He also had the entire Fifth Armored Army in reserve and ready for action. It was not difficult to see where the advantage lay. This climactic action came to be known as 'The Death Ride of Fourth Panzer Army.'

'It's a fine day for a joy ride,' Sepp Dietrich said laconically to the driver of his command tank. 'It won't rain.'

Nor did it. It was a day of intense dry heat. The interiors of the tanks were like ovens despite the air induction systems and fan coolers. The high speed traffic of heavy vehicles over the sandy roads threw up clouds of dust that made it virtually impossible for the *Luftwaffe* to pick out their targets. On one occasion, according to Dietrich, a T34 and a Panther collided head on as they rolled through the dust. 'Ivan had broken through our anti-tank screen and his progeny were streaming like rats all over the battlefield.'

The 'all over' certainly suited the situation. The Fifth Armored Army had come charging into action with all the zest of experienced troops who had waited too long in reserve positions. As the spearhead of the SS *Panzer* Corps rolled towards Prokhorovka it met the full force of this fresh and eager force. Slightly outnumbered, but with more heavy tanks, Hausser's exhausted tank crews met their match. The thick dust prevented the Tigers from making full use of their superior range, and many fell prey to the T34s. The battlefield was littered with burning wrecks – more than 300 tanks were lost by each side. But it was the Germans who could least afford such heavy losses. The onslaught of the *Panzers* was over. By evening the Russians had recaptured Berezowka and cut off 3rd *Panzer* Division and a large wedge of *Gross Deutschland* that had forced its way through the woods to the rescue.

For the Germans, the battle was clearly lost. All the open country between Belgorod, where Seventh Guards Army had broken through as far as the rear echelons of the SS corps, and Orel to the north was possessed by the Russians. Only isolated pockets of Germans were evident in the villages.

From the three hills so fiercely fought for and now relinquished by the Germans, the Russians had a straight line of fire down on to the irrepressible attackers, whose commanders were continually reminding themselves of the Führer's words: 'It must not fail.'

Nevertheless it did fail. The immediate cause of failure, or anyway of termination, was the Führer's own order, relayed through Manstein and radio link to Army Group South's headquarters: 'Operation Zitadelle is cancelled forthwith.'

It is of course impossible to stop a raging battle instantaneously unless both sides are given the same order. A withdrawal meant fighting a rearguard action, and it was two weeks before Hoth's forces got themselves back to their original positions on the starting line – with further considerable losses. In the north, Model's Ninth Army, having advanced so little, had correspondingly little to cover in retreat. The situation at Orel was still critical, however, and Manstein had to order two *Panzer* divisions north to help deal with this threat. He sent two more to the south, where the Taganrog–Stalino sector was also being increasingly threatened.

During the whole of the operation, from H-hour to cancellation, the advances made by the two jaws of the pincer, collectively or by individual units, had never reduced the breach across the base of the salient to less than 60 miles. Twenty *Panzer* divisions, the pride and joy of the *Wehrmacht*, had been bled white, and although on the credit side could be counted the huge number of Russian prisoners and the vast booty and destruction of the battlefield it was only too clear that with Allied assistance the Russians could afford losses on this colossal scale far more easily than the Germans could.

The Death Ride of the Fourth *Panzer* Army signaled the approaching end of the German struggle for Russia. By December, the reconstituted Ninth and Fourth *Panzer* Armies had been pushed back to, and beyond, the Dneiper. The whole of the Eastern Front from Nevel in the north to Kirovograd in the south reflected the turning of the tide, for it had been subjected to unremitting Soviet attacks against the weakening power of Hitler's armies. Now, not even a stalemate could be achieved. The Kursk gambit had been played and had failed.

Sicily (1943)

Hubert Essame

The invasion of Axis-occupied Sicily, Operation Husky, in July 1943 was the greatest seaborne assault of the Second World War. Almost eight divisions – 181,000 troops – were simultaneously put ashore along a hundred mile stretch of the island's coastline. Backing the men was an array of technological expertise and military might that from then on was the hallmark of the Western Allies at war: 14,000 vehicles; 600 tanks; 1,800 guns; 750 warships (including six battleships, 15 cruisers and 128 destroyers) and 5,000 aircraft. For Sicily, the United States contributed her latest inventions – the 'walkie-talkie' radio, and the versatile DUKW six-wheeled amphibious truck. By contrast, in the invasion of Normandy a year later, only 133,000 men were landed over the 45-mile stretch of D-day beaches. Husky marked not only the return of the Allies to the mainland of Europe, but also signalled their determination to knock Mussolini's Italy out of the war.

By January 1943 it was apparent that the Axis forces in Tunis were trapped in the vice being closed by the Allied armies from west and east, and that their destruction was only to be a matter of time. Field Marshal Albert Kesselring, Axis Supreme Commander in the Mediterranean, predicted that the Allies would soon be 'in possession of a jumping-off base for an assault on Europe from the south'. There was an urgent need, therefore, for President Franklin D. Roosevelt and Prime Minister Winston Churchill to meet with their Chiefs of

Staff to decide the next move. They met on 14–23 January 1943 in French Morocco for the Casablanca Conference, with Major General George S. Patton, commanding the United States forces in Morocco, as host.

After discussing – and discarding – the possibilities of a second European front to take the strain off the hard-pressed Soviet Armies, the conference decided that when the North African campaign was over, the Allied forces, under General Dwight D. Eisenhower, should stage Operation Husky – the invasion of Sicily by two armies, one American, under Patton, and one British, led by General Sir Bernard Montgomery, both under command of General Sir Harold Alexander. It was hoped to placate Stalin by drawing German forces away from the Russian front; to open up the Mediterranean to Allied shipping; and to give the war-weary Italians an excuse for overthrowing Benito Mussolini and getting out of the war.

Sicily is about the size of the state of Vermont, and a little larger than Wales. The terrain generally favors the defense. Inland, the ground is rugged and mountainous, with Mount Etna, in the north-east corner, rising to 10,000 ft. Good roads ran along the east and northern coasts; elsewhere they were few, badly surfaced and with many sharp corners and steep gradients. Deployment off the roads would inevitably be difficult. Only in the Plain of Catania could armor move with any degree of freedom. The Allied plan made the capture of the 30 Sicilian airfields a priority, for it was these bases that posed such a threat to Allied shipping in the Mediterranean. They had also sustained the Axis defense in Tunisia. The airfields fell into three groups: the Gerbini group in the Plain of Catania; the Castelvetrano group south-west of Palermo; and the Conte Olivio Comiso group near the south coast ports.

Combined operations were still in their infancy. No one knew to what extent it would be possible to maintain the invading forces over the beaches with the DUKWs, LSTs, LCMs and LCIs. It was therefore considered vital to gain possession of the major ports as soon as possible. Messina, the largest of these, was out of fighter range and known to be strongly defended. Palermo, Trapani and Marsala, also out of fighter range, could maintain about half the invading force; Catania, Augusta and Syracuse, within range, would supply the other half. Operation Husky was proving as formidable to prepare as Operation Torch, the previous (and first) Anglo-American amphibious landing of the war.

For the assault the admirals stressed the advantages of dispersed landings from the naval point of view. The airmen, their case forcibly put by Air Chief Marshal Sir Arthur Tedder, demanded the neutralization of the airfields on the island as a first priority: both British and American logistic staffs insisted that they must have the use of Palermo and the southern and south-eastern ports at a very early stage. After seven invasion plans had been discussed, Eisenhower gave the final decision: the two armies would land side by side, the Seventh US Army about Gela and the Eighth British Army in the south-east corner of the island. July would be the deadline for the landings.

Most post-war comment gives the impression that the Americans and British in the Mediterranean were continually at loggerheads. But the reverse was the case, due largely to the magnanimity and vision of Eisenhower, the Supreme Commander. Seldom did the Allies work together so cheerfully and unselfishly. Eisenhower had in Alexander the most experienced and tactful commander in the British Army to handle his two brilliant but brittle Army commanders – Patton and Montgomery. Finally in Vice Admiral Sir Bertram H. Ramsay, his Deputy Commander, he had the admiral who had organized the largest evacuation in history – Dunkirk – to help him execute the largest combined operation in history.

The air strength of Tedder and Lieutenant General Carl Spaatz (USAAF) was formidable – 267 squadrons, 146 of which were American and the rest British, totalling over 5,000 aircraft and thus outnumbering the 520 Axis planes by ten to one. Immediately after the fall of Tunis, the Allies turned to the task of securing the air dominance over Sicily which must be gained before a single ship could safely approach it or one soldier step ashore. First, the Allied aircraft ranged far and wide against strategic targets in Italy. Then they began an intense bombardment of the enemy airfields and radar stations within striking distance of Sicily and the proposed routes of the convoys. Tedder interrupted the first stage of his air plan to seize Pantellaria; the island fortress Mussolini had constructed as rival to Malta.

Starting in May, the bombardment of this island gradually increased in intensity till 7 June. Thereafter for four days it rose to a crescendo: over 5,000 tons of bombs were dropped. On 10 June, the third anniversary of Italy's entry into the war, a force from 1st British Division approached the island covered by a precision attack by American flying Fortress B17 bombers. The garrison of 4,600 surrendered without a struggle. For the first time victory had been gained by air power alone.

At the end of June, Alexander's plans for the assault were complete. Montgomery and Eighth Army, embarking at ports between Syria and Sfax were to land on a 30-mile front with two corps, 13th Corps (Lieutenant General Sir Miles C. Dempsey) just south of Syracuse and 30th Corps (Lieutenant General Sir Oliver Leese) astride the Pachino peninsula to capture the airfield there. Patton planned to land his Seventh Army on a 70-mile front in three simultaneous seaborne assaults; two on the east flank by Major General Omar N. Bradley's 2nd Corps with 45th Division at Scoglitti and the 1st at Gela, and 3rd Division (Major General Lucian K. Truscott), directly under his own command, at Licata. As a floating reserve he had 2nd Armored Division and part of 9th Division. All were battle-hardened with the exception of 45th Division.

Initially Alexander prescribed the establishment of beach-heads and the early seizure of Syracuse, the Pachino and Ponte Olivo airfields and the port of Licata. Thereafter Montgomery was to seize Augusta, Catania and the Gerbini group of airfields. Patton planned to advance about 15 to 20 miles inland on the first day. Both armies were to link up on a common boundary – the Yellow Line. But what was to be done thereafter was, unfortunately, not clear. Patton suspected (with good reason) that the major role of exploitation would be given to Montgomery. He protested to Alexander but when overruled, like a good soldier for the moment raised no further objection. Both British and American landings were to be preceded by airborne assaults: the British 1st Airborne Division in gliders and the 82nd American Airborne Division parachuting.

Meanwhile, in early June, Generale d'Armata Alfredo Guzzoni had assumed command of the Italian forces on the island with his Sixth Army headquarters at Enna. He found, even by Italian standards at this stage of the war, an appalling situation. There was a total Italian garrison of 30,000 men and 1,500 guns but only four divisions out of 12 were relatively mobile. The rest were scattered in low-grade coast defense units on the scale of 41 men to the mile. Many of them were of local origin and virtually untrained; the standard of their officers was exceptionally low. Most of their arms and equipment were obsolete and the coast defenses, except near the ports, were either perfunctory or non-existent. One Corps headquarters presided over the destinies of these depressing troops at the east end of the island and another at the west. Only German assistance gave cause for any hope.

Guzzoni had attached as adviser Major General Fridolin von Senger und Etterlin, a Bavarian who had distinguished himself at the head of a *Panzer* Corps in Russia. Detached from 14 *Panzer* Corps on the mainland were 15th *Panzer Grenadier* Division under Major General Eberhard Rodt and *Hermann Goering Panzer* Division under Lieutenant General Paul Conrath, a former Nazi police chief, making a total of about 30,000 troops and including a Tiger tank company of 17 Mark VI tanks and approximately 90 Mark IIIs and IVs.

Anticipating landings at opposite ends of the island, as the Allies had originally planned, Guzzoni and von Senger deployed 15th *Panzer Grenadier* Division in the west and the *Hermann Goering* Division in two battle groups; one near Caltagirone about 20 miles north of Gela and the other under Colonel Schmalz in the Catania Plain. With these troops and the *Livorno* Division, south of Caltanisetta near the Ponte Olivo airfield, the Axis counted on holding the ring by rapid counter-attack until reinforced by the rest of 14 *Panzer* Corps from the mainland.

The day before the invasion, 9 July, started hot with scarcely a ripple on the sea. Rear Admiral Louis Mountbatten, the British Director of Combined Operations, with Adm. Ramsay on board the command ship *Antwerp*, watched the six invasion convoys as they passed on their way to the rendezvous south of Malta. Seven and a half divisions, totalling 160,000 men, were afloat in 2,760 ships and landing craft. They came from the Clyde, from Norfolk, Virginia; and ports along the African coast from Beirut to Algiers. Incredibly there was not a single enemy aircraft in the sky.

At noon, a light breeze sprang up from the west; by mid-afternoon it was blowing Force 7. Almost all the troops in the smaller craft were sick. As the British came under the lee of the land, conditions for them improved but for the Canadians and Americans there would be no respite. They would have to land sick to death and soaked to the skin. But the rough weather was not an unmitigated disaster. Most of the defenders of the Sicilian coast retired to bed, deciding that no man in his senses would attempt to land in such conditions.

First to land in the blackest hours of the night were the British 1st Air Landing Brigade in Waco and Horsa gliders. Their target was the Ponte Grande area near Syracuse. But it was disastrous.

Partly owing to the lack of experience of the pilots of their towing aircrafts and due also in part to the high winds their landing was widely scattered. Seventy of the 134 gliders were released too soon and lost in the sea. Only eight officers and 65 men out of a total 2,075 emplaned in Africa, reached their objective. But they managed to hang on until relieved by the 5th British Division. The 82nd Airborne Division (for the same reason) had an equally difficult landing. About 200 paratroopers of 505th Parachute Regiment managed to seize the vital high ground near Piano Lupo to set up and defend road blocks. They were to prove of great value when the expected counter-attack came later that day. Others roamed far and wide, cutting communications and generally spreading despondency and alarm amongst the Italians, rudely wakened from their slumbers.

On the Eighth Army front the guns of the four supporting battleships quickly silenced any coastal batteries and field guns that dared open fire and the landing proceeded smoothly, partly owing to the thorough training the troops had received and partly to the absence of Italian resistance. At one stage, Montgomery received a report that the Royal Marines had been charged by cavalry! In fact they had inadvertently stampeded the horses of the Italian 206th Coastal Division. These they rounded up, mounted and themselves charged inland. By nightfall the British had taken Syracuse and all their objectives for the day.

On the American front, 45th Division at Scoglitti, although delayed for an hour by the gale, had similar good fortune. At Licata, 3rd Division, in the new beaching craft (LSTs, LCIs and LSTs), landed on time and almost without a hitch. Mountbatten was impressed by the coolness, discipline and efficiency of the US Navy crews and the rapid organization of movement inland. By 0830, guns and tanks were freely coming ashore. Only at Gela was there serious opposition.

As Force X, a special force of Rangers attached to 1st Division, approached the shore, the enemy blew up the pier. Simultaneously the coast defense guns opened up. But they were quickly silenced by devastatingly accurate fire from the 5-in and 6-in guns of the destroyer *Shubrick* and the cruiser *Savannah*. As the Rangers touched down they dashed forward into Gela with the leading troops of 1st Division close on their heels. By 1000 Patton, in the headquarters ship *Monrovia* with Vice-Adm. Hewitt, had 3rd Division holding eight miles of coastline and forces moving rapidly inland. At Gela

1st Division held the road junction of Piano Lupo, the town itself and the airfield. The 45th Division reported that its leading troops were five miles inland.

Now that the Allies had shown their hand, Gen. Guzzoni's reaction was prompt but ill-starred. Clearly there was no risk of a landing at the Palermo end of the island. *Kampf Gruppe Schmaltz* could be relied upon for the moment to guard the Gerbini group of airfields. The major threat was posed by the Americans at Gela. Guzzoni therefore set the 15th *Panzer Grenadier* Division in motion towards Enna, thus creating a reserve under his own hand, and ordered the *Livorno* Division, plus two mobile groups and the *Hermann Goering* Division, to make a co-ordinated attack on Gela and drive the Americans into the sea. The orders for the *Hermann Goering* Division went astray: in consequence the Italians attacked on their own at 0830 with infantry and about 20 light tanks. They struck the 16th Regimental Combat Team supported by the guns of the Navy who were in no mood to be pushed aside. Their attack was a costly fiasco.

The German counter-attack during the early afternoon came with greater vigor, accompanied by heavy shelling of the beaches and determined low-flying attacks by the *Luftwaffe* on the mass of shipping now lying offshore. Despite the courage of the Germans it was a muddled affair and came to nothing. About an hour later they renewed the attack, this time supported by Tiger tanks. This too petered out in confused fighting which continued till nightfall, leaving the Americans in possession of all their first day's objectives except the Ponte Olivo airfield.

To Patton it was evident that 11 July would be the crucial day and that his army would have to bear the brunt of a full-dress counterstroke by the bulk of the German armor. To the consternation of the staffs, he therefore scrapped the pre-arranged landing schedules and ordered 2nd Armored Division and the 18th RCT ashore with all speed. Disembarkation proceeded at a frantic rate throughout the night. He was thus ready to meet the thrust on Gela soon after dawn by the *Hermann Goering* Division who attacked in three columns from the east and by the *Livorno* Division from the west. When he disembarked from Adm. Hewitt's barge at 0900, German 88 mm guns were pounding the beach. When his scout car had been de-waterproofed he set off into Gela for the headquarters of the 1st Division. On the way he decided to look in on the HQ of Colonel Darby, one of the Rangers.

It was a lucky decision. In fact, the *Hermann Goering* Division had cut off the 1st Division from the Rangers and a confused battle was raging along the eastern outskirts of the town. From an observation post close to the front, Patton was able to watch a battle between the Rangers, using a captured battery of Italian 77 mm guns and *Livorno* Division. Every gun the enemy could bring to bear was used. They turned Gela into a shambles. In the nick of time, ten Shermans joined in the fray, having driven all the way from Licata. Deadly and accurate fire from the 6-in guns of the *Savannah* was brought to bear on the *Livorno* Division. By mid-morning they had had enough and retired badly mauled.

Patton now moved on to the 1st Division's front which only had two tanks ashore. Outside the town Conrath had flung in all his 60 tanks with orders to hurl the Americans into the sea. Burning tanks soon littered the Gela Plain. The 32nd Field Artillery Battalion, disembarking their guns from DUKWs, went straight into action and engaged the German tanks over open sights. The infantry of the 1st Division stood like a rock. Three miles inland, the Germans reeled back before the 16th Infantry at Piano Lupo. Meanwhile, the tanks of 2nd Armored Division, struggling through the sand of the beaches, roared into action. Deadly and accurate fire from the Navy added to the inferno. The German tanks faltered and then turned back leaving over half their number behind in flames. Patton then got through to Major General Terry de la Mesa Allen, commander of the 1st Division, to congratulate him and at the same time remind him that he still had to take his D-day objective, Ponte Olivo airfield, four miles inland. Meanwhile, farther to the east, the paratroops had put up a magnificent resistance on Biazzo Ridge and disembarkation had continued. By nightfall the bridgehead at Gela was secure. As Patton had foreseen, this was the bloodiest day of the campaign.

An unfortunate incident that night marred a story of outstanding success. Patton had arranged for 504th Parachute Regiment, consisting of two battalions of parachutists, to be dropped on the Gela airfield and had taken every precaution to warn his own troops of the operation. He and his staff were assured that all the anti-aircraft gunners of the huge supporting fleet had also been told. Regrettably, and perhaps due to the 550 Axis air sorties in two days, enemy AA guns in the fleet opened up against the aircraft carrying the parachutists. As a result, the men were dropped far and wide. When daylight came, out of 2,000 men and equipment, all that could be mustered at the landing zone were a scratch company and a few light howitzers.

With both Eighth and Seventh Armies firmly ashore, the first phase of Operation Husky was nearing its end. By the evening of 12 July Montgomery had captured Augusta and was on the point of advancing on a front of four divisions into the Catania Plain. Patton had linked up with him and was nearing the Yellow Line 20 miles inland which was his first objective. Meanwhile, Guzzoni had been moving his armored forces into the Catania Plain and reinforcements from 14 *Panzer* Corps were arriving opposite the British front. The time had clearly come for Alexander to decide which line of advance the Allied armies should take. It seemed obvious to the Americans and others that Patton rather than Montgomery was better sited to strike due north on Enna and the north coast.

On 14 July, Montgomery, in his drive towards Catania, found himself held up by 29th *Panzer Grenadier* Division and two regiments of parachutists flown in from Avignon as well as Battlegroup Schmalz. General Hans Valentine Hube, of 14 *Panzer* Corps, a one-armed veteran of the Eastern Front, had taken charge. Montgomery, without even mentioning the fact to Patton (but apparently with Alexander's acquiescence), now set in motion a left-hook round the foot of Mount Etna on Route 124, which was within the American area of operations. Of the three good roads running north he now had two. That evening, to the consternation of Patton and Bradley, a directive arrived from Alexander allotting to Montgomery the main effort against Messina, on both sides of Mount Etna.

The Americans, cramped for space and resentful of the fact that they had not even been consulted, found themselves relegated to the invidious task of guarding the British left flank. Later, they were to have the consolation prize of a ride to Palermo, when Messina was in Montgomery's grasp. Stung, Patton took off for Tunis to see Alexander and to express his disappointment. Only now did Alexander realize how deeply Patton felt the affront. But it was too late to halt Montgomery. Alexander therefore gave Patton a free hand in advancing towards Palermo and the north coast.

Released from his strait-jacket Patton launched his spectacular all-out drive on Palermo. To this end he created a provisional Corps under Major General Geoffrey T. Keyes, his Chief of Staff. The 82nd and 3rd Divisions were to make for Palermo from the south and south-east, with 2nd Armored Division in their wake for the final

advance on the city. Meanwhile Bradley's Corps was to strike due
north and cut the coast road. During a six-day lightning campaign
in torrid heat Keyes' Corps, with the infantry riding on the tanks,
thrust forward 100 miles and took 53,000 prisoners. On 22 July
Patton, with 2nd Armored Division, entered Palermo in triumph
to the plaudits of the inhabitants and took up his quarters in the
Royal Palace. Next day Bradley's Corps reached the north coast at
Termini Imerese.

After the war attempts were made to detract from Patton's
achievement. It was claimed that, before the campaign started,
contact had been made by Intelligence officers through 'Lucky'
Luciano, head of the Mafia in the United States (and serving a 30-year
prison sentence), with his opposite number in Sicily, Don Calogero
Vizzini, to ensure that the Italian troops put up no resistance to the
invaders. In particular, it was alleged that Mafia agents persuaded
Colonel Salemi's battle group (consisting of a battalion, some field
guns and several Tiger tanks) holding a very strong position in the
mountainous Cammarata area which dominated the two roads to
Palermo, to let Patton's columns through on 20 July. That there were
contacts with the Mafia in Sicily is probably true – they would have
been almost impossible to avoid – but to suggest that their influence
was in any way decisive is ludicrous.

With every justification the Press were jubilant. The Americans
now had a deep-water port capable of handling ships coming direct
from the United States and were no longer dependent on supply over
beaches; the 9th US Division landed at Palermo. Magnanimously
Patton restored his Sicilian prisoners to their families, which reduced
the demand on Allied food supplies. Alexander now directed Patton
to swing along the north coast towards Messina. Montgomery was
to make a short hook with the Canadians about Regalbuto to give
Bradley room to maneuver. Thus the so-called inter-Allied race for
Messina.

Although the Allies had not secured a military decision in Sicily
their progress now finally precipitated the fall of Mussolini and his
government. Hitler was still sane and the time had not yet come
when a policy of 'No withdrawal' would be his strategic panacea. The
disasters at Stalingrad and in Tunisia, and now his appalling losses in
his Russian summer offensive, Operation Zitadelle, at last brought
home to him that his manpower resources were running down. On
26 July, the day Marshal Pietro Badoglio arrested Mussolini, Hitler

gave Kesselring permission to abandon Sicily, before the Allies made their invasion of Italy.

Next day Kesselring, ignoring Guzzoni, told Hube to prepare for evacuation. The chances of success must have seemed slim, for he gave orders that men rather than equipment were to have priority. Hube accordingly planned a slow withdrawal to a series of five defensive positions across the Messina peninsula. The rugged country was in his favor: it gave him magnificent artillery observation; the roads were narrow and winding, often passing through defiles which were easy to block. The anti-aircraft defenses at Messina under Colonel Ernest Guenther Baade were very strong and Captain von Liebenstein of the German Navy had an excellent ferry service across the three-mile-wide straits.

When Patton and Montgomery resumed operations at the end of July they found themselves condemned to attack side by side against a series of excellent defensive positions held by first-class troops, whose morale remained unshaken. For neither the British nor the Americans was there great scope for maneuver: German mines and demolitions harassed their every move. Montgomery had 13th Corps on the right and 30th Corps on his left. In Seventh Army, 45th and 1st US Divisions led first, later giving way to 3rd and 9th Divisions. The weather was hot and the dust appalling. There were many casualties from malaria. Patton, determined at all costs to reach Messina before Montgomery ordered 'a sustained relentless drive until the enemy is decisively defeated'. Inevitably the terrain channelled the advance along narrow lanes or on to ridges and up valleys devoid of cover and in full view of the enemy's artillery observers. Air co-operation on the fronts of both armies left much to be desired. There were far too many incidents of friendly aircraft bombing their own troops.

At Troina, the 1st Division, slogging along rugged hillsides to outflank immensely strong German positions, fought for four days the bitterest battle of the campaign. Allen and his deputy commander were at loggerheads; their men were tired and beginning to feel that they were being called upon to shoulder more than their fair share of the fighting, having been through the whole Tunisian campaign. When Troina finally fell, on 6 August, Patton had to take the decision to relieve both the divisional commander and his deputy.

Exasperated by the delay and worried by the increase in the numbers of men evacuated with battle neurosis, Patton staged three amphibious hooks. But incredibly only enough landing craft could be provided to lift a battalion group. The first run was abortive. The second landed at Brolo on 11 August just behind 29th *Panzer Grenadier* Division's position on the north coast road. It was not strong enough to cut off the battlegroup opposing 45th Division but, helped by the fire of American warships, accelerated the German withdrawal by 24 hours. Regrettably the *Panzer Grenadiers* made up lost time by hanging on to the next position for an extra day. For the night of 15 to 16 August Patton staged a further end run, this time of regimental size. It was a blow in thin air. The Germans had fallen back to the next position and the amphibious force waded ashore not behind the Germans but to meet the leading infantry of 3rd Division.

A similar landing by No. 40 British Royal Marine Commando, just south of Scaletta on the same night, found nothing to stop it except demolitions. But so impeded was their advance into Messina that when they entered the town on the morning of 17 August they found that the 7th Infantry Regiment of 3rd US Division had arrived ahead of them, and Patton had won the race to Messina. He had already accepted the surrender of the city at 1015. There was an element of anti-climax in these last days of the campaign. Despite the overwhelming strength of the Allies in the air and on the sea, Hube had succeeded in evacuating nearly 40,000 German troops with 9,605 vehicles, 47 tanks, 94 guns and 17,000 tons of ammunition. It was a miniature German version of Dunkirk in which typically they had saved a much greater proportion of their heavy equipment than the British. In addition some 62,000 Italians had escaped across the straits.

Baades' 350 dual-purpose anti-aircraft guns had maintained a barrage described as 'heavier than the Ruhr', over the four evacuation routes starting on 11 August, along which 140 small craft plied. From 13 August, von Liebenstein decided to risk working by daylight as well as by night. Losses were remarkably light. Surprisingly, the Allies did not realize until 14 August that the Germans were pulling out. Judged objectively by professional standards, Hube and von Liebenstein were the winners of the race to Messina.

Kesselring was astonished that the Allies should have failed to secure an overwhelming victory, in the last week of the campaign, by landing another amphibious force on the toe of Italy, seize the ferry terminals at Reggio and hamstring the withdrawal across the Straits of Messina. The Allies had ample reserves of troops in North

Africa. Their navies could have provided the landing craft if they had been asked and would not have hesitated to bring their big ships within range of the coastal batteries if ordered. They had unchallenged superiority in the air which they failed to concentrate over the straits.

Finally, Adm. Cunningham was not prepared to risk his warships in the straits at night; the only other foolproof method of disrupting the frantic Axis ferry service. There was no capitulation in Sicily because, before the landing, no agreement had been reached as to whether or not Husky should be followed by the invasion of Italy. It was therefore left to Eisenhower to exploit his victorious landing as he thought fit. As operations progressed, Alexander failed to use his initiative, awaiting orders which never came.

Nevertheless, the campaign had achieved its major objects. It had unseated Mussolini. It had set in motion the negotiations, through the British embassies in Lisbon and Madrid, which would soon result in the Italians abandoning their German Allies and surrendering their fleet. The Mediterranean was at last freed for Allied shipping and in particular for tankers from the Persian Gulf.

Much battle experience had been gained and many good commanders, notably Bradley, had come to the fore. Casualties, at 9,000 British and 8,735 American, were remarkably light. The Germans had lost 32,000 and the Italians 132,000, mostly prisoners of war. And the threat the Allies now offered to 'the soft underbelly of Europe', although it did not swing Turkey over to the Allied side, undoubtedly induced Hitler to call off the ghastly battle of Kursk (Zitadelle) on 14 July and to divert reserves from the Russian front in order to retain his grip on the Italian mainland. The experience gained in the invasion of Sicily, especially in amphibious operations, ensured the success of Overlord, the invasion of North West Europe, less than a year later.

Admin Box (1944)

Patrick Turnbull

In the latter half of 1943, Lieutenant General Renya Mutaguchi, Japanese Fifteenth Army commander, and his divisional commanders, were summoned to a series of conferences at Lieutenant General M. Kawabe's Burma Area Army HQ in Rangoon. They were there to discuss operations for the coming year. The outcome of these meetings – held under considerable strain, since Tokyo had impressed on Kawabe the necessity for speedy victory in Burma to boost flagging morale at home – was the plan for an offensive – Operation *U-Go* – on the central Assam/Manipur front by Fifteenth Army. Its objective was the destruction of 4th Indian Corps, and an advance to the Bengal frontier. It was somewhat optimistically reckoned that success – and it was stressed that failure could not even be contemplated – would spark off a general uprising in India against the British Raj, and what Japanese propaganda was to refer to as 'The March on Delhi'.

But it was not until the general outline of *U-Go* had been approved by Southern Area Commander, Field Marshal Count Hisarchi Terauchi, that a rider for a preliminary, diversionary, operation in Arakan – code name *Ha-Go* – was added. To be carried out by 55th and elements of 54th Divisions under the recently arrived Lieutenant General Tadashi Hanaya, the object of this limited offensive was to pin down, and draw off, British-Indian reserves from the main central front.

Japanese hopes of a resounding victory in Burma seemed justified. Early in 1943, an attempt by 14th Indian Division to recapture the Arakan port of Akyab ended in ignominious failure. Though eventually expanded to six brigades, 14th Division had failed to break through the Japanese defenses on the Donbaik Chaung. This was at no time manned by more than two battalions and by as little as two companies to begin with. Finally, in early April, the recently arrived Japanese 55th Division staged a brilliant counter-attack, driving 14th Division and its replacement 26th Indian Division back well beyond their starting point.

At his Ranchi HQ, Lieutenant-General Sir William J. Slim, commanding 15th Indian Corps, who had been called to take charge of the Arakan battle too late to do other than convert a threatened rout into an orderly withdrawal, was one of the very few not afflicted by the wave of pessimism following this disaster. The jungle, he insisted, was the reverse of the desert – infantry, not tanks and fighter-bombers dominated the battlefield. Therefore until the British copied the Japanese, and made the infantry the *corps d'élite*, there could be little or no hope of victory. Acting on his own theory, Slim devoted the Monsoon period to the intensive battle training of his reconstituted Corps, 5th and 7th Indian Divisions, commanded by Major-Generals Harold R. Briggs and Frank W. Messervy, both veterans of East Africa and the Western Desert, and Major-General C. G. Woolner's 81st West African Division. The Bihar jungle was the scene of tough exercises under active service conditions. Non-combatants – clerks, storemen, wireless operators, cooks – had to join in, warned by Slim that 'in the jungle every man, whatever his job, is likely to find himself engaged in hand-to-hand fighting with the enemy.'

When the 1943/44 dry season operational plans were made known, 15th Corps was gratified to learn that it was to be given the opportunity for a 'return match'. While in Manipur, 4th Corps' activities were to be confined to 'a limited offensive up to the Chindwin', 15th Corps was entrusted with the job of clearing the enemy forces from Arakan, and (possibly) to follow up with the capture of Akyab.

As the Monsoon abated, 15th Corps left Ranchi *en route* for Arakan, but within a few days of setting up his HQ at Bawli Bazar, Slim was called upon to command the newly created Fourteenth Army. His place was taken by Lieutenant-General Philip Christison from 33rd Corps in Southern India.

Arakan's terrain, as 14th Division had found to its cost, heavily favored the defense. A narrow strip oriented north–south, it is bounded on the east by almost trackless jungle-covered hills, the Arakan Yomas and Arakan Hill Tracts, on the west by the Bay of Bengal. What flat ground there is consists of *padi* fields and swamps, furrowed by wide, swift-flowing rivers, and tidal creeks. The Mayu Peninsula, ending at Foul Point opposite Akyab Island, is bisected by a dragon-crested spine of hills, the Mayu Range. Its precipitous jungle slopes rise to 2,500 ft in places, crossed east–west by only three passes. The Goppe and Ngakyedauk Passes were barely fit for mules. But the Tunnels Road was suitable for mechanical transport. This was formerly the track of a narrow-gauge railway connecting the little port of Maungdaw on the west, at the mouth of the Naf river, with Buthidaung on the east, at the point where the tidal Mayu River became the Kalapanzin, and cutting through the range by two short tunnels. This road – 16 miles in length – was the line on which Lt. Gen. Hanaya had chosen to base his main defenses, giving the whole area the picturesque name of 'The Golden Fortress'.

Since the destruction of the Japanese, rather than territorial gain, was Christison's objective, this concentration of enemy forces suited him. Advance was on a two-divisional front, 5th Division to the west, 7th Division to the east of the Mayu Range. After making a wide sweep to the east the West Africans were moving on a pack basis down the Kaladan Valley, acting as a flank guard. Christison had met with only token resistance. By the New Year of 1944, he was poised for the first phase of his main attack; an assault on the Golden Fortress's western bastion, Razabil, just south of Maungdaw. The choice of Razabil as the first objective was dictated by the urgency of securing Maungdaw with its harbor facilities, since, till the port became operational, 15th Corps had to rely on a single supply line. This was a road on the west, coastal, side of the Mayu Range – built the year before by 14th Division's engineers.

In the first week of January, 161st Brigade (5th Division) began to probe the outer edges of the Razabil defensive network. They met such determined opposition that what was hoped would be the decisive blow could not be delivered until 26 January. Though preceded by heavy aerial and artillery bombardments, and supported by the Corps' armored unit – the 25th Dragoons in Lee-Grant medium tanks – hardly any progress was made. After three days of abortive assaults, heavy losses – the Sikh company of 1st Battalion,

1st Punjabi Regiment was reduced to 21 men, while the 4/7th Rajputs lost 27 killed and 129 wounded – Christison had to call a halt.

He planned to switch the main weight of his renewed offensive to 7th Division's front. With this in mind he ordered 25th Dragoons to move to the eastern side of the Mayu Range via the Ngakyedauk Pass, by then capable of taking heavy vehicles, thanks to superhuman efforts on the part of the engineers, since the track included a rise and fall of 1,000 ft in three miles. It was renamed, and since immortalized, as the 'Okey-doke' Pass.

At the same time the eastern exit in the neighborhood of Sinzweya was converted into an administrative area, with petrol and ammunition dumps, vast stores of rations, spare parts, and medical supplies, manned by Ordnance, Service Corps, Transport and Medical units. Its defense against possible tip-and-run raids was entrusted to the 24th Light Anti-Aircraft/Anti-Tank Regiment, commanded by a peace-time solicitor, Lieutenant-Colonel R. B. 'King' Cole.

By 3 February the redeployment was almost complete. The offensive was fixed for 7 February. But unimpressed by the fact that he was outnumbered, and anxious to repeat his division's earlier triumph, Hanaya struck first.

For the tactical execution of *Ha-Go* he detailed a force of roughly 8,000 men under the command of Major-General T. Sakurai (commander of 55th Divisional Infantry Group; an appointment without equivalent in the British Army) which was split into three columns. Though the main striking force of these three was designated *Sakurai* Column, it was in fact led by Colonel S. Tanahashi. He was a dynamic officer who had played a major role in 14th Division's discomfiture. At the head of his own 112th Infantry Regiment, supported by an artillery and an engineer group, his task was to pass through the advanced posts of 114th Brigade (7th Division) strung out on the eastern bank of the Kalapanzin, capture Taung Bazar, then, crossing to the west bank, swing left and 'destroy the enemy forces between the Kalapanzin river and the Mayu Range' – the bulk of 7th Division.

While this was in progress, a smaller column of only one battalion under Colonel Tai Koba, marching rapidly north, was to make a left-wheel near the Goppe Pass, cross the Mayu Range, and establish a road block across 5th Division's lifeline – the Bawli Bazar–Maungdaw road. To pin down forward troops while these outflanking movements were being performed, two battalions, under

Colonel Doi, were to mount a series of holding attacks along the entire front from the Kalapanzin to the sea.

Relying on the element of surprise, *Sakurai* Column took almost suicidal risks when it set out from Kindaung at 2300 on 3 February. In a solid phalanx, 16 men abreast, together with their mules, 112th Regiment marched down a narrow valley, barely 400 yards wide, knowing that units of 114th Brigade were in positions on the ridges on either side. The gamble paid off, helped by the fact that the night was moonless and by a thick mist blanketing the valley. Brigade HQ reported hearing the sound of movement, of muffled voices and the clanking of mule accoutrements, but assumed that the sounds came from Royal Indian Army Service Corps supply columns taking advantage of the cover of darkness. As a result, the few troops installed in Taung Bazar were taken completely by surprise at first light, and wiped out.

By evening most of 112th Regiment had crossed to the west bank. There were indecisive skirmishes with elements of 89th Brigade, divisional reserve, the next day, but by 7 February Col. Tanahashi had reached the Ngakydeauk Pass. Meanwhile Col. Koba had descended on the coastal road near Briasco bridge, spanning the widest of the tidal *chaungs* (Burmese name for watercourses), and overrun a Field Park and a Workshops Company. With only a weak battalion, Koba could not hold his ground. A morning counter-attack beat him back to the foothills after he had set fire to most of the vehicles and damaged the bridge. The vital road was soon reopened, even though convoys were often under fire. Tanahashi on the other hand was soon firmly astride the Ngakyedauk, successfully separating 5th and 7th Divisions.

Christison appreciated from the start the primary importance of retaining the Sinzweya administrative area – from then on referred to as the 'Admin Box'. Having first directed 26th Indian Division, then in reserve at Chittagong, to move forward with all haste, he telephoned Maj.-Gen. Briggs of 5th Division instructing him to order 9th Brigade commander, Brigadier Geoffrey C. Evans, to move immediately with all his spare troops to the Box, and hold it to the last.

Even with the reinforcements Evans could count on in the next hour or so, the chances of holding out against attacks by crack Japanese troops, with a garrison composed mostly of non-combatants, seemed slender. Furthermore all advantages of the terrain lay with the attacker. Never foreseeing that it would become the scene of a major battle, it had been chosen for its flatness and absence of scrub and jungle. Even so, the clearing measured a bare 1,200 yards in diameter. This meant that not a square inch would be out of range of small arms fire. It was a tactical trap; a bowl, the bottom naked, the sides and encircling rim densely covered in jungle. Ammunition dumps piled up at the foot of the western face of a central 150 ft hillock – 'Ammunition Hill' – were particularly vulnerable.

Evans realized that the defenders would be under direct observation, while the enemy could approach unseen to the edge of the perimeter from any direction. Again, although every man from storeman to cook and muleteer would have to take his place in the defenses, there would still not be enough to provide an unbroken line. Concentrating, therefore, on the most likely lines of enemy attack, Evans was obliged to leave the eastern and north eastern sectors dangerously open, counting on his mobile reserve – the veteran 2nd Battalion, The West Yorkshire Regiment, commanded by the experienced Lieutenant-Colonel 'Munshi' Cree, and two squadrons of the 25th Dragoons under their second-in-command, Major Hugh Ley.

Frantic digging was in progress when at 1430 on 6 February, a ragged group appeared from the jungle to the east. It was Maj.-Gen. Messervy, with a number of his staff. His 7th Division HQ had been overrun that morning. Throughout the afternoon more stragglers arrived, giving hair-raising accounts of their escape. By evening Messervy, in touch with his brigades, had resumed command, but had also made it clear that the defense of the Box was to remain in Evans's capable hands. At 1700 the latter called a conference of his commanders, to issue his orders. His instructions were brief – 'Stay put and keep the Japanese out.'

By evening the garrison had been strengthened by the arrival of two companies of the 4/8th Gurkhas – the other two temporarily lost in the jungle – a mortar battery of 139th Field Regiment RA, and a battery of 6th Medium Regiment. A troop of the 8th (Belfast) Heavy Anti-Aircraft Regiment, and two batteries of the 24th Mountain Regiment were ordered to abandon their positions to go to the Box immediately.

During the afternoon there was a low-level attack by Zero fighters, causing a number of casualties, but it was not until midnight that a first assault was delivered at a sector held by an Indian mule company. The muleteers – many of them Pathans – showed exemplary fighting discipline, holding their fire, unflustered by streams of tracer, until the yelling Japanese were almost on top of them. No determined attempt was made to press home the attack – possibly because no serious opposition had been expected.

The next day, the 7th, started badly. A patrol up the Ngakyedauk Pass was ambushed – making clear the fact that the Japanese had severed communications with 5th Division. Then, the two companies of the 4/8th Gurkhas, ordered to occupy a low jungle-covered hillock dominating the 'eastern gate' of the Box (Point 315), were violently attacked before reaching their objective. Forced to give ground, their retreat was followed up by the Japanese who smashed through the perimeter – only to be halted by fire of the 25th Dragoons' 37 mm and 75 mm tank guns, then hurled back in confusion by 'D' Company of the West Yorkshires. The Gurkhas were later able to seize and dig in on part, but not all, of Point 315.

The afternoon and evening were quiet, but in the early hours, Evans heard 'rifle and automatic fire . . . accompanied by screams and cries for help.' A Japanese raiding party had infiltrated the forward positions and entered the Box hospital. This had been set up in three widened and deepened dried-up *chaung* (watercourse) beds, at the foot of a hillock known as MDS Hill. The raiders' first act was to bayonet a number of the badly wounded as they lay helpless on their stretchers. Six doctors were then lined up and shot. An Indian doctor, Lieutenant Basu, escaped by smearing himself with blood and feigning death. When, at dawn, a counter-attack was organized, the survivors, wounded and medical staff alike were used as human shields to protect the retreating Japanese, only to be later murdered in cold blood.

Another crisis developed at first light on 9 February. During the night before, the Japanese manhandled their 70 mm infantry howitzers to the crest overlooking Ammunition Hill, and opened up on the ammunition dumps. Fires were soon raging and crates of .303-in and 25-pounder shells exploding with much the same effect as if the enemy had reached the center of the Box. Having recovered from the surprise, the Dragoons and the Belfast Heavy AA troop engaged the Japanese guns in an extraordinary artillery duel over open sights. As the Lee-Grant's 65 mm (2.56-in) armor was proof against 70 mm shells, it was not long before the enemy batteries were silenced and the surviving crews killed by the West Yorkshires' bayonets. But the burning dumps continued to explode. It was not until late afternoon that the last fires were extinguished.

Early the next morning a partial revenge for the hospital murders was exacted. Regimental Sergeant-Major J. Maloney, 'B' Echelon, 9th Brigade, with a handful of HQ clerks, normally considered too old for combat, held a trench overlooking a dried-up *chaung*. At around 0200 the sound of approaching footsteps and voices was heard. Seconds later, about 50 Japanese headed by an officer came into view. Maloney held his fire until the enemy was level with his trench. Then, at his word of command, a volley of grenades and Sten submachine-gun bursts at point blank range wiped out the entire party. It was a minor victory all the more appreciated when it was found that the dead men's packs were stuffed with hospital rations.

The first phase of the battle was over by 11 February. The Japanese had failed to destroy 5th and 7th Divisions. They had not even thrown them into confusion. On the other hand, rather than mopping up the Golden Fortress, 15th Corps was grimly battling for survival. Yet Christison had sound reason for optimism. Convoys, though sometimes under fire, flowed down the vital coastal road. The isolated *Koba* Force, driven back to the foothills, faced starvation. The Box, despite furious onslaughts, showed no sign of being swamped or running short of supplies. From the 10th the defenders were receiving all they needed, not only in the way of vital rations and munitions, but also such comparative luxuries as toothpaste, mail, rum and spare clothing, by air. Allied Troop Carrier Command's Dakota transports flew a total of 714 sorties, dropping 2,300 tons of supplies without which, starving, their guns silent, Evans's men might well have suffered the fate of Dien Bien Phu.

Over the rest of 7th Division area, the three brigades – 114th, 33rd, and 89th – had dug themselves into subsidiary boxes, and though individually cut off were holding fast and hitting back hard. The advanced elements of 26th Indian Division were in contact with detachments of *Sakurai* Column north of Taung Bazar, while the army reserve, 36th Indian Division was at sea, *en route* from Calcutta to Chittagong.

At this stage, common sense dictated that Hanaya withdraw what was left of Sakurai's original force to the still intact Golden Fortress. His offensive had been halted. Soon his badly mauled regiments would be faced by no fewer than four divisions, two of them fresh to the battle. He had no armor, and the enemy was master of the skies. But he suffered from the besetting Japanese military sin – inflexibility. Once having issued an order, he could not tolerate the thought of modifying it. Furthermore his overconfident dispatches had encouraged Tokyo to broadcast – 'It's all over in Burma.' Sakurai was ordered to press home his attacks with even greater vigor, an order with which he endeavored, loyally, to comply. From 10–18 February the fate of the Box often hung in the balance.

A major onslaught was directed at 'Artillery Hill', held by 24th LAA/AT Regiment, a bare 200 yards from Evans's HQ. Hidden by the jungle, the Japanese advanced to within yards of the gunners' trenches. Their first charge swamped the position, and a hastily organized counter-attack was thrown back.

By then Evans and his commanders had devised a plan for tank/infantry co-operation. It was to prove brilliantly successful. As the infantry left their starting position, the tanks saturated their objective with high explosive, until when, within assaulting distance, the infantry commander fired a Very light. This was the signal for the tanks to switch from HE to solid shot. The Japanese were still forced to keep their heads down, but as they pushed forward the attacking infantry were not exposed to fragmentation. The tanks were, therefore, able to keep up their fire until the leading sections, as close as 15 yards to the enemy, could make the final charge with grenade and bayonet, before the stunned Japanese had time to react. Employing these tactics, 'A' Company of the West Yorkshires, supported by a squadron of the Dragoons, retook 'Artillery Hill' by evening. Only 24 hours later this maneuver was repeated with equal success, after the Japanese had overrun 'C' Company Hill, overlooking the eastern exit of the Pass.

After ten days of ceaseless harassment, Evans could congratulate himself that not one of the Box's main positions had fallen. But casualties were mounting alarmingly. Continuous night attacks, though not on a major scale, were achieving the dual purpose of stopping the exhausted defenders gaining any proper rest and necessitating a frightening expenditure of ammunition.

Efforts were also made to knock out the tanks which at night moved into laager – their machine-guns dismounted and laid on fixed lines. The most determined attack was launched at daybreak from Point 315. Caught in the open by the combined fire of tank guns and machine-guns, the Japanese were all slaughtered before covering half the distance.

Outside the Box, there were setbacks. On the 13th, the 2/1st Punjabis and 4/7th Rajputs (123rd Brigade of 5th Division) overran the key to the Ngakyedauk Pass – the fortified hill feature Point 1070. It seemed the relief of the Box could be only a matter of hours. But during the night, the company of the 1/18th Royal Garwhal Rifles, ordered to hold the position, was subjected to continual *kamikaze* attacks. At dawn the survivors were hurled back down the slopes, leaving the feature firmly in enemy hands. On 10 February a gallant attempt by three companies of the 1st Lincolnshire Regiment (26th Division) failed to clear Point 315 overlooking the 'eastern gate'. One of the company commanders, Major Ferguson Hoey, earned for himself a posthumous VC in this clash.

By the 19th, though the garrison had been strengthened by the 4/8th Gurkhas and the 2nd King's Own Scottish Borderers, general conditions in the Box were deteriorating. The hospital was a shambles as the wounded piled up. Flies by the million infested the primitive wards where the two surgeons labored without rest in the most unhygenic surroundings imaginable. Ammunition proved a constant source of anxiety. Dumps were repeatedly hit. In trying to put out a fire threatening to destroy the entire stocks, 'King' Cole was badly wounded. He refused to leave his post till the siege ended.

On 21 February, however, Point 1070 fell at last to the 2/1st Punjabis, led by Major Sarbjit Singh, holder of the DSO and Bar. This successful assault opened the way to the Box, and 123rd Brigade moved steadily down the Pass, mopping up isolated posts. At last forced to admit failure, Hanaya was obliged to cancel *Ha-Go* while 7th Division's brigades, breaking out of their individual boxes, fanned out into the jungle in an attempt to cut off Sakurai's withdrawal.

But the ordeal of the Admin Box was not over. Night attacks redoubled in their ferocity. On the night of 21/22 February the Japanese broke through to within 20 yards of 9th Brigade HQ. The morning revealed 30 enemy dead ringing the officers' mess. That same morning, a suicidal charge came near to swamping Cole's HQ. But for the murderous volume of fire the Box could then command, it might well have succeeded.

At dawn on 24 February Maj.-Gen. Briggs, who had spent the night at 123rd Brigade HQ, climbed into a Lee-Grant. The last

Japanese had been driven from the immediate neighborhood of the Pass, and the tank 'grumbling out of the eastern entry', crossed the shell-cratered ground until it came to a shattered tree marking Messervy's HQ. Clambering from the turret, Briggs held out a bottle of whisky. 'Messervy grinned and took it, and the two shook hands, and the siege was officially at an end.'

For Hanaya, the failure of *Ha-Go* was a disaster. Out of Sakurai's picked 8,000, less than 3,000, starving, exhausted men fought their way back to the Golden Fortress. He had not only failed to destroy 15th Corps (3,506 casualties), but had not entirely pinned down Fourteenth Army's reserves. When *U-Go* got under way in mid-March, 5th and 7th Divisions were airlifted to the central front where both played a major role in the defeat of Mutaguchi's ultimate offensive.

Compared with the scale of that subsequent battle of Imphal-Kohima, the Box was a minor skirmish. Nevertheless the defeat of *Ha-Go*, like Stalingrad and Alamein, was one of the moral turning points of the Second World War. For the first time in their history as a modern power, the Japanese had suffered a major defeat on land at British-Indian hands.

Anzio (1944)

John Keegan

The little Italian port of Anzio was the scene, in early 1944, of one of the great 'might have been' battles of the Second World War. Like Arnhem which might have ended the war in the west in September 1944, or Army Group Center's offensive in August 1941 which might have defeated Russia in the first four months of Operation Barbarossa, Anzio might have broken the costly stalemate of the Italian front before midsummer of Invasion year, captured Rome, 33 miles to the north, and driven the Germans deep into northern Italy.

This single stroke would have released vitally needed shipping for the D-day operation, brought the Allied bombers closer to their targets in southern Germany and outflanked German positions in the Balkans, one of her major sources of oil and mineral supplies. It would have also dealt a considerable blow to Hitler's prestige and almost certainly cost him a major part of the very large force he maintained in southern Italy to keep the Allied Mediterranean Expeditionary Force at bay. Anzio, in fact, achieved none of these things. Why was the operation, so rich in promise, so empty of fulfillment?

In the early winter of 1943, the Allied armies, landed near Naples in September, were brought to a frustrating halt in the mountains south of Rome. They had run into exceptionally difficult terrain and an unexpectedly severe winter of rain and snow. The Germans also presented problems – there were more of them than the Allied High Command had anticipated and they had built a belt of fortifications, the Gustav Line, which, with the advantages of climate and geography, gave a coherency to their defensive line.

The only progress made by the Allies' two armies, the American Fifth on the Mediterranean coast and the British Eighth on the Adriatic, was by set-piece assaults on strongly defended river lines. These were time-consuming to prepare and costly to execute. Since they had run up against the heavily fortified and well-manned Gustav Line, in early November, they had made virtually no progress at all.

It was against this background that plans for a seaborne invasion behind enemy lines were formulated. The Allied High Command realized that their earlier belief that the Germans would withdraw into northern Italy if heavily pressed was mistaken. General Dwight D. Eisenhower and General Sir Harold Alexander concluded that the enemy's current strategy of making the Allies win Italy inch by inch could be countered only by a seaborne landing in their rear. Alexander, in a directive dated 8 November 1943, laid down a timetable for such an operation: it entailed a triple offensive, first by the Eighth Army to attract German reserves onto the Adriatic coast, then by the Fifth to set the campaign again in motion towards Rome and finally by an amphibious force, landing near Rome, and linking up with the Fifth across the river lines of the Mediterranean coastal plain.

The plan was orthodox – but the means to execute it were not immediately available. The plan demanded ships – but shipping was needed for the coming Normandy invasion and had been directed to leave the Mediterranean forthwith. Troops were needed – but the necessary divisions were also wanted for Normandy. They had begun to leave and had not yet been replaced by the Free French Army which was training in Africa. The plan, code-named Operation Shingle, was, after a feasibility study, therefore shelved. But it was not forgotten. As the winter fighting increased in severity, and apparent futility, the idea of a seaborne descent near Rome came to appear more and more attractive to the protagonists of the original plan, notably Alexander and the British Prime Minister, Winston Churchill.

On 22 December, Shingle was officially canceled; but on the following day Churchill insisted that it be reconsidered. As the author of the heart-breaking Gallipoli failure of the First World War, Churchill's credentials to oversee a revived Shingle did not bear close examination. But he could well argue, if anyone had drawn the parallel, that the Allied position in the Mediterranean was far more favorable in 1944 than in 1915, and that while the objectives Shingle proposed were more limited than those intended at Gallipoli, the investment required was proportionately more limited.

He could and did argue that Shingle made excellent military sense – if only by contrast with the fighting along the narrow mountain roads and hidden defiles to which their current strategy condemned the Allies. There they were unable to disguise either the timing or the direction of their strokes and could gain little advantage from their air superiority. A seaborne movement offered the chance to surprise the enemy both in space and time, and to force him into battle on the naked plain, while supplying themselves plentifully along the broad highway of the Mediterranean. If the enterprise were successful, moreover, it would give them Rome, put the Balkans under threat and perhaps – and here the argument became speculation – even make Operation Overlord, the invasion of Normandy, unnecessary.

It was vital, if Shingle was to work at all, to delay the transfer out of the Mediterranean of the necessary shipping. By direct intervention with President Roosevelt, Churchill secured the retention, first until 15 January, then until 5 February, of 68 Landing Ship Tanks (LSTs), the basic requirement of a seaborne landing. As planning proceeded, Churchill made further requests for logistic supplies and secured them. At the same time he ensured that there was no wavering in the enthusiasm of Gen. Alexander, Army Group Commander, and of Lieutenant General Mark Clark, the American Fifth Army Commander, two of the three men who had chosen Anzio for the invasion point.

In fact, this was unlikely for both had strong, if different, personal motives for wishing the operation well. Alexander, disappointed that Eisenhower, rather than himself, had been appointed Supreme Commander, was resolved that the struggle for Italy should not become a stalemated sideshow – and, without Shingle, it threatened to become just that.

Gen. Clark, who felt that his Fifth Army had not been given the credit its achievements deserved, ached for the glory of capturing Rome. His American and British divisions, now pinned to the river valley floors by fire from the heights of the Monte Cassino range, were 100 miles short of the capital. He counted on Shingle to release them from the stalemate of the plains below Monte Cassino. Seventy miles separate Anzio from Cassino, and Clark thought that, given determination, the launching of concentrated offensives from the two spots should break the German defense on the west coast and lead him into Rome.

This was Churchill's hope and, having secured the necessary equipment for his commanders, he left them to put the plan into action. But the translation of military decisions into effect always reveals unanticipated difficulties. The preparation of Shingle was no exception. Further staff study suggested that the Germans would probably react strongly to the initial landing, and that a two-division landing, for which Churchill had had to commit his personal prestige to find the shipping, might not survive the onslaught. Further shipping, and more men, had to be found to land with three divisions.

The final order of battle, therefore, included, besides the British 1st and American 3rd Divisions, the American 45th Infantry and 1st Armored Divisions, as well as members of American Parachute and Ranger and British Commando battalions. The whole was to be subordinate to a Corps headquarters – the US 6th Corps. This was debatably too small to handle the operations of a force though it had grown from the initial planning figure of 24,000 to a final 110,000. Doubts also emerged about the efficiency of the force itself. At a dress-rehearsal in Naples Bay, both the 1st and 3rd Divisions mishandled their equipment, losing 40 DUKWs (the amphibious lorry on which cross-beach mobility depended) and two batteries of 105 mm howitzers; while the naval parties operating the landing craft made a series of unnerving mistakes. It was not a happy augury.

These events badly worried the already anxious commander of 6th Corps, Major General John R. Lucas. An experienced and respected soldier, Lucas was not happy with the Anzio idea and expressed his doubts strongly and continuously in the pages of his diary. He described himself as unusually tender-hearted for a general in an army which traditionally took a blood-and-guts attitude to the prospect of casualties and he feared he was leading, or worse, sending, his men to their deaths.

Hence his growing obsession, which the weeks of preparation made more and more apparent, with reinforcement and re-supply considerations. It was vital, in his view, that the men in the beach-head should have ashore with them the largest possible quantity of armored vehicles and artillery pieces as well as ammunition and petrol. Given these, and air support, the beach-head troops would be able to repel a counter-attack, which Lucas expected to come swiftly and in strength, despite the different story from Allied Intelligence.

His superior, Mark Clark, an abler man than his posturing suggested, was sensitive to Lucas's anxieties, which to some extent he shared. Consequently, he refrained from giving Lucas the additional responsibility for a decisive breakout from the bridgehead. The orders Clark issued to 6th Corps were for 'an advance on' the Alban Hills – the feature which commands the land between Anzio and Rome – not for an advance 'onto'. This ambiguity gave Lucas the option of halting his troops short of the objective if he felt that the strength of enemy reaction threatened his beach-head.

The Germans were also making their plans. The *Luftwaffe* Field Marshal Albert Kesselring had been preferred to Field Marshal Erwin Rommel for the post of Commander-in-Chief in Italy because of his optimistic and generally correct forecasts of the way events would go in the peninsula. Kesselring was aware that, over a distance of several hundred miles, both his flanks were vulnerable to amphibious assault. He suspected, however, that the coast near Rome was the most likely spot for the Allies to choose, and he accordingly kept two divisions in reserve nearby. They were divisions he could hardly spare, for his armies were at full stretch on the Gustav Line, the cross-peninsula German defense line from which, Hitler had ordered, there was to be no retreat. He was aware, moreover, that even this reserve might not be sufficient to contain a landing, for the Allies might outnumber it before reinforcements, which could only come from southern France, the Balkans and the far north of Italy, had arrived.

On 18 January, and only after receiving the firmest assurances of the unlikelihood of an Allied landing in the near future, from his own and higher Intelligence sources, he agreed to send his two reserve divisions from Rome to Cassino, where Clark's Fifth Army had just succeeded in forcing the line of the Garigliano. General Heinrich von Vietinghoff, commanding the Tenth Army, had represented this breach of his sector of the Gustav Line as potentially catastrophic, for it threatened to outflank the Monte Cassino position on which the whole line hinged. Kesselring was persuaded by his entreaties. What neither appreciated was that Clark, though delighted by this local success, had planned it precisely as a means of clearing the Anzio area of anti-invasion forces. Once Lucas was ashore Clark then intended to launch a major offensive from the Garigliano bridgehead, directed towards Anzio, the Alban Hills – and Rome. The Germans in between, if the strategy proved right, would flee, or surrender to the pincer attack.

Thus Lucas, thanks to an excellent stroke of strategic deception by his own commander, and to the enemy's faulty Intelligence, was to enjoy the most precious advantage an amphibious force leader can obtain – total surprise. His fleet of 240 landing craft and 120 warships made an undetected overnight passage northwards from Naples. In the early morning of 22 January 1944, they began to unload the two assault divisions – 1st British, 3rd US – on beaches left and right of Anzio without interruption from the enemy, apart from some light, uncoordinated cannonading by a few, soon-silenced, batteries. By midnight nine-tenths of the assault force (36,000 men and 3,000 vehicles) had come ashore for a loss of 13 dead, and had established a perimeter between two and three miles inland. The Allied air forces had flown 1,200 sorties, but had not been opposed. The port had been captured intact and was now ready to receive supplies from the fleet which swung untroubled at anchor offshore.

Lucas felt, and rightly felt, that he had done well. Indeed as landings go, the first day at Anzio must be regarded as an impeccable exercise in that particular tactical form. But success did not dispel Lucas's anxieties, for he now feared a major enemy counter-blow. Rather than cripple the expected counter-attack by seizing commanding terrain features and communication centers inland, he redoubled his concentration on building up his base and perimeter defenses. For the next few days the American 3rd Division pushed cautiously inland, the British 1st Division, on its left, rather more boldly. But both failed to reach their obvious objectives, Campoleone and Cisterna, from which an advance on the Alban Hills must start; and neither was urged onward with any fervency by Lucas. He was now directly under the eye of Clark, who had come to see the bridgehead for himself. But even the presence of his superior could not stir him to action, though his diary reveals that it rattled him. When he was ready, he wrote, he would move. He thought he would be ready by 30 January.

Unfortunately for the Allies, the Germans were ready also. If there was one thing at which their staffs had always excelled, it was the rapid improvisation of defense and counter-attack, and this war had given them all the practice they needed at perfecting their procedures. The landing had badly frightened them – Vietinghoff was so alarmed that he had begged Kesselring for permission to withdraw from the commanding Cassino position. But *Oberbefehlshaber* (CinC) Kesselring was not prepared to fall for Clark's ploy and had kept his nerve. He called up his *Alarmeinheiten* and settled down to win the build-up. *Alarmeinheiten* were 'paper' units, formed from clerks, drivers and men returning from leave and all German headquarters had plans to form such units in an emergency. German headquarters in Rome sent several of these units to the beach-head in the first day.

Meanwhile Kesselring called for better units to replace them. From the north of Rome came the 4th Parachute and Hermann Goering *Panzer* Divisions, from southern France the 715th Division, from the Balkans the 114th, from northern Italy the 92nd, 65th and 362nd Divisions and the 16th SS *Panzer* Grenadier Division. From the Gustav Line, which Kesselring insisted should be thinned out, came the 3rd *Panzer*, the 1st Parachute and the 71st Divisions. Not all of these were destined for Anzio. Kesselring had two crises on his hands, the Anzio beach-head and Cassino, and needed a surplus of units with which to juggle his way to stability. By 30 January, he had extracted sufficient force from these newly liberated reserves to have sealed off the Allied bridgehead and to be contemplating his own counter-offensive, which he had scheduled for 2 February.

Lucas's methodical preparation of his offensive had thus ensured the conditions which would bring about its failure. For his postponement of the capture of Cisterna and Campoleone had not only allowed the Germans to build up opposition on the commanding ground of the region; it had also betrayed to them what would be the thrust of his eventual attack. If he had taken these two places, his forces could have moved north-west, north or north-east. Cramped within his original bridgehead, with the coast on his left and the impassable inundations of the Pontine Marshes on his right, he could only attack straight ahead, due north. There the Germans sat and waited for him.

Lucas planned his H-hour, the attack time, for 0200 on 30 January. This timing gave his infantrymen some advantage for

darkness covered the movements of the Ranger force he sent along
the dry bottom of the Pantano ditch towards Cisterna. But it also
concealed the Germans assembling stealthily to ambush them. Of
the 767 Rangers who set out on this commando penetration only
six returned to the Allied lines. Their comrades of the 1st and 3rd
Armored Divisions, following up in a conventional assault, suffered
fewer casualties but nevertheless met desperate resistance and, after
an advance of three miles in three days, which brought them near
to the vital Highway 7, were forced to a halt. Only in the British
sector was there promising progress. Here the veteran 1st Division
had launched its attack from the positions it had won a week before
near Aprilia. (These were 'The Factory', as the Allies termed the
Fascist model farm at Aprilia, and 'The Flyover', a road bridge
which carried a minor road over the Anzio–Campoleone road.) But
it was made at a dreadful price.

The countryside beyond the roads was a maze of gullies or 'wadis',
and these denied protection to the flanks of 3rd Brigade, attacking
up the Anzio–Campoleone highway. Its three battalions suffered
crippling casualties as a result; one, the 2nd Sherwood Foresters,
was almost completely destroyed in the final assault on Campoleone.
'There were dead bodies everywhere,' wrote an American visitor to
the scene, 'I have never seen so many dead men in one place. They
lay so close I had to step with care.'

Though the offensive of 30 January to 3 February was a failure,
in that it cost much for little, fell short of a break-out and further
depressed Lucas at a time when buoyant leadership was becoming
vital to the beleaguered invaders, it did achieve some positive gains
for the Allies. It had inflicted heavy losses on the Germans, who had
no way of suppressing the fire of the Allied fleet or of chasing off
the Allied air force, and had no real answer to the enormous weight
of artillery the Allies could always deliver. Both the British 1st and
American 3rd Divisions had penetrated Kesselring's main line of
resistance; and the upset they had inflicted forced him to postpone
the planned 2 February offensive.

The Allied assault had averted a German offensive designed to
obliterate the Anzio beach-head and sweep the Allies into the sea.
But if it had avoided another Dunkirk, Colonel General Eberhard
von Mackensen, whose Fourteenth Army Headquarters Kesselring
had brought down to oversee German operations at Anzio, was
determined not to let the Allies consolidate. He inaugurated the

first of a series of minor attacks, beginning on 3 February, and chiefly aimed at the British Campoleone salient. All of these were designed to win the ground necessary for a major counterblow. He was unable to shift the British on 3 February but kept them subjected to fierce pressure which, the next day, drove them out of most of their salient. On 7 February, Mackensen attacked towards 'The Factory' and nearly took it. On 9 February he got possession of Aprilia village but failed to take 'The Factory'. It fell next day, was retaken by the British in a counter-attack, and only passed finally from their hands on 11 February.

The British 1st Division had now lost half its strength, which, as always in a stricken infantry formation, meant much more than half its infantrymen. A fresh British division, the 56th, had landed but it was needed elsewhere in the line and could not relieve the 1st and much of its front was, on Lucas's orders, taken over by the American 45th Division with the aim of fighting the Germans out of Aprilia. Lucas seemed to have little fight left in him. Badgered by his superiors, Mark Clark and Alexander, who were frequent visitors to the beach-head; menaced by the appointment of a deputy commander, Major General Lucian K. Truscott, whom he suspected of being kept ready to supplant him, and more distressed than ever by the losses his men were suffering, Lucas busied himself in supervising the preparation of a 'final beach-head line' of strongpoints, roughly following the perimeter of 24 January.

In the coming days the men at the front, who were also frantically strengthening their tactical positions, were to feel grateful for the sense of refuge the final beach-head line offered, for on 16 February Mackensen unleashed his long-prepared offensive. There were two thrusts to the assault. The first, against the British 56th Division on the west bridge-head, was by 4th Parachute and 65th Divisions. The other, and main attack, by 3rd *Panzer* Grenadier, 114th and 715th Divisions, with 29th *Panzer* Grenadier and 26th *Panzer* Divisions in support, was down the now dreadfully familiar axis of the Campoleone–Anzio road. It was spearheaded by a unit chosen specially for the task by Hitler – the *Infanterie Lehr* Regiment. Successor to the *Lehr* Regiment of the Kaiser's Guard, and brother to the mighty *Panzer Lehr* Division, the regiment looked, and thought itself, invincible. In fact, the only activity it was accustomed to were military displays and demonstrations in Germany. It was inexperienced and overconfident. Exposed to the defiant resistance of the American 45th Division, astride the main road, the Nazi regiment suffered heavy casualties and its discipline broke.

Equally disappointing – for those like Hitler, who believed in fancy solutions to old-fashioned military problems – was the performance of the 'Goliath', a remote-control miniature tank. Each of the 13 such tanks used in the attack carried 200 lb of explosive at 6 m.p.h. for a maximum distance of 2,000 ft. It was supposed to open a cheap way into an enemy position. All bogged down on the approach; Allied fire destroyed three, the rest were dragged ignominiously back to base.

But these two reverses were compensated by substantial German successes on 16 February. Although unable to deploy their tanks off the road, just as the Allies had been unable to do during their offensive, Mackensen's divisions had inflicted substantial loss on the British 56th and American 45th Divisions and driven both back. Behind one of their rare air bombardments they continued their attacks during the night, and attacked again early next morning down the main road. A further air raid in mid-morning aided their advance, and by noon they had secured a salient two miles deep and one mile wide in the 45th's front. They were now only a mile from Lucas's 'final beach-head line'. But the Germans could get no farther. Lucas found reinforcements, which included the battered British 1st Division, and with the help of these troops the 45th held out.

The Germans, by the end of the day, had suffered such heavy losses in their engaged infantry battalions, which were down to a rifle strength of 150 to 200 men, that Mackensen persuaded Kesselring that he could only continue if allowed to commit his *panzer* reserve – 26th and 29th Divisions. Kesselring, though not optimistic, agreed. They attacked next day, 18 February, and managed to enlarge the breach considerably. Then they ran into a carefully prepared fire-trap laid on by a 'grand battery' of 200 Allied guns. Five times the Germans tried to break through the barrage that the battery laid around the Flyover on the Anzio road but each time their formations were broken up and driven back. Still they rallied to attack again in the afternoon and only the committal of final Allied reserves from Anzio, and more self-sacrifice by the 45th and 56th Divisions, turned back the assault.

The Germans had very nearly broken through on the afternoon of 18 February and Mackenson continued to attack, at a lower intensity, for the rest of the month. But after 18 February both he and Kesselring accepted that their offensive must end. With the cessation of the great Allied attack on Cassino on 13 February, the reason for the German offensive had gone. They had also, with 5,000 casualties in five days, run out of troops and supplies were low.

The Allies too had suffered heavy losses in men. But their supply line, though occasionally interrupted by the new German radio-controlled glider bomb – most spectacularly when the ammunition-ship *Elihu Yale* was blown up – was never broken and continued to provide ammunition in a quantity the enemy could not hope to match. Profusion of ammunition, after stark bravery, was the principal reason for the Allies' survival in the beach-head. After 20 February the German commanders tacitly accepted that the continued existence of the beach-head was a situation they would have to live with.

For the Allies, however, mere survival fell rather short of a victory. It was enough to satisfy Lucas, but not his superiors who, in the aftermath of the German winter-offensive, promoted him out of his command and into obscurity. With his departure, and the Germans' exhaustion, the beach-head relapsed into a lethal slumber. Maj. Gen. Truscott, who could have won the ground Lucas dared not grasp for, was ironically compelled to oversee a prolonged period of siege-warfare – something for which his predecessor was perfectly fitted.

Yet perhaps it was still not Lucas's sort of battle. For despite the lack of movement on either side, Anzio remained a place of death, the death of young soldiers whom Lucas had cherished more deeply with each day of battle. And the deaths they were to suffer, in this gentle Italian landscape, warming to the spring, were those of a different war in another country – the deaths of soldiers of the First World War in the trenches of Flanders. For at Anzio, as at Ypres, the lines ran within grenade-throwing distance of each other, and men spent their days, throughout the 'lull' of March, April and May, pressed against the earth walls of their bunkers, listening for the distinctive discharge noises of short-range weapons and bracing themselves to withstand the shock of the explosion. Rest, when it came, took tired units no more than three or four miles from the line where shelling, which at least they were spared 'up front' by their proximity to the enemy, was a constant harassment and killer.

There was also the German propaganda barrage. Its message meant nothing to many soldiers; to others it was demoralizing and provocative. Radio broadcasts from Rome warned of the danger and horror of further fighting and encouraged desertion. Leaflets fired over in shells alleged unfaithfulness on the part of wives and girlfriends at home – leaflets for the British troops spoke of English girls enjoying themselves with the Americans encamped in 'Merry Old England' while, for the American soldiers, the villain was the archetypal Jew. One of the most effective leaflets carried the chilling legend, 'The Beachhead has become a Death's Head' and showed a map of Anzio over which a skull was superimposed.

All who survived the 'lull' at Anzio testify to the tension, caused by constant alarms and persistent sense of claustrophobia, they experienced within the perimeter. When orders came, on 23 May, to break out and meet the spearhead probing north from Monte Cassino, they were greeted with the sort of genuine enthusiasm soldiers rarely accord the prospect of risk. The Allies had been too long at Anzio. It had proved no short-cut from the path to Rome.

Ought Anzio to have worked? Mark Clark thought so; Alexander thought so; Churchill continued to think so, long after the war's western focus of effort had moved out of the Mediterranean. Were they all wrong? It depends whether one wants a tactical or strategic answer to the question. Tactically, there seems little doubt that Lucas might have seized the high ground between the beach-head and Rome – the Alban Hills – had he pressed on hard from his perimeter in the first three or four days after the landing. But equally there seems little doubt that to have pressed on farther, to Rome itself, would, even though the city lay temporarily undefended, have resulted in the destruction of his Corps.

Hitler's snap judgement about Anzio was that it betrayed an Allied reluctance to risk a cross-channel invasion and he was willing in consequence to release reserves from much farther afield than usual to crush the landing. Given this reaction, Lucas's caution looks justified. But, his critics argue, bolder action would have frightened the Germans into thinning out the Cassino front which, in turn, would have heightened the chance of the Allies breaking the Gustav Line and dashing to his rescue.

That argument shifts the debate from the tactical to the strategic level. Its validity is dubious also – Cassino and Anzio are so far apart (about 70 miles) that the two Allied forces, given their strength relative to each other and to the enemy's, could not mutually assist each other. A much stronger punch at Cassino, a much bigger landing at Anzio, a weaker Tenth Army, a slower, smaller reinforcement by

Hitler – any of these would have turned the trick for Mark Clark, Alexander, Churchill, perhaps even for the depressive Lucas. But these alterations in the strategic equation presuppose a major revision of priorities in the Allied plans for the conduct of the war in 1944. Not only was there no such revision but American opinion, at the highest level, was rockfast against it.

Roosevelt and Marshall were determined to transfer the focus of Allied war-making out of the Mediterranean and into Normandy, agreed to Anzio with bad grace and resolved to concede it with no more than would pacify Churchill. Given their attitude, the 70 miles between Cassino and Anzio were unbridgeable by any Allied effort. Hitler's hopes and fears – fears that he might be about to lose both the Balkans and Italy; hopes that a brutal extinction of the Anzio beach-head might deter the Allies from risking a landing elsewhere – determined that the Germans would give Lucas and Mark Clark no help either. It was this combination of enemy determination and Allied lack of enthusiasm which robbed the Anzio operation of its chance of success and made the subsequent battle so terrible.

Monte Cassino (1944)

E.D. Smith

When I first saw the monastery it was intact, an ancient and magnificent building set on the top of the steep slopes of Monte Cassino. It dominated the surrounding countryside. As we drove towards the battlefield, at every turning, at the top of every crest, there was the monastery getting bigger and clearer. On a cold February morning in 1944 it presented a noble sight with the pale winter sun shining on the glass of its windows and the great towers and dome outlined against the grey sky.

During the next two weeks, at a comparatively safe distance from the monastery and the town of Cassino, I acted as a supernumary liaison officer, and was a spectator, removed from the fierce struggle that was taking place on the hills across the Rapido valley. Some two or three miles away from our vantage point we could see and hear the battle being waged in the ruined town, among the rocks and scrub on the ridges under the shadow of the monastery, against the background of Monte Cassino, and, to the north, the towering snow-capped peak of Monte Caira where the French wrestled with the elements as well as stubborn German defenders.

Under a clear sky on the morning of 15 February and with token opposition only from the Germans, an armada of bombers made their appearance over the monastery and for four hours wave after wave of bombs pulverized the building; the planes dropped their bombs from heights between 18,000 ft and 10,000 ft. It was an impressive and awe-inspiring spectacle. Even from our remote vantage point we found it difficult to envisage anyone surviving the punishment being meted out. Then, to add to the destruction, the Allied artillery began to batter away as soon as the bombers had returned to their bases. By now the monastery looked like a gigantic decayed tooth and in our innocence most of us thought it would never dominate the valley again. We were wrong. Without scruple, the Germans were now able to use the ruins for defense.

German paratroopers constructed loopholes in the ruined walls from where they could fire in several directions. Artillery and mortar observers kept a ceaseless watch from posts that gave them a perfect view over the terrain below, the ground over which Americans, British, Indians and Poles hurled themselves against defenses until the monastery was abandoned on 17 May 1944.

On 7 March the call came for me to join my battalion, 2/7th Gurkha Rifles, which was holding a position on the hills north of Monte Cassino. The journey forward was on foot and it is etched clearly in my memory. The track up the hills, little used by day, was the life-line of the battalions from 4th Indian Division that were holding the sector around Snakeshead Ridge. Up and down this crude path worn out of the mountainside, went everyone and everything. New, clean soldiers going up, prematurely old bedraggled men returning; some wounded, others acting as escorts to mules. The mules were moving in both directions, being urged on by Italians, Indian and the occasional British voice. How we depended on those mules in Cassino! There was no other way of getting rations, ammunition and other stores up the mountains to the forward positions. It was a dangerous, uncomfortable walk.

The noise of gunfire never stopped. Far behind Mount Trochhio, on the south side of the valley, we could see the flashes of the Allied guns. Ahead we could hear the thump of the German artillery replying, and the sound of tearing silk as the shells flew above our heads in both directions. Occasionally a shell or mortar exploded on the rocks nearby or in a ravine which magnified the noise: no wonder that the climb seemed an eternity though probably it took us less than three hours to reach battalion HQ.

Mules and men, eventually we arrived at our various destinations. The journey up was over. Little did I guess that it would be five weeks before I walked down that trail, all hope of victory gone, our battalion having suffered many casualties, and not one inch nearer

that battered hulk of a monastery. Within those five weeks, two fine
and experienced Divisions, one from New Zealand and the other, the
4th Indian, were to take such a hammering that neither formation
ever reached maximum effectiveness again. Fortunately the future
was not to be disclosed to us when I joined 'A' Company which was
then in a reserve position.

The Company was not holding or defending any ground. The
Gurkha soldiers were sheltering in holes behind rocks or beside
man-made stone 'sangars' from the snow, sleet, winter wind and
the equally unwelcome shelling. It was not long before I had
constructed my own stone shelter, my place of refuge, and thus
we stayed seemingly forever, though my diary tells me it was only
a week. Rarely did we move far from our cramped shelters unless
for the call of nature or for some pressing military chore.

Visits to toilets had to be postponed until evening. Then, at dusk,
it was a common sight to see small groups of bare hindquarters in
the semi-darkness, their owners fervently praying that they might
be allowed to complete the proceedings in peace before the shelling
started.

Our tactical role was to be ready to move up to reinforce any one
of the three forward companies which were in position on the early
slopes of the hill. Fortunately no one attacked those localities while
I was serving with 'A' Company. This was just as well, because a
move forward in full view of the monastery by day would have been
impossible and by night the path would have been difficult.

We had been told that a third attempt to capture Monte Cassino
was to be launched under the code name 'Bradman', but winter
struck with all the violence of a fresh enemy so that the attack was
postponed from day to day because there was no chance of aircraft
even flying, let alone carrying out pinpoint bombing against Cassino
town. Friend and foe, German, British and Indian, clung to exposed
positions on those mountains during the worst storm in an Italian
winter which held us all in its icy grasp. Long-drawn-out days,
followed by nights of activity meant that the morale and physique
of our Gurkhas was severely tested. I wrote in my diary:

> Each night we pray that the following morning will bring a
> change in the weather, a respite from the rain and snow and
> the endless vigil that is never a quiet one because the whine
> and crump of the guns and mortars continue by day and night.

As day succeeds day, anxiety about the next attack has changed into a desperate longing to do anything rather than sit for ever undergoing an ordeal that tests minds and bodies alike.

Such a winter could not go on for ever, even at Cassino, and on 13 March the sky began to clear and the prospects looked brighter. We were told that the long-postponed attack was due to begin on the 15th morning: it was to be preceded by a bombardment of Cassino town by over 500 bombers. Next day dawned clear and at 0830 wave upon wave of bombers arrived, to begin pounding the town which was soon shrouded in billows of smoke and dust. It was a terrifying exhibition, even to us cowering down in our foxholes below Point 569. After a few minutes I felt like shouting – 'That's enough!' but it went on and on until our ear drums were bursting and our senses befuddled. Several bombs fell astride the company position and I found myself shouting curses at the planes.

It's no fun being bombed by anyone, but the feeling of bitterness at being bombed or shelled by your own side is beyond description; the sight of friends killed or mangled by the mistakes of friendly supporting arms arouses the deepest of emotions in the hearts of front-line soldiers. That evening I wrote in my diary: 'What an inferno is Cassino now! Dear God – take pity on those men, if there are any survivors in the town, which I doubt.'

In spite of that terrible ordeal, many German paratroopers survived amongst the collapsed walls and the deep craters caused by the bombs. The German High Command decided to stand firm and, although casualties were heavy, they had been less than expected in proportion to the damage caused by the aerial bombardment. The battle went on. Next day, Maj. Beckett would not let us carry out the mission which had been given us by brigade HQ. Already he had seen too many costly attacks, all of which had ended in failure. Moreover, he was deeply concerned about the safety of Castle Hill itself: an active fighting company of Gurkhas near at hand and ready to help his defenders would be of far more use than another broken band of men who, he knew, would eventually trickle back like their unfortunate predecessors. He refused to let us commit suicide and told brigade HQ accordingly. As a consequence, I lived to write this story.

Later that afternoon a direct hit by a heavy German shell caused one of the castle walls to collapse, engulfing and burying several

Essex soldiers under the rubble. Without hesitation their comrades, British, Indian and Gurkha, began tearing at the stones in an attempt to save their lives. After a few minutes came German paratroopers from foxholes, some only 75 yards away, to join in the rescue operations side by side with our soldiers. In the middle of the Cassino battle there began an unofficial and very local 'ceasefire'. Friend and foe worked together, talked and exchanged cigarettes. My company commander spoke German fluently and he learnt that the enemy's view of Cassino was very similar to ours – it was Hell, the weather bloody, and the end impossible to predict.

It is not surprising that this incident remains clearly in my mind, truly an extraordinary commentary on the senselessness of war. My Gurkha orderly summed it up by saying that the 'Dushman' (enemy) were so like 'our Sahibs' that he wondered if there had not been a mistake somewhere! Why were we not all fighting the Japanese instead? However, his comments and the rescue operations were brought to an abrupt end by the Allied artillery which, for some inexplicable reason, opened up: the German snipers scuttled back and almost as if someone had said 'Let battle commence,' we were shooting away at one another once more. A few men were never released from the rubble.

I was ordered to return and brief 'A' Company who were still waiting at the foot of Castle Hill. Not wishing to retrace my steps along the slippery path at the top of the deep ravine, I sought another route. I met four Indian soldiers, Sikhs, who were hiding behind some rocks on the stony hillside. Their faces reflected fatigue and cold. I greeted them cheerfully, even jauntily, but their hearts were heavy. I asked them the quickest way down to the bottom of the hill. One huge Sikh replied that there was a short cut along the ridge but on this they had lost several men from accurate sniper fire. The alternative path that would take longer, was the slippery precipitous mountain track that I had used before. 'One way you get shot, Sahib, the other you slip to your death.' And he grinned without humor.

Being impetuous and wishing to carry out my mission as soon as possible, I decided to take a chance and dash down the track that snaked its way along the ridge to the base of the hill. I waited and waited. All was quiet. Nothing moved on the path below. Nothing appeared to be moving in the town – indeed there had been a lull in the fighting for some time although, behind me, the sound of battle around the castle continued as fiercely as ever. I rose to my feet at the top of the hill and charged down the track: nothing mattered but to get to 'A' Company. It seemed as if I was going to be lucky when something flicked off my black side-cap as I threw myself behind a rock. I lifted my head and saw the bullet mark. The bullet had only just missed my head. Something had prompted me into diving for cover. It was a cold day, but in a second I was covered in sweat. Cold sweat. Everything seemed to stop: the noise of battle, the guns. Probably less than a minute or two passed. It seemed like an age. I crawled forward and willed myself to make another dash. I prayed with great sincerity, prayed for speed. I prayed that the sniper would think I had already been hit. Into the open, zigzagging down the track at the fastest speed I had ever attempted. Once again the crack, crack, a blow on my haversack and then the safety of another rock. Breathless, I lay as dead until a glance at my watch spurred me on, this time to safety. The Gurkhas welcomed me, surprised to find that I was alive because they had seen me drop twice on the track above.

It had been an exciting day, but it was not yet over. While the company remained at the foot of Castle Hill in close support of the besieged garrison, I was told to make my way through the town and report to brigade HQ to act as liaison officer and, possibly, return with fresh orders. After dark my Gurkha orderly, Rifleman Rambahadur Limbu, accompanied me as we scrambled a way down to the battered Cassino below us. It was not long before I realized that the landmarks that had appeared to be so prominent in fading daylight, from an observation point on the hill, were not nearly so easy to find in pitch darkness among rubble and ruins. After about 10 minutes I was convinced that we were lost. Unfortunately, Rambahadur and I could not agree on the direction we should be taking. We appeared to have gone round in a complete circle but Rambahadur had no doubts whatever: he was sure he knew the way and so, against my better judgement, I agreed to let the Rifleman lead. The town, or the remains of it, was strangely quiet after a day of close-quarter fighting when the noises of machine-guns and grenades had continued to pay testimony to the bitter struggle that was being waged in Cassino.

The two of us shuffled and groped an uncertain way around walls, skirting bomb craters, and scrambling over piles of stones. Occasionally we heard voices or smelt cooking which wafted out of the darkness from improvised cellars and hiding places. It was quite impossible to tell who was friend and who foe: occasionally we saw movement at a distance. Suddenly a dark form appeared in front of Rambahadur and challenged him – in German. As Gurkha and German stood frozen in mutual surprise, I fired at the enemy sentry with my tommy-gun, saw him drop, hit by the burst of fire. We dashed down the remains of an alleyway to throw ourselves behind a wall. Within seconds, several Germans, who had been cooking or eating their evening meal below ground, were shouting furiously at each other and shooting at random. Fortunately no one came to look for us and after about five minutes all was quiet.

This time I took the lead and soon we recognized one of the lost landmarks and, without any further incidents, located brigade HQ. Here we were told to rest but although I was near the end of my tether, the clamor of battle and the nervous strain was too much for me: I could not sleep so back I went to the improvised Operations room where the brigadier informed me that 'A' Company would be returning before dawn. I was to guide them to a quarry nearby which was to be our temporary position until further orders. Rambahadur and I spent some considerable time searching for the best route before meeting them at the outskirts of the town. There was no sleep for any of us that night.

'A' Company had been withdrawn into reserve because a German force had infiltrated its way down the large ravine behind Castle Hill in an attempt to isolate the British defenders by cutting off supplies of food and ammunition. The quarry afforded us some protection from intermittent shelling and mortaring which increased in intensity during the afternoon. As darkness fell, the Germans rushed up to hold a sector and, for the rest of the night, both sides fired indiscriminately at one another without any apparent gains in territorial possession. The next day, 21 March, proved to be just as dangerous – the pressure never relenting for one moment. Throughout the morning the Germans kept up their shelling of our position while we tried to construct stronger defenses and to cover any gaps with mines. By now we were so exhausted that even sleep became impossible. I have never been a good sleeper and I was so wound up that I thought madness was close at hand even if I managed to survive German fire and bullets. Nature eventually saved me when I was going round the company's positions after three sleepless days and nights. My legs buckled under, I hit my head and passed out. At the Regimental Aid Post, the Indian doctor who had already supplied sleeping pills without success, soon diagnosed my comotose state. Events did not let me sleep for more than six hours, but I was restored to sanity again.

So it went on, the merciless shelling and mortaring that claimed many victims. 'A' Company was near the end of its tether. Our Gurkhas' normal resilient cheerfulness, their toughness, their fatalistic attitude towards life generally, all these admirable qualities that make them such magnificent soldiers had evaporated. This was not their kind of soldiering. It provided no opportunities for them to get to close grips with the enemy: for hour upon hour they were targets for mortars, shells and the banshee screams of the *nebelwerfers*. In retrospect, I wonder if we could have held on for another 24 hours, but fortunately our ordeal was nearly over.

During the morning of 22 March, the shelling of our positions became more intense and accurate. It was an inferno all day but early in the evening came the news that saved the lives of the survivors – and our sanity. Later that night we were to move back to rejoin our own battalion which had been resting while we were being hammered.

For five hectic days and nights we had been on detachment away from the 7th Gurkhas. My chief recollection was the noise that never stopped. It was to be two days before we recovered our spirits. Fortunately our colonel decided to send us back to act as reserve company again, while the other three rifle companies held the front line near the Snakeshead Ridge.

Unbeknown to us, however, the generals above had realized that 4th Indian Division was exhausted and would have to be withdrawn. We had shot our bolt and had little to show for our efforts. Our friends of the 1/9th Gurkha Rifles, still clinging to the isolated position on Hangman's Hill, were ordered to begin their withdrawal after dark on 25 March. By a miracle they made their way down the hillside and through German outposts without any major incident. Eight officers and 170 Gurkha ranks abandoned Hangman's Hill without relief: later the Germans claimed to have counted 185 dead Gurkhas in and around their old position, the price that battalion paid for the nine days spent under the walls of the monastery.

And our turn was soon to come. In the early evening of 25 March, an advance party from the Lancashire Fusiliers arrived to begin the take-over of our positions. For me the relief could not have been delayed because by that time I was suffering from a nasty bout of diarrhea. In my diary I wrote: 'Now very weak – how long can I continue?' Next morning brought confirmation that we were to be relieved by 78th British Division during that night, a complicated and dangerous operation of war because the German outposts were, in some places, less than 100 yards from ours. And then we faced a long march back across the valley of the Rapido to our waiting transport.

The distance was probably less than five miles, but during the time in the front line many men had hardly walked at all for six weeks. We had been cramped in foxholes, we were unfit, mentally exhausted, and many of our soldiers had lost their willpower. Even though the ordeal was nearly over, the fact did not seem to be understood. The Germans did little to hamper or harass us – indeed I believe they were relieving their own units but this was not known at the time. All we knew was that our group of dejected, tired soldiers, had to be across the valley before the sun rose the next morning. No one looked back. They just stared ahead with eyes that seemed to see nothing and kept on following the man in front, trying to force one foot past the other.

Never will I forget that nightmare of a march. Officers, British and Gurkha, shouted at, scolded, cajoled and assisted men as they collapsed. At times we had no alternative but to strike soldiers who just gave up; all interest lost in everything, including any desire to live. By dint of all the measures we could think of, most of our battalion reached the waiting transport and survived to fight another day, elsewhere, in Italy.

Cassino for us was over – a few weeks later it was to be over for the Germans as well. The third battle had been a grim struggle with few prisoners being taken, by either side, with every yard contested and no quarter given. Like many others who fought at Cassino, I remember how the decencies of war were observed to an astonishing degree. There were many examples of feelings, akin to comradeship, recounted by soldiers who fought at Cassino. Many wounded men survived because stretcher bearers were allowed to carry out their missions of mercy under the Red Cross flag in the forward areas: the contestants had a mutual respect and understanding of each other's problems. The German High Command's cautious claim to a victory was a true assessment because their defenders had won the battle: it was a victory, however, dearly bought because their losses were as distressingly high as ours.

When we left Cassino, the monastery still glowered down at us, an impregnable fortress. The ruins did not fall to any direct assault or succumb to the heaviest weapons available to the Allies. Monte Cassino continued to dominate the lives of the soldiers that fought under its shadow.

Omaha Beach (1944)

Nigel Bagnall

'You guys going to stay here until you're all dead? Like to see me attack alone?' The American lieutenant rushed towards the barbed-wire entanglement and blew a hole in it with an assault charge. 'Come on, let's go!' Three hundred exhausted men of the 1st US Division, 5th Corps, death staring at them on their bitterly contested toehold of Nazi Europe, flung themselves after the lieutenant. At last the Americans began to move forward from the slaughter of 'bloody Omaha' beach on D-day 6 June 1944, the first day of the Allied invasion of Europe.

At 2130 on Sunday 4 June Group Captain Stagg, senior meteorologist, reported to General Dwight D. Eisenhower, Supreme Commander Allied Forces, and his senior commanders that the bad weather, which had already forced one postponement of the Allied invasion, was improving.

A rain front over the planned assault area was expected to move in two or three hours and the clearing would last until Tuesday morning. Stagg expected the high winds to moderate and cloud conditions to permit bombing during Monday night and Tuesday. But a heavy sea would still be running and the cloud base might not be high enough to permit spotting for naval gunfire.

Eisenhower faced a critical decision. Such weather conditions would be barely tolerable but to decide on another postponement meant that the invasion would have to wait until 19 June before the right conditions of moon, tide and daylight returned. The choice was between a risky disembarkation of troops or postponement – and the longer the delay, the shorter the likely duration of good campaigning weather on the Continent. Admiral Sir Bertram Ramsay, Commander-in-Chief Allied Naval Forces, reminded the Supreme Commander that he had to make a decision within half an hour for by then, if the invasion were to go ahead, orders must be given to the first convoys to sail. Turning to General Sir Bernard Montgomery, Ground Force Commander, Eisenhower asked, 'Do you see any reason for not going on Tuesday?' 'I would say Go,' replied Montgomery. At 2145 Eisenhower announced his decision. 'I am quite positive we must give the order . . . I don't like it, but there it is . . . I don't see how we can do anything else.'

With the decision taken, the detailed plans that had been prepared over the years began to unfold. The invasion would take place along the 40 miles of coastline between the Vire Estuary and the River Orne in western Normandy. This area offered several advantages – it was near the ports in southern and south-western England, the beach-heads would be within Allied fighter range, it was near the major port of Cherbourg which, hopefully, would be captured early, and Allied air attacks on railways and bridges might be able to isolate the assault area and slow up the arrival of German reinforcements and supplies.

The initial assault landings were to be carried out by 21st Army Group, under Montgomery's command, consisting of six reinforced infantry divisions landing from the sea, and three airborne divisions. On the east was the British 2nd Army and on the west the United States 1st Army. Five beach-heads had been selected – 'Utah' and 'Omaha' for the United States 1st Army; 'Gold', 'Juno' and 'Sword' for the British 2nd Army.

A number of factors governed the selection of D-day. A long period of daylight would enable maximum advantage to be gained by Allied air power. The moon should be nearly full to aid the airborne troops and the tide should be strong. Beach obstacles would thus be fully exposed at low water and vehicle landing craft could ground, unload and withdraw on a rising tide. The requirements of the actual timing of the landing, H-hour, also entered into the calculation.

The Allies had learnt several lessons from previous amphibious operations and these had to be considered in selecting H-hour. At Tarawa, the Americans learnt that naval fire support could not be relied on to neutralize beach defenses, unlocated gun positions, or to provide close fire support for the assaulting troops. Admiral Ramsay studied the full report and observed that 'the heaviest casualties were caused by the failure to neutralize enemy positions during the period immediately before and after the touch down of the assault.'

The final period selected for D-day was between 5 and 7 June and H-hour was to be staggered, varying by about an hour from the easternmost British and westernmost American landings, because of the different tidal and beach conditions.

On the German side, an invasion in the west had been expected since 1942. To protect the 3,000 miles of coastline Germany controlled, an 'Atlantic Wall' was planned. This fortification existed largely in Hitler's mind and though it was good propaganda it was never completed. Their manpower situation was also discouraging. On paper there were between 50 and 60 German divisions in the west but they rarely had more than 25 efficient, full-strength field divisions available at any one time.

The 5th Corps assault at Omaha was planned to extend over 7,000 yards of beach which curved landward in a slight crescent, flanked at both extremities by 100-ft-high cliffs rising almost directly out of the sea. Above high-water mark there was a sloping bank of shingle, in places 15 yards wide, which extended into sand dunes on the eastern two-thirds of the beach. On the remaining western third of the beach, the shingle butted against a sea wall, between 4 ft and 12 ft high.

Behind the dunes, which formed an impassable barrier to vehicles, was a shelf of sand some 200 yards wide in the center but narrowing sharply at either end. Beyond this sand shelf, the grass-covered ground rose sharply to between 100 ft and 180 ft before opening on to a plateau of rolling farm land. Four small wooded valleys extended inland from the beach area to provide natural corridors onto the plateau. Near the eastern end, there was a fifth, less distinct, exit.

Below the high-water mark the beach sloped very gently but with an 18 ft tidal range, some 300 yards of firm sand would be exposed at low tide. Here the Germans had built three bands of obstacles which would be concealed at high tide. None of the bands was unbroken but together the three formed one continuous obstacle over 100 yards wide and 250 yards out from the high-water mark at its seaward edge. The first two belts consisted of waterproofed Teller mines fixed to iron frames and upright logs and the third comprised a series of metal 'hedgehogs' designed to hole assault craft that had avoided the mines.

The German shore defenses at Omaha were based around 12 strongpoints though not all of them had been completed by June. Each of these strongpoints was a small complex of pill boxes, gun casements and firing trenches, surrounded by minefields and wire. Only two of the complexes were bomb-proof. Deep trenches or tunnels connected the various components and there were underground living quarters and ammunition stores. The strongpoints were mainly sited to block the valley exits from the beach though they could also cover the tidal flat and the whole beach with both flanking and direct fire. Machine-gun emplacements, weapon pits, barbed wire and minefields fortified the areas between the strongpoints. In all there were 35 pill boxes with artillery pieces of various sizes and/or automatic weapons, four artillery batteries, 18 anti-tank guns, six mortar pits, 35 rocket-launching sites, each equipped with four 38 mm rocket tubes, and 85 machine-gun nests.

There was no heavy coastal artillery in the Omaha sector and only two batteries of mobile field guns in the immediate vicinity, but there were about 60 light artillery pieces within the strongpoints. The Allies had been informed that the defensive positions were held only by a reinforced infantry battalion, 800 to 1,000 strong, belonging to the 716th Infantry Division. Fifty per cent of these were supposed to be non-Germans. But this intelligence assessment was wrong.

Field Marshal Erwin Rommel, Army Group B Commander-in-Chief, and responsible for coastal defenses between Denmark and the Pyrenees, knew from his experience in North Africa that it was folly to use massed armor against an enemy who had air superiority. If the German army could not fight the Allies on something like equal terms, then its only chance of offering a successful defense was to fight from the strongest natural positions. The battle for the West, Rommel considered, would be decided at the water's edge, and the decision would come within the first 48 hours of the Allied landing. He therefore wanted to move the German armored divisions forward into the coastal areas, so that at least elements of them could intervene.

But Rommel was overruled by von Rundstedt. He was only permitted to make a few moves forward nearer to the coastline. This proved to be very fortunate for the Allied troops at the Omaha beach-head. Allied intelligence estimated that the nearest German reserves to the Omaha sector were two more battalions of the 716th Division, but they judged that it would take them two to three hours to arrive, and then they would be able to do little more than help contain the Allied landings. A full scale counter-attack would have to await the arrival of the 352nd Infantry Division, thought to be in the St Lo–Caumont area some 20 miles farther inland, and the Allies believed that it was not capable of delivering such an attack until the afternoon of D-day.

The objectives of 5th Corps were then laid down with the aim of gaining an adequate foothold or lodgement area as quickly as possible. The assault echelons (an echelon is a formation of troops in parallel divisions, each with its front clear of the one ahead) were to break through the beach defenses within two hours of landing, and then clear the exits leading out through the valley by H + 3 hours. This achieved, 5th Corps' D-day objective was to advance four miles inland and secure the plateau up to the river Aure, where the Corps was to be prepared to repel German counter-attacks. Later 5th Corps was to push southwards towards Caumont and St Lo, conforming with the British 2nd Army on its left flank.

Fifth Corps consisted of three infantry divisions; the 1st Division, which had seen action in the Mediterranean, and the 2nd and 29th Divisions. Since the Corp's subsequent operations were to develop on a two-divisional frontage, it was necessary to land elements of both divisions in the assault echelons, so as to avoid having to pass one formation through another within the restricted bridgehead. There was neither sufficient shipping nor room on the beach to allow both formations to assault at once.

The Corps would then conduct its landing in four basic echelons, the two assault ones each consisting of some 15 waves of landing craft. The first echelon (Force O) and the second echelon (Force B) were commanded by the headquarters of the 1st and the 29th Divisions respectively but were made up from elements of both formations. The 2nd Division formed the third echelon, and a miscellany of units the fourth and last.

Embarkation of Forces 'O' and 'B' began on 31 May and 1 June and both were completed by 3 June. The numbers of men and vehicles involved was enormous – for Force 'O', the first assault echelon, 34,000 men and 3,300 vehicles were loaded into 300 landing craft. Two battleships, three cruisers, 12 destroyers, 33 minesweepers and 105 other ships supplied the escort, minesweeping and fire-support requirement. In addition, 600 vessels of different types were ready for a variety of support and service work. The main convoy of Force 'O' left Portland harbor in Dorset on the afternoon of 5 June and made an uneventful crossing of the English Channel under continuous Allied air cover.

At 0300 the armada arrived at a point 12 miles off Omada. The wind gusted between 10 and 18 knots and waves were 3 ft to 4 ft high. Into this swell the assault craft were unloaded from larger ships. Some were winched down fully loaded, but to get into others soldiers had to scale the scramble nets over the sides of the parent ships. This was a hazardous operation as the craft were tossing and bucking in the heavy sea. The men were heavily laden – each soldier was equipped with weapons, a rubber life-preserver, a gas mask, a first-aid kit, entrenching tools, a canteen, knives and rations and extra ammunition and explosives.

Ten small craft sank almost at once, throwing 300 heavily laden men into the sea. The assault craft circled the transport area, getting into formation. As dawn lightened the sky, the craft edged towards the beaches. Discomfort followed the soldiers as waves sloshed over the blunt bows of the landing craft and they had to bail out with their helmets. Seasickness added to the misery.

The sea also took a toll of the guns and armor that were to follow the assault craft. Thirty-two amphibious tanks were launched too early into the swell and sank within minutes. Some crews escaped, others drowned in their vehicles. Ninety-six tanks were planned to follow the soldiers onto the beaches – a third of that number had now been lost without ever coming under fire. The DUKWs that were to ferry support artillery ashore also ran into difficulties. The small, heavily laden craft foundered – the 111th Field Artillery Battalion lost all but one of its 105 mm howitzers and the 16th Infantry Cannon Company and the 7th Field Artillery fared little better.

With 40 minutes to go to H-hour, when the troops would reach the beaches, the Allied aerial and naval bombardment of the enemy defenses reached a climax. The Allies had a massive air superiority on D-day. A total of 3,467 heavy bombers, 1,645 medium, light and torpedo bombers, 5,409 fighters and 2,316 transport aircraft were stationed in England on 6 June. Against this the Germans could muster only 319 aircraft, of which 100 were fighters. Field Marshal Hugo Sperrle, Commander of *Luftwaffe* Air Fleet III, had requested more aircraft before D-day – the *Luftwaffe* simply could not spare any from the defense of Germany's industrial centers. German naval patrols had been canceled on 5–6 June because of bad weather and the ships stayed in port. In fact the German navy did not consider the weather suitable for an invasion and, because they had no weather stations in the west, they were unable to detect the improvement in the weather noted by the Allies. German E-boats did approach the Allied fleet by accident but the mighty steel shield of warships that protected the invasion force was impenetrable. One German rating, on seeing the Allied force, said in astonishment that 'It's impossible. There can't be that many ships in the world!'

At Omaha, 500 heavy bombers of the US 8th Air Force mounted a concentrated attack on the German defenses. The US battleships *Texas* and *Arkansas* poured 3,500 shells into the enemy positions from their total of ten 14-in, 12 12-in and 12 5-in guns. A variety of fire-support craft softened up the landing areas. But even this did not convince German High Command that the invasion point was between Cherbourg and the Seine and not the Pas de Calais area which, to strengthen the illusion, the Allies had bombed extensively in the days leading up to 6 June.

In the assault craft the cold and miserable vanguard of the invasion, bailing frantically to remain afloat, paused to look up and cheer the flying shells that were to destroy the German coastal defenses. The landing craft moved closer and closer to the shore of occupied Normandy and still no response came from the enemy defenses.

It was a silent prelude to disaster. The naval bombardment had overshot many of the front-line enemy positions. Some had been neutralized but only temporarily. The final aerial bombardment did not deliver a single bomb on the beaches – for fear of hitting their own men the aircraft crews had delayed a few seconds in dropping their bombs. They fell three miles inland. The landing craft, in a strong lateral current, had tended to drift eastward: the landmarks, seen so often in aerial photographs and in training exercises, were shrouded in smoke and dust and early morning mist. And so the troops, trained for specific tasks in their planned landing areas, found themselves in a confused and unexpected situation.

But this was the least of their immediate problems. The German shore batteries opened up, crashing into the bobbing, awkward landing craft. Artillery, mortars and machine-guns thundered all along the four-mile stretch of Omaha beach. Those units whose job it was to ensure that the successive waves of assault craft could beach safely and disembark their men and equipment on the rising tide suffered badly. The special Engineer Task Force was responsible for clearing gaps through the belts of obstacles during the first half-hour of the landing. Only five of the 16 assault ferries carrying the Engineers landed in the correct sectors and of these, three of the teams had no infantry or tank support. Sixteen bulldozers were to have come ashore with the task force – only six reached the beach and three of these were quickly disabled by artillery fire. Much of the equipment needed to mark lanes through the obstacle belts was lost or destroyed.

To add to the Engineers' problems they came in behind schedule and became mixed up with infantry, some of whom sought shelter behind the obstacles the Engineers were intended to blow. The Germans singled them out for special attention, with sniper fire detonating the mines fixed to the obstacles while the Engineers were working on them and mortar fire detonating rows of mines. At the end of the day there were 50 per cent casualties among this special unit.

Despite the difficulties, the Engineers managed to clear six lanes through the belts of obstacles before the incoming tide submerged them. Four of these lanes were in the 16th Regiment's sector and two in that of the 116th Regiment. But only one of these lanes could be marked and this created casualties and confusion as waves of assault craft, unaware of the situation, approached the areas. One craft struck a mine and disintegrated, showering the Engineers with debris and spreading blazing fuel over the water.

On 5th Corps' right flank, the invasion plan was for the 116th Infantry Regiment to land four companies in the first assault wave on each of their four beaches – code-named Dog Green, Dog White, Dog Red and Easy Green. A Ranger Company was to land slightly farther to the right on Charlie beach and from there it was to assault a strongpoint just to the west of Vierville. The 16th Infantry Regiment should also have landed four companies in the first assault wave in Easy Red, Fox Green and Fox Red.

Because of the general eastward drift of the landing craft few touched down in the correct sectors and sub-units became hopelessly mixed. Few landing craft made dry landings, most of them grounded on sandbanks up to 100 yards from the beach and in some places troops were disembarked into water that was neck deep.

F and G Companies came ashore on Dog Red and Easy Green.

Although under heavy fire and disorganized by landing in the wrong place, many of them crossed the 200 yards of tidal flat to shelter behind the sea wall and shingle. Those who stopped at the water's edge were under direct German observation and suffered casualties. The right wing of 5th Corps' assault wave had practically disintegrated and the four companies of the 116th Infantry Regiment were no longer a fighting force. A Company had been cut to pieces on the shore line, F Company was disorganized by heavy casualties, scattered sections of G Company were trying to find their correct sector and E Company had veered widely off course, landing on the eastern extreme of the 116th Regiment, on the left flank.

To the west of the 116th Regiment, on the extreme right flank of Charlie beach, the 2nd Ranger Battalion had suffered severely. Their objective was an enemy strongpoint to the west of Vierville. One of their two landing craft was sunk by artillery fire and the other came under direct machine-gun fire as soon as the ramp was lowered. By the time the soldiers had reached the base of the cliff, 200 yards from the water's edge, only half the 65-strong unit was still alive. By nightfall, only 12 remained.

There were heavy casualties on the left flank, in the 116th Regiment's sector, but the majority of the supporting tanks had got ashore. Four tanks landed on Easy Red, a mile-long beach marking the junction point of the 116th and 16th Infantry Regiments, but only about 100 men landed with them – unfortunate for the Allies, for here enemy resistance was light. E and F Companies were scheduled to land on Easy Red but the bulk of both companies drifted too far to the east. The result was that only elements of these companies, together with part of E Company of the 116th Regiment, came ashore in the right sector in the first assault wave and these were bunched on the extreme eastern part of the beach.

Some of the troops were disembarked in waist-high water but then had to cross a deep channel to get to the beach. This pulled them even farther to the east and though casualties were light, with only two men killed, most of their heavy equipment such as flame throwers and mortars and some personal weapons were lost. Others landing slightly farther to the east were less fortunate – not only were they disembarked in deep water but they came under heavy fire. Only 14 men reached the shingle.

Stiff enemy resistance, faulty navigation and delays contributed to the critical situation that was now developing on Fox Green.

Two companies from the 116th Infantry were scheduled to land in the first assault wave but the bulk of four companies, including elements of E Company of the same regiment, landed hopelessly intermixed in a comparatively restricted sector. Few casualties had been incurred in the final approach to the beach but as soon as the leading landing craft lowered their ramps and disembarkation got under way interlocking enemy machine-gun fire swept the water and inflicted heavy casualties. The survivors struggled to the water line and here, with most of their officers dead or wounded, they stopped.

I and N Companies of the 16th Infantry Regiment, which should have formed the first assault wave on Fox Green, were delayed – and they missed the disaster. I Company drifted widely off course and were an hour behind schedule. N Company was 30 minutes late and landed beyond the eastern limit of Fox Green. The company lost a number of men at sea and during the landing but it disembarked at a point where the tidal sand reached almost to a steep escarpment. This was the only company, of the nine that formed the first assault wave, that was ready to act as a unit.

At 0700, 30 minutes after the first assault wave had landed, a second group of five follow-up waves approached the beaches. These included the support battalions of the two leading regiments and was timed to go ashore at 0740. None of the follow-up assault waves arrived under the conditions that were expected. The tide had risen nearly 8 ft and now covered most of the beach obstacles. Only six lanes through the obstacles had been cleared and these were still not properly marked. The initial assault waves had not advanced beyond the sea wall or shingle and neither the surviving tanks nor the infantry from the first wave were in a condition to provide more than spasmodic covering fire. Nowhere had the enemy defenses been neutralized.

The troops in the second wave were organized, briefed and equipped to do no more than mop up any enemy positions that had been by-passed by the first wave. They were then to move inland, by boat loads, to their respective battalion assembly areas. Only a few sections of the second waves had special assault equipment – flame throwers, demolition charges and bangalore torpedoes for clearing lanes through minefields once ashore.

The troops in the second waves, as they approached the shore, could see the carnage wrought among the first wave. Debris from

sunken assault craft bobbed among half submerged bodies and struggling survivors. Broken or discarded stores, weapons, lifejackets,
equipment of every kind littered the shore line. Silent, wounded
soldiers were grouped among the desolation, many in severe shock.
One sergeant recalled a 'terrible politeness among the more seriously
injured' and a soldier of the 741st Tank Battalion saw a man sitting at
the water's edge, oblivious to the machine-gun bullets that spattered
about him, 'throwing stones into the water and softly crying as if his
heart would break.' Medical orderlies, there to treat the wounded,
did not know 'where to start or with whom'.

On the right wing, in the 116th Infantry Regiment's sector, the 1st
Infantry Battalion had landed only A Company in the initial assault
wave; the other three companies in this wave belonged to the 2nd
Infantry Battalion. The 1st Battalion's three remaining companies
were to come ashore in the second wave on Dog Green in echelon
formation at ten-minute intervals. They assumed that A Company's
assault wave had cleared most of the enemy positions.

At 0700, B Company started to come ashore but it was badly
scattered over an area extending to nearly a mile on either side of
its intended sector. A few assault craft beached in the correct area but
were subjected to the same heavy fire that had decimated A Company
30 minutes earlier. The survivors of B Company struggled ashore to
mingle with those of A Company along the shore line. Only three
widely dispersed groups on the flanks played any effective part in
the subsequent battle.

C Company was scheduled to land directly behind B Company at
0710. A major navigational error prevented it from doing so – and
it was saved the disastrous fate of B Company. The company came
ashore 1,000 yards to the east on Dog White beach. One of its six
assault craft became entangled on the mined obstacle belt and it took
20 minutes of gentle maneuvering before it got free. The remaining
five assault craft approached the shore in reasonably good order but
the vessel carrying the special assault equipment capsized in the
surf when its ramp jammed and the entire load was tipped into
4 ft of water. The unit recovered from this set-back and suffered
only six casualties in disembarking and crossing the sand, largely
because smoke from grass fires in the escarpment obscured enemy
observation. C Company moved up to the sea wall and started to
reorganize.

At 0720 D Company began to disembark having lost two assault craft, one swamped and the other hitting a mine. The remainder of the company got no farther than the shore line, having come under fire as soon as they disembarked. Most of the heavy support weapons were lost. To add to the disruption, the three assault craft carrying the battalion command group, the Headquarters Company and the Beachmasters party for Dog Green were widely scattered several hundred yards to the west. They came in directly under the cliffs and suffered heavy casualties in doing so. They stayed in the same position for most of the day and played no part in co-ordinating the scattered remnants of the battalion.

The 2nd Infantry Battalion had landed three of its companies in the initial assault wave – now only G Company survived as a fighting unit. Machine-gun fire ripped into the ranks of the supporting H Company and of the battalion headquarters as the ramps were lowered. Men scrambled for shelter behind disabled tanks near the water's edge. The battalion commander, together with his command post and elements of H Company, braved the fire, running up the open beach to the shingle bank where they joined the leaderless survivors of H Company. Because of the faulty radio communications it was over an hour before further progress could be organized. Eventually an attack by about 50 men was mounted against the enemy positions in and around Les Moulins, but it was beaten back to the crest of the shingle bank.

While this was in progress, the four sections of G Company, trying to move along the beach to get near their objectives on Dog White, gradually lost cohesion. One by one individuals or small groups stopped to take cover, only to become mixed and separated as they progressed westwards along the shingle bank crowded with survivors of other companies. By the time the remnants of G Company had reached their correct sector at about 0830, the main action was already over.

The 3rd Battalion of the 116th Infantry Regiment was scheduled to arrive directly behind the 2nd Battalion on Dog White, Dog Red, and Easy Green between 0720 and 0730. But the battalion was ten minutes late and came in well to the east on Easy Green and Easy Red along a thousand-yard frontage. Only a few scattered elements of the first assault wave had landed in this sector. K and I Companies came in behind them in close formation on Easy Green, and suffered only a handful of casualties in crossing the tidal flat to the shingle, but having arrived there safely they appear to have become immobilized.

L Company disembarked on either side of the junction between Easy Green and Easy Red, where they met only light enemy fire, which many men seem not to have noticed. M Company landed farther to the east on Easy Red and, encountering enemy fire on first disembarking, they stopped at the water's edge. Eventually, when the rising tide began to push them forward, the whole Company moved to the embankment as a body and, as one of them later remarked, 'the Company learned with surprise how much fire a man can run through without getting hit.'

Although the enemy defenses had not been breached, the second assault group suffered much less severe casualties than the initial one. Altogether five of the eight companies of 116th Infantry Regiment were capable of developing and holding a precarious toe-hold which they had established. Troops who were demoralized and lacked inspired leadership found this supplied when, at 0730, the Command Group of the Regiment, which included the assistant divisional Commander Brigadier General Cota and Colonel Canham began to land on Dog White. Both men were fearless soldiers and could not have arrived at a more opportune moment nor at a better place to influence events. To their left troops were crowded along the embankment of a few hundred yards, while the main Ranger contingent was about to land in the same area. Ahead of them, behind the embankment, smoke from burning grass obscured the enemy's view and rendered his fire largely ineffective.

The experience of the 16th Infantry Regiment was similar to that of the 116th. Although the initial assault wave all landed on Fox Green, leaving the large 2,000-strong force on Easy Red beach with only a handful of infantry operative, the second group started to land, and casualties were high. The main problem was the dislocation of command posts, faulty landings, casualties, the loss of radio sets and the physical difficulty commanders experienced in imposing control. Except for those immediately around them, they could exert little influence over the many men lying against the sea wall – a shelter they were all too reluctant to leave. Behind them the troops could see successive waves battling through the same fierce defense they had been through and the bodies of dead and dying comrades, and in front of them lay the enemy and a beach flat littered with minefields and wire obstacles.

The situation looked critical and further vehicles and support weapons could not come ashore until the exits had been cleared.

But slowly, desperately slowly, inspired leadership and individual heroism began to turn the tide. General Cota and Colonel Canham, the latter already wounded, walked up and down the beach oblivious to enemy fire and bluntly directed officers and NCOs to get their men moving. Slowly groups of men, often from different units, and in other places units of company size, started to move forward supported by the few remaining tanks. Behind Easy Red beach an engineer lieutenant and a wounded sergeant walked forward under fire to clear a lane through the wire obstacles. Their task done they returned and looking down in disgust at the men huddled behind the shingle, exhorted them to get forward before they were killed where they lay. Advances were made in a world of smoke and confusion, each group isolated from its neighbors. An impetus developed, however, as successive penetrations brought a slackening of enemy fire.

The most significant advance in the 116th Regiment's sector came from Dog White beach. Here C Company and the 5th Ranger Battalion were spurred forward by General Cota at about 0750.

German defenses in this area consisted of lightly manned weapon pits connected by deep trenches sited just on the crest of the escarpment. The machine-guns were mainly sited to provide flanking fire down other sectors of the beach, rather than to deal with a direct assault. On the opposite side of the sea wall there was a double apron wire obstacle which had to be breached before the infantry could get through. After an initial setback, a gap was eventually blown by a bangalore torpedo and the infantry started to filter through under cover of heavy smoke from the grass fire drifting eastward along the face of the escarpment.

The leading infantrymen were joined by others who had cut their way through the wire and together they moved forward to the high ground giving access to the plateau. Progress was slow here through fear of mines, and the company advanced in column following an indistinct track. On gaining the top of the escarpment the enemy positions were found to be unoccupied and, after suffering only six casualties since leaving the shelter of the sea wall, the advance was resumed for a farther 200 yards when, still moving in column, the company encountered machine-gun fire from a flank and went to ground.

At 0810 the 5th Ranger Battalion, without knowing exactly what C Company was doing ahead of them, crossed the beach flat after blowing four lanes through the wire and started to climb the escarpment. Heavy smoke forced some of the men to put on their respirators and contact was lost between the various sub-units. However, for the loss of only eight men, the few enemy positions still holding out on the edge of the escarpment were overrun, and, after pausing to reorganize, the Rangers resumed their advance.

By 0830 a penetration 300 yards wide had been made and the last groups of infantrymen were leaving the sea wall. It was not in itself an advance of great significance but similar actions, frequently on an even more reduced scale, were being conducted all along the beaches. These isolated penetrations were then gradually linked together, expanding the bridgehead laterally and, what was of equal importance, giving it some depth so that further reinforcements of both men and equipment could be brought ashore as the beach exits were first cleared and then developed.

On the 16th Regiment's front, a gap opened up by G Company became an exit for movement off the beach during the remainder of the morning. The Regiment's command group landed in two sections at 0720 and 0815. The second section included Colonel Taylor who got his disorganized and leaderless men moving with terse instructions: 'Two kinds of people are staying on this beach, the dead and those who are going to die – now let's get the hell out of here!' As soon as the engineers had cleared gaps through the wire obstacles and scattered minefields, the infantry were organized into haphazard groups and sent forward under the command of the nearest available officer or NCO. As they moved forward through the gap, there was intermittent enemy fire from both flanks and the already congested route became a scene of even greater confusion as leaderless groups stopped to shelter below the crest.

Strenuous efforts by the officers who had landed with the various command groups in the later waves encouraged the troops forward onto the plateau and gradually the bridgehead was extended. Progress inland was aided by a few isolated but determined groups of Rangers who had landed to the flanks of the main assault, and then fought their way forward unaware of what was happening elsewhere. As the penetrations which had been made between 0800 and 0900 started to link up, a new but still fragmented phase of the battle began. German defenses along the immediate coastline had begun to crumble and there were no significant reserves available to the enemy in the Omaha sector. A more immediate threat to the Germans came on the flank of 5th Corps attack. Here the British 2nd Army had broken through the German defenses in a number of places, and to the west, the American 7th Corps was firmly ashore with men and vehicles pouring across the beaches almost unhindered.

The inland battle behind Omaha developed into three generally unconnected and largely uncoordinated actions around Vierville, St Laurent and Colleville. Although there was only scattered resistance from small but determined enemy groups, seldom as much as company strength, progress was slow for a variety of reasons. Little fire support was available since most of the tanks and heavy support weapons had been lost during the landings, vital communication links were missing, units were frequently still hopelessly mixed, and control amongst the thick hedgerows was extremely difficult.

By 1100, however, Vierville had been cleared after a frontal attack by two battalions of the 116th Regiment, who then tried to extend the bridgehead laterally to link up with the Rangers who had landed farther to the west. By late afternoon this advance had been halted and Colonel Canham decided to withdraw and concentrate on the defense of Vierville, where the scattered Engineers, with only a quarter of their equipment, struggled to open up the beach exit giving access to Vierville. East of the Les Moulins valley, the 3rd Battalion of the 116th Regiment fought their way forward in small groups until they were stopped just short of St Laurent. Farther to the east, two battalions of the 16th Regiment fought a series of confused and fragmented actions in an advance towards Colleville, which was halted short of the town by a local German counter-attack.

At sea, the 115th Infantry Regiment had been held as a floating reserve only to be committed if the situation became critical. The desperate situation which had developed during the 116th Regiment's landings on the right wing of 5th Corps assault demanded their committment so the 115th Regiment was ordered to land at H+4 (1030) to give immediate support. The same eastward drift which had disrupted the earlier assault waves dislocated the landings of the 115th Regiment. Pulled eastward by the incoming tide sweeping up the English Channel, the Regiment landed on top of the 18th Infantry Regiment in the process of disembarking east of St Laurent. It was not until early afternoon that the confusion on the congested beaches could be sorted out and the 115th Regiment headed for its assembly area south-west of St Laurent. After an unsuccessful attempt to take the town, the regiment halted short of the St Laurent–Colleville road.

The 18th Infantry Regiment, whose disembarkation had been disrupted by the unscheduled arrival of the 115th Regiment in their rear, was tasked with taking over the 16th Regiment's D-day objectives. However, because of delays and enemy resistance, their orders were changed and it was directed onto the high ground beyond the St Laurent–Colleville road to fill a gap between the 16th Infantry on the right, but at dusk it had not managed to reach the road.

At the end of the day 5th Corps had established two footholds, the first in a narrow sector between St Laurent and Colleville, nowhere more than a mile and a half deep; the second, slightly farther to the west, around Vierville. The cost of these modest gains had mounted to 2,000 killed, wounded and missing, together with the loss of a large amount of equipment which included about 50 tanks and 26 artillery pieces. The whole of the landing area was still under enemy artillery fire and of the 2,400 tons of supplies planned to be onloaded during D-day, only about 100 tons had actually arrived. Beach obstacles were only about a third cleared, even after a low tide during the afternoon had enabled the Engineers to resume work on them; beach exits had not been developed, nor had the essential beach organization, necessary to ensure the orderly handling of successive landings, been properly established.

The principal cause of 5th Corps' setback was the unexpected degree of enemy resistance. Not only were prisoners taken from the 726th Regiment which was known to be in the area, but also from the fully combatant 352nd Division whose presence on the coast came as a complete surprise. How much of the 352nd Division was actually in the Omaha area is not known – certainly not the whole formation, since elements of it were encountered as far east as Bayeux in the British 2nd Army sector. The division appears to have been moved into the area between Grandchamp and Arromaches – in order to stiffen the second-line coastal formations deployed within the immediate beach defenses. In this manner, all the prepared strongpoints and their various interconnecting weapon pits were fully manned and the artillery of the 352nd Division, consisting of three field and one medium battalion, was at least in part able to support the German troops confronting the Omaha landings.

Had it not been for the massive assistance of the Allied navies and air forces during this critical period of 5th Corps' landing, it is doubtful whether the shaken and depleted troops of the assault waves would have been able to recover, reorganize and then develop an offensive which was to deepen and widen their bridgehead in the succeeding days.

Omaha is a story of near disaster but no shame. Largely unseasoned troops, subjected to all the hazards of a vast and complex amphibious operation, further compounded by unfavorable weather conditions and stubborn opposition, were initially near paralysed by shock but, under the shield of fire provided by the allied navies and air forces, rallied and resumed a dogged offensive.

Aachen (1944)

Hubert Essame

The greatest US involvement in ground fighting during the Second World War was not in the battle of the 'Bulge' nor the recapture of the Philippines, but in the little-known battles of Aachen in the autumn of 1944. They were in some respects akin to the Meuse–Argonne offensive of 1918 which holds a similar place in the First World War, but the Aachen battles were not ultimately successful. After three months two US armies only penetrated 22 miles into Hitler's Reich at a cost of 140,000 casualties, then they were subjected to a totally unexpected German winter counter-offensive in the Ardennes. Allied hopes of victory in 1944 died with the protracted and frustrating campaign on the Siegfried Line.

Back in the heady days of the Normandy breakout, comparatively little stress had been laid on the spectacular success of Lieutenant General Courtney H. Hodges ' First US Army in their helter-skelter advance from the Seine, in accordance with General Dwight D. Eisenhower's 'Broad Front' policy, towards the Aachen Gap and Cologne. Hodges, in the last days of August, advancing on a three-Corps front with Major General 'Lightning Joe' Lawton Collins' 7th Corps on the right flank suddenly swung it NE towards Mons. Approaching this area were disjointed elements of 20 routed German divisions flushed out of Normandy by the British. Neither had been forewarned of the other's approach and both stumbled into an impromptu battle which ended in more than 2,000 Germans being killed and another 30,000 POWs being rounded up. First Army in fact had destroyed the last reserves of both Seventh and Fifteenth Armies leaving the way ahead to Liege and Aachen virtually open. It was this little-advertised victory which enabled US patrols to be first across the Belgian border into Germany west of Aachen on 11 September. The First Army closed up on the west bank of the river Wurm.

Thereafter Eisenhower gave priority for supply to Field-Marshal Sir Bernard Montgomery's airborne carpet thrust towards Arnhem. Hodges closed down offensive operations on 22 September to shorten his front and bring forward another Corps to fill the gap in the Ardennes between his army and Patton's. Ahead on either side of Aachen from Geilenkirchen to the Huertgen Forest stretched one of the strongest parts of the West Wall. Hodges also knew that whatever its military value Hitler would not lightly let Aachen go. The days when cities could be carried at a run in the confusion of the pursuit were over. First Army would once more have to face new problems demanding novel techniques. In Normandy it had been hedgerows, now it would be concrete pillboxes, minefields and all the bedevilments of fighting in a densely populated industrial area. Inevitably success would depend more on the courage and skill of the individual infantryman than on air support or armored strength.

On purely military grounds retention of Aachen had little to recommend it, surrounded as it was by hills and lying within two defensive belts of the West Wall. The city's roads were relatively unimportant as First Army had already found adequate ones leading towards the Rhine both north and south of the city. Over a millennium before, however, in the days of the Emperor Charlemagne, Aachen (Aix-la-Chapelle) had been capital of the Holy Roman Empire and thus had become identified with the mythology of National Socialism. To strike at Aachen was to strike at a symbol of Nazi faith. Hodges therefore decided to encircle it using 30th Division and 2nd Armored Division of 19th Corps to strike south to link up with 7th Corps NE of Aachen near Wuerselen and thereafter reduce the city at leisure. West and north of Aachen lay a densely built-up urban area. Major General Leland S. Hobbs, commander of 30th Division, therefore chose to make the first penetration of the West Wall on a narrow front along the Wurm nine miles north of Aachen where the country was more open.

On 26 September over 300 guns began a systematic attempt to

knock out all the pillboxes on the divisional front; results were disappointing. Heavy bomber support was arranged with the proviso by 30th Division that the USAF should avoid bombing them instead of the enemy as they had done with disastrous results at St Lo in Normandy – 75 men killed and 505 wounded by American bombs. Bad weather resulted in the attack's postponement until 2 October. When the air strike went in, many of the medium bombers missed their targets – one group bombed a town in Belgium 28 miles away! The fighter-bombers, although they found their target area, failed to knock out a single pillbox. The 117th Infantry Regiment had to fight its way forward supported only by its own artillery, mortars, heavy machine-guns and tanks. There followed a day of small battles amongst the houses of Marienberg and Palenberg.

A volunteer flame-thrower operator of Lieutenant Robert P. Cushman's platoon, Private Brent Youenes, advanced within 10 yards of the first of two pillboxes and squirted two bursts into the embrasure. Private Willis Jenkins then shoved a pole charge into it. Out came five badly shaken Germans, lucky to be still alive. The platoon next shot up a machine-gun crew in a trench outside the pillbox and, creeping round the back of another, tossed hand-grenades through the embrasure. Pte Youenes squirted it with flame and the garrison surrendered. The platoon then dealt with three more pillboxes in like manner. An observer's comment, 'These infantrymen have guts' erred on the side of understatement. Meanwhile the Engineers worked on treadways across the quagmires of the Wurm to enable the tanks to cross; none, however, could get into action before nightfall.

On the next day house-to-house fighting in Palenberg often lapsed into hand-grenade duels. One rifleman, Private Harold G. Kiner, spotted a hand-grenade that landed between him and his fellow riflemen, threw himself upon it and saved his companions at the cost of his own life. He was posthumously awarded the Medal of Honor. On the right flank of 117th Infantry, the 119th Infantry Regiment established a shallow bridgehead along the Wurm in the face of intense artillery fire.

Close infighting like this characterized the struggle among concrete and wire for the next three days. On 4 October the Germans staged a full-dress counter-attack with tanks and assault guns supported by well-directed artillery fire: even the *Luftwaffe* made an appearance. They got nowhere despite goading by Field Marshal Walther Model.

By the 6th, superior American morale and armament swung the issue in their favor. On the left, 2nd Armored Division attacking SE carried all before it; on their right. 30th Division, despite fatigue, burst into the ghost town of Arlsdorf and the squalid streets of Merkstein. It was here that Private Salvatore Pepe refused to take cover but, rushing forward alone firing his rifle and tossing hand-grenades, wounded four Germans and caused 50 more to surrender. The 30th Division was now only three miles from Wuerselen, the planned point of junction with 7th Corps attacking from the south. Inch by inch the advance continued. By the evening of the 7th, Hobbs, justifiably exuberant, could report to his Corps Commander, 'We have a hole in this thing big enough to drive two divisions through . . . this line is cracked wide open.' His division and 2nd Armored had literally ruptured the West Wall in the face of a surprisingly large concentration of heavy and medium artillery and over 50 assault guns. Both divisions had taken in their stride the shock of the abrupt change from exhilarating pursuit to a grim battle in fortified zones.

It was now the turn of 7th Corps to strike north with 1st Division and complete the encirclement of Aachen by advancing to Wuerselen. Major General Clarence R. Huebner of 1st Division planned to do this with the 18th Infantry Regiment. Only a two-and-a-half-mile advance was involved, but it would take them through a dense maze of pillboxes and over exposed hill crests. To take these hills was no easy task; holding them thereafter under heavy artillery bombardment would be even more difficult. In Aachen itself there were about 12,000 Germans. Furthermore, unknown to the Americans, Field Marshal Gerd von Rundstedt had promised to provide 3rd *Panzergrenadier* Division and 116th *Panzer* Division under 1 SS Corps for counter-attack when the situation was ripe. Huebner's preparations included the provision of special pillbox assault teams equipped with flame-throwers, Bangalore torpedoes and pole and satchel charges. A battery of 155 mm guns and a company of tank destroyers were also provided to hurl point-blank fire against the pillboxes.

Attacking at night on 8 October and again on the 9th, the 18th Infantry fought their way forward to Verlautenheide, halfway to Wuerselen. Here they had to endure the most intense artillery fire yet encountered in the campaign. Despite fatigue, the 18th Infantry faced the prospect of a counter-attack with determination. It came in full force during 15–16 October. German losses were heavy; over 250 dead were counted in front of 16th Infantry Regiment. Altogether a third of the attackers were killed to no avail.

Meanwhile, from the north, 30th Division had turned southwards to meet 1st Division, in the process attracting particularly vicious attacks by 1 SS *Panzer* Corps. Amidst the slag heaps and pit heads around Bardenberg the reserve battalion of the 120th Infantry Regiment knocked out six tanks and 16 half-tracks, the CO, Major Howard Greer, personally accounting for two with his bazooka. Almost hourly fresh German units were fed into the struggle. But divisional morale remained unshaken, despite 2,020 casualties sustained in the past ten days. All efforts on their part to get forward still continued to meet vicious and obstinate resistance. The pressure on Hobbs from his superiors to close the now mile-wide gap and get on to Wuerselen became almost unendurable. On 16 October he struck again with 119th Infantry as his spearhead against the dug-in tanks and pillboxes blocking the way forward. In the mid-afternoon, 18th Infantry in the south spotted American troops on the ridge SW of Wuerselen. They were the two survivors of a patrol of 119th Infantry, Privates Edward Krauss and Evan Whitis. At 1615 these two, quickly reinforced, had the honor of closing the ring around Aachen.

Aachen itself, already a wilderness of rubble as a result of RAF attention earlier in the year, now found itself the target of 7th Corps artillery and fighter-bombers of 9th Tactical Air Force. An ultimatum to surrender delivered under a flag of truce, broadcasts on Radio Luxembourg and leaflets shot into the ruins by artillery on 10 October were all scornfully rejected by the garrison commander, Colonel Gerhard Wilck. Huebner had to commit 25th Infantry to a tedious battle within the ruins 'from attic to attic and sewer to sewer'. German resistance, reinforced by SS Battalion *Rink*, continued obstinate to a degree. Methodically, 26th Infantry inched their way forward. Outside the perimeter all attempts by 1 SS *Panzer* Corps to re-establish contact with the encircled garrison came to nought. Finally on the 19th Model abandoned the city to its fate.

But Col. Wilck issued an order of the day, 'The defenders of Aachen will prepare for their last battle. Constricted to the smallest possible space we shall fight to the last man, the last shell, in accordance with the Führer's order.' Over the air he continued to affirm his 'unshakeable faith in our right and our victory'. By the night of 20 October, 26th Infantry, reinforced by two battalions of tanks, had corralled his few remaining soldiers into the western and SW suburbs. Next morning, Lieutenant Colonel John T. Corley's battalion, supported by a 155 mm gun, approached a big air raid bunker at the northern end of the city. Faced by the threat of being blasted into eternity, Colonel Wilck surrendered. He had fought to a finish. The battle for Aachen was over; the once proud city, the first city of the Reich to be captured, lay in utter ruin. Burst sewers, broken gas mains and dead animals raised an overpowering stench.

It had been a costly battle. The 30th Division lost over 3,000 men, the two battalions of 26th Infantry 498. Throughout the armor had been forced to fight in penny packets cheek by jowl with the infantry. It had been a soldiers' battle in which Allied air power and material superiority counted for less than the fighting spirit of the infantry and the tank crews. Between them 1st and 30th Divisions had taken some 12,000 prisoners. What was surprising was the skill with which the German commanders had handled the many miscellaneous elements thrown piecemeal into the fighting as the days went by. Even more surprising was the tenacity with which their troops continued to fight.

Long before the battle it had become evident that Model, commander of Army Group B, whose frontage coincided almost with that of General Omar N. Bradley's 12th Army Group, had succeeded in establishing a well-organized defense of the West Wall astride the Aachen Gap. The morale of his troops was high, and even his second-class troops, established in fixed defenses, built-up areas and woods, could be formidable. Stolberg's 4,000 defenders put up a week's street fighting. Much bitter fighting in ever-shortening hours of daylight and deteriorating weather would have to be faced before the line of the river Roer, 12 miles ahead, let alone the Rhine, could be reached.

It is an indisputable fact that on the whole the German Army still outclassed the Allies in the flexibility and simplicity of its organization and in the professional skill of its battle-experienced corps and divisional commanders and their staffs. In the debacle at the end of August and the first week of September, although the Seventh and Fifteenth Armies had been reduced to skeletons, most of their staffs had survived and still continued to function. With the aid of Military Police and *Waffen* SS detachments they succeeded in regaining a measure of control. Hitler rushed forward First Parachute

Army to fill the gap between what remained of Seventh and Fifteenth Armies.

Heinrich Himmler, commanding the Home Army in addition to his duties as Minister of the Interior, Chief of Police and Head of the SS, had put all his weight behind the drive to fill the ranks of 43 *Volksgrenadier* (the People's Grenadiers) Divisions now being formed. To supplement the artillery Hitler ordered 12 motorized brigades (about 1,000 guns), 10 *Werfer* Brigades, 10 assault-gun battalions and 12 machine-gun battalions to be raised. Himmler diverted the best of the manpower and equipment into the *Waffen* SS which now composed one third of the *Panzer* and one fourth of the *Panzergrenadier* divisions. The great strength of these divisions lay in their young officers – Nazi to a man, coarse, arrogant and cruel, but well trained and ruthless in battle. From them Hitler planned to produce a new generation to replace the regular officers of the *Wehrmacht*.

'Unconditional surrender' and the announcement of the Morgenthau Plan on 24 September, which revealed the Allied intention of turning Germany into a third-class agricultural state, reinforced Joseph Goebbel's propaganda appeals to the German people. Now that the enemy stood on the sacred soil of the Fatherland a deeply felt, instinctive love of country prompted all, soldiers and civilians alike, to fight on in the belief that the Führer in some mysterious way would emerge finally triumphant like Frederick the Great when all seemed lost in the Black Year of 1759. Behind the ramparts of the West Wall and depths of the Huertgen Forest they would fight on as the nights grew longer and the autumn rains slowed down the Allied armies and diminished the threat from the air.

As a matter of strict nomenclature, defined by the US Army Military History Department, the battle of Aachen ends with the fall of the city. Popularly, in the Allied Armies of the time and in European eyes, especially German, it also embodies all the operations of First and Ninth Armies east and west of Aachen in November and the first half of December.

At Brussels on 18 October Eisenhower revealed to the Army Group commanders his intention of continuing the battle on the Aachen front with First and Ninth Armies as a first step towards enveloping the Ruhr. He made it clear that serious logistic difficulties must first be overcome. Until the mouth of the Scheldt was cleared, enabling the port of Antwerp to be opened, no large-scale offensive could be sustained. Two other serious supply problems were causing him great anxiety. Surprisingly, US factories had failed to keep up with the Army's needs and an acute shortage had developed, which would take some time to make up. Eisenhower broadcast a personal appeal to the United States. Casualties, especially infantry riflemen and tank crews, had been much heavier than anticipated. Drastic steps had to be taken to comb out and retrain as infantry men from other arms. For these reasons and the vagaries of the weather affecting air support a resumption of the battle was deferred for nearly a month. If there was no fog over the airfields in Great Britain there was always fog over the target area and vice versa. As a result, autumn, with overcast skies, damp depressing fogs, persistent rain and ever shortening hours of daylight, was already far advanced when on 16 November Bradley renewed his offensive towards the Rhine.

Immediately south of Aachen, First Army, now numbering 12 divisions, was to make the main effort. In particular it was to take the seven Roer dams at Schmidt, so that Eisenhower's future plans for the Second British and Ninth Armies could be implemented. North of Aachen the Supreme Commander brought in the Ninth Army, fresh from America, to advance simultaneously and protect First Army's northern flank. Some seven miles ahead and almost parallel to the front lay the river Roer, initial objective of both Armies. To reach it First Army would have to fight its way through the dense Huertgen Forest, three miles deep, flanked by extensive built-up areas. On Ninth Army's front the country was more open for tanks and for controlling the large forces now to be engaged.

By this time, although the Allies had not an inkling of his intentions, Model's plans for an Ardennes counter-offensive in December with Fifth and Sixth *Panzer* Armies and Seventh Army were already far advanced. Facing First and Ninth Armies he had Fifth *Panzer* Army and Seventh Army; in their immediate rear Sixth *Panzer* Army had already started to assemble. Altogether some 30 divisions would be concentrated here and large stocks of fuel and ammunition built up. Model had over 1,000 guns centrally controlled and plenty of ammunition. His losses of the early autumn had been replaced and his intentions were crystal clear – to fight the Americans in the Devil's Garden of the West Wall and Huertgen Forest; under no circumstances would he allow the Americans to cross the Roer. Furthermore, the Sixth *Panzer* Army, destined to execute the main effort in the Ardennes, must be kept out of the battle on the Aachen front but look like joining it.

Bradley imagined that an overpowering aerial bombardment would shatter German morale and then he intended to blast his way through with massed artillery. Over 1,200 heavy bombers of 8th USAAF and RAF Bomber Command were to 'take out' the towns of Duren, Julich and Heinsberg on the Roer. The forward troops would have 750 fighter-bombers on call. Late on the morning of 16 November vast fleets of aircraft passing over First and Ninth Armies signalled the start of Bradley's offensive. Results were disappointing – the 9,400 tons of bombs, for safety reasons, were dropped so far behind the German forward troops that they almost completely missed them. The attacking troops, four divisions on a 25-mile front, although supported by 1,000 guns, found themselves greeted by deadly small arms, artillery and mortar fire. It was small consolation and no help to them that six miles ahead three towns on the Roer had been destroyed in the heaviest tactical air bombardment yet launched.

Thus inauspiciously began the month-long battle of attrition which occupies a place and significance in the history of the American Army similar to that of Verdun for the French and Passchendaele for the British. In the end it absorbed some 17 divisions, resulted in severe casualties both from enemy action and sickness and severely tested the morale of the troops. It was fought in vile weather – damp grey mist alternating with heavy downpours reduced the battlefield to a ghastly quagmire and precluded effective air support. Everything favored the enemy. In the Huertgen Forest, First Army plumbed the depths of misery. Here, hidden from view amongst the closely planted trees, protected by barbed wire, anti-personnel mines, log bunkers, log-covered foxholes and machine-gun emplacements, a few men could hold up whole battalions. There were so many mines that the attackers were reduced to using pitch forks to uproot the new wooden and glass types. Charles B. Macdonald, American Official Army Historian, vividly recorded the fighting in *The Siefried Line Campaign*:

It was attrition unrelieved. Overcoats soaked with moisture and caked with freezing mud became too heavy for men to wear. Seeping rain turned radios into useless impedimenta. So choked with debris was the floor of the forest that men broke under the sheer physical strain of moving supplies forward and evacuating the wounded. The fighting was at such close quarters that hand grenades were often the decisive weapon. The minefields seemed endless. A platoon would spend hours probing, searching, determining the pattern, only to discover after breaching one minefield that another just as extensive lay 25 yards ahead. Unwary men who sought cover from fire in ditches or abandoned foxholes might trip over lethal booby traps and turn the promised sanctuary into an open grave.

The swollen bodies of the dead in grotesque positions added to the general horror. So bitter was the fighting that the village of Huertgen changed hands 14 times and the village of Vossenack eight times. Inevitably there were unfortunate incidents in which both officers and men cracked under the strain. More than 24,000 killed, missing, captured and wounded fell a prey to the fighting here; a further 9,000 succumbed to the misery of the forest itself, the wet and the cold, trench foot, respiratory diseases and combat fatigue. To some extent, too, the torpor which comes from prolonged exposure without relief to shellfire and bad weather was reflected at command level.

In the more open country on the northern part of the front Ninth Army had better fortune and reached the Roer from Julich to Linnich on 28 November. Thanks to realistic training in the United States and the support of more lavishly supplied British artillery, the army stepped off on the right foot in this its first battle. It would be another two weeks, however, before First Army was able to close up with the river opposite Duren. The testimony of British officers who saw the American troops at this time should also be recorded. During the battle many officers and men of Guards Armoured Division were exchanged with the Americans. Their impression was that 'their methods might be somewhat curious and unorthodox, but there could be no doubt about the excellent results when put into practice. Divisions such as the 29th and 30th Infantry who fought in this battle could have challenged comparison with the finest of our own.' Lieutenant-General Sir Brian Horrocks, commanding the British 30th Corps on the extreme left flank of the offensive, and with the 84th US Infantry Division under his command, was most impressed by their performance in their first battle, their bravery, initiative and ability to learn from experience.

The first snow fell on 9 December; thereafter the days were chill and the sky overcast. By 15 December First and Ninth Armies, having advanced eight miles in a month, had reached the high ground overlooking the river Roer. But three miles to the south the Germans still held Schmidt and the vital dams despite persistent attack. Attempts by the RAF to burst them with their heaviest bombs had failed. On their right, on a 100-mile front in the Ardennes, Bradley only had some four divisions, two new to battle and two badly mauled in the Huertgen Forest. The Germans, fighting what was an essentially defensive action, had reinforced the front with 11 divisions including two *Panzer*. Of these, however, only one, 10th SS *Panzer*, was scheduled to take part in the now imminent Ardennes offensive. American losses, mostly in front-line units, in killed, wounded or missing in the Aachen battles since September now totalled 68,000, plus over 70,000 sick as a result of fatigue, exposure, accidents and disease.

Fifty years later it is fair comment to say that First Army fought in the wrong place. They would almost certainly have had greater success if they had advanced in September, as originally planned, south of the Ardennes in conjunction with Patton's Third Army. Better still, they could have been sent through the Ardennes, which, as the Germans had proved in 1940 and would soon confirm, were not the barrier to large-scale military movement they had traditionally been assumed to be.

At 0530 on 16 December in darkness and fog from south of Monschau came the rumble of 2,000 German guns, their heaviest artillery barrage of the whole campaign. Model launched 13 infantry and seven armored divisions, followed by a further ten, a thousand tanks and 250,000 men into the Forest of the Eifel. The battles of Aachen were over. Another had begun.

Ardennes (1944)

Peter Young

Not since Pearl Harbor had the Americans received so rude a shock as when the dawn of 16 December 1944 was broken by the thunder of a thousand guns: German guns, heralding a most determined onslaught.

Ever since July, Hitler, with a strategic sense which one is compelled to admire, had been building up a reserve, a *masse de manoeuvre*, of 250,000 men. It was little enough for a two-front war, nor were they the soldiers of 1940, but it was still a force capable of delivering a heavy blow. And it was commanded by von Rundstedt, a man of whom miracles could still be expected. He had already performed one when he stabilized the German line on the Western Front after the débâcle in Normandy. Now he performed another by concentrating Hitler's last army (Model's Army Group B) in the Eifel area without attracting the attention of the American High Command. How did the Allied intelligence fail to see a quarter of a million men, their vehicles and 1,100 tanks? They saw what they wanted to see. The Germans, they thought, were licked – and anyway who would think of mounting an offensive in the Ardennes in the middle of winter? A certain number of suspicious troop movements were reported by prisoners, civilians, and by airmen, but their significance was discounted. As the Germans hoped, these were thought to be reinforcements for the fighting round Aachen.

Although von Rundstedt was to command the offensive, he did

not favour it. It was Hitler's own brain-child. Physically the Führer was not the man he had been before the bomb attempt of 20 July. Lt-General Hasso von Manteuffel saw him as 'a stooped figure with a pale and puffy face, hunched in his chair, his hands trembling, his left arm subject to a violent twitching which he did his best to conceal, a sick man apparently borne down by the burden of his responsibility. When he walked he dragged one leg behind him.' But this miserable, shambling creature could still make himself obeyed. Whatever his physical condition his willpower was unimpaired. Temperamentally unstable, he was incapable of playing a waiting game. He deliberately sought a decision. Moreover, that acute if unbalanced mind could detect certain factors in favour of his plan.

In 1940 the Ardennes had been the weak link in the French chain. Now the Monschau–Echternach sector was the weakest part of Eisenhower's front. Lt-General Courtney H. Hodges (First Army) was holding 85 miles with only five divisions and three of them (2, 4, and 28) had suffered heavily in the recent fighting round Aachen. Only about 100 miles to the NW was Antwerp, the great Allied supply base, which had recently been opened to seaborne traffic. The German commanders knew the narrow roads of the Ardennes with their hairpin bends and steep hillsides very well. They had come that way in 1940. Bad weather could be expected to nullify the Allied air superiority. Otto Skorzeny's Panzer Brigade 150, disguised in American uniforms, would cause confusion behind the lines.

Von Manteuffel had a conversation with Hitler on 2 December, when the latter admitted that there was

> a certain disparity between the distant objective of Antwerp and the forces which were to capture it. However, he said, this was the time to put everything on one throw of the dice, 'for Germany needs a pause to draw breath.' Even a partial success, he believed, would retard the plans of the Allies by eight to ten weeks . . . Temporary stabilization on the Western Front would enable the Supreme Command to move forces from there to the threatened central sector of the Eastern Front.

The German generals were not unnaturally concerned about the question of air cover. After the Berlin conference Manteuffel told Hitler that 'in our sector of the front we never saw or heard a German aeroplane these days.' He received this curious reply: 'The *Luftwaffe* is being deliberately held back. Göring has reported that he has three thousand fighters available for the operation. You know Göring's reports. Discount one thousand, and that still leaves a thousand to work with you and a thousand for Sepp Dietrich.'

When the attack came the SS General Sepp Dietrich with the Sixth SS Panzer Army fell upon the US V Corps (Major-General Leonard T. Gerow) and thrust towards Liège. The Americans were driven back to the Eisenborn Ridge, but in three days' desperate fighting they denied the enemy the direct road to Liège, the main communications centre of Bradley's Twelfth Army Group. A German armoured column did succeed in thrusting forward through Malmédy, Stavelot, and Stonmont, but as luck would have it narrowly missed not only the Allies' main fuel dump but Hodges' HQ at Spa. By 19 December it had been brought to a halt.

Fifth Panzer Army, though weaker than Sixth, made much more progress. Von Manteuffel achieved tactical surprise by attacking without a preliminary bombardment, relying on close co-operation between his armour and his infantry. His onslaught shattered the US VIII Corps (Major-General Troy H. Middleton), which was strung out upon a long front. On Manteuffel's right a corps cut off two regiments of the inexperienced US 106th Division in the Schnee Eifel. On his left two panzer corps broke through the US 28th Division, and reached the outskirts of Houffalize and Bastogne.

Seventh Army (General Erich Brandenberger) was supposed to cover Manteuffel's left flank by thrusting forward towards the Meuse. It made some progress at first especially on the right, but after a few days was held up by the US 4th Infantry Division and elements of the 9th Armoured Division.

Dietrich's failure meant that the Germans were not going to retake Antwerp. Hitler determined nonetheless to exploit Manteuffel's narrow breakthrough.

In 1940 Gamelin had had no theatre reserve, no *masse de manoeuvre*. Eisenhower had the XVIII Airborne Corps; this he now sent to General Hodges.

Eisenhower ordered General Omar N. Bradley (12th Army Group) to attack each flank of the German breakthrough with an armoured division. But he saw that if Model succeeded in widening the shoulders of the breakthrough Bradley's army group might be split right down the middle. Practical as ever, he placed all the US forces north of the breakthrough (First and Ninth Armies) under

Montgomery (21st Army Group), leaving Bradley in command of the forces to the south.

Like Joffre in 1914, Eisenhower was willing to give up ground rather than let his line break. Patton (Third Army) was to disengage, make a tremendous left wheel, and drive northwards. The 6th Army Group in Alsace would have to take over Patton's sector in the Saar even if this meant giving ground in Alsace and perhaps abandoning Strasbourg. General de Gaulle was *not* pleased. But in fact the Germans were in no position to mount another offensive, and although the northern corner of Alsace was evacuated, Strasbourg itself was saved.

While Eisenhower was taking a grip on the situation, his front-line troops, though hard-pressed, were putting up a fight which compared more than favourably with the resistance of the French IXth Army in 1940. The unfortunate Corap had had few if any tanks. It was the American armour that won time for Eisenhower's measures to take effect. The 7th Armoured Division denied St Vith to the enemy until 21 December. Part of the 10th Armoured Division delayed von Manteuffel just long enough to allow 101st Airborne Division to establish itself in Bastogne.

Bastogne stood like a rock. Fifth Panzer Army, unable to drive through, had to go round, shedding considerable forces to contain the improvised fortress. Summoned to surrender 22 December Brigadier-General Anthony McAuliffe, a modern Cambronne, curtly answered 'Nuts'.

The Germans had not quite shot their bolt. Sixth Panzer Army got going again and Manteuffel's two panzer corps drove on westward and on Christmas Eve his 2nd Panzer Division was in sight of the Meuse, near Celles, three miles east of Dinant. But the attack had lost its momentum.

Meanwhile, the Allied counter-attack was getting under way. The weather had cleared and 5,000 Allied planes were strafing the transport strung out nose to tail all the way to the German frontier. In the words of General Arnold 'We prepared to isolate the battlefield.' Moreover it was air supply that saved Bastogne, while Patton pushed up from the south to its relief.

In the line north of the gap Montgomery had three American corps under Hodges (V, XVIII Airborne, and VII) with the British XXX Corps in reserve on the Meuse. Hodges' centre was still vulnerable and to shorten it Montgomery evacuated a salient round Vielsalm – *reculer pour mieux sauter* is no bad tactical axiom.

The US 2nd Armoured Division (VII Corps) cut off and destroyed Manteuffel's spearhead at Celles on Christmas Day. Next day the US 4th Armoured Division broke through to Bastogne. Thus ended the first phase of the battle.

By Christmas Day von Rundstedt realized that the battle had been lost, but Hitler was not the man to admit defeat or to cut his losses. Instead he thought up a new double offensive. He would begin by taking Bastogne and then, wheeling north, would take the First Army in flank while a secondary attack engaged it from the direction of Roermond. In the New Year he would mount yet another offensive in Alsace.

At the same time Eisenhower was planning a counter-offensive which had rather more substance. Bradley and Montgomery were to strike simultaneously.

Bastogne was still the storm centre. The corridor to the town was only a mile wide in places. Patton was determined to drive off the two German corps that were squeezing its lifeline. At the same time Manteuffel was concentrating for the attack which would rid him once and for all of this thorn in his flesh. On 30 December they met head on, and locked in a deadly winter battle which ranged blindly and fiercely through the snow-clad woods and ravines of the Ardennes.

By the time the battle died down the Germans were spent. On 8 January 1945 Hitler reluctantly agreed to limited withdrawals, and next day Patton broke out of Bastogne. Model, helped by a break in the weather, began to disengage his forces. On the 13th, owing to the Russian winter offensive, the German Supreme Command withdrew Sixth SS Panzer Army from the Ardennes battle, and permitted a general retreat. Patton and Hodges joined hands at Houffalize on the 16th and Bradley was able to resume command of his army and restore his original line. By 28 January it was all over.

The battle cost the Allies 76,980 casualties, but it ruined Hitler's last reserve army both morally and physically. The Germans lost 70,000 casualties and 50,000 prisoners, besides 500–600 tanks and 1,600 planes. The Russians had launched their great winter offensive on 12 January, and Hitler no longer had his *masse de manoeuvre* to meet it: a terrible price to pay for the six weeks delay it imposed on the Western Allies.

It was a great victory. Even so the Germans, though less well trained than three years earlier, had hacked a wound 50 miles deep in the American line. They had fought with all their old devotion. The more credit to the Americans who beat such men.

The part of the air forces must not be underrated. The *Luftwaffe* was still able to send over 700 aircraft on New Year's Day, 1945, to attack Allied airfields and to destroy nearly 200 planes on the ground. On 22 January the Anglo-American air forces claimed to have destroyed 4,200 pieces of heavy equipment; railway engines and trucks, tanks, motor and horse-drawn vehicles.

There are those who regard General Eisenhower as a very indifferent general, little more than a sort of Grand Liaison Officer. It is true that in the battle of the Ardennes his original lay-out was faulty. Major-General Fuller even goes so far as to say: 'The enormity of Eisenhower's distribution can be measured by supposing that it had been made in May, 1940. Had it been, then there can be little doubt that his armies would have suffered a similar fate to Gamelin's.' But this is going altogether too far, and ignores the fact that up to mid-December 1944 Eisenhower had had the initiative on the Western front, and was not simply sitting waiting to be attacked. Once the battle began he made the right decisions and he made them in time. In the event his 33 divisions mauled 26 German divisions. One can only judge a general by his works, good or ill, and it seems to the present writer that Eisenhower's stature is greatly enhanced by this macabre winter battle.

> *Few, few shall part where many meet*
> *The snow shall be their winding sheet*
> *And every turf beneath their feet*
> *Shall be a soldier's sepulchre.*
>   (Thomas Campbell, *Hohenlinden*)

Berlin (1945)

John Strawson

In all the talk that went on in the last months of the Second World War about strategy and objectives and partitioning Europe, one vital point was overlooked by everyone. It was that the only military objective whose capture or elimination could actually bring the war to an end lay in the person of one man – Adolf Hitler. It was Hitler's will alone which kept the German people on their dreadful path to destruction. He had made his intention clear to his generals on the eve of the Ardennes offensive in December 1944: 'We must allow no moment to pass without showing the enemy that, whatever he does, he can never reckon on a capitulation. Never! Never!' Indeed he had already said it countless times – in *Mein Kampf* and in his endless table talk years before. 'We shall not capitulate – no, never. We may be destroyed, but if we are, we shall drag a world with us – a world in flames.'

The battle for Berlin turned this reckless prophecy into the reality of *Götterdämmerung*. Albert Speer, technocrat, and Minister of Armaments and War Production, described the helplessness to which Hitler's miscalculations had reduced the once mighty Reich: 'Howling and exploding bombs, clouds illuminated in red and yellow hues, droning motors and no defence anywhere – I was stunned.'

Before 1945, when it was hard to see how it could be done, both the Russians and the Western Allies had repeatedly named Berlin as their goal. But such definitions made little sense unless it was possible to make a proper plan to capture the city. This was not feasible until the beginning of 1945. Once the *Wehrmacht* had at last recognized that there was nothing left but a strategy of defense, in the East on the Vistula and in the West on the Rhine, once Germany itself was on the point of being invaded, that is in January 1945, the battle for Berlin – then only a few hundred miles away from each main enemy army – was on.

Planning the final battle of the war began in the Soviet High Command in October 1944. It was intended to advance from the Vistula to Berlin and beyond in six weeks. The offensive was to start on 20 January 1945. Later the date was brought forward to 12 January. Three army groups or 'fronts' were to attack – 1st and 2nd Belorussian commanded respectively by Marshals Georgi K. Zhukov and Konstantin Rokossovski, and 1st Ukrainian under Marshal Ivan S. Koniev – 2.5 million men against fewer than a million Germans. The Russians' material superiority was even greater. When the attack started it had immediate and startling success. The Eastern Front collapsed, as Colonel General Heinz Guderian, Chief of the German General Staff, had forecast, like a house of cards. By early February the Red Army had reached the River Oder opposite Berlin. They were only 40 miles from the city. Here they paused.

Why did Stalin not push on after his first brilliant success? Was it simply that with Berlin virtually in the bag he wanted to get his hands on as much of SE Europe as he could? Still more interesting is the question he put to his generals: 'Who is to capture Berlin, we or the Allies?' – and this at a time when it had already been agreed with the Americans that they would halt their armies well to the west of the city.

Zhukov maintained that because of so many casualties to men and equipment suffered during the January battles, difficulties of supply and air support, as well as the German counter-attack capability, further advance was impossible. Colonel General Vasili I. Chuikov, on the other hand, commanding 8th Guards Army under Zhukov, claimed that the war could have been ended in February. He also recorded that when on 4 February the advance on Berlin was being discussed, Stalin telephoned Zhukov and told him to halt the advance on the city and attack the German forces in Pomerania instead.

The result was that the final thrust on Berlin did not start until 16 April. Broadly, Zhukov was to take the city while Koniev would cut off the German Army Group Vistula from Berlin and secure Zhukov's southern flank. Zhukov had no illusions about the problems facing him:

> The unusual and highly complex offensive against Berlin required the most careful preparation at all front and army levels. Troops of the 1st Belorussian front were expected to break through a deeply echeloned defense zone extending from the Oder River all the way to heavily fortified Berlin. Never before in the experience of warfare had we been called upon to capture the city as large and as heavily fortified as Berlin. Its total area was almost 350 square miles. Its subway and other widespread underground engineering networks provided ample possibilities for troop movements. The city itself and its suburbs had been carefully prepared for defense. Every street, every square, every alley, building, canal and bridge represented an element in the city's defense system.

Yet four days after the attack started, his artillery opened up on Berlin and on 21 April the leading troops of three armies, 3rd Shock, 2nd Guards Tank and 47th broke into the outskirts of the city. The last phase of the battle had begun. Eleven days later on 2 May, General Helmuth Weidling, Berlin Commandant, surrendered. It was all over. The battle between 16 April and the German capitulation had cost the Red Army a terrible 300,000 casualties.

'How pitiful is their Berlin!' announced Marshal Zhukov after his troops had captured it. It was the Red Army and Allied bombing which had made it so. Yet the courage and perseverance of the Berliners themselves should not be forgotten. The long road to Berlin had cost the Russians 20 million men since that day almost four years earlier when the two great armies had clashed head on. And all of it had been brought about by the man who at the height of the fighting for Berlin conducted, or thought he conducted, the battle which he claimed would cause the Russians to suffer their bloodiest defeat.

That it was the Russians and not the Americans who reached Berlin first was because of decisions and actions taken during the first two weeks of April 1945. Lieutenant General William H. Simpson's US Ninth Army crossed the Elbe astride Magdeburg on 12 April, and reached Tangemunde – only 50 miles from Berlin. The Russians'

next offensive was not planned to start for another four days, 16
April, and they were at this time 40 miles from Berlin on the Oder.
The day before, Simpson asked General Omar N. Bradley to let his
troops expand the Elbe bridgehead and push on in force for Berlin.
That he would have got there seems more or less certain for he had
suffered very few casualties and opposite him were only scattered,
ill-equipped and untrained formations of General Walther Wenck's
Twelfth Army which had no air support at all. Wenck commented:
'If the Americans launch a major attack they'll crack our positions
with ease. After all what's to stop them? There's nothing between
here and Berlin.' But Eisenhower vetoed the idea.

On the same day Stalin sent a message to the American Ambassador in Moscow to the effect that the Red Army was about to
renew the offensive. The main thrust would be on Dresden with
a subsidiary one on Berlin. This information was hardly accurate.
The main Russian forces were directed at and astride the German
capital. Could the *Wehrmacht* withstand the forthcoming Russian
steamroller? Colonel General Gotthard Heinrici in command of
Army Group Vistula (still called this although it had long since
left the Vistula far away) had two armies – General Theodor Busse's
Ninth Army, directly in the path between the Red Army and Berlin,
and General Hasso von Manteuffel's Third *Panzer* Army which was
on the Oder 30 miles NE of the city and was deployed as far
north as Stettin. He would be attacked by three Russian Fronts –
Rokossovski's aimed at Stettin, Zhukov's at Berlin and Koniev's at
Dresden.

It took the Red Army only ten days from 16 April to surround
Berlin. But it was by no means a walkover for them. The battle for
the Seelow Heights, a critical position, was hard and costly. Despite
all their superiority in artillery, the Russian troops came under heavy
AT and machine-gun fire which took such a toll of the advancing
troops that they were stopped. This caused Stalin to order Koniev
to direct his armored forces on Berlin so that on 17 April two Soviet
fronts were making for the city. This was too much for Busse's Ninth
Army, and by 20 April the Germans defending the approaches to
Berlin were overrun. One Russian witness, Konstantin Simonov,
saw the remnants of a German battle group:

In front of us lay Berlin, and to our right a forest clearing,
now a chaos of jumbled tanks, cars, armored cars, trucks,

special vehicles and ambulances. They had uprooted hundreds of trees, probably in an attempt to turn round and escape. In this black, charred confusion of steel, timber, guns, cases and papers, a bloody mess of mutilated corpses lay strewn along the clearing as far as the eye could see . . . Then I noticed a host of wounded men lying on greatcoats and blankets or leaning against tree trunks; some of them bandaged and others covered in blood, with no one to tend to them.

Before the Russian attack on the Oder position started, Heinrici had explained to Speer that there would be no proper battle for Berlin because the two wings of Army Group Vistula would simply withdraw respectively north and south of the city. But when it was clear to him that Zhukov had broken through, Heinrici did make an attempt to organize the *Volkssturm* (home guard) battalions to establish some defenses to the east of the city. But *Volkssturm* battalions without transport and with inadequate supplies of ammunition could never stop the Red Army.

On 20 April Soviet artillery began to shell Berlin. Next day 2nd Guards Tank, 3rd Shock and 47th Armies – all Zhukov's formations – reached the outskirts of the city. At the same time Koniev was moving forward with 3rd Guards Tank Army. Then with two huge pincer movements, the Russians encircled the German Ninth Army to the SE of Berlin and Berlin itself, while their spearheads pushed on to the Elbe. By 25 April the Russians had surrounded Berlin and contacted US forces at Torgau. Now there was only one thing left to do – take Berlin and finish the war in Europe.

Col. Gen. Chuikov has left his recollections of it all:

A battery of heavy howitzers was stationed on an open grassy space beside a wood. Dark, ragged clouds were sailing across the sky. The earth seemed to doze, shivering a little from time to time from shellfire in the distance. The gun crews had already run out the howitzers, and were awaiting the command to fire. The muzzles were trained on Berlin . . . on the fortifications of Fascist Berlin – 'Fire!' The heavy shells flew up, cleaving the air with a whistling sound. The path had been opened. In the morning I went up to my observation post. It was in a large five-storeyed building near the Johannisthal aerodrome. From a corner room here,

where there was a jagged hole in the wall, one got a view of
the southern and south-eastern parts of Berlin. Roofs, roofs
without end, with here and there a break in them – the work of
landmines. In the distance factory chimneys and church spires
stood out. The parks and squares, in which the young leaves
were already out seemed like little outbreaks of green flame.
Mist lay along the streets, mingled with dust raised by the
previous night's artillery fire. In places the mist was overlaid
by fat trails of black smoke, like mourning streamers. And
somewhere in the center of the city ragged yellow plumes
rose skywards as bombs exploded. The heavy bombers had
already started their preliminary 'working-over' of the targets
for the forthcoming attack . . . Suddenly the earth shuddered
and rocked under my feet. Thousands of guns announced the
beginning of the storming operation.

The 'Fascist beast' himself had made much of making *Festung
Berlin* an impregnable fortress. It was a myth. In March 1945 a
'Basic Order for the Preparations to Defend the Capital' had been
signed and issued, but little had been done to turn Berlin into a
proper defensive position. The city was defended more by words than
deeds. The battle for Berlin would decide the war, Hitler claimed.
So it did, but not in the way he meant. The Basic Order envisaged
an outer perimeter about 20 miles out, another one 10 miles out, a
third following the S-Bahn (the railway serving the suburbs), and a
final citadel around the government buildings.

A plan was all it was without troops and weapons, ammunition
and supplies or a proper command system to control everything.
The battle for the city itself never really developed. It was simply
a gigantic mopping-up operation. The Red Army isolated Berlin
with overwhelming numbers. Then it slowly crushed the city's
life. It was impossible to fight a full-scale battle there with nearly
two million inhabitants, mostly old men or women and children
living in shelters. Allied bombing had forced them below ground.
In any event the military organization defending the city was a
lame skeleton. So-called *Panzer* divisions had a mere dozen or so
tanks and armored vehicles. After engaging the advancing Russians,
they inevitably retreated, leaving the dead and wounded lying in
the streets. The fighting itself was done in the midst of civilians
who had themselves either been killed by rockets and shells, were

cowering in cellars or desperately trying to find further cellars behind the retreating soldiers in order not to fall into Soviet hands. The streets were littered with bodies. Yet in some extraordinary way the spirit of the Berliners survived. They scrawled defiant messages on walls, proclaiming ultimate victory in spite of retreat. It was not the *Götterdämmerung* that Hitler had foreseen. But it had its moments of glory.

Up to 22 April Hitler was still nominally in charge of operations. One day earlier he directed his last battle. How did he conduct himself? First, he gave exact instructions to General Karl Koller, a *Luftwaffe* officer and Goering's Chief of Staff. When Goering had left the Bunker, Koller stayed. Like so many others he was unable to stand up to Hitler. Earnest and fussy, he would accept the Führer's raving invective and threats with misgiving but without dissent. Instead he would wring his hands and examine his conscience. On this occasion, as so often before, Hitler's orders were given in the greatest detail. He selected precisely which troops were to be brought back into reserve from the northern part of the city in order to launch a counter-attack on the Russians in the southern suburbs. He laid down exactly which ground units of the *Luftwaffe* were to be employed and in what way. The attack would be an all-out and final attempt to turn the tide. Every man, every gun and every tank would be committed, the *Luftwaffe* would put every available plane into the skies. All would be staked on a final desperate blow. An SS general, *Obergruppenfuehrer* (Lieutenant General) Felix Steiner, would command the operation.

The tactical plan for Steiner's attack was that it would be launched from the Eberswalde into the gap between von Manteuffel's Third *Panzer* Army and Busse's Ninth Army, so smashing the spearhead of Zhukov's drive on the city. But Army Group Steiner was a figment of Hitler's imagination. It had nothing like the strength required to mount an attack of the sort envisaged. Nonetheless Hitler told Steiner on the telephone to withdraw every man available between Berlin and the Baltic up to Stettin and Hamburg. The order was absurd. Steiner had no communication with any of these troops. Even had he the means of giving orders, there was no transport to move them. Yet when Steiner protested, Hitler broke in with an assurance that the Russians would suffer their bloodiest defeat before the gates of Berlin.

The shortage of troops was made up for by an abundance of

threats. Commanding officers who did not thrust home would not live to tell the tale. Steiner's written instructions contained a specific promise that he was answerable with his life for the execution of his orders. 'The fate of the Reich capital depends on the success of your mission.' Koller too was assured that his own head would guarantee both the vigilance of the effort to be made and the success that would result. All was in vain. Hitler's granite willpower was powerless now. Skeleton German battalions could never hold back the fully manned and equipped Russian divisions. The attack never came off. It did not even cross the start-line. German withdrawal in the north simply allowed Russian tanks to stampede through to the center of Berlin. The Steiner attack had made a desperate military position still more hopeless.

Weidling, on the other hand, who became Commandant of Berlin on 25 April, knew the city was almost surrounded. That evening on reporting in the Bunker to the Führer and his entourage, he showed them from a sketch map that the ring around the city would soon be finally closed. In fact the ring was already closed. After explaining the dispositions of enemy and German forces, Weidling gave his view that despite the defenders' efforts, the Russians were slowly and surely advancing to the center of Berlin. The encirclement involved eight Soviet armies. On the same day, 25 April, Hitler ordered the *Wehrmacht* to re-establish contact with Berlin by attacking from the NW, SE and south – so bringing the battle of Berlin to 'a victorious conclusion'. The only troops Weidling had, would ever have, were some *Volkssturm* battalions, *Luftwaffe* ground personnel and Hitler Youth units, and the remainder of his own 56 *Panzer* Corps. These he organized into defense sectors.

Despite all these difficulties Weidling made a plan which he put to the Führer on 26 April for effecting Hitler's escape from the city. Hitler rejected it. He was not prepared to be caught wandering about somewhere in the woods: 'I stay here to die at the head of my men. But you must continue to defend the city.' While inspecting defenses that day Weidling saw little to comfort him:

> The Potsdamer Platz and the Leipziger Strasse were under strong artillery fire. The dust from the rubble hung in the air like a thick fog . . . shells burst all round us. We were covered with bits of broken stones . . . The roads were riddled with shell craters and piles of brick rubble. Streets and squares

lay deserted. Dodging Russian mortars we made our way to the underground station by jumps. The roomy underground station was crowded with terrified civilians. It was a shattering sight . . . Colonel Barenfanger, who commanded in this sector, pressed me for more men and more ammunition. I could promise him neither. Most of his men were *Volkssturm* troopers who had been sent into the exceptionally severe fighting with captured arms . . . No ammunition for these guns could be found in the whole of Berlin.

Exactly how Berlin would finally fall remained to be seen. Lieutenant Colonel Pavel Troyanovski, a 'Red Star' correspondent, was there on the same day as Steiner's abortive attack:

It seemed as though we were confronted not by a town, but by a nightmare of fire and steel. Every house appeared to have been converted into a fortress. There were no squares or gardens, but only gun positions for artillery and mine throwers . . . Our guns sometimes fired a thousand shells on to one small square, a group of houses or even a tiny garden. Then the German firing points would be silenced, and the infantry would go into the attack . . . From house to house and street to street, from one district to another, mowing their way through gunfire and hot steel, went our infantrymen, artillery, sappers and tanks . . . On 25 April the German capital was completely encircled and cut off from the rest of the country. At the height of the street fighting Berlin was without water, without light, without landing fields, without radio stations. The city ceased to resemble Berlin.

On 23 April Stalin laid down the boundary between Zhukov and Koniev. The *Reichstag* (Parliament Building), where the Soviet flag was to be raised, was given to Zhukov. His soldiers captured the *Reichstag* and ran up the Red flag at about 1430 on 30 April – an hour before Hitler committed suicide. But German resistance, recalled one German soldier, continued in the hands of an SS officer:

The close combat boys went into action. Their leader was SS-*Obersturmführer* [First Lieutenant] Babick, battle commandant of the *Reichstag*. Babick now waged the kind of war he had always dreamed of. Our two battery commanders, Radloff and Richter, were reduced to taking orders from him. Babick's command post was not in the *Reichstag* itself but in the cellar of the house on the corner of Dorotheenstrasse and the Hermann Goring Strasse, on the side nearer the Spree. There he ruled from an air-raid shelter measuring some 250 sq ft. Against the wall stood an old sofa and in front of it a dining table on which a map of the center of Berlin was spread out. Sitting on the sofa was an elderly marine commander and next to him two petty officers. There were also a few SS men and, of course, SS-*Obersturmführer* Babick bending over his map. He played the great general and treated everyone present in the dim candle-lit room to great pearls of military wisdom. He kept talking of final victory, cursed all cowards and traitors and left no one in any doubt that he would summarily shoot anyone who abandoned the Führer.

Babick was tremendously proud of his successes. He was hoping for reinforcements. From somewhere or another, marines had come to Berlin on the night of 28 April, led by the very Lieutenant-Commander who was now hanging about the cellar with nothing to say for himself. Babick never moved from his map, plotting the areas from which he expected reinforcements and even the arrival of 'Royal Tigers' [heavy tanks]. Babick was still bubbling over with confidence. For one thing, he thought himself perfectly safe in his shelter. SS sentries were posted outside, others barred the corridor to the *Reichstag*, and Royal Tigers, our finest weapons, were apparently just around the corner. He had divided his men into groups of five to ten. One group was commanded by SS-*Untersturmführer* [Second Lieutenant] Undermann; he was posted south of the Moltke Bridge in the Ministry of the Interior (the building the Russians called 'Himmler's House') and the bridge itself lay in his line of fire.

Then an SS ensign, aged about 19, came to Babick with the report that Undermann and his men had come across some alcohol and that they had got roaring drunk. As a precaution he had brought Undermann along; he was waiting outside. Babick roared out the order: 'Have him shot on the spot!' The ensign clicked his heels and ran out. Seconds later we heard a burst of fire from a submachine-gun. The boy reappeared and reported:

'Orders carried out.' Babick put him in charge of Undermann's unit. Our ranks in the *Reichstag* got thinner and thinner. Part of our battery gradually dispersed, and by the night of 30 April, no more than 40 to 50 people, soldiers and civilians, were left in the cellar. This remnant was now busy looking for the safest possible hiding-places. There we intended to sit tight until the Russians came. But they kept us waiting for another 24 hours. At dawn on 1 May, we heard over our portable radio that the Führer had 'fallen in the battle for the *Reich* Capital,' his wife at his side. Goebbels and his family had gone the same way. We were our own masters, at long last.

The only thing still to be done was to negotiate with the Russians in order to surrender what was left of the city. By this time all that was left in German hands were the Government buildings, part of the adjoining *Tiergarten* and the area between the Zoo and the Havel river. Hitler had forbidden Weidling to capitulate but he had authorized a break-out. After Hitler's death Martin Bormann, the Deputy Führer, had sent a telegram to Admiral Karl Dönitz in Plön, appointing him as Hitler's successor. Dönitz, not realizing that Hitler was dead, replied: 'My Führer! My loyalty to you will be unconditional. I shall do everything possible to relieve you in Berlin. If fate nevertheless compels me to rule the Reich as your appointed successor, I shall continue this war to an end, worthy of the unique, heroic struggle of the German people.' But Goebbels and Bormann were trying above all to put an end to the pointless bloodshed. They therefore made contact with the Russians who agreed to receive a German representative.

This was Lieutenant General Hans Krebs, Chief of the General Staff since Guderian's dismissal on 28 March, who spoke Russian and had been in Moscow as Military Attache. He met Gen. Chuikov, Commander of the 8th Guards Tank Army, at Schulenburgring near Tempelhof Airport, at 0400 on the morning of 1 May. He had been authorized to negotiate only a truce or armistice, but the Russians, despite suspicions that the Western Allies were contemplating a separate peace with the German armies in the West, refused to consider anything except unconditional surrender. When Krebs referred to 1 May as a day which their two nations shared as a holiday, Chuikov drily observed that it might be a fine day in Moscow, but he could not say the same for Berlin. Thus Krebs failed and he committed suicide after returning to the Bunker. Next Weidling tried to negotiate. On the following morning he crossed the line dividing the two armies and surrendered the Berlin garrison with its 70,000 troops. The battle for Berlin was over. The question now was how would the Russians behave?

Rape, looting, burning and murder became commonplace. Hitler's very last War Directive of 15 April had made it clear what fate threatened a defeated Germany: 'While the old men and children will be murdered, the women and girls will be reduced to barrack-room whores.' Even at the end Hitler's reliance on propaganda and foresight did not desert him. But better things were on the way for Berlin. The Red Army positioned more disciplined regiments there: American troops reached the city on 1 July; the British arrived next day.

Iwo Jima (1945)

Paul M. Kennedy

Iwo Jima made an unremarked appearance on the island-littered map of the Pacific when, over 70 years ago, an underwater volcano spewed out ash and mud. The eight square miles of barren ash and soft, freshly formed rock might have remained in obscurity but for the strategic significance of this speck of land in the battle for the Pacific in the Second World War. Vital to the American campaign of rolling back the newly acquired Pacific empire of the Japanese to attack the enemy homeland, the grim battle for the tiny island lasted over a month and at the end 5,800 Americans and nearly 22,000 Japanese lay dead. Seizure of the island would deny the Japanese an excellent strategic base and give the Americans a bomber base only 660 nautical miles from Tokyo. Previous bombing missions had flown from the Marianas, 2,800 miles from Japan – a range which precluded fighter escort and led to heavy B29 Superfortress casualties. Iwo Jima was also a necessary link in the air defenses of the Marianas and it had to be captured, not merely isolated. There was a final consideration – the island was traditionally Japanese territory, administered from Tokyo, and its fall would be a severe psychological blow to the enemy.

Such blows were important. The Japanese had expanded their empire at a phenomenal rate. In the first five months of 1942 they had captured territory stretching from Burma in the west, through the Malay archipelago, to the central Pacific island groups of the

Gilberts and the Marshalls. Control of these islands, small in size, gave them air command of the surrounding area, and command of the skies was vital to control of the seas.

The Americans responded in two ways. They built up fast carrier-based forces which could gain command of the air in disputed areas, from which land and sea control could follow. To gain land control they devised sophisticated amphibious assault techniques to capture island bases. The land targets were so small that such invasions were, in reality, direct attacks on fortified positions and the landing was not an orthodox preliminary move, it was the battle itself.

Naval victories at the Coral Sea on 7 May 1942 and a month later at Midway, on 4–5 June, started the American comeback. On 7 August, 19,000 Marines under Major General Alexander A. Vandegrift landed on the island of Guadalcanal in the southern Solomons. The move took the local Japanese commanders by surprise and there was no need for an amphibious assault. On the nearby island of Tulagi, however, the Marines had a grim struggle with the local garrison and learned their first lesson – that the Japanese soldier, even if his position was hopeless, would fight to the death rather than surrender.

The next step in the Pacific re-conquest was a two-pronged assault. General Douglas MacArthur thrust into the south-west Pacific, taking the Solomons, isolating Rabaul on the island of New Britain, and 'hopping' along the northern coast of New Guinea. Admiral Chester W. Nimitz's central Pacific forces captured the Gilbert, Marshall and Mariana groups, and isolated the Carolines. So swift was the American drive that on 20 October 1944 the re-conquest of the Philippines began, against which the Japanese could offer only sporadic resistance after their naval defeat at Leyte Gulf.

The US Marines played a decisive part in the drive across the Pacific, particularly in the central Pacific advance. In their first attack, against the Gilbert Islands in November 1943, the Corps suffered heavy losses in the confused and bloody assault on Tarawa. Yet they learned a lot from the assault and in later and larger operations in the Marshalls and Marianas the benefits of earlier experience were clearly revealed. Now, at the beginning of 1945, with Japan pushed almost back to her national boundaries, the Marines were preparing for their toughest assignment yet – the assault on Iwo Jima.

The Japanese were also aware of Iwo Jima's importance and

began speedy reinforcement towards the end of 1944. A garrison of 23,000 men under Lieutenant General Tadamichi Kuribayashi was sent to the island with orders to hold out as long as possible – American air and naval superiority ruled out further reinforcement. Kuribayashi was a courageous and dedicated soldier, described by Tokyo Radio as one whose 'partly protruding belly is packed full of strong fighting spirit.'

The Japanese took with them 120 big guns of over 75 mm caliber, 300 anti-aircraft guns of over 25 mm, 20,000 small guns, including machine-guns, 130 8 cm and 12 cm howitzers, 20 20 cm mortars, 70 20 cm rocket-guns, 40 47 mm and 20 37 mm anti-tank guns, and 27 tanks. The building of pillboxes began in October 1944 and five months later 360 were complete. A superb network of deep, interconnected caves, which were almost impervious to naval bombardment, was built. All this on an island of eight square miles.

Adm. Nimitz entrusted overall control of the Iwo Jima operation to Admiral Raymond Spruance's Fifth Fleet which, with its fast carrier and battleship units supported by a mobile fleet train, was the most powerful naval body in the world. Its rôle was to give distant cover against enemy air or naval attack and to participate in the bombardment of the island. Rear Admiral Richmond Kelly Turner, probably the most experienced leader of amphibious operations during the Second World War, was given command of the landings. The US troops, 84,000 in all, were to come from 4th and 5th Marine Divisions, with 3rd Marine Division in floating reserve, along with Major General Harry Schmidt's 5th Marine Amphibious Corps.

Major General Groves B. Erskine's 3rd Division had fought at Guam and Bougainville and the 4th Division, under General Clifton B. Cates, had seen action at Saipan and Tinian. Major General Keller E. Roche's 5th Division did not have combat experience but they were trained and strengthened by many veterans. Lieutenant General 'Howlin' Mad' Smith, the vigorous leader of the Marine Division at Guadalcanal and now commander of the Fleet Marine Force, Pacific, was the commanding general of the Expeditionary troops. With such a tried team of commanders and good calibre soldiers, there was little doubt about the eventual outcome of the invasion. The question was, how easy – or difficult – would the Marines find the assault?

From late 1944 the most intensive softening up yet of the Pacific War began. Army bombers flew raids by day, Marine ones by night with ever-increasing intensity in the weeks leading up to the invasion, which was scheduled for 19 February 1945. Three days before the landings, Admiral William Blandy's Amphibious Support Force, which included five battleships, began an intensive bombardment of the island. At the same time, Spruance supervised carrier forces in their aerial attacks on Honshu to prevent any possible Japanese air strikes against the invasion fleet.

The shelling of Iwo Jima proved completely inadequate, as Schmidt had forecast in repeated requests for a longer, ten-day bombardment. The Americans received a shock on 17 February when 11 of 12 gunboats supporting beach demolition teams were sunk by enemy fire. Blandy realized from this that the island's defenses were far heavier than had been expected and accepted Schmidt's advice to concentrate bombardment on the beaches and nearby areas. Iwo Jima, like Tarawa, was so small that it was virtually all beach – unless enemy fire could be neutralized before the assault the Marines would be completely exposed.

The 'gunboat incident' benefited the Americans in two ways. It forced a reassessment of the enemy defenses and also exposed many Japanese gun positions. It seems unlikely that the orders to open fire came from high-ranking commanders – the first of Kuribayashi's 'Essential Battle Instructions' demanded that 'while the enemy bombardment is going on, we must take cover in the dugouts and we must keep our casualties to a minimum.' Kuribayashi was swift to order redeployment of the guns that had opened fire.

With a broad rocky plateau in the north and the extinct volcano of Mount Suribachi at the southern tip of the pork-chop shaped island of Iwo Jima, the only place a full-scale invasion could be mounted was on the black cinder beaches along the south-east coast. From this point it was only a short distance to airfield No. 1; but a landing here also meant that the open beaches would be subjected to an intense fire from higher ground to the north and the south.

At 0640 on 19 February, just before sunrise, Blandy's ships, now reinforced by two battleships and 13 cruisers from Spruance's fleet, opened up with a stupendous close-range bombardment of the island. The astonishing number of 450 ships ringed the island. Blasted by shells ranging from five-inch to 16-in in diameter, the beaches seemed to be torn apart. Shortly afterwards, rocket-firing gunboats attacked the Motoyama plateau while other gunboats lobbed mortar rounds at Mount Suribachi. Then, as the firing was temporarily checked and the various ships moved into their final positions, carrier aircraft and

heavy bombers from the Marianas showered the areas surrounding
the beaches with rockets, napalm and bombs. After a further ten
minutes the naval shelling recommenced, joined by ten destroyers
and over 50 gunboats which steamed as close inshore as possible
in an effort to screen the approaching invasion armada. The whole
co-ordinated action was immensely impressive – one history of the
battle describes the bombardment as 'a power-laden deployment
packing the utmost momentum yet devised by the mind and
engineering of man. This was the acme of amphibious assault.'

As the naval bombardment, now a creeping barrage, reached its
crescendo, the landing-ships lowered their ramps and the first of the
five assault waves emerged, 5,500 yards from the shore. Each wave
consisted of 69 amphtracs, armored amphibian tractors which could
take 20 troops each right onto the beach and scramble over coral reefs
if necessary. The first wave, the 4th Marine Division on the right,
the 5th on the left, moved virtually undisturbed towards the shore.
At 0902, after 30 minutes' steaming, the amphtracs hit the beach,
spewing out their men and the armored mortar and rocket-firing
vehicles.

They were immediately up against two unexpected physical
obstacles – black volcanic ash into which men sank up to a foot
or more, and a steep terrace 15 ft high in some places, which only a
few amphtracs managed to climb. Most stayed on the beach, getting
in the way of oncoming waves, while the troops jumped out and
struggled through the ash. One Marine described how he 'tried to
sprint up the terrace wall but my feet only bogged in the sand and
instead of running I crawled, trying to keep my rifle clean but failing.'
Fresh waves of assault troops arrived every five minutes and soon
10,000 men and 400 vehicles were on the beach. Despite inevitable
confusion the first combat patrols pushed 150 yards inland, then 300.
And then the enemy opened up.

From rabbit-holes, bunkers and pillboxes, small arms and machine-
gun fire crashed into the Marines. Heavy artillery and mortars, from
deep emplacements and caves on Suribachi and the Motoyama plateau, and trained exactly on the beaches well in advance, thundered
out, destroying men and machines. The Japanese garrison, true to
their orders, had withheld fire during the landings – only five
amphtracs were lost from the early waves. As the momentum of the
assault slowed at the terrace and the creeping barrage out-distanced
the Marines, the defenders nearest the beach were able to recover

and man their weapons. The ash on the beach cushioned all but direct blasts from the mortars and artillery – but one war correspondent stated that 'nowhere . . . have I seen such badly mangled bodies.' It soon became clear that to stay on the beach was near-suicide – but to move off it meant moving into fire from the well-developed defense system.

At this point – and probably only here – the outcome of the battle was in doubt. If the Japanese had mounted a counter-attack, they might have routed the disorganized Marines. But the lessons of Tarawa, Roi-Namur, Saipan and Guam were that furious counter-assaults upon the invaders simply exposed the defenders to the overwhelming American firepower. Kuribayashi's task was to deny Iwo Jima to the enemy for as long as possible and his troops were ordered to stay strictly on the defensive. Many of the guns were firing only sporadically to conserve their ammunition, although no one at the beach-head would have believed this. The initiative still lay with the Marines – they and their equipment were successfully ashore. Now they could, they *must*, go forward.

Slowly, desperately slowly, the Marines pushed inland, a confused collection of small groups rather than a united force. Each bunker, each rabbit-hole meant a fight to the death. Each enemy position was supported by many others – the Japanese would disappear down one hole and pop up at another, often behind rather than in front of the advancing Marines. The Marines struggled on, pouring bullets, grenades and flame into enemy positions. Flail tanks rumbled forward with the Marines, detonating land mines, tank-dozers carved channels through the terrace and ordinary tanks relieved the pressure on the Marines by knocking out machine-gun nests and pillboxes. But it was no pushover, even with the armor. Facing 4th Division's lines, for example, were ten reinforced concrete blockhouses, seven covered artillery positions and 80 pillboxes. A battalion commander asserted that 'whenever a man showed himself in the lines it was almost certain death.' By mid-afternoon the reserve battalions of four regimental combat teams and two tank battalions had been committed to the battle to relieve the pressure on the leading units.

As dusk fell on this first, bloody day of the campaign, the numbers of Marines had risen to 30,000, with the committal ashore of the reserve regiments for both divisions. On the left flank Colonel Harry B. Liversedge's 28th Regiment had pushed across to the ridge which overlooked the beaches on the south-west; but fierce enemy opposition had halted its progress towards its main target, Mount Suribachi. Next in line was Colonel Thomas A. Wornham's 27th Regiment, which had similarly been brought to a halt in its efforts to overrun airfield No. 1. Farther to the right were the two regiments of the 4th Division, Colonel Walter W. Wensinger's 23rd Marines and Colonel John R. Lanigan's 25th Marines; both had come under extremely heavy fire from the entire Motoyama plateau area, and the 25th Regiment, being farthest on the right, suffered many casualties – one battalion had only 150 men left in the front line.

Although the Marines had failed to reach their first day's objectives, they had secured a foothold and, aided by the inflow of reserves, were digging in to await the expected counter-attack. It didn't come. Instead, the Japanese kept up a deadly accurate mortar and artillery fire against the beaches, causing great damage and loss of life. Most feared of all were the 60 kg and 250 kg bombs which the Japanese had converted into rockets, which came screaming out of the blue to burst upon impact. 'A nightmare in hell' was one description of the scene.

On the second morning, after a 50-minute naval bombardment, the Marines moved on again. But progress was, if anything, even slower than on the previous day. Liversedge's 28th Regiment, making repeated attacks upon the approaches to Mount Suribachi with the aid of artillery, half-tracks and destroyers positioned nearby, advanced only 200 yards that day. To the north the 4th Division reached their objectives on No. 1 airfield and then swung right to face the rising ground that constituted Kuribayashi's first major defense line. Here, too, early progress soon petered out. On the next day this line remained virtually static but the 28th Regiment, again assisted by naval and aerial bombardment, penetrated almost to the foot of Suribachi.

The rugged volcanic mountain, rising steeply out of the sea to a height of 556 ft, was not of central importance to the defense of Iwo Jima. Yet it offered fine observation and artillery siting positions and, because of its imposing appearance, control of it tended to symbolize mastery of the island. Recognizing that it would soon be cut off, Kuribayashi had allocated only 1,860 men to its defense; but to its natural advantages had been added several hundred blockhouses, pillboxes and covered guns around its base together with an intricate system of caves in the slopes. As always, each position had to be taken separately, using a variety of weapons: mortars, tanks, rockets, flame-throwers and dynamite. When the Marines reached the caves, they went in with knives to kill the Japanese in close combat. Some of the defenders, out of ammunition, were reduced to rolling stones down the slopes, but still they fought on. By the morning of 23 February, the Marines were approaching the summit and 40 men under Lieutenant Harold Schrier carried an American flag to signify their victory. At 1020 it was raised amid cheers while fighting was still going on in the vicinity; and at noon it was replaced by a much larger flag. The planting of the second flag was photographed by Joe Rosenthal of Associated Press and the picture became probably the most famous of the entire war.

The end of the campaign was far from in sight – the worst had yet to come. Anticipating a fierce struggle, the Americans had committed the 3rd Marine Division on the same day to the middle of the front line, with the 4th on the right and the 5th on the left, and General Schmidt had come ashore to take direct control of what was the largest group of Marines yet to fight under a single command. Only 2,630 yards of island were left but it was obvious that every one was to be paid for dearly.

Kuribayashi had systematically turned the plateau region into an armed camp. Rockets, artillery and mortars, one a 320 mm weapon that lobbed 700 lb shells, were in good supply and blockhouses and pillboxes were numerous. Caves were elaborate and well fortified – one could hold 2,000 troops and had 12 exits – and the defenders were well trained and in high morale. They were prepared to hold a position to the death, infiltrate Marine lines, or throw themselves under an enemy tank with a bomb strapped to their backs. It was all deadly, frighteningly inhuman. Admiral Turner called it 'as well defended as any fixed position that exists in the world today.'

Fortunately this kind of operation was exactly what the Marines were trained for. During the Pacific War, as they fought from one atoll to the next, the Marines endured a much more personal and individual form of combat than that seen in actions in Western Europe or North Africa, and against a fanatical enemy who would not surrender.

To reduce the casualties of the attacking force, weapons of modern military technology were brought to their aid. The Japanese positions were bombarded by the guns of warships, they were battered by heavy bombers, the rockets and machine-guns of fighters, as well as dive-bombers. Tanks, artillery, mortar and rockets hammered the positions, flame-throwers scorched them, and dynamite blasted them. But the Marines knew, as they looked ahead over the next ridge, along the next gully, that the capture of virtually every position also involved close-in fighting – with machine-gun, pistol, grenade, knife, digging-tool, even hands – before the defenders were fully overcome. This was how the hell on earth of Iwo Jima had to be taken.

The battle for the second airfield, sited almost in the dead center of the island, was typical of this form of fighting. There the Japanese had constructed hundreds of pillboxes, rabbit-holes and concealed emplacements, which defied the concentrated American firepower for two days. On 24 February, the two battalions of the 21st Marine Regiment rushed forward to take the enemy lines with bayonet and grenade, the terrain being too difficult for tanks. Not only did the Japanese fire upon them from all their entrenched positions, but many rushed into the open and engaged in a struggle reminiscent of some medieval carnage, with the bayonet as the key weapon. Casualties rose steeply on both sides. The Marines, thrown back by this fierce counter-attack, re-formed and charged again. By nightfall of the next day, they had captured the airfield and were pressing towards Motoyama village, with only the prospect of another bitter struggle ahead: to the right of them lay the formidable Hill 382, a position which became so difficult to secure that the Marines referred to it ominously as 'the Meat Grinder'.

The fighting in the days following was the same. The Americans had to take the higher, central part of the enemy's lines first, for whenever the 4th and 5th Divisions pushed ahead on their respective flanks they were heavily punished by the Japanese who overlooked them. The problem was that it was this middle zone where it was hardest to deploy tanks and artillery, or to direct the naval support fire with accuracy. Although the elements on the flanks helped, the Marines had the main job, the slow and deadly job, of clearing the area. By the tenth day of the fighting, though, the supporting fire for the 3rd Division had been substantially increased and the forward battalions found a weak spot in the Japanese line, and poured through. By evening Motoyama, now a heap of stones and rubble, was taken and the Marines could look down upon the third airfield. Once again, though, further momentum was broken by Kuribayashi's second major defense line, and there remained many areas to wipe up. Hill 382 was fiercely held by its defenders for two more days, and Hill 362 in the west was equally difficult. The whole operation was taking much longer than the ten days Schmidt had estimated for it, and the Marines were tired and depleted in their ranks: some units were down to 30 per cent of their original strength.

On Sunday 5 March, the three divisions regrouped and rested as best they could in the face of Japanese shellings and occasional infiltration. On that day, too, the Marines had the satisfaction of seeing a B29 with a faulty fuel valve returning to Tinian from a raid on Tokyo make an emergency landing on airstrip No. 1. Iwo Jima was already fulfilling its function.

For the Japanese, the situation was serious. Most of Kuribayashi's tanks and guns and over two-thirds of his officers had been lost. His troops were in a serious position, reduced to such desperate measures as strapping explosives to their backs and throwing themselves under American tanks. The Marines were moving relentlessly forward, however slowly, and this forced a gradual breakdown in Kuribayashi's communications system. This meant that, left to their own devices, individual Japanese officers tended to revert to the offensive. This may have been more appealing to the Samurai but it exposed the greatly depleted Japanese forces to the weight of American firepower. One attack, by 1,000 naval troops on the night of 8–9 March, was easily repulsed by 4th Marine Division with Japanese losses of over 800 men. The pressure on the defending forces was starting to tell; they were losing their cohesion.

On the afternoon of 9 March, a patrol from the 3rd Marine Division reached the north-eastern coast of Iwo Jima and sent back a sample of salt water to prove that the enemy's line had been cut in two. There was no stopping the American advance but even now there was no sign of Japanese surrender – the only indication of their desperate condition was the increasing number of 'banzai' charges. Kuribayashi's reports, however, describe the deteriorating situation: 10 March. American bombardment 'so fierce I cannot express nor write of it here'; 11 March. 'Surviving strength of northern districts (army and navy) is 1,500 men'; 14 March. 'Attack on northern district this morning. Much more severe than before. Around noon one part of the enemy with about ten tanks broke through our left front line and approached to 220 yards of divisional HQ'; 15 March.

'Situation very serious. Present strength of northern district about 900 men.'

On 14 March the Americans, believing all organized resistance to be at an end, declared Iwo Jima occupied and raised the Stars and Stripes. Yet underground, in their warren of caves and tunnels, the Japanese lived on. Kuribayashi told the survivors on 17 March: 'Battle situation come to last moment. I want surviving officers and men to go out and attack enemy until the last. You have devoted yourself to the Emperor. Do not think of yourselves. I am always at the head of you all.'

Clearing out pockets of organized resistance with tanks, demolition teams, rifle fire and flame-throwers took until 26 March. On this day the Japanese staged their last desperate fling when 350 troops rushed an Air Force and Seabee (Civil Engineers of the US Navy) construction camp. They were destroyed by a Marine pioneer battalion after a day of wild fighting. Kuribayashi committed suicide in the northern corner of Iwo Jima in the last few days of the battle. He promised that to help revive the Japanese army after his death, 'I will turn into a spirit.' One US Marine hoped that 'the Japs don't have any more like him.'

Only 216 Japanese had surrendered by 26 March; 20,000 were dead. In the following two months 1,600 Japanese were killed and another 370 captured as sporadic resistance was crushed. The American casualties, considering their air and sea control and their superior firepower, were equally daunting. A total of 275 officers and 5,610 men of the Marine Corps were killed and 826 officers and 16,446 men were wounded. Thirty per cent of the entire landing force and a staggering 75 per cent of the infantry regiments of the 4th and 5th Divisions were battle casualties. So depleted were some units during the action that one battalion commander commented that 'the appearance of a war dog and its handlers seemed like heavy reinforcements.' Twenty-four Medals of Honor were awarded and there were 2,648 'combat fatigue casualties' – both facts telling evidence of the gruelling nature of the battle for Iwo Jima.

Iwo Jima soon justified the strategic value which the Joint Chiefs of Staff and, in particular, the Air Force had attached to it. Before the end of the war against Japan, more than 20,000 crewmen in crippled planes had landed upon the island's airstrips; and from 7 April onwards, thanks to the efforts of the Seabee construction units, Mustang fighters were able to escort the daylight raids of the Superfortresses against Tokyo and other Japanese cities.

General Smith called the battle 'the toughest we've run across in 168 years' but also insisted that 'When the capture of an enemy position is necessary to winning a war it is not within our province to evaluate the cost in money, time, equipment, or most of all, in human life. We are told what our objective is to be and we prepare to do the job.' Admiral Nimitz summed up the achievement of the assault troops: 'Among the Americans who served on Iwo Island, uncommon valor was a common virtue.'

6
The Korean War

Inchon (1950)

Sydney L. Mayer

The Inchon landings of September 1950 were to prove the turning point of the war in Korea. General Douglas MacArthur conceived of the landings as a way of breaking the Communist stranglehold on the South. When UN forces had succeeded in taking Inchon they were to push on to the main prize – the South Korean capital, Seoul. The struggle for the control of this city was to prove the most savage of the whole war.

On Saturday 24 June 1950 United States President Harry S. Truman heard some grim news. Secretary of State Dean Acheson telephoned – the North Koreans had invaded South Korea. He advised the President to call on the United Nations Security Council to declare that an act of aggression had taken place. The following day Acheson called again. There was no doubt that a full-scale invasion had taken place but the United Nations was unlikely to do more than call for a ceasefire – and the call would probably be ignored. The United States therefore had to decide what degree of support, if any, it would give to South Korea.

The Japanese surrender in August 1945 left the US and Russia in Korea and they decided on the 38th Parallel as a purely military demarcation line between their two forces. In September 1947 the US turned the Korean problem over to the UN. By this time Korea had become a pawn in the rivalry between the two major world power blocs. A UN call for all-Korean elections was ignored by the Russians and elections were held in the South only. In August 1948 the Republic of Korea (ROK) was established in the south under the veteran nationalist Dr Syngman Rhee. In September the Democratic People's Republic of Korea was created in the north, with former guerilla leader Kim Il Sung as premier. There were now two mutually antagonistic Korean regimes, each claiming rights to the whole country and each backed by one of the two world power blocs. Sporadic fighting took place along the 38th Parallel and though the US believed an invasion of the south was possible, Acheson admitted that 'its launching in the summer of 1950 did not appear imminent.'

Despite appearances, it had happened. President Truman, like most Americans, was acutely aware of the dangers of appeasement. The dictators had not been stopped in 1931 when Japan invaded Manchuria; in 1935 when Mussolini invaded Abyssinia or in 1938 when Hitler marched into Austria. The result was a massive and bloody war. If the US did not react to the agression, so the reasoning went, the Communists would seek to extend their conquests and this would inevitably lead to a third world war. There were pressing domestic considerations too – failure to act would encourage the arch witch-hunter of Communists, Senator Joseph McCarthy, to charge the government with appeasement, possibly fostered by subversives within the President's own staff.

In Washington, the State and Defense Departments presented joint recommendations. General Douglas MacArthur, then stationed in Japan, was ordered to evacuate all Americans from Korea but to attempt to keep the key airports open. The US air force was to remain south of the 38th Parallel and ammunition and supplies for the South Korean army were to be delivered by air drop and other means. The Seventh Fleet was to sail to the Formosa Strait to prevent any possible conflict between the nationalist Chinese on Formosa and the Chinese Communist mainland. American policy had altered – Korea and Formosa now fell within the US defense perimeter.

To MacArthur, news of the invasion was like a nightmare, a repetition of Pearl Harbor. As soon as he received orders from Washington he sent aircraft to evacuate Americans from Korea but did nothing else. But soon, orders came to commit US troops to the field and MacArthur took immediate action.

Events had given MacArthur a new role. After a successful military career in the Second World War and a smoothly run administration of post-war Japan, MacArthur had little more to look forward to than an honored retirement. Now, as commander of US, and later UN, forces in Korea he had another chance of glory and fame in the field. Thrilled by the challenge, MacArthur prepared his staff for his last great military campaign.

In the meantime, the UN voted to support American operations in Korea. MacArthur was now leader of a nominal UN force – nominal because, especially at the start, the only active participants were the retreating South Koreans and whatever American forces could be shipped or flown from Japan.

By the start of July, North Korean forces had crossed the Han river, pushing streams of dispirited ROK forces before them. At the same time, the first US combat troops arrived in Korea. MacArthur's arrogant hope that the North Koreans might 'turn round and go back when they found out who was fighting' came to nothing and on 19 July North Korean tanks smashed through American defenses at Taejon and rolled towards the Naktong river, the last major natural obstacle guarding the Pusan perimeter.

The Pusan perimeter was a 140-mile line running west and north of Pusan, from the Korea Strait to the Sea of Japan. Organized by Lieutenant General William Walker, commander of the US 8th Army in Korea, the Pusan perimeter held out against intensive North Korean pressure while US tanks, artillery and troops arrived through the port to reinforce the bridgehead. UN aircraft flew sorties against North Korean supply lines and the enemy's failure to mass forces for a decisive penetration at one point along the perimeter also contributed to the Americans' ability to hold the line.

By September 1950, the situation was deadlocked along the Pusan perimeter. Although North Korean forces seemed unable or unwilling to launch a major attack against the perimeter line, ROK and American forces were not of sufficient strength for a land assault on the enemy lines.

MacArthur considered that the only way out of the impasse was to attempt an amphibious landing behind enemy lines. The risks involved in such an action were enormous. Failure would result in irreparable damage to UN credibility in Korea and devalue the stature of the organization. Its ability to effectively intervene in any crisis situation would be greatly impaired.

The idea of landing at Inchon dated back to MacArthur's first visit to Korea following the start of open war between North and South. North Korean supply lines were stretched to the limit. A landing at Inchon would force the enemy to fight on two fronts. The result of this, MacArthur calculated, would be the total breakdown of enemy supply lines. As a result, they would be forced to withdraw from the Pusan perimeter within weeks.

If a landing at Inchon was successful the UN would enjoy a considerable propaganda boost. It would also make possible the recapture of Seoul, the South Korean capital, 18 miles to the east.

Codenamed Operation Chromite, plans for the Inchon landings went ahead. Meanwhile, thousands of reservists were sent from the West Coast of the United States to Japan. The first objective was to capture the island of Wolmi-do, at the entrance to the port of Inchon. Once taken, large numbers of troops could be brought forward, and the island would act as a springboard for the invasion proper.

The next step was to capture the city of Inchon itself. The prime objective – the recapture of Seoul – would now be in the UN forces' grasp. To make this possible, Kimpo – Seoul's major airport – had to be taken. At the same time as preventing the North Koreans from bringing in reinforcements, control of the airport would allow the UN to do just that.

MacArthur fervently believed that the North Koreans would be forced to retreat. He thought that, while fleeing, they would be trapped between the UN troops controlling Seoul and the forces heading north – freed from their 'prison' behind the Pusan perimeter.

Once the plan for the Inchon landings had been constructed, it was necessary to select the right personnel to head the operation. It was decided that the 10th Corps, commanded by General Almond, would be landed at Inchon by Rear Admiral James H. Doyle. Doyle was Amphibious Group Commander of the Pacific Fleet. His flagship, Mt McKinley, was anchored at Tokio. The landing force was to be in two groups – a marine division to push south and the 7th Division to cover their flank. Both these divisions would then form a defensive buffer against the North Koreans as the 8th Army moved north from the Pusan perimeter.

From the moment the idea of an amphibious landing had been mentioned, the Joint Chiefs supported it. But they were not so keen about the choice of Inchon as a landing place. Their reasoning was that because Inchon was far to the north and so near Seoul, the

North Koreans would almost certainly put up a savage defense. Also, Inchon's unusually high tides would make a quick and easy landing very difficult. UN casualties could be enormous before they even reached dry land. There was little room for failure. In contrast to the attitude of the Joint Chiefs, MacArthur had supreme confidence in his own judgement.

After much pressure, the Joint Chiefs finally gave MacArthur the go-ahead on 28 August, and the plan was finally ready for operation on 4 September. The assault on Inchon was set for 15 September. This date was chosen because the tide would be at its highest. Some doubts were voiced by navy and marine personnel – and rightly so. On that day the morning tide was at 0659 and the evening tide at 1919. A tide of at least 23 ft was necessary to enable the LSTs to navigate their way to the narrow peninsula of Wolmi-do, from where the landings were to be staged.

It was planned that a Battalion Landing Team (BLT3) of the 5th Marines would land at Green beach. This was to take place at 0630 with the morning tide. The sea front of Inchon itself, *Red beach*, was to be taken by BLT-1 and 2 at 1730. Back-up forces bringing tanks, bulldozers and engineers in eight LSTs would be brought forward. The 25 ft of tide would be just enough. Three heavily armed battalions would be landed at Blue beach simultaneously. Their task was to be the most demanding of all – to move forward and seize the main road and rail links between Inchon and the capital Seoul. Precise timing was vital for this operation. No margin of error could be afforded. Because of the tide, landing craft had to arrive and depart within a strictly laid-down timetable. Otherwise they ran the risk of being stranded on a sand bar.

MacArthur suspected that the Marines would have to use ladders to go into Inchon. This suspicion was confirmed when Lt. Eugene Clark was sent to inspect the beaches in the landing zone. He discovered that the mud was waist-deep at the harbor wall.

To complicate matters still further, the North Koreans launched an offensive against the Pusan perimeter in early September. General Walton Walker, in the perimeter, feared that if the Marines left for Inchon the North Koreans would have taken over Pusan by the time the landings took place.

MacArthur insisted that his plan to land at Inchon was the only way to avoid a protracted conflict, as well as a likely UN defeat in

Korea. So, after further argument and appeal to President Truman for confirmation, MacArthur had his way.

About 70,000 men had to be transported from Japan and Pusan to Inchon. An armada of 260 ships from the United States, France, Britain, Canada, New Zealand and Holland was formed. They were to link with support units at a prearranged series of points.

Things seemed to be going smoothly when a typhoon blew in from the Pacific with wind speeds of up to 125 m.p.h. The ships held their course. Any delay would have wrecked the whole plan. Remarkably, the typhoon passed – causing little harm.

The flagship *Mt McKinley*, with MacArthur aboard, arrived off Inchon on 14 September. By this time the coast had been under almost continuous bombardment for five days. Wolmi-do was singled out for the heaviest of the fire in order to clear the way for one of the three planned landings.

A thin causeway linked Wolmi-do with the mainland. If one of the mainland landings failed, UN troops could defend the island for some time while awaiting reinforcements. But for this to be feasible, Wolmi-do had to be captured swiftly.

The 5th Marines started to land on Green beach, on Wolmi-do, at 0633 on the 15th. It was held lightly and they encountered only scattered resistance. The total enemy presence on the island was around 350 men. By 0655 the 'battle' was virtually over and UN forces raised the flag on Radio Hill – the highest point on the island. This first step in the Inchon plan which had caused the Chiefs of Staff so many sleepless nights, was completed by 0800. Wolmi-do had been captured without a single fatality.

UN forces bombarded Red beach from sea and air for the rest of that day. But the landing had to wait for the evening tide, 1730, and as the tide flowed in the landing operation began. This time, things did not go so easily for the UN forces.

There was a fierce battle for the control of Cemetery Hill in the city of Inchon itself. A North Korean bunker held down the Marines below a sea wall. But by midnight the Marines had established a firm line across Observatory Hill – and had complete control of Red beach. Within six hours, UN forces had entered the very heart of Inchon.

So far, things seemed to be running smoothly and to plan. A number of landing craft became stuck in mud some 300 ft out from Blue beach, forcing Marines to wade ashore, and some vehicles stalled when a road collapsed. After a sea wall was dynamited, however, the landings at Blue beach were made easier. The Marines reached their objective by midnight and by the following day the North Koreans had fled Inchon.

Inchon had been taken at the cost of 196 casualties, including about 20 dead. The Joint Chiefs' fears had been proved unfounded and MacArthur's stock had never been higher. But it still remained to capture Kimpo airfield and Seoul itself. This had to be done quickly, but it was not going to be so easy.

The North Koreans had decided to abandon Inchon to avoid unacceptably high losses. However, they intended to dig in their heels at Seoul. The capital was turned into a virtual fortress.

Once Inchon was theirs, MacArthur, Almond and Admiral Struble visited the battlefields. MacArthur believed that he could take Seoul within five days. Almond thought it would take almost a fortnight. Almond was right.

The first target – Kimpo airfield – was captured on 18 September. As it happened, Kimpo was hardly used at all by the North Koreans, but within days it became one of the world's busiest airports as the Americans airlifted in reinforcements. It seemed inevitable to the Americans that Seoul must fall very soon. But they had reckoned without the ferocity of the North Korean defense of the city. The Americans had to bombard the city with all the firepower they possessed. Many civilians were trapped and burnt to death in an inferno from which there was no escape.

MacArthur was a great respecter of the virtues of technology. He believed that tanks, artillery and aircraft should be used to the full in order to save lives. The North Koreans, however, were not equipped with so much sophisticated hardware and, consequently, thought quite differently. Almost all they had was men. They were to fight to the last.

To the Americans, Seoul was a political symbol of the first importance. If this had not been the case, it would have been possible – and certainly wiser – to by-pass the city and join up with the northward bound 8th Army. MacArthur, however, was determined to capture the city and had to pour in more and more forces in the attempt to do so. In Seoul itself there were 20,000 North Koreans who were determined to fight it out until every one was dead.

This was unfortunate for the citizens. Living in Seoul soon

became a nightmare. Prior to the Marines moving into the city, aerial bombardment had devastated whole districts. The badly built wooden dwellings of most of the people were burnt to the ground. Often, their owners went with them. North Korean suicide squads threw themselves at the advancing tanks but failed to slow them in any way.

When the Americans finally entered the city, most of the defenders were dead. Thousands of civilians – men, women and children – had been slaughtered and many more were horribly maimed by fire. Panic-stricken homeless refugees were everywhere.

The situation was made still worse as the surviving North Koreans fought a last-ditch, street-by-street battle with the Americans. This fighting was desperate and vicious. Intense heat from the burning buildings added to the horror. The fighting continued until 27 September when the Marines reached the 'Capitol of the Republic of Korea' and raised the American flag above it. By the time the North Korean defenders were finally overcome, more than 130,000 prisoners had been taken.

On 29 September MacArthur entered the shattered city and in the South Korean National Assembly pronounced that Seoul was restored as the seat of government. On that same afternoon he returned to Tokio. As a city, Seoul suffered one of the greatest hammerings to be perpetrated in modern warfare. Thousands of its people were dead or homeless. Its buildings were mostly rubble. MacArthur had confounded his critics and scored the greatest triumph of his military career.

Imjin River (1951)

A. H. Farrar-Hockley and E. L. Capel

The Stalinist regime of North Korea launched a major offensive in the Korean War on 22 April 1951, breaking through the line held by the United Nations west of Chungpyong Reservoir. The situation was only saved by the stand of the Gloucestershire Regiment at Imjin River against a much larger enemy force, composed mostly of Chinese communists. The Glosters' action was later termed 'the most outstanding example of unit bravery in modern warfare' by the UN Commander in Korea, General James Van Fleet. A. H. Farrar-Hockley, the co-author of this account of the Glosters' stand was the Adjutant of the regiment during the Imjin River battle.

The battalion moved back towards the battle line on 21 March 1951, a monumental date for the past and, did they but know it, for the future. But the first step towards the Imjin river was neither very demanding nor challenging: Colonel Carne was ordered to site and dig a battalion position covering Uijongbu. The sector belonged to the 3rd United States Division and its Commander was anxious to have a long stop on the road leading south from the river through the hills at this point. Though little more than a rough track it had been used successfully by the Chinese less than three months previously as a main thrust line to Seoul. It was, indeed, an ancient invasion route by the armies of Imperial China. So the Glosters dug and wired, grumbling cheerfully as British soldiers do when they are obliged to prepare defences without an enemy in sight.

Even when, at the beginning of April, they moved north through the hills along this route to the Imjin itself, there was no sign of the enemy, and this was in many ways a comfort; for though the river formed the front edge of the UN defensive line 'Kansas', there were so few troops to man it that the gap between the Glosters' left and the nearest ROK unit was three miles. On the right, the nearest friendly element was a company of the Fifth Fusiliers, almost two miles distant. Thus isolated, the battalion was required to deny to the Communist Forces the use of the road running south.

The Glosters relieved the PEFTOK (Phillipines Expeditionary Force, Task Organization Korea) and these small, brown, friendly men withdrew to the south. They had been in the position only a few days and had very little intelligence about enemy locations or strengths. It seemed to Colonel Carne that he had better do something to remedy this lack of knowledge as soon as his companions had settled. 'A' Company, under Major Pat Angier, was left forward on the old Castle Site, a high point (148) west of the village of Choksong. 'D' under Major 'Lakri' Wood, were on the hill feature south-east of the village. 'B' Company, commanded by Major Denis Harding, somewhat to the east guarded the right flank approaches. 'C' (Major Paul Mitchell) lay in reserve on the high ground directly above battalion headquarters. The headquarters site was at a point where the road running south entered the hills and swung across a shallow stream. The open valley mouth towards the river was held by the Drums. Troubled by a triangular-shaped height immediately to the west overlooking this site, the colonel put out on it his only uncommitted force, the assault pioneers under Captain 'Spike' Pike.

It was a carefully considered deployment which made the best of a frontage of seven miles and depth of five. Any enemy approach would lie through the small arms fire of at least two companies, and two sections of the Vickers machine-guns. The guns of 45 Field Artillery Regiment, backed potentially by the United States 3rd Divisional artillery, the mortars of 'C' Troop, 170 Mortar Battery and the Glosters own 3-inch mortar platoon were able between them to cover both companies and approaches with shell or bomb. The difficulty was to detect enemy movement by night. A change in darkness to a tight defensive position was not practicable because of the shortage of defence stores. It took eight days to get the first truckload of barbed wire and the second did not reach the battalion until it had been in position for 17 days. Much had happened in that time.

An active patrol programme confirmed that the ford across the Imjin river, carrying the road from Seoul northwards, was intact and the enemy defences covering it on the far bank empty. But there had been movement in the high ground immediately to the north amongst a series of bunkers. 'A' and 'D' Companies combined in a night operation to close on these and sweep them at dawn. Apart from a radio mishap at the outset, this was most successful, though when the troops searched the bunkers these were also found to be abandoned. Where had the enemy gone?

A major sortie followed in daylight: two company groups and Major George Butler's squadron of the 8th Hussars moved north across the Imjin to a distance of seven miles in an operation named 'Cygnet' – young swan. At last a few half-starved and very miserable Chinese soldiers were captured. Was this the rearguard of the mighty Chinese Peoples' Volunteers?

As a matter of fact it was. Weakened by the severity of the winter and defeated by the advancing United Nations forces, the mass of Chinese divisions had broken away from their pursuers during March. There had thus been no pursuit into the heart of North Korea as in 1950. General Ridgway had now replaced General MacArthur as Supreme Commander, Allied Powers, and his orders were to hold on or about the line of the 38th Parallel of latitude – the old demarcation line between north and south – which, in this sector, was roughly along the course of the Imjin. A few exhausted Chinese and North Korean units had been left to hold an outpost line while, 20 miles to the north over a period of six weeks, the Chinese commander-in-chief, Peng Teh-Huai, refreshed, replenished, and reinforced his armies. Then, with the winter finally past, he gave orders on 13 April for a fresh offensive. Small reconnaissance parties were sent south to discover and infiltrate between the UN positions, travelling only by night, resting and watching by day. On the night of the 21st, the mass of the attacking armies began to march south after them, amongst them the 63rd Army of three divisions* – the 187,

---

* A Chinese Communist Forces (CCF) Division was about 9,000 strong, mostly infantry with six to eight batteries of light artillery and about twice this number of medium and heavy mortars.

188, 189 – with orders to force open the ancient route to Seoul.

Various sources of intelligence had disclosed to the United Nations commander in Korea, General James van Fleet, that an offensive was impending. All units were ordered to be ready and thus all were watchful. A little after midday on 22 April, the Glosters' artillery observation posts saw 20 enemy moving south in file . . . dressed in dark uniforms. A larger body of moved round behind hill . . . immediately north of the Imjin ford known as Gloster Crossing. Air recce began to search as Colonel Carne accompanied a patrol to a vantage point close to the river from which to observe. The adjutant joined the colonel and the intelligence officer, Lieutenant Henry Cabral, on the bank. Five more enemy parties between 10 and 20 strong were observed occupying the old positions on the high ground immediately to the north, in which they were severely shelled. But otherwise the colonel's orders, sent back to the adjutant, were clear: the companies were to take pains to lie low and conceal themselves from what were obviously enemy scouting parties. A fighting patrol was to be prepared in 'C' Company – one platoon – to lay an ambush on the south side of the ford as soon as it was dark. Meantime, 'A' Company's observation post was to watch this sensitive point until dusk and to shell and mortar any attempt to seize it in daylight.

The afternoon passed in an atmosphere of excitement. Everyone in the battalion sensed that a major clash was imminent. Men rested in all positions. At 5 p.m. the hot evening meal was eaten and before dusk a comprehensive check of weapons and ammunition had been completed. Half the reserve ammunition was brought forward from 'A' Echelon to the headquarters site. As the light waned, the ambush party from 'C' Company, Lieutenant Guy Temple's platoon, came down from their hilltop and made their way to the river and ford.

The task of the 'C' Company platoon was to surprise and destroy the enemy attempting to cross to the south of the Imjin. It was only partially successful for two reasons. First, because the weight of the enemy seeking to cross were far greater than had been expected from air reconnaissance and ground observation reports during the afternoon and evening. At dusk on the 22 April, the main body of the enemy were not within 12 miles of the river. They closed on the Imjin in a forced march of three hours carrying all their battle gear. Lieutenant Temple's platoon destroyed the enemy's advanced party attempting to seize the crossing by *coup de main* early in the night but were then pressed by a battalion backed by two more. Seventy

Field Battery, 'C' Troop of 170 Mortar Battery, the mortar platoon and the small arms of the ambush fired continuously for some hours but they could not stem indefinitely the flood of Chinese soldiers.

Meantime, unknown to the Glosters, a second enemy brigade was crossing the Imjin at another ford, of which they were unaware, one-and-a-half miles downstream. This was the second reason for the limited success of the ambush and a consequence of the excessive frontage held by the battalion. Even while the ambush held the enemy to its front in check, a strong assault was being launched against 'A' Company on the Castle Site by about two battalions while a third crossed the road to the east to attack 'D' Company.

Upstream, the left flank company of the Fifth Fusiliers holding a ridge overlooking the river and lateral road had been attacked and forced to withdraw. A battalion from this area moved south to attack 'B' Company of the Glosters. Not long after midnight, therefore, the three forward rifle companies of the Glosters were in action, 'A' Company being critically pressed by an enemy outnumbering them by six to one.

At battalion headquarters, Captain Reeve-Tucker, the signals officers, entered the command vehicle with a message from the ambush party.

'They're still trying to cross in hordes, sir,' he said to the colonel. 'In another five minutes, he [Temple] reckons they'll be out of ammunition.'

The colonel looked across at Major Guy Ward, the battery comander, and the adjutant.

'Tell him to start withdrawing in three minutes,' he said to the adjutant. 'Guy, I'm going to ask you for one last concentration, and then start dropping them short of Gloster Crossing as soon as the patrol is back at the first cutting south of the river.'

The advantage of the United Nations' Forces as their line was, almost everywhere, assailed that night was in the power of their weapons, particularly artillery, to drop destructive fire accurately into the enemy masses. Their weakness lay in the length of front which resulted in numbers of fragmented battles, each of which needed to be won by the defence if Line Kansas was to be held. The artillery could not engage so many targets adequately. The morning light would permit the UN air forces to add their weight of firepower. The question was, would it be enough?

At a number of points, air strikes forced the enemy to withraw temporarily by 9 a.m. on the morning of the 23rd but there were none available to the Glosters.

Before dawn on the 23rd the battalion Command Post had moved up to the ridge held by 'C' Company. From there, in a bunker constructed under RSM Jack Hobbs' supervision some days before, the colonel could overlook the battle on the two hill positions to the north. The desperate nature of the struggle was manifest before the morning sun rose. By night, the calls for fire support, each fresh report from 'A', 'B' or 'D' Company headquarters and the artillery radio links had made it all too clear that the attack was in strength. Just after dawn, in the command post, Corporal Walters told the adjutant that Major Angier, commanding 'A' Company, wished to speak to him.

'I'm afraid we've lost the Castle Site. I'm mounting a counter-attack now but I want to know whether to expect to stay here indefinitely or not. If I am to stay on, I must be reinforced as my numbers are getting very low.'

When the message was passed to the colonel he was already considering what his options were now that daylight had come. Two questions were in his mind: would the Chinese continue to press their attack in daylight with the threat of intervention by UN aircraft; and, secondly, how long would it be before the Chinese discovered that both battalion flanks were completely open and encircle his battalion?

He questioned Major Angier briefly and then gave his orders: 'You will stay there at all costs until further notice.'

At all costs and until further notice . . . The need for 'A' Company to hold its position was this: notwithstanding the loss of the highest point of their position, they had still observation over the approaches to 'D' Company as well as forward to the two river crossing points. If the company was precipitately withdrawn, the Chinese would reinforce freely the force on the south bank, overwhelm 'D' Company, and in turn, 'B'.

The adjutant sent forward a supply of ammunition in a pair of Oxford carriers under Lieutenant Cabral.

'Don't worry about us,' said Major Angier on the radio; 'we'll be all right.' He returned to the fight. The counter-attack was in progress to regain the Castle Site on which, in one of the company's bunkers, the Chinese had installed a medium machine-gun. Lieutenant Philip Curtis led his platoon forward as the guns of 70 Field Battery fired in support. But the overhead cover in the bunker protected the enemy machine-gun crew and they fired freely into the attacking platoon, driving them back within half a minute. Amongst the wounded dragged into cover was Lieutenant Curtis. Corporal Papworth of the Royal Army Medical Corps began to attend to the injuries. Curtis did not wait for his attention.

'We must take the Castle Site,' he said.

'Just wait until Papworth has seen you, sir,' said a soldier at his side. But he would not wait. Alone he ran forward painfully, a pistol in one hand, a grenade in the other. Possibly waiting until this single figure advancing reached point-blank range the Chinese machine-gunners held their fire. Curtis pulled the pin from his grenade and threw it. As it flew through the air, the Chinese opened fire and killed him; but were themselves killed a few seconds later as the grenade landed directly in the bunker opening and blew away the muzzle of their gun. Then, as Major Angier was directing a platoon to close upon this key point, he was killed and command of the company passed to the only surviving officer, Lieutenant Terry Waters. By the time he came up to take over, the opportunity to recover the Castle Site had passed.*

To the east, 'D' Company was under command of Captain M. G. Harvey.† By about 0830 on that morning, 23 April, it was apparent that neither 'A' nor 'D' Companies could hold against the weight of successive attacks unless air support was available. At 0730, the brigade commander had given permission to Colonel Carne to withdraw his forward positions. When it became clear about 50 minutes later that the Glosters' request for air strikes would not be satisfied, the colonel gave the order to withdraw. 'A' and 'D' Companies were brought into positions immediately north-west and west of battalion headquarters and 'B' Company to a hill feature below the great height of Kamak-San to the east of the road.

In breaking away from the enemy, the whole fire potential of the battalion, Captain Frank Wisbey's heavy mortar troop and the three batteries of 45 Field Regiment was used against the enemy of the 187 CCF Division. Their dead and wounded lay in heaps on the hill slopes they had occupied and in the gulleys along which they

* Lieutenant Curtis was to receive a posthumous Victoria Cross for his gallantry.
† Major W. A. Wood was away with a leave party in Japan.

had sought to infiltrate past the main position. With 'A' and 'D' Company positions in their hands, they had had enough and by noon the battlefield fell quiet.

The adjutant recalled a series of incidents of that day, 'clear in themselves but joined by a very hazy thread of continuity.'

Colour Sergeant Buxcey organizing his Korean porters with mighty loads for the first of many ascents to the new 'A' company positions . . . When Buxcey's anxious face has left my mind, I can still see Captain Bob Hickey, the doctor, working at the Regimental Aid Post, one hand still wet with blood as he turns round, pausing for a moment to clean himself before he begins to minister to yet another wounded man. The ambulance cars are filled; the jeep that Bounden drives has been out time and again with the stretchers on its racks. Sergeants Baxter and Brisland, Corporal Mills, the whole staff of the RAP is hard at work with dressings, drugs, and instruments . . . I remember watching the slow, wind-tossed descent of a helicopter that came down for casualties to whom the winding, bumpy road back south would have meant certain death . . . Shaw, my driver, and Mr Evans, the Chief Clerk, went off to Seoul . . . Captain Carl Dain, the counter-mortar radar officer came in to say, 'I'm sending my vehicles back, except for my jeep. I've decided to stay with you to make up your numbers of Forward Observation Officers . . . Lieutenant Donald Allman, the assistant adjutant, was sent to reinforce 'A' company, now under its second-in-command, Captain Anthony Wilson . . . That morning the Padre, Sam Davies, said a funeral service for Pat Angier, whose body had been brought back on one of the Oxford carriers by Lieutenant Cabral. Pat's body was the only one to which we could pay our last respects – but we did not forget the others. Three of us stood by while the solemn words were said: then we saluted and walked away, each busy with his own thoughts. Pat lay at rest beside the soft-voiced stream, quiet in the morning sunlight.

Later that morning, the battalion second-in-command, Major Digby Grist, came forward to see what was to be done by way of support for the battle which must surely come to life again as soon as darkness fell. While discussing the prospect, news came that rear battalion headquarters ('A' Echelon) five miles back, had been attacked and forced to withdraw: the enemy had infiltrated strong patrols this far south. The colonel said, 'I think you'd better go back at once, Digby, to see what is happening.' Well aware that he was almost certainly about to run a gauntlet of fire, the second-in-command set off calmly with his driver, Bainbridge. Thirty minutes later, they were driving for their lives through an enemy ambush.

On the right flank, Major Harding had managed to withdraw from his former position secretly and his new site was unknown to the enemy. He was determined not to reveal it until compelled to do so. When observers reported the approach of enemy patrols, Sergeant Pethrick was sent out to lay an ambush on the most likely approach. Not long after he had settled, expecting to catch a patrol, about 200 Chinese obligingly entered his position and a fire fight began. The Chinese, part of 188 CCF Division, reinforced and began to work round the flanks of the ambush. Sgt Pethrick was ordered back while other detachments from his company went forward, greatly assisted by medium and heavy mortar fire, to hold the enemy off the main position. Backwards and forward, all among the little knolls that lay below the peak of Kamak-San, engagements flared up and died, only to be renewed elsewhere.

Notwithstanding the capture of the forward company positions of the Glosters, the commander of 63 CCF Army was dissatisfied, as we are now aware, with the progress of his force after 24 hours of attack. The 187 Division had failed to destroy the battalion holding the old road running south through Solma-ri. On the night of 23/24 April, it had been planned that 188 Division should march down this road to cut in behind the bulk of the British 29th Brigade and the 3rd United States Division. Due to the casualties inflicted on the 187 Division, the 188 had now to complete the elimination of the Glosters though, as the battle line stood, the tactical opportunity seemed still to be open to the 63rd Army. The 29th Brigade and 3rd Division were fighting in positions east-north-east of the Glosters: if the latter could be disposed of during the first hours of darkness of that night, it should prove possible to march rapidly down the road to Uijongbu. For this reason, Chinese patrolling and probing attacks began early in the evening, particularly against 'B' Company, with the aim of finding a route into the heart of the battalion's position and a bypass along which part of the division might slip to the south.

Under the arrangements of Sergeant Smythe, the signal sergeant, telephone cables had been run to all new company positions. At ten minutes to midnight on 23 April, Major Denis Harding telephoned the battalion command post.

'Well, we've started. They're attacking Beverly's [Lieutenant Gael's] platoon now – about 150 I should think.'

This explained the noise from this direction. Captain 'Recce' Newcome, the artillery FOO, was directing defensive fire from the guns. From 'C' Company came similar news. The 188 Division was attempting to force the right flank of the battalion while simultaneously making for the highest ground in the area, the peak of Kamak-San. In character, the assaults on the rifle companies followed the pattern of the previous night: wave after wave of men armed with grenades and sub-machine-guns stormed the positions under cover of medium machine-guns and mortar fire, were halted by the fire of the defence – small arms, mortars, guns – and driven back with heavy loss.

At the outset of the engagement on the night of 23/24 April, the Chinese were at a disadvantage. The information gained by their patrols was faulty largely due to Major Harding's deceptive tactics: they attacked late and obliquely the battalion right flank, so that the assaults, pressed blindly for the first few hours, were struck by enfilade fire. Some time after two o'clock in the morning of the 24th there was a lull during which it seems probable that a fresh regiment came forward, with a truer idea of the Glosters' positions.

About a quarter to three, intense enemy mortar and machine-gun fire fell among 'B' and 'C' Companies. The soldiers waiting – regulars, national servicemen, recalled reservists; west country-men predominantly, with a scattering from London and almost every other county of the British isles; but long since moulded in comradeship by the fortunes of war – stood to their weapons to face another onslaught. Despite the slaughter inflicted on the enemy by their courage and skill, the Glosters' numbers were dwindling. There seemed to be no limit to the casualties the Chinese commanders were prepared to sacrifice to their aim. There was a limit to the casualties that the British battalion could accept if it was to sustain an effective defence.

At three o'clock the telephone from 'C' Company rang in the

command post. Major Paul Mitchell spoke to the adjutant. 'I'm afraid they've overrun my top position and they're reinforcing hard. They're simply pouring chaps in above us. Let me know what the colonel wants me to do, will you?'

The colonel had no doubt as to what had to be done. With the enemy in strength on the commanding ground of 'C' Company's ridge, the right half of the battalion had been cracked open. Below this lay the headquarters site with the radios connecting the battalion to brigade headquarters and the guns, the regimental aid post with the wounded sent down during the night, the battalion 3-inch mortars and the artillery heavy mortars.

'Pack the headquarters up,' the colonel said to the adjutant, 'and get everyone out of the valley up between "D" Company and the anti-tank platoon position. I'm going to withdraw "C" Company in ten minutes; and I shall move "B" over to join us after first light.' The withdrawal of 'C' Company was an extremely difficult operation in darkness, and as a result only one-third of the Company eventually joined the battalion on Hill 235 – the final position.

By dawn, all but 'B' Company were on the high ground overlooking the valley from the west. The next problem was to disengage 'B' Company and bring them into the main position; a taxing problem because they were still under attack. By fortunate chance, the local Chinese commander decided to concentrate his force against one platoon, Lieutenant Geoffrey Costello's, and no less fortunately Costello's platoon held firm, the wounded standing with the unwounded. Across the valley in the main position, Captain Dain was able to bring shellfire down amongst the Chinese infantry scrambling up the hillside and Sergeant Syke's section of Vickers opened fire effectively into this target at 2,000 yards range. At first slowly and painfully, Major Harding managed to draw away what remained of his company. With the rearguard of Lieutenant Arthur Peal's platoon, Harding himself broke away at last. A group of the enemy followed them, closing as they approached the foot of the Glosters' hill but were driven back as Private 'Lofty' Walker of 'C' Company, entirely of his own initiative, ran down to meet them, firing a Bren light machine-gun from the hip into the approaching foe. Twenty of 'B' Company survived the journey. Colonel Carne combined them with the remnant of 'C' Company under Major Harding's command.

During and after the movement of 'B' Company, three important matters had to be attended to: the detailed knitting together of the defences in the new position on Hill 235* against renewed attack; the clarification of the battalion's position in relation to the remainder of the battle in the sector; and a check of physical resources in weapons, ammunition, radio batteries, water, medical supplies and food. The colonel was engaged in the first between seven o'clock on the morning of the 24th, when the sun broke through a haze of grey clouds, and 0845. His round of the battalion was not without incident. Prior to 'B' Company's move he came across a group of Chinese infiltrating forward and, supported by two of the regimental police and his driver, he drove them back with the loss of two dead.

'What was all that about, sir?' asked his adjutant as he came back over the ridge.

'Oh, just shooing away some Chinese.' He continued on his way. A few minutes later, the brigade major† came on to the radio to answer the adjutant's request for information about tactical intentions. He had cheering news. PEFTOK – the Filipinos – were on their way forward to reinforce the battalion and on 25 April armour and infantry in brigade strength would come up in relief. The battalion should be back in reserve by the evening of the 25th.

Meantime, it had to maintain its powers of defence. An expedition was arranged to descend the steep path to the headquarters site to collect ammunition and all the other supplies which were needed. RSM Jack Hobbs and CSMI 'Muscles' Strong of the Army Physical Training Corps assembled men and porters. Major Guy Ward got together a parallel party of gunners to pick up batteries for their radios. Captain Dain screened the sortie with smoke shells and discouraged Chinese intervention by an occasional salvo of shrapnel. By nine o'clock all had safely scrambled back, heavily laden.

Through the morning and afternoon came several reports about the progress of the relief column. They were not encouraging: Chinese forces were said to be blocking the southern entrance to the hill road. Tanks of the 8th Hussars were sent to help them but in the afternoon the news was that the latter had lost its leading troops in an ambush. The tank carcases were blocking the road in a gorge. But this was

---

* Later to be called Gloster Hill.
† Major Jim Dunning, who was acting in place of Major K. R. S. Trevor, on leave.

not all. The brigadier came on the radio to say that the unrestricted passage of the Chinese past the Glosters would lead to the remainder of the 3rd Division, including the 29th Brigade, fighting to the east, being cut off from their withdrawal route. Though unlikely now to be reinforced on 25 April, it was essential for the Glosters to remain in position.

The colonel had been studying his map as he listened to this statement. When Brigadier Brodie had finished he put his map on top of the radio and replied.

'I understand the position quite clearly,' he said. 'What I must make clear to you is that my command is no longer an effective fighting force. If it is required that we shall stay here, in spite of this, we shall continue to hold. But I wish to make known the nature of my position.'

It was a plain statement of fact. The numbers in the position capable of fighting were about 350, many of whom were wounded. A lot of weapons had been smashed. There had been no resupply of ammunition since the 22nd. Radio batteries might last a further 12 to 15 hours. Once darkness fell, the battalion had no means of stopping the enemy from using the road below.

The brigadier recognized this but stressed that by remaining in position the battalion must pose a threat to the Chinese. They would be obliged to keep attacking and thus retain forces close to the Imjin which would otherwise be used to the south against division and corps.

Seen from the view of the commander of the 1st United States Corps, Lieutenant-General Frank W. Milburn, it was essential for the battalion to remain. This did not ease Colonel Carne's difficulties of holding fast against a third night of attacks. Yet with a calm face he set off up the hillside to the topmost ridge to consider night positions while the adjutant settled arrangements for emergency resupply by Auster aircraft and a full supply by Fairchild Packets the next day. There would be no helicopter for the wounded that night, but perhaps that also might manage to reach the Glosters' hill next morning. For the moment, a night battle had to be reckoned with: dawn on the 25th was 12 hours distant.

The remainder of the afternoon passed. Colonel Carne arranged to draw in his force tightly round spot height 235, the centre of the feature: on the north-west, 'A' Company; to the east, 'D' Company; south, 'B' and 'C'; south-west, Support Company, now grouped together under their commander, Major Sam Weller. Battalion headquarters was to be sited between 'A' and Support Companies. At dusk, when the Chinese could no longer see their movement, the Glosters moved together, carrying their wounded among them.

The ridge was generally bare apart from patches of sere dwarf oak and a copse of scrubby trees. The ground was rocky; tools were few. But none doubted the need to dig and, where this was impracticable, rock sangars were raised. By 2000 hours all was quiet.

It was a time for contemplation among the defence. Some of those awaiting the enemy attack were fearful and all were apprehensive of a series of desperate battles ahead. Yet there were no signs of panic or recrimination; none of despair. A sense of determination to fight the battle out successfully was manifest. It was a mood which owed a good deal to individual valour but stemmed, too, from the immense confidence all felt in their commanding officer. He had been amongst them a good deal that day, making the occasional, quiet remark as he was apt to do, neither purveying false confidence nor betraying fears. He gave the impression of being unshakeable and they believed that he was.

By the night of the 24th/25th, according to Chinese prisoners-of-war, the 188 Division had lost over 4,000 killed and wounded since it had cross the Imjin. 189 Division began to cross the river at dusk with orders to clear away the Glosters once and for all. Commanders of the leading regiment had crossed earlier in the day to study the ground and plan the night attack. It was to begin quite silently, the assault companies creeping forward to a range at which they might effectively throw grenades – say, 25 yards. So six companies marched from their assembly area behind the Castle Site to the foot of Hill 235 as soon as it was dark and began stealthily its ascent.

The Glosters had put out trip wires with tins to rattle. These warnings revealed the enemy's approach at 2045 and within a few minutes the faithful guns of 45 Field Regiment were firing into the densely packed enemy. Even so, several hundred Chinese got right up to the Glosters' defences, blowing trumpets and whistles, calling commands shrilly as they sought to overwhelm their dogged foes. Gradually, they were driven back until 2300 hours when all became quiet once more. The Glosters set aside their dead in hollows and sent back the wounded to Captain Bob Hickey in his makeshift RAP.

Three hours later, the Chinese returned. Again the guns, the rifles and machine-guns fired, grenades were exchanged, the battle swayed to and fro. Towards dawn fresh numbers began an ascent across the little valley to the east with many trumpets directing them.

'It will be a long time before I want to hear a cavalry trumpet playing after this,' said the colonel to the adjutant.

'It would serve them right, sir,' said the adjutant, 'if we confused them by playing our own bugles. I wonder which direction they'd go if they heard Defaulters played!'

'Have we got a bugle up here?' asked the colonel. The adjutant called down the question to Drum-Major Buss on the eastern slope.

'Got one in my haversack,' came the reply.

'Well, play it, Drum-Major,' said the adjutant.

'What shall it be, sir?'

'It's getting towards daylight; play Reveille – the Long and the Short. And play Fire call – in fact, play all the calls of the day as far as Retreat, but don't play that!'

There were a few preliminary peeps from the Drum-Major as he tried out his lips and then his calls rang in the morning air: Reveille, Defaulters, Cookhouse, Officers Dress for Dinner, Orderly NCOs and many more. When the last sweet note died away there was silence. Certainly surprised, perhaps confused and apprehensive of a counter-attack, the Chinese stopped their movement for a while.

The attacks began again after dawn, principally from the north, assault after assault. 'A' Company were driven back from their position, being reduced to one officer, CSM Gallagher and 27 soldiers. The adjutant took them back in a counter-attack and remained to command. He asked the guns of 54 Field to fire deliberately on the restored company position when a Chinese assault flowed into it. This ejected them but they massed again. The forward observation officer with the company, Captain Ronnie Washbrook, brought in with great skill a series of air strikes using napalm against those on the northern slopes. It was a joy to the defenders to see six more pairs of F 8os attack concentrations of troops from Hill 235 to the Imjin. Daunted at last, the Chinese drew back. It was 0610 on the morning of 25 April.

The morning news came from brigade headquarters. Pressure on the route to the east had become so great that all forces were falling back towards Uijongbu. There were no troops available to fight a way forward to the Glosters. The battalion was to fight its own way back, given maximum support from the guns. Orders were passed to Major Weller, the adjutant, Captain Harvey, Lieutenant Temple representing Major Harding, Henry Cabral, Major Ward of 70 Battery and Captain Wisbey of the heavy mortar troop. Captain Hickey was present from the RAP. After pointing out the route to be taken and giving orders for tactical movement, the colonel paused and looked at the doctor.

'Bob, I'm afraid we shall have to leave the wounded behind.'

'Very well, sir. I understand our position.'

Ten o'clock was to be the hour of disengagement from Hill 235. In each defensive location beforehand, everything of value was destroyed, to prevent it falling to the Chinese. At 1000, the colonel met the adjutant.

'Let Sam Weller know that I have just been told by the brigadier that the guns are unable to support us – the gun lines are under attack themselves. Our orders are quite simple; every man to make his own way back.'

Word was hastily passed: soon officers and men were hurrying down the hillside in the warm sunlight. The adjutant passed the RAP. 'Come on, Bob,' he called to the doctor. 'The colonel will be off in a moment and that will be the lot.'

'I can't go,' he said. 'I must stay with the wounded.'

Soon none of the battalion was left on Hill 235 but the dead, the wounded and the gallant RAP staff, Padre Sam Davies amongst them.

The long ridge two miles to the south of Gloster Hill was held in strength by the Chinese and thus blocked the attempts of the Glosters to break out. Some of those running and marching away were shot down and some were captured by the enemy sallying down from the hilltops or advancing to oecupy the abandoned hill.

A group under Captain Harvey took fortuitously a route first north and then west and some of this number survived a hail of fire to reach friendly lines (a total of 46 all ranks).

By the evening of the 25th, about 350 of the battalion and its supporting Arms were being marched north across the Imjin River as prisoners of war. So too were the 63 CCF Army which had been so mauled that its remnants were withdrawn over the river to recover.

At brigade headquarters, Brigadier Brodie had written in the operations log his own documentary: 'No one but the Glosters could have done it.'

So passed Lieutenant-Colonel Carne's battalion of the 28th/61st

Foot from view – at least for a time. But almost at once a new battalion came into being. The remaining fragment of the Glosters was ordered to the rear until a decision could be taken as to the future. This disposal reckoned without the character of Major D. B. A. Grist who had assumed command. He gathered in every officer and soldier, including those who had just escaped from the line, returned from leave or arrived from the reinforcement camp and formed them into a fighting body. Replying to a special message of encouragement from the Colonel-in-Chief, he signalled, 'we are already operational again.' Thus continuity was maintained. As it happened, the main battle was fast waning: the Chinese strength was insufficient to carry the battle across the Han and CCF units north of Seoul began to draw back on 30 April.

From 26 April to 23 May, the Glosters with the remainder of the 29th Brigade were deployed on the Kimpo Peninsula, watching the right flank of the UN line. It was a quiet sector and here all units were reinforced and equipped anew. Major Grist was promoted to lieutenant-colonel and confirmed in command of the battalion. Officers, warrant officers and NCOs of the regiment came from far and wide to fill out the companies; many had hastened to return of their own volition as soon as they heard the news of the battalion's loss. Comrades old and new shared a unique occasion when, on 8 May, General James van Fleet, presented a Distinguished Unit Citation to the battalion and 'C' troop, 170 Heavy Mortar Battery, by command of the President of the United States.

In the last week of May, once more at full strength, the British brigade returned to the Imjin, the Glosters holding the reserve position but taking an active part in patrolling north of the river. Those who had been there before were happy to see tons of defence stores arrive. The front was covered with wire; trenches were properly revetted and covered. In August, the battalion moved forward from reserve into many of their old positions and, finally, in September, to a sector north of the river where a new line, 'Wyoming', was dug and wired. From its place in this sector, the battalion was relieved by 1st Battalion, The Welsh Regiment, in November 1951.

A year and a month after leaving, the 28th/61st returned to England. Despite the pleasure of being safely at home once more, the thoughts of many of its members were often with those left behind in the prison camps.

Two main columns of British prisoners had been formed up at

the end of April from those captured out of the British 29th Brigade. Amongst them were a few members of the United States Air Force shot down in the same battle area. As they marched, certain individuals and small groups escaped but the majority were secured effectively by the Chinese guards as the columns marched nightly in stages of 12–15 miles until a point was reached beyond the range of day-fighter/ground attack aircraft of the United Nations. Thereafter the marches were made by day. Some of the prisoners were passed over to the North Koreans for intelligence interrogation at the notorious 'Pak's Palace' at Pyongyang, in which conditions were so bad that hundreds of UN prisoners died. The majority were marched to Chiangsong on the Yalu river where a dull life was not enlivened by daily political lectures aimed at subverting the loyalties of United Nations prisoners.

In the officers' camp, Colonel Carne was singled out for prolonged isolation and beatings due to his immense prestige. Many of his officers and soldiers were also confined and beaten, and some were tortured for escape or defiance of Chinese demands for information. Less than one per cent of the British prisoners co-operated with their captors against their own country or fellow prisoners.

With the failure of their offensive in the spring of 1951, the Chinese had abandoned the hope of driving the United Nations Forces from Korea. Their problem was how to end a war which they saw they could not win, and which was unduly expensive in war material, without sacrificing all political prospect for the communist camp. Armistice negotiations dragged on from May 1951 until August 1953. Only then, at last, were the prisoners-of-war able to move south to be exchanged at Panmunjon, close to the 38th Parallel. Amongst the whole body of prisoners originally taken, many had died of neglect or starvation. Among the 33 dead of the Glosters' group none had died more honourably than Lieutenant Terry Waters, attached to the 28th/61st from the West Yorkshire Regiment, who had chosen to die of his wounds rather than make propaganda broadcasts against his own nation.*

In the autumn of 1953, what remained of Colonel Carne's battalion sailed back into Southampton water. Sirens and hooters sounded as

---

* Lieutenant Waters was posthumously awarded the George Cross.

they came ashore to be reunited with wives and families. They were astonished and a little embarrassed to find themselves famous as men who had made history. Such is the way of the British soldier: may it always be so.

7
Vietnam

Dien Bien Phu (1953)

Charles Mey

Dawn is about to break over the North Vietnamese airfields of Gia-Lam and Bach-Mai, just outside Hanoi in the north-east corner of Vietnam. Over 1,800 French and South Vietnamese are ready in full fighting kit, tense and waiting to go into battle. With them are their three commanders, Major Marcel Bigeard, Major Jean Brechignac and Major Jean Souquet, all seasoned veterans of the Indo-China war. On the runway, 67 C47 Dakotas sit, their crews ready to take off. It is 20 November 1953.

Another Dakota, 190 miles away, is circling over a valley shrouded in mist and drizzle. Three French officers, Lieutenant General Pierre Bodet, Brigadier General Jean Decheaux and Brigadier General Jean Gilles, are aboard. They will soon give the go-ahead for the dropping of three parachute battalions who are waiting to attack a small village held by the Viet Minh. It is the village of Dien Bien Phu.

Suddenly, at 0700, the sky clears. An order goes to the parachute battalions outside Hanoi. It is the beginning of Operation Castor. Over Dien Bien Phu, the swarming Dakotas fill the air with their roar and thousands of Thai peasants stare up in surprise. The planes discharge their cargoes of men, and hundreds of white parachutes blossom against the blue sky. Viet Minh soldiers rush to their battle stations. On the dropping zone (DZ) Natasha, a Viet Minh company on exercise has already skirmished with Maj. Bigeard's paratroopers of the 6th Colonial Parachute Battalion. The DZ covers a large area and already the recovery of the tons of equipment parachuted into it is becoming difficult. Machine-guns, 81 mm mortars and radio sets litter the ground. But many of the radios have not survived the drop. Worse, some of the mortars cannot be found.

Farther to the south, on DZ Simone, Maj. Brechignac's paratroopers, from the 2nd Battalion of the Parachute Chasseurs Regiment, have been dropped in difficult conditions and it is proving difficult to rally the soldiers and get them into action as a concerted force. Without waiting for support, Bigeard has left the DZ to attack the village of Dien Bien Phu with three of his four companies. But the Viet Minh regular soldiers defend doggedly. At 1500, Souquet's 1st Colonial Parachute Battalion, who have jumped in support of Bigeard, arrive to take part in the mopping-up action. The 148th Regiment of the People's Army withdraws in good order and the villagers flee into the mountains. French losses are only 13 dead and 40 wounded. It is confirmation of the value of surprise blows struck by well-trained parachute units.

On the second day, 21 November, a second force of paratroopers jumps into the valley of Dien Bien Phu. These are the legionnaires of the 1st Foreign Legion Parachute Battalion and the soldiers of the 8th Vietnamese Parachute Battalion, with their commanding officers, Lieutenant Colonel Pierre Charles Langlais – who breaks a leg on landing – and Gen. Gilles, commander of the whole Dien Bien Phu operation. Heavy supplies are now dropped on DZ Octavie, but one of two bulldozers parachuted in buried itself in the ground after its chute had failed to open fully. The French forces on 22 November are 4,560 men, after a fresh battalion of Vietnamese had arrived. It was time to begin the construction of defensive positions.

After the airborne landing of 20 November, Dien Bien Phu is soon to be a fortified zone, capable of holding 12,000 soldiers. Why is it sited in such an area? Because the French High Command's patience is wearing thin. Embroiled in a war with Ho Chi Minh's revolutionary army since 19 December 1946, a spectacular victory is badly needed. And with Gallic daring, they have chosen to occupy Dien Bien Phu, a base 200 miles inside the enemy's territory.

The French High Command at Saigon is not sure about the role which Dien Bien Phu is being called upon to play. Is it a rallying point for the Lai Chau garrison? A 'hedgehog' in an essential strategic position? Or a start point for an offensive, as Major General Renee Cogny declares? Perhaps it is a trap sprung for the army of General

Vo Nguyen Giap, of the Vietnamese People's Army. Or could it be a diversion in anticipation of an attack on the Red River Delta?

Before being replaced by General Henri Navarre, General Salan, Chief of Staff of the French Expeditionary Force in Indo-China, said that Laos could only be defended by holding Dien Bien Phu, as well as Na-San and Lai-Chau. Navarre will come under severe criticism for his action here in establishing Dien Bien Phu as a fortress, sited as it was in the bottom of the valley. But he saw the ten-mile-long and six-mile-wide valley floor as an ideal base. From it he could make sorties to attack the Viet Minh. He felt that the enemy could not surround his fortification, nor could they effectively use artillery against the airstrip from the hills ten miles away.

For some time, Dien Bien Phu is almost a tourist venue for many high-ranking French officers and politicians, together with their Government's military visitors. The fortress is praised from all sides, although one man, General Blanc, has his criticisms about the area in times of monsoon. His warning is not heeded. Among the visitors are General Spears, British Military Attache and High Commissioner Malcolm McDonald, many American Generals including John ('Iron Mike') O'Daniel, US Army Commander in the Pacific. But none of these highly expert people question the ability of Dien Bien Phu to withstand attack.

There is a collective blindness on the part of senior French officers. And this notwithstanding the fact that the archives hold details of defense preparation, backed by information from the Deuxième Bureau on the movement and capability of the enemy forces.

But from December 1953, events will show that if Navarre has set the scene, it is Giap who will script it. The situation created by the French airborne landings at Dien Bien Phu on 20 November is analyzed by the Viet Minh Council of War. Orders are given to the 316th Division to attack Lai-Chau so that it will be compelled to fall back to Dien Bien Phu. But in December 1953 the French forestall the Viet Minh plans. The Lai-Chau garrison is evacuated in 183 sorties by air transport four days before the arrival of the North Vietnamese troops. Over 2,000 men who had to be left behind have to try to make the 60-mile jungle journey to Dien Bien Phu on foot. But only 175 T'ai soldiers make it. The rest die in ambush. Many desert.

With the Viet Minh fallen back from Dien Bien Phu, the offensive and reconnaissance missions ordered by Gen. Cogny immediately begin to be costly. Two missions, Operations Ardèche and Régate, are undertaken by a paratrooper task force commanded by Lt. Col. Langlais. They leave the base to link up with the Laotian light infantry and Moroccan *Tabors* from Laos. The rendezvous is to be in the Sop Nao region, a mountainous area with thick jungle, providing perfect ambush sites. The task force is harried by a mobile enemy and the losses make it necessary to abandon these long-range penetrations and to concentrate efforts on the mountains that surround Dien Bien Phu itself.

In the fortress, information from French intelligence is that the 351st, 308th and 312th Divisions are moving towards Dien Bien Phu. Soon Giap is mobilizing his forces and the French are preparing for a siege. Their engineers calculate that enormous quantities of equipment will be needed – 36,000 tons. This would take an impossible 12,000 Dakota trips from Hanoi. All the engineers get is 4,000 tons – and 75 per cent of that is barbed wire.

There is another battle between the French and the Viet Minh. It is one of logistics. And the French will lose this one too. All their fortification work is accurately mapped. It can be seen clearly from the surrounding high ground. The smallest trench stands out clearly in the bare earth. As for the French, they see nothing of the enemy's movements in the dense jungle. They do not know that 55,000 regular and locally raised troops surround them. Giap's forces open five routes through the jungle towards Dien Bien Phu. They are used by 600 Russian-built 2.5-ton lorries which travel by night with all lights extinguished. The French air attacks on the passes of Lung Lo and Phadin cause sections of these precarious roads to slide into ravines, and torrential rains make fords impassable and turn valleys into marshes.

But traffic is never interrupted for more than a few days. Thousands of coolies work day and night maintaining the Viet Minh supply routes. In addition, on the narrow tracks pack-horses, mules and convoys of bicycles, each one laden with 220 lb, head towards the battlefield. Nothing can stop this conveyor belt of human ants. But the fortress can count only on transport aircraft. Everything has to come from Hanoi.

Ten M24 Chaffee tanks stripped down (each requiring five C47s and two Bristols to lift them), 105 mm and 155 mm guns, rations for 11,000 men, generators, water-purifiers. But French airpower, even with the help of a squadron of C119s supplied by the Americans, could not meet the demands of Dien Bien Phu.

Even before the real trial of strength begins the French have lost the logistics battle. When the airstrip is destroyed and the parachute is the only means of supply, the consequences will be disastrous for the French.

Gen. Giap's artillery strength around Dien Bien Phu is impressive. On the day before the attack the besiegers have 144 field-howitzers (American 75s and 105s), 48 120 mm heavy mortars, 30 75 mm recoilless guns and 36 37 mm AA guns. And during the course of the battle 12 siz-barrel Katyusha rocket-launchers will come into action. The physical effort of dragging these guns into place over wet and slippery slopes by human muscle power must have been enormous.

On D-Day, Giap has at his disposal stocks of shells far greater than the French thought possible. From 13 March to 8 May 1954 his guns will fire about 150,000 shells, about 30,000 of them from the 105s. And the French artillery will need an airlift of incredible proportions to keep the guns firing. A total of 95,000 rounds of 105 mm and 8,500 rounds of 155 mm ammunition are parachuted into the base. But a quantity falls beyond the ever-shrinking perimeter into Viet Minh territory.

The besieged French have six batteries (24 guns) of 105 mm, one battery of four 155 mm howitzers and 32 120 mm heavy mortars. Colonel Piroth, who commands the base artillery, considers they can stop any enemy infantry attack, and are good enough for effective counter-battery work. He said: 'No Viet Minh gun will fire three rounds without being destroyed.' The French have underestimated the enemy's artillery strength, the supply of ammunition, the skill of his gunners and the effectiveness of his camouflage.

Bur Dien Bien Phu's firepower inferiority is also the result of other factors. Contrary to expectations the Viet Minh guns are served by excellent crews, trained in camps in south China. Their fire is directed and controlled by observers with uninterrupted views of the airfield and the unprotected French batteries. From the first day of the attack their power and their precision will come as a bitter shock. The French counter-battery work is random and will have no effect.

The Viet Minh 105s, in fact, are undetectable and practically invulnerable, because they are well dug-in, though this is at the expense of wide fields of fire and large handling crews. Dummy guns are used by the Viet Minh to deceive the French spotters in the base. And so the battle of Dien Bien Phu was going to start under unfavorable conditions for the defenders. Their officers either know or sense it and it seems that Navarre and Cogny have their doubts. But by this time the die has been cast.

'Gentlemen, it is at 1700 tomorrow.' Colonel Christian de la Croix de Castries had just completed his briefing on the evening of 12 March 1954. The unit commanders have been waiting this moment for several weeks. Less than six miles away, Giap issues his final orders for the attack. He knows the importance of the battle and its cost: 'We will have to sustain losses in the course of the battle. Victory is bought at the price of blood and paid for, like all revolutionary conquests, with sacrifices.'

At D-day the attackers have a superiority of eight to one: there are only 6,500 French front-line troops against the 50,000 seasoned combat troops of the elite 308th, 312th, 316th, 304th, the 351st (engineers and artillery) divisions and the 148th local regiment. The French have five Foreign Legion battalions, but eight others are composed of Algerian and Moroccan riflemen, Thais, Vietnamese, Montaguards and mobile police. On 13 March Viet Minh movements are spotted around Beatrice and Gabrielle strongpoints, as two regiments of the 312th Division move up to their start-lines less than 100 yards from the French defenses. Two C47s and a fighter are destroyed by artillery fire on the airstrip.

At 1715 the first 105 mm shells land on Beatrice which is held by 3rd Battalion, 13th Demi-Brigade of the Foreign Legion. Two 105 mm guns in the position are destroyed and Colonel Gaucher, the commander, killed. The Viet Minh infantry attack in the failing light after sappers have blown paths through the wire. Regardless of casualties the enemy move forward, overrunning bunkers and dug-outs. Hand-to-hand fighting with grenades occurs in the trenches and amongst the ruins. At 2100 only one strongpoint is still holding out. Shortly after midnight a heavy silence settles over Beatrice. The garrison of legionnaires has lost 75 per cent of its numbers and fewer than 200 men regain the main French lines.

In the entrenched camp the French are dumbfounded. A strongpoint, defended by the Legion, overrun in six hours! Thousands of men look towards the lost position and try to understand. Col. de Castries, who has sat up all night by his telephones and has lived out the agony of Beatrice, alerts his HQ in Hanoi. He is promised reinforcements and air support. The airfield is all but closed and enemy shelling forces those fighter-bombers still intact to escape to Laos. In addition a quarter of the French 105 mm ammunition has been exhausted in one night.

On the next day, 14 March, the 5th Vietnamese Parachute Battalion is dropped in reinforcement and de Castries contemplates a counter-attack on Beatrice. But low cloud and a violent storm make close air support impossible, besides which it is known that Giap's next objective will be Gabrielle. At 1800 the Viet Minh batteries begin their shelling of the strongpoint, which is held by a battalion of Algerian riflemen and eight Foreign Legion 120 mm mortars. The Viet Minh send in 88th and 165th Regiments of the 308th Division to the attack. It is eight battalions against one. Benefiting from their in-depth defense the Algerians resist the first onslaught. But by dawn on 15 March only one redoubt is still in French hands and awaiting a promised counter-attack by the main part of the garrison.

The counter-attack consists of two companies from the Legion and one battalion of Vietnamese paratroopers supported by six M24 tanks. It fights its way to within 1,000 yards of the position and enables 150 men to regain the French lines before the thrust is called off. The second outlying strongpoint has gone. Within two days of the start of Giap's offensive the French illusions have been shattered. Dien Bien Phu is a trap. Gen. Navarre is directing the battle from his office in Saigon, more than 1,000 miles from the fighting. Gen. Cogny, installed in Hanoi, has the immediate responsibility for the battle. Knowing of the setbacks of 13 and 14 March and realizing what they portend, another battle is to be fought in secret between these two officers.

Navarre finally arrives at Hanoi where a message signed by Cogny awaits him: 'One has to envisage the possibility of a defeat at Dien Bien Phu with the attendant loss of our personnel who are at present located there.' Cogny, having recognized inevitable defeat, wishes to make certain that responsibility for it does not fall on him. Henceforth, relations between the two generals conducting the same battle will be restricted to exchanges of written notes. But this does not stop them trying to find scapegoats – the engineer officers who designed the fortifications, the photographic interpreters, the transport and ground-attack crews, and – of course – the French civilian government.

At this point both Navarre's and Cogny's responsibilities are crushing and it is made worse by the fact that knowing the enemy's capabilities, they themselves chose the ground on which the battle is being fought. In 1953–4 the Vietnamese People's Army is a well-balanced force of divisions, regiments, battalions and companies, all well-equipped with up-to-date weapons and well led and disciplined. In addition it is fighting for its own country and for a cause in which it passionately believed. To present this modern army as a collection of rebel bands was perhaps necessary for propaganda's sake but to believe it was absurd.

By 15 March morale in the Dien Bien Phu garrison is at its lowest ebb. During the night Col. Piroth, unable to face the defeat of his artillery, takes a hand-grenade and kills himself in his dug-out. In the command post, several officers have cracked. And de Castries hesitates, overwhelmed and overtaken by events. He lacks neither courage nor panache but rather the qualities needed to direct a battle of this magnitude. Later he will be taken to task for his passivity. But it must be remembered that he was ordered to defend Dien Bien Phu after several generals and colonels had 'declined the honor'.

A soldier of much sterner stuff is the hatchet-faced Langlais, commander of the airborne troops. On 24 March de Castries effectively hands over command of the entrenched camp to him with the exception of Isabelle which is put under the control of Colonel André Lalande. It is an unofficial transfer of authority and a tacit recognition of the plight of the garrison. Langlais is also aided by Bigeard, sent back to the valley some eight days earlier with his battalion. Bigeard is to be Langlais' adjutant. Ultimately the paratroop 'Mafia' will take over the defense of the base.

Taking advantage of several days rest from shelling, all those capable of wielding pick and shovel have been put to work reinforcing the dug-outs and bunkers. But on 16 March the 3rd Thai Battalion on Anne Marie sense that things are going against them. They decide to leave the field and return to their villages. And several hundred North African and Vietnamese desert and go to ground in the dug-outs on the banks of the Nam Yum.

Giap and the Front Military Committee have considered the lessons of the first phase of the offensive. Losses have been very heavy and it is decided to pursue the policy of strangling the base. In ten days his front-line troops will dig more than seven miles of trenches and approach routes. A 50-yard tunnel will be dug to place an enormous explosive charge under the position known as Eliane. On the night of 30 March, after a violent preliminary artillery bombardment, the 312th and 316th Divisions launch their attack on the five hills that make up Dominique and Eliane. The battle rages for four days with hand-to-hand fighting for positions that are lost, recaptured and lost again. On one day, the defenders fire 13,000 rounds of 105 mm ammunition. This is largely responsible for the enemy's terrible losses and their failure to take their objectives. But they have made some progress and continue to erode the defended area.

The situation becomes critical on 2 April after units from the 308th Division are thrown against Huguette. At this point Bigeard scrapes together forces for a counter-attack and Viet Minh units break off the action, leaving 800 dead on the wire. The morale of the besieged forces soars and is maintained when Bigeard and his paratroopers recapture one of Eliane's lost strongpoints. Into a harrowing battle, Giap throws four battalions but in vain. Overall, the French position has not improved. Several thousand men are still isolated and trapped. There is little they can do but delay defeat. The Viet Minh divisions have been exhausted by their efforts. Giap is forced to launch a campaign for the 'mobilization of morale and rectification of right-wing tendencies.'

But on 1 May he orders a general offensive to begin at 2200. On that day there remains for the garrison three days' rations, 275 rounds of 155 mm, 14,000 rounds of 105 mm and 5,000 rounds of 120 mm mortar ammunition. Two strongpoints fall in the first assault, but Langlais and Bigeard hope to be able to hold on with reinforcements of men, supplies and ammunition parachuted into the base.

But the advantage of the attackers is overwhelming. Towards midday on 6 May Giap orders his Katyusha rocket-launchers, the 'Stalin Organs', into action to blow up the dumps and spread terror in North African and Vietnamese ranks. By dawn on 7 May the base has been reduced to a rectangle of half a square mile. Incredibly Bigeard mounts another counter-attack with two companies supported by the last Chaffee tank. By 1800 all firing had ceased. The base does not surrender, it is simply overwhelmed.

The price paid in the 56-day defense of Dien Bien Phu is more than 2,000 French dead, 7,000 wounded and missing, and 7,000 prisoners *en route* for the death camps. And it has cost Giap 8,000 lives and 15,000 wounded to secure his 'revolutionary conquest'.

The French High Command was relying heavily upon the firepower of its medium and fighter-bombers to destroy the supply lines of Giap's divisions and to smash those artillery batteries which had escaped the fire of the base's 155 mm guns. It was mistaken reliance. In fact, the French Expeditionary Corps' air support is ridiculously weak, no more than a hundred strike aircraft, of which three-quarters are committed to the battle at Dien Bien Phu. More pitifully still, there are only 80 transport planes and too few pilots.

Dive-bombing attacks on the supply lines, just as those on the edges of the entrenched camp, have only a limited effect because of the meticulous camouflage of the Viet Minh. Napalm, which had been used with devastating effect two years earlier at Vinh Yen, on the edge of the Red River defenses, is rendered less effective by the different thicknesses of vegetation in the dense forest. On the other hand, the Viet Minh anti-aircraft weapons (36 37 mm cannon and 50 12.7 mm machine-guns) are very formidable. It is soon obvious that French airpower cannot change the course of the battle.

In December 1953 Navarre had studied the operation which, coming from Laos, would crush the Viet Minh army brought to Dien Bien Phu. He had given this the name Condor. By April this was to be the last hope of relief for the defenders of Dien Bien Phu. Three thousand men, two-thirds of them Laotian Light Infantry, would march on the base to attack the Viet Minh's rear areas. At the same time the guerillas of Colonel Trinquier's Mixed Airportable Commando Group would be mobilized, together with Mollat's commandos and all those groups of irregulars fighting in the Viet Minh areas. And an airborne task force would be sent as reinforcement in good time.

But on 22 April Navarre cancels the promised reinforcements and leaves the units already engaged freedom of action to continue or break off. These troops will get close to the perimeter and recover the 78 men to escape from the valley but on 7 May they will receive the order to pull back.

A breakout and withdrawal of the Dien Bien Phu garrison towards Laos would have been, without any doubt, fraught with danger. But it was the only chance to escape annihilation. Capture of all the garrison, if it remained where it was, appeared inevitable. There was a possibility of trying to break out on 3 May under the code name Albatross. But the breakout, covered by all the guns and combat aircraft, would only have been towards the south-east by those still capable of carrying four days' rations and their personal weapons. In the effort to save some of the 6,000 men still able to fight, the wounded would have to be abandoned. But HQ in Hanoi vetoed the plan as being dishonorable. The forces inside the entrenched camp were left to their fate, to fight on heroically without hope until overwhelmed.

The debacle of Dien Bien Phu was due to a number of grave errors in the siting, supply and quality of the French defensive positions. Its ultimate destruction was due to the inability of the French to sustain an adequate supply of men, ammunition and provisions for the besieged garrison. To this must be added the brilliance of General Giap's powers of leadership and the unexpectedly high quality of his battalions.

The loss of Dien Bien Phu was not only the end of a battle, it was the first time an Asian subject people had beaten their European masters in battle. And it was the finish of France as a colonial power in Indo-China.

Ia Drang (1965)

Ian Westwell

On 22 October 1965 Major-General Harry W. O. Kinnard, Commanding General of the 1st Cavalry Division (Airmobile), received the message he had been anxiously waiting for. Short and to the point it stated: 'Commencing first light 23 October First Air Cav deploys one Bn TF [Task Force] minimum 1 Inf Bn and 1 Arty Btry to PLEIKU, mission to assist in defense of key US/ARVN [Army of the Republic of Vietnam] installations at PLEIKU or reinforce II Corps operations to relieve PLEI ME CAMP.' Since the division's arrival in South Vietnam it had had a few brushes with small bands of local Viet Cong guerrillas and, although Kinnard knew his men had performed well, he remained aware that they had yet to face the cream of the North Vietnamese Army.

Kinnard was a great believer in the value of airmobility and had been involved with the division from its early days. Indeed, as a brigadier-general, he had led the 11th Air Assault Division, where his enthusiasm and firm but relaxed style made him popular with the men. Close attention had been paid to their training and he felt sure that the successful completion of an operation lasting more than a few days would silence those critics who complained at the cost of the division.

Kinnard knew the men of the 1st Cavalry were special. They had to be: helicopters were temperamental beasts. A large part of the division would be used to keep them in the air. Pilots needed the skill to fly at tree-top level at over 100 m.p.h. The division's strength was speed and firepower. Eagle Flights, the basic tactical unit, consisted of six UH-1C Hueys, armed with 2.75-in rockets and a minigun capable of saturating an area the size of a football pitch in a few seconds, and seven UH-1Ds for carrying combat troops. Going into action they flew in a V-formation to give all-round vision and mutual protection. It worked in theory – would it work in practice?

Good up-to-the-minute intelligence on the strength and position of the enemy would be essential to the mission. A few days after the initial attack on the Plei Me Camp Captain William P. Gillette, the Air Cavalry Squadron intelligence officer, was able to give a full and remarkably accurate report. It was clear that the NVA assault on the camp, 40 km south-west of Pleiku, was meant to be the beginning of a full-scale offensive aiming to cut South Vietnam in two. Two enemy regiments were in the area: the 33rd around Plei Me and the 32nd, lying in ambush ready to destroy any ground force attempting to relieve the camp. The month-long battle that was to follow became known as the Battle of the Ia Drang Valley. It was to be a major test for the 1st Cavalry Division and was the first time that regular NVA troops controlled by a divisional headquarters fought a conventional battle against US forces.

Initially the 1st Cavalry Division acted in support of the South Vietnamese Army. The Cav's 1st Brigade, ordered to secure Pleiku, to provide artillery backup and to furnish a reserve force, was soon in action. At 1730 hours the NVA hit a relief column at two points and the air cavalry was called up. The brigade was quick to respond – its helicopters were in the air in 10 minutes – and the firepower it deployed was widely recognized as the decisive factor in the defeat of the enemy. Plei Me camp was relieved on 25 October.

It soon became clear that a major opportunity for the full deployment of the air cavalry was unfolding. The NVA was pulling back after receiving a bloody nose and a quick response might give them a further mauling. General William C. Westmoreland, Commander of the US Military Assistance Command, Vietnam (MACV), flew up to the front and after a brief conference ordered the cavalry in pursuit. For Kinnard it was the chance he had long waited for. He was given a free hand and his job was no longer just reinforcement and reaction but unlimited attack. A pattern for future actions was being born: the division was to engage in hard-hitting search-and-destroy missions against NVA forces operating in the difficult terrain of Vietnam's Central Highlands.

It was not just the enemy that caused problems. Much of this part of South Vietnam consisted of dense vegetation, and jungle composed of 30 m high trees. Rocks hidden by man-tall elephant grass could flip a helicopter on its side. Most clearings were too small for even a single Huey, but by using the tail-rotor as a chain-saw – strictly against regulations – pilots could hack a way to the ground. A slight error of judgement, all too easy after six hours in the saddle, would be costly, and maybe fatal.

For the next 12 days much of the 1st Brigade was deployed to the west of Pleiku. Most of their operations involved fierce fighting and most of them proved successful. On 1 November, for example, a routine reconnaissance patrol flying 12 km west of Plei Me spotted some unusual ground activity beneath the jungle canopy and ordered in units of the 1st Brigade. The enemy had no time to melt back into the undergrowth. Seventy-eight were killed and 57 captured. More damaging was the capture of a complete field hospital – dozens of cases of essential medical supplies, including morphine and penicillin, were stacked to chest height over a large area.

The 1st Squadron, 9th Cavalry, again drew blood two days later in a perfectly executed ambush on an enemy unit of company strength moving along an east–west trail just north of the Chu Pong mountains. The troopers had to wait an agonizing 90 minutes before the unit entered the ambush zone, but their training taught them to wait until the leading elements had gone by. With a deafening roar eight claymore mines were exploded and then the cavalrymen fired continuously for two minutes. There was no return fire. But the Cav did not have things entirely their own way this time. Back at base they came under sustained, almost fanatical, attacks from three companies of NVA regulars and by midnight their perimeter was in grave danger of being overrun. Now, however, the advantages of airmobility became apparent. Help was soon at hand, as Company A, 1st Battalion, 8th Cavalry, located 20 km to the north, flew in. The first platoon was on the ground and in combat 40 minutes after midnight.

These first sustained combats by units of the 1st Brigade though small in scale were, for Kinnard, ample justification of the airmobile concept. Scout ships were regularly finding enemy forces. Highly mobile rifle units were then being flown in to fix the enemy before massive air and ground firepower was used to inflict maximum damage. Many lessons were learnt through combat experience.

In their first skirmishes many cavalry troopers were disconcerted by the suicidally close ranges at which they came to grips with the enemy. Several units were almost dropped into the laps of the NVA and firefights often took place at ranges of less than 20 m, where the firepower of Soviet and Chinese-built assault rifles could be devastating. It was often difficult to organize artillery support and the emergency medical evacuation of casualties was delayed because of the lack of equipment to clear landing zones.

The early encounters of the Ia Drang campaign were also remarkable for the successful deployment of airborne units at night. The battle of 3 November, for example, was the first time a defensive perimeter under heavy fire was reinforced in the dark by airborne toops flown into an unfamiliar landing zone. It was also the first time that aerial rocket artillery was used at night and as close as 50 m to US troops.

Basic training taught the pilots to fly low and fast – they would be away before the enemy could get them in their sights. That was the official line, but most pilots took it as a sick joke. Fully laden they had to fly low, but there was no way they could fly fast.

Flying at night or dropping into a vicious firefight from 500 m was every pilot's nightmare. No amount of training could prepare them for it. The enemy always knew they were coming. Helicopter engines were noisy and in the jungle-quiet could be heard several miles away. Over the drop zone tracers would shoot up out of the undergrowth. Beautiful but deadly, a 0.5-in calibre round would go through anything. If the enemy were lucky they might hit the 'Jesus nut' that held the rotor blades in place. There would be no survivors after a hit like that.

On 9 November the 1st Brigade was withdrawn from the Ia Drang battles. Its deployment had clearly been a major success and some 200 North Vietnamese soldiers were killed and an estimated 180 wounded. More importantly it had destroyed over 100,000 rounds of 7.62 mm ammunition, two 82 mm mortars and three 75 mm recoilless rifles and captured over $40,000 worth of medical supplies.

The 1st Brigade was replaced by the 3rd, consisting of the 1st and 2nd Battalions, 7th Cavalry. For the battles in Ia Drang it was supported by the 2nd Battalion, 5th Cavalry. By this stage Kinnard's major concern was that the NVA might slip away and that the cavalry would fail to capitalize on its earlier successes. He ordered Colonel Thomas W. Brown, the 3rd Brigade commander, to initiate patrols south and south-east of Plei Me. Colonel Brown, well versed in airmobile techniques, started a vigorous hunt for the enemy. Intelligence reports suggested that the 33rd NVA Regiment was reorganizing between the Ia Drang river and the Chu Pong mountains. It was also believed that the 32nd Regiment was nearby and that other reinforcements had arrived.

On 14 November the 1st Battalion, 7th Cavalry, commanded by Lieutenant-Colonel Harold G. Moore, began a sweep along the base of the Chu Pong range. The battalion was, however, short of helicopters, only 16 UH-IDs were available. Fire support, the most essential part of any airborne assault, was to be provided by two 105 mm batteries located at landing zone (LZ) Falcon, 9 km east of the search area. Like the senior officers of the 1st brigade, Moore was conscious that his men had yet to be tested against a large NVA force.

LZ X-Ray, 10 km west of Plei Me, and capable of taking up to ten UH-IDSs at one time, was chosen by Moore as the best place for the opening air assault. The co-ordination of all arms was of crucial importance in the early phases. At 1017 hours a preliminary bombardment by 105s began and was quickly followed by an aerial attack. The LZ was saturated with fire – helicopter gunships fired 50 per cent of their rockets in 30 seconds. Company B of the 1st Battalion was the first to drop. On landing the troops spread out to secure a perimeter around the LZ, and Companies A and C quickly followed.

By 1330, however, the North Vietnamese had made further reinforcement extremely hazardous. At ground level the LZ was ringed by sparse bush which, with elephant grass and anthills, provided ideal cover for the enemy who were able to pin down the cavalrymen. Several Hueys carrying the leading elements of D Company were hit and, though none was shot down, Colonel Moore forbade a further eight from landing. A and B Companies were ordered to pull back and prepare a tight defensive perimeter for the night. Of the two, Company B was in the worse position. One of its platoons had become separated and could not be precisely located.

LZ X-Ray was hot. Sitting in a pilot's seat, the target of all surrounding hostile fire, the men who flew the helicopters were desperate for the troopers to get out of the craft as quickly as possible; and then there was the agonizing wait as the wounded were loaded aboard. Crews counted themselves lucky if they got back into the air in under a minute. It was a hell of a long time to wait. A pilot who was present recalled the atmosphere of tension:

'Orange One, abort your landing. Fire on the LZ is too heavy,' a pathfinder called from X-Ray. Orange flight turned and we followed. There was a whole bunch of yelling on the radios. I heard two ships in the LZ call out they were hit badly. What a mess. Finally we heard Yellow One call to take off, and we saw them emerge from the smoke on the left of the LZ, shy two ships. They had waited in the heavy fire while the crews of the two downed ships got on to other Hueys. One crew chief stayed, dead. One pilot was wounded.

By mid-afternoon on 14 November Moore knew he was in a major battle and his men were fighting for their lives against the 66th and 33rd NVA regiments. It seemed obvious to Colonel Brown at Plei Me that the enemy were intent on destroying the 1st Battalion, 7th Cavalry. He prepared to send in reinforcements to strengthen the landing zone. Company B of the 2nd Battalion, 7th Cavalry, arrived at X-Ray by 1800 hours, and night landing facilities were set up.

The situation around the perimeter was by this stage less dangerous and it was only the isolated platoon of Company B that was causing concern. Although reports suggested it was holding its own with morale still high, eight men had been killed, 12 had been wounded in action and only seven remained unhurt. The platoon faced several attacks but all were beaten off by small arms and artillery fire. Dawn revealed dozens of enemy dead around their position. Savage close fighting went on inside the perimeter. The 1st Platoon leader of C Company was found dead with the bodies of five NVA soldiers around his foxhole and one trooper was found with his hands locked around the throat of an adversary. By 1000 hours on 15 November air strikes and aerial rocket artillery units firing 2.75-in rockets and miniguns had blasted the North Vietnamese out of their positions.

Moore was confident that the enemy was no longer capable of attacking the landing zone in any strength and at 1330 ordered his tired men to pull out. The troopers were quick to realize they had inflicted a heavy defeat on the enemy. Many bodies littered the battlefield, and heavily bloodstained bandages suggested that far more had been very badly wounded. By noon a relief force, the 2nd Battalion, 5th Cavalry, reached Moore's position and the relief of the isolated platoon was little more than a formality. The troops at LZ X-Ray were ordered to sit tight and await the arrival of the 2nd Battalion, 7th Cavalry, who had been detailed to act as a relief force. By 0930 hours on 16 November its leading elements began to arrive and Colonel Moore's men were airlifted out.

The two-day battle around LZ X-Ray was the high point of the 1st Cavalry campaign in the Ia Drang Valley. Colonel Moore's men suffered nearly 200 casualties but the NVA lost many more: 634 known dead, 581 supposed dead and six taken prisoner. Large amounts of their equipment fell into the cavalry's hands. It was clear to both sides that there would now be no full-scale offensive in South Vietnam's Central Highlands. The 3rd Brigade continued to sweep the Chu Pong area until 20 November and the 2nd was withdrawn on the 26th.

The 1st Cavalry Division fought in the Ia Drang Valley for 35 days and during that time changed the nature of the war in Vietnam. No longer would US forces have to footslog through dense undergrowth in search of an elusive foe. Air cavalry units could respond to any situation in a short time and maintain contact with the enemy for longer than was previously possible. Commander-in-chief General Westmoreland was full of praise. 'The ability of the Americans to meet and defeat the best troops the enemy could put into the field of battle was once and for all demonstrated beyond any possible doubt as was the validity of the Army's airmobile concept.'

Hamburger Hill (1969)

John Pimlott

In the aftermath of the Tet Offensive in early 1968, the Americans and their allies in South Vietnam enjoyed a distinct military advantage. Despite the failure of the Communists to trigger a countrywide revolt, by the end of February the Communists had suffered grievous manpower losses and had been forced back to their border bases. With half a million troops in-country, the Americans could contemplate offensive operations into such bases, inflicting yet more casualties while impressing upon the North – about to engage in peace negotiations in Paris – that the costs of continued aggression would be crippling.

General Westmoreland, in his last weeks as MACV commander, looked particularly toward the A Shau valley on the far western edge of Thua Thien province in ICTZ. About 28 miles long and up to 2 miles wide, this 'slash in the mountains', close to the Laotian border, had long been a natural route for NVA troops and supplies entering South Vietnam. Surrounded by towering, jungle-covered mountains, the valley was isolated and exceptionally difficult to penetrate, especially during the monsoon with its torrential rain and thick fog.

US and South Vietnamese Special Forces had established camps at A Loui, Ta Bat, and A Shau village, but the first two were abandoned in December, 1965, and the third was overrun by the NVA in a bruising battle the following March. Since then, the A

Shau valley had been abandoned to the Communists, something that Westmoreland found deeply frustrating. In April, 1968, he ordered the 1st Cavalry Division to mount an offensive – codenamed Delaware – to reassert Allied control.

US aero-rifle teams entered the valley on 14 April, intending to seize the former Special Forces camp at A Loui in the northern sector. They encountered a wall of anti-aircraft fire which 200 B-52 and 300 fighter-bomber sorties failed to quell; and, although battalions of the 7th Cavalry did take A Loui, conditions were appalling. Low cloud and rain effectively negated the advantages of airmobility; Delaware was called off on 11 May.

This pattern was repeated in August, when the 101st Airborne Division entered the valley in Operation Somerset Plain. The only answer seemed to be the construction of a road from the coast into the A Shau, reducing the dependence on helicopter resupply. By the end of 1968, this had been pushed to the eastern edge of the valley, but if it was to go further, operations would have to be carried out to clear the way.

These began in January, 1969, with Operation Dewey Canyon – a Marine assault south through the Da Krong valley into NVA Base Area 611 astride the Laotian border. It enjoyed a degree of success, persuading the new MACV commander, General Creighton Abrams, to order a follow-up offensive.

In March, the 2nd Brigade, 101st Airborne, air assaulted the central sector of the valley in Operation Massachusetts Striker. It culminated in a three-day battle at Dong A Tay ('Bloody Ridge'), in which the 1/502nd Infantry lost 35 men killed and over 100 wounded. The NVA were clearly prepared to fight.

Massachusetts Striker forced the NVA back toward the north-western sector of the valley, around a mountain (Dong) known as Ap Bia, but marked on US maps as Hill 937. Situated close to the Laotian border, 937 and its neighboring ridges – Hills 900 and 800 to the south and Hill 916 to the south-west – were covered in thick jungle, tangled vines, and impenetrable bamboo. In residence since 1964, the NVA had fortified the area, building log-covered bunkers and camouflaged spiderholes to protect all avenues of approach. By May, 1969, when the A Shau valley was chosen as an objective of the 101st in Operation Apache Snow, Ap Bia was being held by over 1,200 men of the crack NVA 29th Regiment.

Apache Snow began on 10 May with helicopter assaults by five

Allied battalions (three from the 101st Airborne Division and two from the 1st ARVN) into the northern A Shau. At LZ2, about 2,000 yards north-west of Hill 937, Lieutenant Colonel Weldon Honeycutt's 3/187th Infantry landed without incident and began to conduct RIF (reconnaissance-in-force) operations toward the mountain and Laotian border. A more permanent LZ and battalion command post was set up closer to 937 and, with no reaction from the NVA, Company B was ordered to seize the summit.

Starting out at 1640 hours, the paratroopers followed a trail to the south-east of the new LZ which took them into thick jungle, enclosed by tall trees, matted vines, and bamboo. Moving forward over fallen trees, the lead scouts trod warily while their comrades, sweating in the dank, humid air, plodded behind. As they crossed a low saddle, the NVA struck, firing RPGs (rocket-propelled grenades) and AK-47s into the American column. Airstrikes were called in, and, as dusk was gathering, the company pulled back into an NDP (night defensive position).

With only three men wounded, the skirmish was hardly significant, but when another ambush was sprung in the same area the following morning, killing three Americans, it was obvious that the enemy had been found. This suited Honeycutt, who immediately revised his plan. Recalling Company C from its RIF along the Trung Pham River, he ordered it to attack, parallel to Company B, along a ridge that ended between Hills 900 and 937, while Company D worked around the northern edge of the mountain. The aim was to have all three companies in position to assault the summit by first light on 13 May. It did not work.

The companies moved out at 0830 hours on 12 May, after intense air and artillery 'prepping' fire. They entered a nightmare of close-quarter fighting that was to continue with little respite for eight days. During that time, the 3/187th was to be shattered, both mentally and physically, as enemy resistance hardened and conditions deteriorated. On Company B's line of advance, the NVA drew the Americans closer to the mountain, into a clearing that sheltered line after line of bunkers, each of which seemed impervious to airstrikes or artillery strikes.

Day after day, the company moved up, attacking the bunkers with grenades, recoilless rifles and machine-guns, only to be forced to pull back, dragging their wounded to safety. By 15 May, Company B was exhausted and had to be replaced by Company D, itself less

than strong after terrible experiences farther north. On 12 May,
the company had found its way blocked by a steep-sided ravine.
On reaching the bottom 24 hours later, they had been ambushed
and forced to reverse their journey, in the dark and under torrential
rain, manhandling seven of their wounded (including the pilot of a
downed medevac helicopter) up a virtually sheer slope. They had
then returned to recover seven dead, killed in the initial ambush.

Horrific as all this was, it did not match the experiences of
Company C as it pushed along its designated ridge. Once again, the
NVA drew the Americans closer to the mountain before springing a
carefully prepared ambush on 13 May. The company lost two dead
and 35 wounded in a matter of minutes: Honeycutt had no choice but
to withdraw the survivors to his command post, sending Company
A to take their place. It fared no better, stalling in front of a line
of bunkers which defied all efforts at destruction. Meanwhile, the
1/506th, ordered to move from the south toward Hills 916 and 900,
made little progress amid a maelstrom of enemy fire and violent
thunderstorms.

By 16 May, all attacks had ground to a halt, and soldiers were
beginning to react to the appalling strain of the situation. Honeycutt,
with his repeated demands for action, became the focus of the men's
discontent: 'If that sonofabitch wants to take this . . . mountain so
bad, why don't he do it himself?'

But the fighting did not end. On 17 May, the 1/506th edged closer
to Hill 900 and, 24 hours later, the weary assault companies of the
3/187th made enough progress to suggest that one final effort would
take the summit of 937. They were blocked, not by the enemy, but
by one of the most spectacular thunderstorms yet experienced. As
visibility declined to zero, the rain turned the slopes of 937 – by
now devoid of vegetation – into a sea of sticky mud. The attack was
called off.

During the night of 18/19 May, Major General Melvin Zais,
commanding the 101st, ordered three fresh battalions – the 2/501st,
2/506th, and 2/3rd ARVN – to join the battle. They landed without
incident on the 19th, taking up blocking positions to the south-east
and north-east of Ap Bia. On 20 May, all five battalions attacked,
surrounding the NVA and cutting them off from their bases
in Laos.

As the 2/501st and 2/3rd ARVN climbed the precipitous north-
eastern and eastern faces of 937, respectively, the 1/506th put in a

three-company assault across Hill 900 and into a deep draw – the major NVA escape route – to the south-west. At the same time, Honeycutt's men continued their attacks over familiar ground, gradually clearing the bunker lines and reaching desperately for the summit.

Enemy fire did not slacken, even when small groups of Company C scrambled onto the western edge to set up a defensive perimeter. But once they were joined by squads from Company A, the paratroopers were able slowly to clear the mountaintop. By 1655 hours, the fighting was dying down.

In any other war, the Battle of Dong Ap Bia – soon to be dubbed Hamburger Hill by the 3/187th, 'because they say this mountain turns men into hamburgers' – would have been hailed as a great victory. Despite heavy casualties – the Americans lost 70 killed and 372 wounded in the ten days of fighting – over 630 enemy bodies were found, and a well-defended base had been taken. But Vietnam was different, and, as news of the battle filtered out, controversy began.

Publicly condemned by Senator Edward Kennedy as 'senseless and irresponsible', the action fueled the anti-war lobby, particularly when, on 5 June, the 101st abandoned Ap Bia and allowed the enemy to return. Military arguments that the strategy was to impose casualties, not occupy real estate, cut little ice, especially when, on 27 June, *Life* magazine ran a misleading feature on 'The Faces of the Dead in Vietnam. One Week's Total.'

Many readers imagined that the 241 photographs shown were all of men killed at Ap Bia. Under considerable political and public pressure, President Nixon ordered Abrams to cease offensive operations in NVA-controlled territory, accelerating the process of Vietnamization to allow US troops to be withdrawn. US involvement in Vietnam was drawing to a close.

8
The Six-Day War

Jerusalem (1967)

Ashley Brown

Shortly after 0930 hours on the morning of Tuesday, 6 June 1967, Colonel Mordechai Gur, commander of the Israeli 55th Parachute Brigade, spoke on the radio net to his waiting paratroopers. 'We stand on a ridge overlooking the Holy City. Soon we will enter the city, the Old City of Jerusalem about which countless generations of Jews have dreamed, to which all living Jews aspire. To our brigade has been granted the privilege of being the first to enter it.'

The capture of Jerusalem was the most potent symbol of Jewish victory in the Six-Day War of 1967, for the control of the Holy Places, such as the Temple Mount and the Wailing Wall, was enormously important to the young state of Israel. The honour of being the troops who would physically take possession of this great prize had been earned by Gur's men, who had shown great courage and skill over the past two days. In particular, they had wrested control of northern Jerusalem from the experienced and well dug-in forces of the Jordanian Army in the early morning of 6 June.

Tension had been building between Israel and her Arab neighbours for some time when, on the morning of 5 June, the Israeli Air Force launched a sudden strike against the Egyptians. This was totally successful, but in the confusion of that morning's events, King Hussein of Jordan was led to believe that the Israelis had themselves been hard hit, and agreed to send his forces in to attack Israel. At 1100 hours a bombardment began from the Jordanian side of the heavily fortified border, and the Jordanian Air Force flew sorties into Israeli air space. This was a foolhardy move that Hussein was to regret bitterly. Within hours, the rampant Israelis had put his entire air force out of action, and Major-General Uzi Narkiss, in charge of Central Command, was putting into operation his contingency plans for an offensive against Jordanian territory.

The Israelis had to cope with an unpromising strategic situation. Their main problem was that a long, narrow finger of land, inviting attack or artillery barrage from the Jordanian territory on either side, was the only link with the Israeli-held areas of Jerusalem. This corridor had to be made secure, and so Narkiss used the tanks of Colonel Ben Ari's 10th Mechanized Brigade to push north of the corridor and seize the ridge linking Jerusalem with the important centre of Ramallah; at the same time, Latrun was attacked and overrun. Meanwhile, to the south of the corridor, the 16th Jerusalem Brigade launched a series of attacks that cut the main Jordanian communications with their forces in Hebron. The success of these two sets of operations, greatly helped by the command of the air that the Israeli Air Force was now exerting, gave the situation a new complexion. Far from being the side with the strategic initiative, the Jordanians were now vulnerable, and their position in Jerusalem under threat.

Within Jerusalem, the possibilities and prospects for either side were complicated by two factors. First, there was a substantial Israeli enclave within Jordanian territory on Mount Scopus, comprising the Hadassah Hospital and the Hebrew University. A prime Israeli goal was to relieve this enclave (which had been maintained, under United Nations auspices, since 1948) while the Jordanians in turn wished to overrun the position. The second factor affecting operations in the city was that in the two decades since the establishment of the existing frontier, both sides had built up complex sets of fortifications. These networks of deep concrete bunkers, carefully sited linking trenches, mines and barbed wire promised to make a frontal offensive a difficult, if not impossible, task.

The main Jordanian force in the city was the 27th Infantry Brigade, under Brigadier Ata Ali. Further brigades were in support to both north and south, while a tank battalion was stationed behind the main built-up areas in the Kidron valley. The Israeli Air Force made every effort to cut the communication lines of these forces with the Jordanian concentrations further to the north and east, but Ali was a competent officer and he had been reinforced. His men, basically the former Arab Legion under a different name, were well trained and confident of the strength of their defensive positions. Against them, the Israelis decided to throw in one of their crack formations – the 55th Parachute Brigade.

The 55th Parachute Brigade was a body of men trained to expect shock action and to be in the forefront of any Israeli offensive. Under its experienced commander, Colonel Mordechai Gur, were many veterans of raids on Arab territory, although some of the most senior officers had not yet seen action. Raised to a fever pitch by the days of waiting before the air strike that marked the beginning of the Six-Day War, the paras had expected to be used against the Egyptians in the Sinai, and at noon on the 5th were told to prepare for a jump against El Arish, to give impetus to the northern axis of advance. However, such was the pace of the Israeli success that by 1600 hours the decision was taken to use the whole brigade against the Jordanians in Jerusalem.

The basic plan was for the 66th and 71st Battalions of the 55th Brigade to attack along a front running from the Mandelbaum Gate to a point opposite the Jordanian-held Police School building. When a breakthrough had been made, the 28th Battalion would push through to exploit southwards, towards the walls of the Old City. Some support would come from the tanks attached to the Jerusalem Brigade, but the paras would have to fight their way through an awesome set of obstacles with only minimum support before the attack could gather momentum.

The staff of the 55th Brigade urgently prepared for the assault. It was due to go in as soon as possible, but in the event, the battalions would not be ready before 0215 hours on the 6th. The crews manning the 81 mm mortars were especially concerned, because the shells they needed were very slow in arriving. They were anxious to start rangefinding, but could not risk running short of ammunition. Units were getting lost as they struggled to find their place in the line and Jordanian shells, falling at random, were causing casualties. In addition, the deputy commander of B Company, 71st Battalion, had mistakenly attached his men to the convoy of buses carrying mortars forward, and with him was all the communications equipment for the battalion. But eventually all was just about in position and, at 0215 on 6 June, the barrage began.

With buildings on the Jordanian side bursting into flame and lines of tracer flicking through the darkness, the first Israeli platoons approached the Jordanian positions. They thrust bangalore torpedoes below the coils of barbed wire, and then hastily pulled back and hit the deck. The 71st Battalion in particular had trouble in their sector: bangalore torpedoes were not exploding, and then further wire obstacles were looming up after the first breach had been made. The delays meant that men moving forward to exploit the expected breach caused overcrowding, and the milling soldiers could have been very vulnerable to Jordanian shells. Eventually the way through was cleared. Waving green torches (usually the recognition signal for assembly after a night jump) to indicate that the path was open, officers led the platoons through into the next phase of the assault.

Once through the wire, the 66th Battalion was to exploit northwards, through the Police School, taking the important position of Ammunition Hill, while the 71st Battalion was to move through the Sheikh Jarrah area and the American Colony towards the Wadi El-Joz. The men of the 66th knew that they would face enormous difficulties. Ammunition Hill was a vital point, and the Police School itself was well fortified. The paras were heavily laden, carrying extra magazines for their Uzi sub-machine-guns and knapsacks stuffed with grenades. In some cases, men were unable to get up when they fell over, and in one narrow trench Israeli troops got stuck because they were too bulky to pass along.

Giant searchlights illuminated the white walls of the Police School; Jordanian flares suddenly lit up the whole scene. Blazing houses made the darkness around them seem even darker, and the constant explosions of tank, mortar and Jordanian 25-pounder shells provided a deadly backdrop as the paras pushed ahead. It was impossible to see exactly where the enemy small arms fire was coming from. If a trench or emplacement was seen, then it could be attacked and wiped out, but the main priority was to push on to the important objectives. In spite of their loads, and in spite of the fire, the men of the 66th Battalion kept going.

First into the Police School was A Company, cutting a way through a cattle-fence outside. The long passages inside were completely dark, a darkness rendered even more impenetrable by the sudden shell flashes outside. Groups of four men cleared the rooms, two throwing in a grenade and then spraying a room with fire, while the other two moved on to the room next door. But the paras kept tripping and falling in the pitch blackness; in the end, the officers had no option but the dangerous one of using torches. When they had taken the school, A Company moved on towards the Ambassador Hotel, together with D Company; B and C Companies moved towards Ammunition Hill.

As dawn broke (at about 0340 hours) the paras were engaged in a deadly, exhausting fight for the hill. In the trenches and bunkers it was often very difficult to tell friend from foe, and the fighting was further confused by Jordanian sniping from hills to the north. Tanks came up in support, but close-quarters fighting against prepared positions is a tanker's nightmare, and they needed infantry protection against bazookas and recoilless rifles. Soon, the paras had emptied the spare loaded magazines they had brought with them, and had to refill magazines by hand from ammunition boxes – a tiring, fiddly task when under fire. But gradually, the hill was cleared, and the final, so-called 'great bunker' was taken at 0515.

Meanwhile, the 71st Battalion was also meeting stiff resistance in its attack. Having had the most problems in assembling for the assault, this battalion also had difficulty in finding its way once it was into the Jordanian lines. The difficulty of finding the right road in the darkness with only photographs to guide them was magnified by the need to clear hidden Jordanian positions. Dropping grenades into emplacements, and carefully moving along the sheltered sides of streets, the Israelis began clearing the area between the frontier and the Nablus Road, and had a stroke of luck when the Jordanian defenders of the street leading to Wadi El-Joz were taken by surprise. A company of paras moved rapidly down the street to set up positions at this important intersection.

Although the advance was generally going well, the Jordanian support weapons soon picked out the assembly area of the Israelis, and the brigade's mortar crews and recoilless rifle operators suffered casualties as artillery fire began to zero in on them. The breaches in the front-line defences were soon being crossed by the wounded returning from the fight up ahead, some stoical but others screaming with pain. The medical resources of the brigade were becoming dangerously stretched by the mounting casualties in the attacking battalions and among the support units that were under artillery and machine-gun fire.

One heavy machine-gun in particular had caused great concern as it swept the breaches with fire before it was knocked out by a bazooka; and in spite of many efforts, a light machine-gun proved endlessly troublesome. It would stop as soon as a shell burst near it, then open up again. A group of staff officers from the 28th Battalion volunteered to finish it off; but when they tried to approach it they were caught in a trap, and the commander of the support company, leading the attempt, was seriously wounded.

With bullets flying and shells bursting around them, the men of the 28th Battalion moved off to begin their part of the assault soon after the 71st Battalion had gone through the breach in the wire. One shell chanced to injure the deputy commander of D Company, while there were serious officer casualties when a Jordanian 25-pounder struck lucky and hit battalion headquarters. After a seemingly interminable wait, it was dawn before the first members of the 28th Battalion had got to the Jordanian side of the wire, and then they had to fight their way south.

Fighting in the daylight proved, in some ways, worse than the night fighting. Now, snipers could fire without the flash of their muzzles giving away their position, and Jordanian artillery observers had a better view of events. Some of the districts through which the men of the 28th were moving were supposed to have been cleared, but the Israelis soon found that enemy troops could easily infiltrate back into good positions. The building of the Moslem Council had to be cleared three times to make certain that a single shot, or a carefully lobbed grenade, would not take its toll of the advancing Israelis.

The task of moving down Saladin Street was given to C Company but, unable to identify the area properly, it went down Nablus Road. Here the paras had to flush out the YMCA building, from which there was considerable fire. Entering it cautiously, they found most of it empty, finding only the base of a machine-gun mounting. Suddenly the squad that was investigating the situation was fired upon, and men went down wounded. Time was too short to waste it on just one obstacle, and a hand-to-hand combat would have resulted in further casualties. The squad pulled out, and a supporting tank put two shells into the upper stories; the advance went on.

About 0500, there was a lull and the men of the 28th Battalion were ordered to halt. This was a nerve-racking moment, because the risk of a sniper's bullet, or of a well-aimed salvo of artillery shells was as great as ever. Then the advance began again with more tank support. The main task now was to get to the Rockefeller Museum, an imposing new building that dominated the approaches to the north-east corner of the Old City. The roar of the tank guns when they fired almost deafened the paratroopers as the sound echoed between the high buildings. The paras also found it difficult to communicate with the tank crews because the cables for the external telephones had been cut by shrapnel, or were turned off so that the tankers could listen to the stream of orders they were getting on their radio net. But in spite of these problems, the tanks were a real boon, for they drew fire away from the men on foot and they certainly gave the Jordanian defenders second thoughts about opening up at short range.

By 0800, the 55th Brigade had performed brilliantly. All its objectives were secured, and it had set the scene for further advance. From Ammunition Hill in the north through Sheikh Jarrah, the Ambassador Hotel, and down to Wadi El-Joz, a line had been established that gave contact with the slopes of Mount Scopus and promised imminent relief for the besieged garrison; while in the south, the capture of the Rockefeller Museum made an assault against the Old City a practical possibility. Indeed, paras of the 28th Battalion had set themselves up in the Rivoli Hotel opposite Herod's Gate, and when they were not engaging the defenders of the walls of the Old City they were able to sample the delights of the hotel's kitchens, and have a bath.

The casualties sustained by the brigade in reaching these objectives had been horrific – but the achievement had been immense. Gur visited the troops at the Rockefeller Museum. Although many had no previous experience of real action, he noted that already they were comporting themselves like veterans; they knew exactly where enemy fire might come from, and where to find precisely the safest places to sit and relax.

The ranks of the three battalions were thinned by the pounding they had taken during the assault, but there was no shortage of volunteers to replace the dead and wounded. The mortar crews and anti-tank personnel were now anxious to get into the front line – especially as the Old City was beckoning. Morale was sky-high, and Gur prepared to move the 66th Battalion further south for another day's fighting.

Narkiss, desperate to finish things off and to get into the Holy City, ordered Gur to concentrate on taking the last Jordanian strongpoint in the region, the Augusta Victoria Hospital on a ridge to the south of Mount Scopus, and then to prepare an encirclement of the Old City. The plans for the assault were swiftly drawn up, and it was decided to wait until after 1930 hours, when darkness fell, before attacking.

The assault on Augusta Victoria Hospital got off to a bad start, when some troops strayed too close to the walls of the Old City and were fired on from there; and then, at 2140, Gur was informed that 40 Patton tanks of the Jordanian Army had been seen on the reverse side of the slope his men were to attack. With only four Shermans as support, Gur could not risk the assault. He decided to wait until the next day, when aerial support could be called in. Anti-tank dispositions were made and then the soldiers tried to sleep.

Gur's new plan was to attack at about 1130 hours on 7 June, by which time the Israeli Air Force should have dispersed the Pattons. The Israeli high command decided, however, that the attack should go in much earlier in the morning, at 0830. Again, there was frantic haste to reschedule operations, for the new attack was to be mounted from Mount Scopus as well as from across the Kidron valley.

Had the Israelis known it, such frenzied preparations were hardly necessary. Far from being able to bring up substantial armoured reinforcements, Brigadier Ata Ali had been completely cut off by the success of Israeli moves to north and south, and by the Israeli Air Force's devastating attacks on Jordanian road convoys. His troops began a skilful withdrawal in the early hours of 7 June.

At 0804, just before his attacks were to start, Gur was at last given the order that he was so anxious to receive: he was told to take the Old City. Immediately after the air attacks on the Augusta Victoria Ridge, his men stormed over it, and at 0930 he was able to give the historic order to his brigade that the time for waiting was past.

The entry into the Old City was to be via the Lion's Gate, which was the only one able to take tanks, and as the armoured support of the paratroopers approached this point of entry, there was some sporadic defensive fire. Gur himself led the entry into the Old City, and his troops met only light resistance from isolated snipers. At about 1000, he reached the Wailing Wall. The brigade's ordnance officer produced a bottle of whisky, and passed it round. The 55th Brigade had won a victory that no one in Israel would ever forget.

9
The Falklands War

Wireless Ridge (1982)

John Frost

The British Army's Second Battalion of the Parachute Regiment fought in all the major battles of the 1982 land war between Britain and Argentina for the Falkland Islands (Malvinas). After spearheading the landings at San Carlos on 21 May, the battalion fought its way to Port Stanley against determined Argentinian resistance, via Bluff Cove, Goose Green and Wireless Ridge. The most famous of these battles is undoubtedly Goose Green (where 2 Para commander, Lieutenant-Colonel 'H' Jones, won a posthumous Victoria Cross for his charge against an enemy position), but the engagement at Wireless Ridge on 13–14 June was no less dramatic and arguably more decisive. The Ridge, a spur on the north side of Port Stanley, was heavily defended by troops from the Argentine 7th Infantry Regiment and the Argentine 1st Parachute Regiment.

The origins of the Parachute Regiment lie with an initiative of Winston Churchill who, after noting the success of German paratroop operations during Germany's invasion of Holland and Belgium, suggested the formation of a British airborne elite force. The first units began training in June 1940, with volunteers from the units forming the Parachute Regiment in August 1942.

2 Para's task was to capture the Wireless Ridge features, keeping

west of the telegraph wires, and Colonel Chaundler's plan called for a two-phase noisy night attack. In Phase 1, A Company would take the northern spur where the ponds were, C Company having secured the start-line. Once this was secure Phase 2 would come into operation, and B and D Companies would pass through from the north to attack the main Wireless Ridge feature itself. B Company would go to the right (the western end of the ridge), while D Company attacked the rocky ridge-line east of the track.

The mortars would move forward from Mount Kent to a position in the lee of the hillside south of Drunken Rock Pass, and this would also be the site for a static Battalion Headquarters during the attack. H-hour was to be at about 0030. The importance of digging in on the objectives was emphasized once more, since Wireless Ridge was dominated by both Tumbledown and Sapper Hill, and if enemy troops should still be there at dawn they could make 2 Para's positions untenable.

The orders were straightforward, and the plan simple, involving the maximum use of darkness. As the 'O' Group ended the company commanders were told that they would now fly up to Mount Longdon to look at the ground over which they would operate.

The CO went on ahead with the Battery Commander to meet Lieutenant-Colonel Hew Pike, CO of 3 Para, and Major William McCracken, RA, who controlled the artillery 'anchor' OP on Mount Longdon. They discussed and arranged for co-ordinated fire support, with 3 Para's mortars, Milan teams and machine-guns all ready to fire from the flank, and Major Martin Osborne's C Company, 3 Para, in reserve.

Back at the gully all was peaceful in the bright sunshine. Suddenly this was shattered as nine Skyhawks appeared further to the north, flying very low in formation and heading due west towards Mount Kent. The effect was electric, for no one expected that the Argentines could still flaunt their air power in this way.

At 'A' Echelon, behind Mount Kent, there was no doubt as to who the jets were aiming for. As they came screaming up over the col and rose to attacking height, the formation split: three went for the area where the artillery gun-line had recently been, three went for 3 Commando Brigade HQ, and three attacked 'A' Echelon. All the machine-guns opened up, claiming one possible hit as the bombs rained down. Amazingly, there were no casualties from this minor blitzkrieg. But the accuracy of the attack, and its obvious definiteness of purpose, left people wondering if the enemy had left concealed OPs behind, watching Mount Kent, or if satellite photography had shown up the various targets or, possibly, if Argentine electronic-warfare equipment had picked up radio signals from Brigade HQ.

The air raid created delays to all helicopter movement, but eventually the CO was able to fly on to Brigade HQ, while the company commanders were dropped on to Mount Longdon for their own recces. Colonel Chaundler had already been updated on the actual strength of the enemy, which was greater than had been thought, and a new Argentine position had been detected to the east of the pond-covered spur, on a knoll overlooking Hearnden Water and the mouth of the Murrell River.

While the CO was at Brigade HQ, the company commanders were able to study Wireless Ridge in detail from the commanding position on Longdon. It at once became obvious that much of the information so far given to them was inaccurate. What was thought to be C Company of 3 Para proved to be nothing of the sort: Major Dair Farrar-Hockley noticed that it was an *enemy* position of about company strength, situated dangerously on the flank of the 2 Para axis of attack, west of the northern spur. It was also clear that Wireless Ridge proper was heavily defended, with positions which stretched a long way to the east beyond the line of telegraph poles that marked the 2 Para boundary. Strangely, no harassing fire was being brought to bear during the day on any of the Argentine positions, and their soldiers were free to stand about in the open.

The company commanders flew back to Furze Bush Pass, but clearly a major change in plan was necessary. The CO returned from Brigade HQ as evening approached and was told of the situation. 'Go away and have your supper. Come back in 45 minutes and you will have a new set of orders,' he said. Meanwhile the move-up of mortars and the adjustment of artillery had been delayed, and as a result the changes to the fire-plan had to continue into the night, directed by the OP on Longdon and using illuminating rounds.

Unfortunately for the company commanders, normal battle procedure had already ensured that relevant details of the first plan had permeated to the lowest level. Platoon and section commanders had had time to issue clear and well-constructed orders to their subordinates, but now their efforts were all useless, for by the time the company commanders returned with the CO's revised plan, it was too late to go into new details. Such a sudden last-minute change did little for the men's faith in the system, but it was unavoidable and, in any case, the soldiers had by now become stoical, while the cynics among them were not disappointed by this evidence of fallibility at higher levels. Nevertheless, the battalion was able to adapt and change its plans and moved off on time. But Phil Neame had his misgivings about what the SAS to the east of his line of advance was *meant* to be doing, and there was no knowledge of what the SAS was actually *going* to do. Furthermore, no one really knew what was beyond Wireless Ridge to the south, in the Moody Brook area, and everyone would have liked to have known exactly when the 5 Brigade attack on Tumbledown was timed to begin.

The battalion's new plan was for a four-phase noisy night attack. In Phase 1 D Company would capture the newly discovered enemy position west of the northern spur; A and B Companies would then assault the pond-covered hilltop; Phase 3 called for C Company to take the knoll to the east; and finally D Company would roll up the enemy on Wireless Ridge itself, with fire support from A and B Companies, starting in the west and finishing at the telegraph poles.

Fire support was to be lavish in comparison to Goose Green: two batteries of 105 mm guns, HMS *Ambuscade* with her one 4.5-inch gun offshore, and the mortars of both 2 and 3 Para, totalling 16 tubes. Ammunition was plentiful, and the battalion's mortars had been moved complete from Mount Kent by helicopter, and were thus fresh for action. The Machine-Gun Platoon had also been flown forward. Between the six guns they had enough ammunition to provide a massive weight of fire, and the men were fresh and rather proud of their earlier achievement behind Mount Kent against the Skyhawks. The Milan Platoon was already forward with the battalion – the experience of Goose Green had demonstrated the capability of this precision guided missile against static defences. Finally the light tanks of the Blues and Royals would be there, Scimitars with their 30 mm automatic cannon and Scorpions with 76 mm guns, and both equipped with very high quality night-vision equipment and having superb cross-country performance. All available support was allotted first to D Company, then to A and B in their assault, and finally to D Company again as it traversed the ridge.

As night closed in the tanks, the mortars and the Recce Platoon, which was to secure the start-line, moved up. By now the promise of the day had vanished and snow and sleet were falling, considerably limiting the effectiveness of all the gun-sighting equipment, and reducing visibility.

At about 0015 a storm of fire from the supporting artillery and mortars was unleashed upon the Argentine positions. A and B Companies passed by, led by C Company patrols to the new start-line secured by Corporal Bishop's patrol in the relatively safe ground overlooking Lower Pass. At 0045 hours on Monday 14 June, D Company moved over its own start-line further to the west, and headed towards the identified enemy position.

As the company moved forward, the tanks of the Blues and Royals and the machine-guns provided fire support while the artillery increased its rate of fire. Enemy mortar fire in retaliation became heavy. In the rear of the company, Private Godfrey of 12 Platoon had a near miss as a piece of shrapnel cut through his windproof and dug into his boot. He dived for cover – straight into an Argentine latrine!

The weight of supporting artillery and mortar fire was singularly effective, for the enemy on the D Company objective could be seen running away as the company pushed forward, although 155 mm air-burst shelling increased as the Paras began to clear the Argentine trenches, now abandoned except for a few enemy killed by the barrage. The darkness of the night and the extent of the enemy position caused the company to spread out, creating problems of control. Lieutenant Webster of 10 Platoon counted up to 20 trenches on his right, with more over to the left, where 2nd Lieutenant Waddington's 11 Platoon found the other half of the assault formation.

Occasionally as they moved forward, men would suddenly disappear into the freezing water of an ice-covered pond. Privates Dean and Creasey of 11 Platoon went in up to their necks, and had to tread water to stay afloat until their platoon sergeant, Sergeant Light, dragged them out.

Fire support for the company was immaculate. The tanks used their powerful image-intensifier night-sights to pinpoint targets. Once enemy positions were identified, they fired. As soon as the battalion's machine-gunners saw the strike they, too, opened up. Occasionally the machine-gun fire was too close for comfort, even for D Company, and in the end 10 Platoon Commander called for it to stop.

The opposition had fled, and D Company took its first objective in record time, remaining *in situ* while A and B Companies began their part of the battle. Enemy artillery fire was increasing, however, and Neame therefore decided to push forward for another 300 m into relative safety, to avoid the worst of the barrage.

Several of those waiting to move on the A and B Company start-lines were reminded of scenes they had seen from films of the First and Second World Wars. As shells landed all around, men lay huddled against the peat, with bayonets fixed. There could be no denying that, for the soldiers, fear of the known was in this case worse than blissful ignorance of the unknown. In the shelter of the peat bogs some smoked, watching the display of illuminants above.

Just as the time came to move, the shelling claimed its first victim, for Colour Sergeant 'Doc' Findlay was killed in the rear of A Company, and soldiers from Support and HQ Companies were also wounded. The advance began, the two companies moving southwards parallel to each other, on either side of the track. The men crossed the stream in the valley north of their objective with the tanks firing over their heads. The effect upon the enemy was devastating. In their night-sights the tank crews could see Argentine soldiers running or falling as the accurate fire took effect. The boost to morale that this form of suppressive fire gave was considerable; fundamentally, the battle was being won by supporting arms, the infantry being free to do their own job, which is actually clearing and securing the ground.

On the left, all was going well with A Company. Command and control had been well practised back at Goose Green and now the junior officers and section commanders were quite expert in maintaining direction. Silence was unnecessary and orders were shouted backwards and forwards. The enemy were still shelling as the companies advanced, but now counter-battery fire was being provided by our own artillery. From his own position the CO could see the two companies in extended formation, moving quickly up the hill, the whole battlefield brightly lit by starshell.

Co-ordinating the two assaulting companies' advances was difficult, however. The track provided a boundary of sorts, but controlling upwards of 200 men during a noisy battle over difficult terrain is not easy. Colonel Chaundler had another worry. Earlier, before the battalion had moved up, he had been shown a captured Argentine map which indicated a minefield directly in the path of the assaulting companies. There was only 15 minutes to go before 2 Para set off – far too late for a change of plan. The CO only had time to brief OC B Company, while John Crosland had none in which to warn his men, and in any case was told to push on regardless, since there would be no time to clear the mines. Only afterwards did Major Crosland tell his men that they had actually moved directly through the minefield without knowing it. Miraculously, no one was blown up on the way.

The ponds on the spur claimed a victim, however, when Private Philpott of 5 Platoon suddenly plunged into over 6 ft of water. He was dragged out and his section commander, Corporal Curtis, immediately organized a complete change of clothing from the other men in the section, which probably saved Philpott's life.

The two companies consolidated on the objective. There was some firing from the trenches, swiftly silenced as the men of both companies ran in to clear them. Once more the enemy had fled, leaving only 20 or so of their number behind, quickly taken prisoner as they were winkled out of their holes. Radios were still switched on, and several dead lay around the positions. As the men dug in, the enemy shelling increased and it was to continue for the rest of the night at the same level of intensity. Most thought it was worse than Goose Green, but fortunately the abandoned enemy bunkers provided reasonable shelter, although a number of casualties occurred in A Company.

It was now C Company's turn. Already they had had a minor scare on the A and B Company start-line when a Scorpion tank had careered towards Company Headquarters in the darkness. It was hopelessly lost and its commander had to be evacuated after a dose of 'hatch rash' – the effect of placing the head in the path of a rapidly closing hatch. The confused vehicle was soon heading in the right direction, but now under the command of Captain Roger Field, who had seized this opportunity to revert to a more honourable role than foot-slogging.

With A and B Companies now firm, C Company was ordered to check out the Argentine position further to the east that had been spotted from Mount Longdon on the previous day. Major Roger Jenner was glad to be moving again, for it seemed that the supporting artillery battery had developed a 'rogue gun' and every sixth round meant for the enemy was coming in uncomfortably close to his company. He and his men set off, taking cover occasionally on the way as shells fell close by. There had been no firing from the company objective during the battle, and soon the platoons were pushing round the side of a minefield on to the knoll.

As the Recce Platoon advanced, they could hear noises of weapons being cocked. The bright moonlight left them uncomfortably exposed on the hillside. On the forward edge of the slope were two parallel lines of rock, and on the second line the platoon found a series of shell scrapes, suggesting recent occupation by a body of troops. Once again it seemed that the enemy had left hurriedly, leaving tents and bits of equipment behind in the process. Away over to the east Jenner's men could see the bright lights of Stanley airfield, and could hear a C-130 landing. The company was ordered to dig in, but since an enemy attack on this feature was extremely unlikely the CO changed the orders, and C Company moved up to the pond-covered hill.

If any particular group deserves special praise for what was done that night, then it must be the tanks of the Blues and Royals. Their mere presence had been a remarkable boost to morale during all the attacks that had taken place, and the speed and accuracy of their fire, matched by their ability to keep up with the advancing Paras, had been a severe shock to the enemy. Lance-Corporal Dunkeley's tank, which Captain Field had taken over following the injury to its commander, had alone fired 40 rounds from its 76 mm gun.

2 Para was performing superbly, its three first objectives taken with great speed and a minimum of casualties, despite heavy and accurate enemy artillery fire. Whenever the enemy in trenches had sought to return fire they had been met by a withering concentration of fire from the rifle companies' weapons which, coupled with very heavy support, had proved devastating. It is not known whether the Argentines had gathered that they were facing the men from Goose Green, but there can be no question that 2 Para knew.

D Company was now ready to go into the final phase of the attack and began moving forward again to the west end of Wireless Ridge. The tanks and support weapons moved up to join A and B Companies on the hilltop overlooking the D Company objective, and endured the artillery fire as well as anti-tank fire from Wireless Ridge to the south.

12 Platoon was now in the lead. Lieutenant John Page, who had taken over from the tragically killed Jim Barry, looked for the fence, running at right-angles to the ridge, that would guide him to the

correct start-line for the assault. Unfortunately there was little left of the fence marked on the maps, and Corporal Barton's section, at the point of the platoon, could only find a few strands of wire to follow. The number of ice-covered ponds added to the difficulty and the intense cold was beginning to affect men's reactions, as they worked their way south to the western end of Wireless Ridge.

Once more, massive fire-power began to soften up the enemy, who apparently still had no intimation that they were about to be rolled up from a flank. The initial idea had been for D Company simply to sweep eastwards along the ridge without stopping, with 11 Platoon on the left, 12 Platoon on the right and 10 Platoon in reserve. There was still uncertainty as to whether Tumbledown to the south had been taken or not, and clearly a battle was still in progress on that mountain as the Scots Guards fought to drive out the Argentines on its summit. But Neame and his D Company had no intention other than to push on regardless, although they knew that if Tumbledown was still in enemy hands by daylight then 2 Para would be extremely vulnerable.

The bombardment of the western end of the Wireless Ridge continued as the platoons advanced. It seemed to have been effective, since no enemy were encountered at all, although, to be certain, 11 Platoon cleared any bunkers they came across on the reverse slope with grenades.

The first part of Wireless Ridge was now clear and across the dip, where the track came up, lay the narrower rocky outcrops of the remainder of the objective. Fire was concentrated on these areas from A and B Companies as tanks, Milans and machine-guns provided an intense concentration on to three enemy machine-gun posts that remained.

Efforts to switch artillery support further forward and on to the area of Moody Brook had unfortunate results. Five rounds of high explosive crashed on to the ridge around and very near the leading D Company platoons. 3 Section of 11 Platoon was caught in the open and, despite screams to stop the firing, it was too late. Private Parr was killed instantly, and Corporal McAuley was somersaulted into some rocks, completely dazed, and had to be picked up by a stretcher party.

There was a considerable delay while a livid Major Neame tried to get the gunners to sort themselves out. It seemed that one gun was off target, as C Company had noted, but at the gun-lines they did not know which, since in the dark it was impossible to note the fall of shot, even if there had been time, and the other battery was not available owing to shortage of ammunition. In the meantime the CO was growing increasingly impatient, urging the D Company commander to press on.

As soon as the gunners could guarantee reasonable support, and with increased efforts from the Blues and Royals, Neame was off again. All through the wait constant harassing fire from the enemy had been landing around the company, so none were sorry to move. Despite the fire pouring on to the ridge-line ahead, enemy machine-gunners continued firing from well-sited bunkers, and were still staunchly in action as the platoons advanced.

They moved with 11 Platoon on the left, 12 Platoon ahead on the ridge itself, with the company commander immediately behind and, in the rear, 10 Platoon. 12 Platoon came across an abandoned Argentine recoilless rifle, an anti-tank weapon, as they crossed the start-line, which may well have been the weapon that had earlier been engaging the tanks on the A and B Company positions. The platoon moved down into the gap between the two parts of the ridge line, but as the soldiers passed by some ponds, very heavy machine-gun fire began from their front and illumination was called for as the platoon answered the firing. Corporal Barton came across some orange string, possibly indicating a minefield, but his platoon commander urged him on regardless.

The enemy appeared to be surprised by the direction of the assault, and as the Paras advanced, they could hear an Argentine voice calling out, possibly to give warning of this sudden attack from the west. 10 Platoon came across a lone enemy machine-gunner who lay wounded in both legs, his weapon lying abandoned beside him.

Corporal Harley of 11 Platoon caught his foot in a wire, which may have been part of a minefield, and, fearing that it might be an Argentine jumping mine, unravelled himself with some care. The platoon pushed on, skirmishing by sections until they met a concertina of wire. Fearing mines, Sappers were called for from Company Headquarters, but these could do little in the darkness except tape off the suspect area. In fact channels could be discerned between the concertinas, and these were assumed, correctly, as it turned out, to be safe lanes.

While 11 Platoon was extricating itself from the minefield, Neame pushed 12 Platoon on and brought 10 Platoon out to the left to maintain the momentum. Suddenly an intense burst of firing brought the company to a halt. It was a critical moment. For a short time, *all* commanders had to do everything in their power to get things going again, with platoon commanders and sergeants and section commanders all urging their men on. It was a real test of leadership as several soldiers understandably went to ground.

A brief fire-fight ensued, with 12 Platoon engaging the enemy as they pushed forward on the right overlooking Moody Brook below, where lights could be seen. The moment of doubt had passed, however, and once more the men were clearing bunkers and mopping up with gusto. 10 and 12 Platoons now moved on either side of the company commander. Maximum speed was needed to keep the enemy off balance as they fell back, conducting a fighting withdrawal along the ridge. The tanks continued to fire, directed by the company commander. Unfortunately his signaller had fallen into a shell-hole and become separated, thus creating considerable frustration for the CO, who wanted to talk to Neame about the progress of his battle.

During 12 Platoon's brief fight Private Slough had been hit and died later in hospital, and another soldier was wounded.

Enemy artillery fire continued to make life uncomfortable. Fortunately D Company's task was no longer difficult, as most of the enemy bunkers had now been abandoned. 12 Platoon reached the telegraph wires and consolidated there, while the other platoons reorganized further back along the ridge. Shellfire intensified and snipers began to engage from enemy positions further to the east along the ridge.

Neame went up to see the platoon commander, Lieutenant Page. Snipers in the rocks were still firing on the platoon and it seemed that the enemy might be about to counter-attack from the direction of Moody Brook, to the right.

On several occasions the company commander was nearly hit, and his perambulations began to be the cause of some comment. Sergeant Meredith shouted to him, 'For God's sake push off, Sir – you're attracting bullets everywhere you go!'

A hundred metres or so to the east, Argentines could be heard shouting to each other, as though rallying for a counter-attack. John Page called for fire support, and then ordered his own men to stop firing, for by so doing they were merely identifying their positions. They felt very isolated and vulnerable.

For two very long and uncomfortable hours the company remained under pressure. Small-arms fire mingled with all types of HE fell in and around 12 Platoon's position as the men crouched in the abandoned enemy sangars and in shell-holes. John Page continued to move around his platoon, organizing its defences, and suffering a near-miss in the process. He was hit by a bullet, which passed between two grenades hanging on his webbing and landed in a full magazine in his pouch. He was blown off his feet by the shock. 'It was like being hit by a sledge-hammer and having an electric shock at the same time,' he later described the moment. As he lay there a round exploded in the magazine, but fortunately the grenades remained intact, and he was soon on his feet.

Meanwhile the CO was still trying to get in touch with Neame to know the form. Lieutenant Webster, OC 10 Platoon, was momentarily elevated to commanding the company since he was the only officer left near Company Headquarters. As he talked to the CO, voices could be heard below in the direction of Moody Brook. Corporal Elliot's section opened up and automatic fire was returned by perhaps ten to fifteen men. 11 Platoon moved forward to join 10 Platoon in a long extended line along the ridge, the men firing downhill towards the enemy position. Eventually the CO got through to the company commander, who had had a hair-raising time walking along the ridge to discover what was happening. He now informed the CO of his fears of imminent attack.

Sporadic enemy fire from Tumbledown added to D Company's danger, and all the earlier fears of the consequences of delay to the 5 Brigade attack came to the fore. The CO offered to send tanks up but Neame declined, since they would be very exposed on the forward slope fire positions they would be forced to adopt. He would have preferred another company to hold the first part of Wireless Ridge, which as yet remained undefended.

The company reorganized, leaving Corporal Owen's section forward as a standing patrol while 10 and 11 Platoons found dug-outs on the reverse slope. 12 Platoon stayed in its positions near the telegraph poles.

There was little more that the Companies on the northern spur could now do to support D Company. Two of A Company's trained medical orderlies had been wounded by the shelling that still continued, so the platoons had to look after their own casualties – once again the value of the medical training for all ranks was vindicated. Fortunately the helicopters in support that night were fully effective, evacuating casualties with minimum delay, and other casualties were taken back to the RAP on one of the tanks. The enemy artillery fire gave the remainder every incentive to dig, and the possibility of being overlooked by Mount Tumbledown in the morning was an additional spur.

For A and B Companies it was now a matter of lasting the cold night out, which was not without incident. Privates 'Jud' Brookes and Gormley of A Company's 1 Platoon had been hit by shrapnel. The rule was to switch on the injured man's easco light, normally used for night parachute descents, to ensure that he would not be missed in the dark. Sergeant Barrett went back to look for Brookes, whose light was smashed.

'All right, Brookes – me and the Boss will be back to pick you up later.'

'Ee, Sarge,' he replied in a thick Northern accent, 'Ah knows tha f— will.'

Unknown to them, the men of 3 Platoon were actually sitting next door to 13 Argentine soldiers, who were taking cover from their own shellfire. Only later in the morning were they found and taken prisoner.

In B Company, the state of Privates Carroll and Philpott of 5 Platoon was a cause for concern, since both were now suffering from hypothermia after being immersed in one of the ponds. Their section commander, Corporal Steve Curtis, decided to tell the platoon commander. As he ran out into the shelling, a round exploded close by, shredding his clothes almost completely yet, amazingly, leaving him unharmed.

The mortar teams had been busy all night. By now they had moved on to the side of the A and B Company hill to avoid shelling, which had been uncomfortably close at their first position in the bottom of the valley to the north. Improvised bins had helped to reduce the tendency of the mortar tubes to bed into the soft peat, although not completely, and another problem was that tubes would at times actually slip out of their base-plates under recoil. To prevent this, mortarmen took turns to stand on the base-plates as the tubes were fired, and by the end of the night four men had suffered broken ankles for their efforts. The fire they had been able to provide was very effective, however, and all concerned had been determined that, this time, there would be no question of running short of ammunition or of being out of range. The 3 Para mortars on Longdon did sterling work providing illumination.

The Machine-Gun Platoons, too, had been hard at work, their six guns providing intense heavy fire throughout the night. Re-supplied by the tanks and by the splendid work of WO2 Grace's Pioneer Platoon, they had had no worries about ammunition. But gradually the guns broke down, and by dawn only two of the six were still in action.

In Battalion Headquarters the second-in-command, the Operations Officer and Captain David Constance had taken turns at duty officer. At one point the second-in-command, Major Keeble, had been able to see the flashes of the enemy 155 mm guns as they fired, but no amount of reporting back produced any counter-measures. Once the drone of a low-flying Argentine Canberra jet was heard, and amidst the din of artillery even larger thuds reverberated as the aircraft dropped its bombs. Private Steele of the Defence Platoon was unlucky: as he lay on the ground a piece of shrapnel caught him in the back. He hardly felt it, thinking that it was only a piece of turf from the explosion – only later did he discover a rather nasty wound where the metal had penetrated.

The CO's party had not escaped either. A stray round hit Private McLoughlin, a member of the Battery Commander's group, and actually penetrated his helmet at the front. The helmet deflected the round, however, and McLoughlin walked away unharmed.

The snipers were in great demand. Their night-sights enabled them to identify the enemy infra-red sights and to use the signature that then appeared in the image intensifier as an aiming-mark. The Commando Sappers had had a relatively minor role to play in the battle, since there were no mines that it was imperative to clear. But, as at Goose Green, they provided a very useful addition when acting as infantry.

On Wireless Ridge at first light, 12 Platoon was still being sniped at from behind and to the right. Further back along the ridge, Corporal Owen had searched a command post. While rummaging in the bunker, he found a map showing all the details of the Argentine positions, as well as some patrol reports. These were quickly dispatched to Company Headquarters and on to Brigade.

Private Ferguson, in Owen's section, suddenly noticed four or five men below them. The corporal was uncertain as to who they could be – possibly 12 Platoon – and told Ferguson to challenge. The latter

yelled 'Who's there!' and was instantly greeted with a burst of fire
that left them in no doubt. Grenades started to explode around Owen
and his men as the enemy counter-attacked. The section opened fire,
and Corporal Owen shouted for the machine-guns to engage.

10 Platoon meanwhile were firing on either side of the section, and
Owen himself blasted away with eight M-79 rounds. The section was
soon short of ammunition, and the men began to ferret for abandoned
Argentine supplies. Just then the remainder of the platoon moved up
to join the section; though uncertain as to exactly where the enemy
were, they were determined to prevent the Argentines from regaining
the ridge.

Private Lambert heard an Argentine, close in, shouting, 'Grenado,
grenado!'

'What a good idea,' he thought, and lobbed one of his own in the
direction of the voice. There were no more shouts.

11 Platoon also saw a group of four men to its front. 2nd
Lieutenant Chris Waddington was unable to make out who they
were and, thinking they might be 10 Platoon, shouted to them to
stop. The four men took no notice, so he ordered a flare to be put
up – the figures ran off as the platoon engaged with small arms and
grenades. The orders not to exploit beyond the ridge-line meant that
not all the enemy positions had been cleared during the night, and
it seemed that some stay-behind snipers had been left there, and it
was probably these that had given 12 Platoon so much trouble. But
the counter-attack, such as it was, had fizzled out. Artillery fire was
called down on Moody Brook to break up any further efforts at
dislodging D Company. Down below the ridge a Landrover could
be seen trying to get away. Lance-Corporal Walker fired at it and
it crashed.

11 Platoon now came under extremely accurate enemy artillery
fire, possibly registered on the flashes of their weapons. Major
Neame therefore ordered them to cease firing with small arms,
intending to continue the battle with artillery alone. Moody Brook
was deserted, however. In the distance the men of D Company
noticed two Argentine soldiers walking off down the track as if at
the end of an exercise.

In the light of dawn it appeared to the Paras on the ridge that a large
number of enemy troops were moving up to reinforce Sapper Hill to
the south-east. Neame called for artillery with great urgency, but no
guns were available. After a further 20 minutes or so, by which time

the enemy had reached the top, the target was engaged. Meanwhile other Argentines could be seen streaming off Tumbledown and Harriet – 5 Brigade had won its battles.

As D Company began to engage this new target the CO arrived. He confirmed Neame's orders to fire on the enemy retiring towards Stanley, and the company now joined in with machine-guns in a 'turkey shoot'. John Greenhalgh's helicopters swept in and fired SS-11 rockets and, together with two other Scouts, attacked an Argentine battery. The enemy AA was still active, however, and all the helicopters withdrew.

The retiring Argentines on Tumbledown had made no reply to the helicopters, and their artillery had stopped. It was obvious that a major change had occurred. The news was relayed to the Brigadier, who found it difficult to believe what was happening. But the CO realized how vital it was to get the battalion moving into Stanley before the enemy could rally, and A and B Companies, together with the Blues and Royals, were ordered to move as fast as possible up on to Wireless Ridge. The Brigadier arrived, still disbelieving until Colonel Chaundler said, 'It's OK, Brigadier, it's all over.' Together they conferred as to what to do next. D Company ceased firing on the fleeing enemy on the far hillside, and the order was given that men were only to fire if fired upon first. Permission was then given for the battalion to move on.

B Company, by now on the ridge, was ordered down into Moody Brook. Corporal Connors's section of 5 Platoon led the way, still expecting to come under fire from the 'Triple As' on the race-course. The other two sections covered him forward. He cleared the flattened buildings of the old barracks and Curtis's section took over, clearing the bridge over the Murrell River and the building on the other side, while all the time their platoon commander was exhorted, 'Push on, push on!' They remained cautious, fearing booby traps or a sudden burst of fire.

A Company now took the lead as B Company, covering A's advance, moved south on to the high ground on the far side of the valley, above the road, passing through three abandoned gun positions on the way. The tanks of the Blues and Royals moved east along Wireless Ridge to give support if it should be necessary. A Company was well on the way down the road into Stanley, with C and D Companies following, when Brigade announced a cease-fire. Cheers went up, and red berets quickly replaced steel helmets.

Bottles of alcohol miraculously appeared to celebrate with. Relief, elation, disbelief – all in turn had their effect.

Major Dair Farrar-Hockley led his men towards the race-course, past the abandoned guns that had been spotted so many hours earlier yet had remained operational in spite of requests for artillery fire. According to civilians afterwards, the Argentines still on the outskirts of Stanley simply broke and ran when they heard that 'the Paras' were coming. The leading elements of the battalion arrived in Stanley at 1330 hours, on Monday, 14 June some five hours before the official cease-fire, with 2nd Lieutenant Mark Coe's 2 Platoon the first into the town. They were the first British troops into the capital.

Eventually all the companies were brought into the western outskirts, finding shelter amongst the deserted houses, a few of which had suffered from stray shells. One or two dead Argentine soldiers still lay in the street where they had been caught by shellfire. On the race-course the Argentine flag was pulled down and Sergeant-Major Fenwick's Union Jack once more served its purpose.

10
The Persian Gulf War

Desert Storm (1991)

Jon E. Lewis

In the vast winter silence of the desert night the ominous keening of aircraft high overhead could be heard. Everywhere along the Saudi–Kuwaiti border troops looked anxiously skywards from their foxholes. The jets were flying east, and mud soldiers of the Coalition shivered a sigh of relief. Ours. At the wet, temporary HQ of Britain's First Armoured Division a single voice rang out clear into the sandy darkness: 'Yellow Alert. We are at war.'

It was 11.30 p.m. on the evening of 16 January 1991. Operation Desert Storm, the effort to remove Saddam Hussein from his occupation of Kuwait, and the biggest concerted military action since the Second World War, had begun – just five months and 13 days after the Iraqi dictator had sent his tanks rolling across the Kuwaiti border. If the invasion of Kuwait had been a military success, it had also proved to be the biggest political mistake of Saddam's career.

No sooner had Saddam ordered his 500,000 victorious invasion troops to dig-in along the Kuwaiti–Saudi Arabian border, than the Americans had, under the flag of the United Nations, garnered together a considerable Coalition of anti-Saddam forces dedicated to ejecting him from Kuwait. Wars are seldom fought for moral principle, and the war which would be fought in the Persian Gulf was no exception. Though politicians would declare that force was necessary to deal with the 'bully' Saddam (while ignoring similar illegal occupations of smaller neighbours by Israel and Turkey, among other nations) the truth was always more prosaic: Saddam's occupation of Kuwait threatened to restrict the free access of the major economic nations to its huge subterranean seas of oil, as well as upsetting the area's fragile Arab balances of power.

As the US had taken the diplomatic lead against Iraq, so the US provided the overwhelming bulk of men, women and arms which would fight Operation Desert Storm; nearly 450,000 troops. In recognition of this, an American, General H. Norman Schwarzkopf, was appointed Commander-in-Chief of Coalition forces in the Gulf. (As a courtesy to the host country, Schwarzkopf was officially subordinated to the Saudi defence Minister, General Prince Khalid, but in practice operational command remained wholly with Schwarzkopf and his US CENTCOM; the only non-American on Schwarzkopf's central planning staff was Britain's Lieutenant-General Sir Peter de la Billiere, an acknowledgement of the fact that Britain provided the second largest troop contingent, 40,000 soldiers.) 'Stormin' Norman', as he became dubbed, was a 56-year-old Vietnam veteran, of some irascibility. Whether by luck or design, in him the Americans had appointed a commander who was a canny user of the media – many American officers still blamed TV for defeat in Vietnam – and a master of the soundbite. At the end of the campaign, Schwarzkopf was asked by a journalist what he thought of Saddam Hussein as a military strategist. Using the fingers of his left hand to count off Saddam's 'attributes', Schwarzkopf replied: 'As far as Saddam Hussein being a great military strategist, he is neither a strategist, nor is he schooled in the operational arts, nor is he a tactician, nor is he a general, nor is he a soldier. Other than that, he is a great military man. I want you to know that.'

Schwarzkopf himself, however, was all the above. A near-genius at battlefield strategy and tactics, his Operation Desert Storm would draw comparisons with Cannae and El Alamein.

Following his arrival in Saudi Arabia in August 1990, Schwarzkopf had initially been concerned only to secure the east Saudi border (Operation Desert Shield) against Iraqi incursions. Two months later Washington, mindful that economic and diplomatic sanctions might well fail to persuade Saddam to withdraw his forces from Kuwait, directed the general to prepare contingency plans for an offensive.

On paper, at least, the Iraqi Army was a formidable opponent and CENTCOM planned for the worst. Intelligence suggested that the

Iraqi Army was as big and as dangerous as Saddam Hussein himself claimed. It contained over a million men, and possessed a devil's feast of modern weaponry: around 6,000 tanks (including a number of Soviet T-72s), 4,000 armoured personnel carriers, between 800 and 1,000 combat aircraft and 3,200 artillery pieces, including some which could outgun those of the Coalition. Moreover, the Iraqi Army was reputed to be battle-hardened after its grinding 1980–8 war with Iran, and extremely adept at defence. It had already fortified the border with Saudi Arabia with a continuous belt of obstacles, including sand berms and oil-filled trenches which could, with the touch of a torch, be turned into a wall of fire. Most dangerous of all the Iraqi forces were the armoured divisions of the 'elite' Republican Guard, held as a theatre reserve in southern Iraq and northern Kuwait. Uncomfortable at not having the classic three to one ratio of advantage that military wisdom says an attacker should have in order to guarantee victory, and worried that an offensive might break down into an attrition battle or *slugfest*, Schwarzkopf decided to exploit the Coalition's huge air force to reduce Saddam's military capability, especially in the Kuwaiti Theatre of Operations (KTO). This would be the preliminary to a ground offensive with air support (in line with the AirLand Battle Doctrine adopted by the Pentagon in 1982) which would outflank the main Iraqi defences in the west beyond the point at which the Iraqi, Saudi and Kuwaiti borders meet – and where the Iraqis had failed inexplicably to build fortifications. This massive outflanking drive into the KTO from the west would be accompanied by direct attacks from the south and a feint amphibious landing from the east, where 17,000 US Marines were waiting offshore. The Iraqis would be crushed and caught in a massive envelopment. Though it was apparently bitterly contested by some of his staff, Schwarzkopf stuck to the essentials of his plan, finally getting it approved in mid-January 1991.

The plan was no sooner approved than it was called into use. The deadline for the implementation of United Nations Resolution 660 (Iraqi withdrawal from Kuwait) expired on midnight 15 January. The first Coalition aircraft were in the air twenty-four hours later, flying the first of a total of 110,000 sorties against targets across Iraq and Kuwait. Radar-guided American Stealth bombers executed pinpoint attacks with so-called smart bombs, accurate enough to be deposited down the airshafts of Iraqi bunkers. Other planes, wave after wave of them, F-15Es, F-A18 Hornets, A-6E Intruders and RAF Tornadoes bombed Iraqi military and communications targets and destroyed much of Saddam's air force before it could leave the runway. In the first day of the air campaign, US warships in the Gulf launched more than 100 Tomahawk Cruise missiles (each armed with half a ton of high explosive); observers in the Iraqi capital, Baghdad, watched in wonder as the Cruise missiles flew between buildings and turned corners before hitting their targets. Baghdad shook under the weight of the bombardment. Iraqi anti-aircraft fire turned the sky white.

Over the following weeks the air campaign drastically degraded Saddam's ability to fight a battle, destroying his highly centralized communications and command system, his arms and his army's morale. The Coalition achieved complete air supremacy. In Schwarzkopf's phrase, the removal of the Iraqis from the skies 'blinded' Saddam. For this, the Allies were to lose a total of 67 aircraft.

The one black cloud in the Coalition's silver-lined air campaign was Iraq's Scud missile capability. Saddam began firing his Soviet-built Scud missiles on the second night of the air war, the first targets being Tel Aviv and Haifa in Israel. Although the six missiles which landed in Israel killed no one, and did not contain the feared chemical or nuclear warheads, the impact was psychologically and politically explosive. Israel threatened to take unilateral retaliatory action, something which would have wrecked the anti-Iraqi alliance, even perhaps starting a new Arab–Israeli war. Frantic diplomacy by the Americans, together with the dispatch of Patriot ground-to-air missile systems to shoot down Scuds, managed to persuade Israel from immediate punitive measures. The Patriots, though, were only of minimal effectiveness, failing even when they intercepted incoming Scuds always to destroy the warhead. Covert operations by British SAS and US Special Forces teams, dropped behind Iraqi lines, and the hunting of mobile Scud launchers by the Coalition air force did better. In the end, the Israelis suffered only 13 fatalities from Scuds. The Iraqis' most effective Scud launch was one of those aimed at Saudi Arabia. In the dying hours of the war a Scud landed on a US barracks in Dhahran, killing 28.

Such was the effectiveness of the air campaign that senior Coalition air force officers began to question whether a ground offensive was necessary. Schwarzkopf, however, along with the army and the Marines, was mindful that a war has never been won by airpower alone. Consequently, as the air campaign continued its attrition of enemy units, Schwarzkopf continued the deployment of the coalition army, most crucially of all the move west of the bulk of his forces: the US XVIII Airborne Corps, including the French Light Armoured *Division Daguet*, farthest west, its task a lightning drive to the Euphrates which would simultaneously protect the left flank of the invasion and cut off an Iraqi escape; then, to the right of XVIII Airborne, VII Corps, including British 1st Armoured Division, the steel *schwerpunkt* of the offensive which would smash north and then north-east towards Kuwait, hitting the Republican Guard in the flank. This remarkable movement of XVIII Airborne and VII Corps to their start positions was accomplished across several hundred miles of desert by thousands of tanks, trucks and other support vehicles. In order both to tie down Iraqi troops and confirm Iraqi expectations of a frontal attack on Kuwait City, Coalition Arab forces and the US 1st and 2nd Marines, together with the 1st (Tiger) Brigade of the US 2nd Armoured Division were deployed in the south of the battlefield, along the Kuwaiti–Saudi border.

While Schwarzkopf made ready, time was trickling away for Saddam Hussein. If the air war had degraded his military capacity it had done nothing to diminish his rhetoric or his will to hold onto Kuwait, promising the Coalition 'the Mother of All Battles' should it try to force him out. A Soviet attempt to broker talks failed. On 22 February US President Bush gave Saddam the ultimatum to withdraw from Kuwait or face the consequences. In the best fashion of the Western, Bush's deadline expired at noon – noon (EST) on Saturday 23 February. Saddam refused to blink. That night, with singular appropriateness, American Forces network radio in the Gulf played 'Saturday Night's All Right (For Fighting)'. As Elton John sang, soldiers along the front line were making ready for combat, Marine bulldozers breaching Iraqi defences. Sand berms were demolished, trenches filled with oil burned off, and minefields cleared.

As Saturday night edged into Sunday morning, Coalition air force and navy began a massive bombardment of the Iraqi lines. It started raining. And then at 4 a.m., US and Saudi Marines in the coastal area that was the easternmost point of the battlefield began moving forward through the Iraqi defences, the vaunted 'Saddam Line'. The ground war had begun.

The Marines breached the Iraqi barriers with relative ease, the minefields posing fewer problems than expected: many mines had become exposed by shifting sand, while some Marines crossed the minefields by walking on anti-tank mines, knowing that they could not be detonated by the weight of a man. By the end of the first day of the ground war (G-Day) the 1st Marine Division had secured Al-Jaber airfield, halfway to Kuwait City, having bypassed some Iraqi units who were poised to fight but failed to counter-attack. The battlefield, eerily quiet and shrouded in acrid smoke from the Kuwaiti oil wells set on fire by the Iraqis on 22 February, was littered with burnt-out wrecks of Iraqi trucks and tanks, victims of the Coalition air force.

At the opposite end of the Allied line, the French *Division Daguet* and its attached US 82nd Airborne Division (the Screaming Eagles), given the task of sweeping around the Saddam Line and securing the offensive's left flank, penetrated rapidly into Iraq, brusquely subduing the Iraqi 45th Infantry Division with artillery and HOT anti-tank missiles from French-built Gazelle helicopters. The 101st Airborne Division, immediately to the east, after a hold-up due to poor weather, mounted one of the biggest airmobile operations in history with some 300 Chinook helicopters ferrying troops to establish an advance position, FOB Cobra, 70 miles inside Iraqi territory.

Iraqi resistance to the Coalition incursions was everywhere so minimal that by late morning Schwarzkopf decided to deal the enemy a further reeling blow, bringing the second phase of the offensive forward to the afternoon of G-Day instead of the morning of G+1. The US 24th Mechanized Infantry Division – Schwarzkopf's old division – along with the 3rd Armoured Cavalry began rolling forward at midday, its mission to cross nearly 250 miles of Iraqi rock and sand and establish itself near the town of Basra, where it would cut off Iraqi forces and engage the Republican Guards. As the 24th roared across the desert it passed weary US Long Range Surveillance Detachments, who had been in Iraq for weeks sending back HUMINT (human intelligence). Also at midday, VII Corps – with 1,300 tanks the biggest armoured corps in history – led by the 'Big Red One', the US 1st Infantry Division (Mechanized), began its breach of the Iraqi line, with the divisions of the Corps following through over the next 24 hours. The British 1st Armoured Division went through the breach in the morning of G+1, the 'anvil' on which the rest of the Corps would hammer the Republican Guards.

To the right of VII Corps, east of Wadi al-Batin, Arab forces from Egypt, Syria, Saudi Arabia and Kuwait began their advance in the afternoon of G-Day, proceeding more circumspectly than their neighbours, the US Marines, in part because they faced one of the most fortified sections of the Saddam Line. The Egyptians found themselves in front of walls of burning oil, but managed the breach in less than five hours after pushing sand into the trenches with their tanks and bulldozers.

By evening all Coalition forces had advanced well beyond their schedule, progress only improved by the Coalition's continuing deception operation, with thousands of Marines – apparently set for a seaborne invasion – waiting off Kuwait's shore, and a highly visible demonstration by the famous 1st Armoured Cavalry Division (the Air Cav) in the Wadi al-Batin. Casualties had been minimal. Among the worst losses of the day were those suffered by the British in a 'friendly fire' incident, when an American A-10 'Tankbuster' mistakenly eliminated a British Warrior Armoured Vehicle; nine soldiers died.

As dawn broke on 25 February, G+1, the scale of the Iraqi rout and disorientation became more apparent. The fast-moving *Division Daguet* had hardly encountered a living soul and continued its spectacular dash throughout the day, reaching As-Salman airfield, 70 miles inside Iraq, by evening, where it had to be ordered to pause. Eastward down the line the 24th Infantry Division (the Victory Division) rolled ever onwards, also without opposition, while the British 1st Armoured Division engaged and defeated the Iraqi 12th Armoured Division before becoming delayed by the throngs of Iraqi soldiers eager to surrender. Elsewhere over the battlefield it was the same story of Iraqis throwing down their weapons. The crush of POWs, indeed, posed more of a problem than the Iraqis who tried to fight; 25,000 prisoners were captured during the day. Only in a handful of places did the Iraqis put up serious resistance. An armoured division counter-attacked the US 2nd Marine Division near Al-Jaber but was heavily repulsed. Iraqi armour which tried to block the path of the 2nd Marine Division and the Tiger Brigade also fared badly. Perhaps the fiercest encounter of the day was at the Burgan oil field near Kuwait International Airport, where the 1st Marine Division met with well-entrenched Iraqi units. These were flushed out by a massive 'time on time' artillery bombardment and then decimated by USMC tanks and Cobra attack helicopters. The Iraqis lost 50 tanks for no USMC loss.

If the Coalition needed any proof that things were going well, it came on the morning of the next day, Tuesday 26 February (G+2), when Baghdad Radio announced that Iraq was prepared to withdraw from Kuwait. Washington's response was brusque: 'The war goes on.' In Kuwait City itself, panic-stricken Iraqis began to commandeer vehicles and flee northwards on the road to the Mutla Gap causing, as one commentator quipped, 'the mother of all traffic jams'. A dozen Coalition F-15s bombed the front of a 1,000-vehicle Iraqi convoy, and then bombed its rear. Coalition aircraft then swarmed down on the luckless trapped Iraqis in a turkey-shoot reminiscent of the destruction of the Wehrmacht as it tried to escape through the Falaise Gap in 1944.

The reason for the Iraqi haste in quitting Kuwait City was that the Coalition's southern groupings were now only miles from the suburbs, although the US 1st Marine Division had run into a sizeable formation of Iraqi armour determined to make a fight for the International Airport. The battle would last throughout the day and into the next, the sky so dark with smoke from oil well fires that flashlights had to be used to read charts. The Tiger Brigade and 2nd Marine Division also met opposition as they curled north around Kuwait City to prevent any retreat.

Meanwhile, far to the west, with the *Division Daguet* holding the left flank secure against Iraqi reinforcements, the XVIII Airborne Corps had consolidated its hold on the Euphrates valley, with the 24th Infantry Division reaching Highway 8 and then surging eastwards down it towards Basra, its helicopter attack regiment in the van. The 24th had the smell of success in its nostrils and was now riding towards the Republican Guard. A brigade of 57 Iraqi T-72 tanks unlucky enough to cross the 24th's path was decimated, the T-72s no match for the 24th's M1A1s and Apache attack helicopters.

Likewise closing on the Republican Guards was VII Corps, with the 2nd Armoured Cavalry making contact with the Guard late in the evening. After completing its rout of the 12th Iraqi Armoured Division, the British 1st Armoured Division had overrun the 17th and 52nd Armoured Divisions, eliminating 300 enemy tanks and armoured vehicles in the process. At midnight the British division reached its main objective, codenamed Waterloo, at the south end of Phase Line Smash. Caught between an anvil and a descending hammer, the Republican Guard realized too late that the target of XVIII Airborne and VII Corps was not Kuwait but the Guard itself.

Over the next 32 hours, by 8 a.m. Thursday 28 February (G+4), the Iraqi Army disintegrated. They surrendered in their thousands, waving anything white they could find. The Iraqi force at Kuwait International Airport was finally overcome, with the triumphant Marines opening their lines to give the honour of liberating Kuwait City to the Kuwaiti 35th Mechanized Brigade, who entered the city at 9 a.m. on 27 February to an ecstatic welcome. Much of the city was anyway already in the control of Kuwaiti resistance fighters.

Along the Iraq–Kuwait border, meanwhile, XVIII Airborne and VII Corps engaged the Republican Guard in what would be the classic tank battle of the campaign, lasting into the morning of G+4. Although some of the Iraqi units in the Basra Pocket put up a brave fight, especially those from the Guard's best-equipped divisions (Tawakalna, Medina and Hammurabi), it was always a one-sided contest. The Iraqis had no air cover and very poor communications, while the attack–attack tactic of the US forces never allowed them time to consolidate. The Coalition was fighting a multi-dimensional modern war while the Iraqis wanted a static war of First World War vintage. The Republican Guard left the field with its pretensions to military elitism in tatters. In truth the Guard was never the force Saddam claimed it to be, or the Coalition feared it to be. Its experience fighting the Iranians had left it not so much combat-ready as combat-fatigued. Moreover, the Guard – its primary function being the protection of Saddam's Ba'athist dictatorship – selected most of its officers for political reliability, not military ability. What was arguably the best Guard unit, *Amn al-Khas* (special security), was judged too important by Saddam to fight in the war, and was kept in Baghdad. Other Iraqi units, made up overwhelmingly of conscripts, had second-rate equipment and little desire to die for Saddam's lost cause. Nor were there as many Iraqi soldiers in the KTO as the Coalition had estimated (500,000); in all probability they numbered fewer than 300,000 – 200,000 fewer than the Coalition.

With the Iraqi Army almost completely encircled, Schwarzkopf would have liked to have continued the war to ensure its destruction. As it was, 700 Iraqi tanks escaped the net. The Coalition's Arab members had no wish to see the complete disintegration of Iraq – which would have unleashed a wave of protest in their countries, where support for Saddam was sizeable – and at 9 p.m. (EST), in a televised address, President Bush announced a ceasefire from midnight – 8 a.m. on 28 February in the Gulf. By the close of the ground war the Iraqis had suffered around 8,000 casualties; another 86,000 Iraqis had surrendered to the Coalition. The Iraqi Army had not only been driven from Kuwait, it had been routed. Coalition casualties during the ground war were minimal: 150 KIA, a quarter of these victims in 'friendly fire' incidents. The Mother of All Battles had taken exactly 100 hours.